A CONSUMER'S GUIDE TO TESTS IN PRINT

Second Edition

DONALD D. HAMMILL
LINDA BROWN
BRIAN R. BRYANT

pro·ed
An International Publisher

8700 Shoal Creek Boulevard
Austin, Texas 78757

Copyright © 1992, 1989 by PRO-ED, Inc.

Library of Congress Cataloging-in-Publication Data

Hammill, Donald D., 1934–
    A consumer's guide to tests in print / Donald D. Hammill, Linda
Brown, Brian R. Bryant. — 2nd ed.
        p.   cm.
    Includes bibliographical references.
    ISBN 0-89079-548-7
    1. Norm-referenced tests—United States—Evaluation. I. Brown,
Linda, 1950– . II. Bryant, Brian R. III. Title.
LB3060.32.N67H36 1992
371.2′6—dc20   92-3041
                                                            CIP

A Consumer's Guide to Tests in Print is available from

8700 Shoal Creek Boulevard
Austin, Texas 78757

4 5 6 7 8 9 10 11 12 13 14 15 16   04 03 02 01 00 99

CONTENTS

INTRODUCTION TO THE CONSUMER'S GUIDE

A Consumer's Guide to Tests in Print was developed to provide professionals with objective information about the technical characteristics of the norm-referenced tests that they use every day or that they are contemplating using. In this chapter we discuss reasons why the guide is needed, describe the project, and explain how the material in the *Consumer's Guide* can be used to evaluate tests.

THE NEED FOR THE CONSUMER'S GUIDE

At present, professionals have no source of objective information that they can consult when evaluating standardized norm-referenced tests. That is, no sources exist that apply objective criteria to specific tests and rate the tests according to the adequacy of their statistical properties.

This void is particularly surprising since criteria for identifying good tests are so easily accessible. One good source is assessment textbooks. Of the many textbooks that are available, those by Aiken (1988), Anastasi (1988), Gronlund and Linn (1990), Nunnally (1978), and Salvia and Ysseldyke (1991) are prime examples. Another useful source of criteria is the booklet *Standards for Educational and Psychological Tests*, published by the American Psychological Association (1985). This booklet was developed by a joint committee composed of representatives of the American Psychological Association, the American Educational Research Association, and the National Council on Measurement in Educa-

tion. These sources set forth and justify their psychometric criteria, but they do not apply those criteria to specific tests. That important task is left to their readers, who may or may not possess sufficient psychometric knowledge to evaluate tests properly and who therefore may produce evaluations that are idiosyncratic, subjective, or otherwise inadequate.

Of course, test reviews are readily available to individuals who need information about various instruments; but the content, comprehensiveness, and value of those reviews vary widely. For example, the compilation by Sweetland and Keyser (1991), *Tests: A Comprehensive Reference for Assessments in Psychology, Education, and Business*, does not purport to evaluate any of the several thousand tests included. Instead, it provides the reader with short, concise descriptions of such nontechnical characteristics as title, author, appropriate ages for use, publisher, and price. In brief, it provides the reader with a test's "name, rank, and serial number."

On the other hand, the equally comprehensive *Mental Measurements Yearbook* (Conoley & Kramer, 1989) does emphasize critical reviews of tests. In this volume, tests are evaluated by professionals who are presumed to have some credibility in the assessment field. The most popular tests generally are reviewed by several experts.

Many textbooks (e.g., McLoughlin & Lewis, 1990; Salvia & Ysseldyke, 1991) include reviews of tests, and some books (e.g., Compton, 1984) are devoted entirely to test reviews. And many professional journals such as the *Journal of Psychoeducational Assessment*, the *Journal of Learning Disabilities*, and *The Reading Teacher* also print test reviews on a regular basis.

Unfortunately, the competence of the reviewers used to critique tests in these sources varies widely, and the evaluative criteria that they apply are often unspecified or inconsistently used. As a result, the reviews are frequently contradictory, biased, subjective, or otherwise inadequate. For example, after studying the same set of reliability coefficients, one reviewer may laud a test for its "high" reliability coefficients while a second reviewer may condemn the same test for having "low" reliability. Occasionally a reviewer will overlook a test's critical elements and fixate on its superficial qualities. For example, a reviewer may fail to mention a test's good normative data and write endlessly about the need for an easel, colored pictures or photographs, a carrying case, or some other irrelevant aspect. The *Consumer's Guide* project was undertaken to avoid or at least to minimize these problems.

A DESCRIPTION OF THE CONSUMER'S GUIDE PROJECT

The first step in designing the *Consumer's Guide* was to develop an objective method for obtaining and codifying test reviews. The Reviewer Evaluation Form was constructed for this purpose. Subsequent steps involved selecting expert reviewers to evaluate test scores, choosing the tests to be reviewed, and initiating the test review process.

Developing the Reviewer Evaluation Form

Before a Reviewer Evaluation Form could be designed, the measurement principles that were to be evaluated in the *Consumer's Guide* project had to be identified. Next, objective criteria had to be formulated by which these principles could be evaluated. Finally, the criteria had to be stated in a simple, straightforward, and standard manner and incorporated into a record form that was quick to complete and easy to interpret.

The Reviewer Evaluation Form is time-efficient in that reviewers simply check the appropriate rating within each section being evaluated. Comments or lengthy responses are required only in those few instances when the standard evaluative categories do not account for some unusual or highly specific piece of information provided in a test manual. The Reviewer Evaluation Form is easy to interpret in that all reviewers complete the same form for every test score that is evaluated. This uniformity creates a consistent body of information that can be collected and interpreted readily. The Reviewer Evaluation Form is also objective, since the evaluative criteria are based on widely accepted psychometric practices rather than on the personal preferences of the reviewers.

At this point the reader should turn to Appendix F and study the Reviewer Evaluation Form. The front side is devoted to nontechnical, descriptive information about the test being rated. This information includes the content being measured, the time required to administer the test, the response formats employed, and so on. This portion of the Reviewer Evaluation Form is discussed in detail in Chapter 4.

The reverse side of the Reviewer Evaluation Form contains sections for rating the three measurement areas evaluated in the *Consumer's Guide*: norms, reliability, and validity. A section is also provided for reviewers to record personal remarks concerning research designs or statistical analyses. This space also is used to justify ratings that are not based on the descriptive statements contained in the Reviewer Evaluation Form. For example, the stated criteria might not be appropriate or might not account for an acceptable procedure. This part of the Reviewer Evaluation Form is described in detail in Chapter 3.

Selecting the Review Panel

We knew that the *Consumer's Guide* reviewers would be required to sift through vast amounts of technical information, to consider that information critically and carefully, and to evaluate it objectively. For these reasons, we recruited professionals who had extensive experience in test construction and appraisal and who also had an intimate, working knowledge of statistics and research design. The names and professional affiliations of the *Consumer's Guide* reviewers are listed in Appendix C.

Selecting the Tests

The *Consumer's Guide* includes reviews of individually administered, norm-referenced tests. The first edition of the *Consumer's Guide* contained reviews of tests selected from an extensive pool created by combining the 50 most cited tests in *Tests in Print* (Buros, 1983), tests nominated by our panel of reviewers, and promising new tests. We also included tests that were frequently cited in our own extensive review of research published in professional journals in the fields of education and psychology. Tests published or revised after 1989 were reviewed for this latest edition of the *Consumer's Guide*. In both editions, the list of tests reviewed was further shaped and reduced by our goals for the *Consumer's Guide* project.

First, the reviews in the *Consumer's Guide* were limited to norm-referenced tests, which we defined as tests in which an individual's performance is interpreted in terms of its relationship to the performance of the members of a specified reference group. We recognize that valuable information can be obtained from criterion-referenced tests, direct observation, informal checklists and rating scales, case histories, interviews, cumulative records, or permanent products analysis. These important and useful techniques were not included in the *Consumer's Guide* because the measurement principles and statistical procedures associated with them are different from those associated with norm-referenced tests. To include these techniques in the current *Consumer's Guide* would have required the development of different evaluative criteria. It also would have tripled the number of instruments to be reviewed. In short, a project of that scope would have exhausted our resources and our patience!

We also limited our evaluations to tests designed primarily for use with school-aged students in Grades K–12. We decided to focus on tests that are given individually for diagnostic, screening, or identification purposes and to exclude tests that usually are administered to large groups or on a school-wide basis. Therefore, such test batteries as the *Metropolitan Achievement Test*, the *Stanford Achievement Test*, and the *California Achievement Tests*, among others, are not included in the *Consumer's Guide*. In addition, we eliminated quasi-normed tests designed primarily for clinical use rather than for norm-referenced use.

Obviously, many old tests that are no longer used or are no longer available for purchase were excluded from the *Consumer's Guide*. In many cases, where a test has been revised one or more times, we chose to evaluate the two most recent editions.

Rating the Tests

Finally, after developing the Reviewer Evaluation Form, recruiting expert reviewers, and assembling the list of tests to be evaluated, the actual rating of tests began in earnest. Each test on the *Consumer's Guide* list was assigned to two reviewers. The reviewers then completed a Reviewer Evaluation Form for every score generated by the test. For instance, reviewers assigned to the *Wechsler Intelligence Scale for Children–Third Edition* completed 20 Reviewer Evaluation Forms: one for each of the 10 principal subtest scores, one for each of the 3 supplemental subtest scores, one for each of the 3 quotient scores, and one for each of the 4 performance indexes.

When the two or more sets of reviews on a given test were completed, they were compared by the project staff. If the reviewers agreed on every point, then the Reviewer Evaluation Forms were scored and the results were recorded in Appendix A. When the reviewers disagreed, we reconciled the evaluation by reexamining the data and descriptive information reported in the test's manual.

USES OF THE CONSUMER'S GUIDE

The *Consumer's Guide* has many practical uses. Obviously the basic value of the work is that it saves the reader time in choosing good tests. This is done by providing the reader with objective evaluations of tests that are based on the application of accepted criteria and that are made by two or more professionals experienced in test construction or measurement. It also has value as a means of instructing professionals how to evaluate and to improve tests.

Using the Consumer's Guide to Select Appropriate Tests

Many individuals will use the *Consumer's Guide* because they know what area they want to measure (e.g., reading comprehension) but are undecided about the most appropriate test to choose. In such instances, the user will turn to the Taxonomy in Chapter 4, find the code number for the Reading Comprehension category, and then locate this number in the taxonomic list in Appendix B. That list contains the names of all reading comprehension tests having an Overall Rating of A (Highly Recommended), B (Recommended), and F (Not Recommended). Obviously users will want to choose tests that have an A or B rating. When readers have the names of the A and B tests, they can consult the alphabetic list in Appendix A to learn which of the acceptable tests satisfy their nontechnical requirements for such things as age of the student being tested, input/output modalities, administration time, and so on. Users who have a particular test in mind and only want to know its *Consumer's Guide* rating will turn directly to the alphabetic list in Appendix A.

Occasionally a professional will need to know the psychometric adequacy of a test that was not reviewed in the *Consumer's Guide*. When this happens, he or she should study the criteria presented in Chapter 2, complete the Reviewer Evaluation Form, and rate the test in question using the procedures described in Chapter 3.

Using the Consumer's Guide as an Instructional Tool

The *Consumer's Guide* also has value as a means for teaching college students or others how to evaluate tests. When used in this manner, the students study the *Consumer's Guide* and then evaluate a variety of tests using the Reviewer Evaluation Form as a guide. The student's rating can be compared with the ratings in the *Consumer's Guide* or can be judged by the teacher, who presumably is familiar with the tests that are evaluated.

Whenever students or professionals rate tests, we would appreciate receiving copies of the Reviewer Evaluation Forms. When this is done, please include a vita or biographical sketch of the reviewer. We are especially interested in receiving forms on tests that are not presently included in the *Consumer's Guide* or that are rated differently from those recorded in the guide. In this manner we can perfect our evaluative criteria, correct any errors in the ratings, and add new tests to appendices of future editions.

Using the Consumer's Guide to Improve the Quality of Tests

We hope professionals who build and revise tests will find the material published in this volume to be useful in their endeavors. At the very least, new and revised tests should be constructed to satisfy the evaluative criteria presented. The rating should be of particular interest to test authors who are engaged in revising or updating their tests since the ratings depict the strengths and weaknesses of the existing test. The ratings indicate which of the statistical properties of the test are adequate and which are in need of perfecting.

2

PRINCIPLES OF MEASUREMENT

Three fundamental measurement areas are of particular concern when the technical adequacy of norm-referenced tests is evaluated: norms, reliability, and validity. In this chapter we discuss the importance of each concept, set forth the statistical procedures usually associated with them, and state the criteria used to operationalize these principles in the *Consumer's Guide*. Our discussions are admittedly brief. Readers desiring in-depth discussions of these topics are referred to the primary sources cited throughout the text.

NORMS

In this section we discuss the process by which normative data are acquired and reported. Particular attention is paid to the nature of the normative sample and to the various kinds of normative scores that are commonly derived from a test's raw scores. This section concludes with a discussion of how the principles governing norms were operationalized as evaluative criteria for the *Consumer's Guide*.

Normative Sample

The process of administering a test in a systematic and consistent way to a large, representative sample of individuals for the purpose of preparing comparative scores is called *norming*. The normative sample should be representative of the specified group or groups of people with whom the test

developers intend their instrument to be used. This reference group may be the nation as a whole, some particular local or geographic sample, students in a specific school district, or an even more limited group such as 10th-grade algebra students, female medical students, or individuals with a particular disability. Generally, national norms are more useful than other types of norms because they are more widely applicable; but they are inherently no better than norms based on the performance of more limited or specific samples.

Regardless of the intended reference group, test developers should demonstrate that the test's normative sample is, in fact, representative of the specified reference group. This is easy to accomplish with national norms because a considerable amount of demographic information is known about a nation's population as a whole and is readily available through such publications as the most current *Statistical Abstract of the United States* (1990). Similar information is available for Canada, Australia, Mexico, and other countries as well. Detailed information about gender, education, occupation, family income, geographic dispersion, domicile, racial and ethnic makeup, and native language of a country's population is available. Evidence of national representativeness rests on the extent to which test developers show that the important demographic characteristics of their normative sample approximate those of the reference population as a whole.

Representativeness of a sample can be assured in several ways. One way is to select subjects on the basis of some stratified procedure. With this method, knowledge of the characteristics of a population is used to choose the sample. For instance, if a national sample is needed, the nation might be divided according to major census districts. The sample representing a particular district would be selected so that the percentage of subjects in such categories as gender, ethnicity, and social class matches the percentage of subjects in those categories within the census district as a whole. As much as possible, random selection procedures are used to choose individual cases. This manner of selecting a sample is most highly recommended.

When norms are based on the performance of a specified reference group that is not national, the test developer must specify the important demographic characteristics known or believed to be present within the population and then must demonstrate the representativeness of the normative sample that was selected. For example, the characteristics of states, counties, cities, and school districts are available from census data, and a local normative group should have a similar demographic makeup.

Sometimes the characteristics of the population are unknown (e.g., the population of adults who are mentally retarded). On these occasions a detailed description of the sample's characteristics is all that is possible. In some instances it may be both feasible and desirable to develop norms by testing the entire population rather than to select a normative group from within that population.

Representativeness also implies currency, as Salvia and Ysseldyke (1991), among others, have pointed out. A reading test normed on a representative sample obtained in 1950 is not especially helpful in interpreting the scores of students who take the test in 1988. Not only have the national demographics shifted considerably since the original standardization of the test, but the patterns of reading performance also might have changed in 38 years. This is particularly true of academic areas that are subject to change in curricular content or instructional methods. In a rapidly changing world, normative data can become outdated fairly quickly.

Obtaining a representative sample also is a function of sample size. The sample must be large enough to ensure that demographic representativeness can be achieved. The larger the sample, the more likely it is to be representative without resorting to the selection of subjects on a nonrandom basis or by otherwise manipulating data. In addition, Salvia and Ysseldyke (1991) suggested that "in a normally distributed array of scores, one hundred subjects is the minimum number for which a full range of percentiles can be computed and for which standard scores between ±2.3 standard deviations can be computed without extrapolation" (p. 115).

Normative Scores

Normative scores are obtained by transforming the raw scores of the individuals in the normative group into scores that are normally distributed or are associated with age or grade. We will discuss three broad categories of normative scores: standard scores, percentile ranks, and age or grade equivalents.

Standard scores.   Standard scores are deviation scores with a stated distribution. They are derived from the cumulative frequency of the raw scores made by the individuals in the normative group. A standard score has a specified position in the normal curve distribution that identifies the score's distance from the mean (M) of the normative group relative to the standard deviation (SD) of the distribution.

Depending on the preference of the test developer, raw scores can be converted into a variety of standard score distributions. The most popular of these are stanines (M = 5, SD = 1.96), T-scores (M = 50, SD = 10), z-scores (M = 0, SD = 1), and deviation quotients (M = 100, SD = 15). Standard scores are particularly useful because they are interval data and therefore can be combined, averaged, and otherwise manipulated statistically. They also are closely related to percentile ranks.

Percentile ranks.   Percentile ranks indicate the percentage of people in the normative group who achieved raw scores that were higher or lower than a particular score. They are easy to interpret. A percentile rank of 40 indicates that the person who earned the score achieved at the same level or better than 40% of the normative sample and scored lower than 60% of that group. Because of this, they are easily understood by parents and children as well as by professionals.

Deciles and quartiles are similar to percentile ranks. Whereas percentiles range from 1 to 100, deciles range from 1 to 10 and quartiles from 1 to 4. The advantages and disadvantages of these scores have been explained fully by Aiken (1988), Salvia and Ysseldyke (1991), and Wallace, Larsen, and Elksnin (1992).

Age and grade equivalents.   Age and grade equivalents are derived by computing the average raw score made by people of a given age or at a particular grade level. That point is recorded on a graph that has raw scores along one axis and age or grade levels on the other axis. Points are plotted for the scores obtained at different ages and grades and a line is drawn to connect these points so that one can determine easily what age or grade corresponds to each raw score.

Age and grade equivalents are reported in test manuals primarily because they enjoy a false reputation as easily understood and useful scores. Despite the continuing popularity of age and grade equivalents, most knowledgeable psychometrists have suggested that they should be avoided whenever possible. In particular, the International Reading Association (1980) and the American Psychological Association (1985) have advocated abandoning these scores.

Among the problems associated with age and grade equivalents is that their use promotes a concept of normal performance that is inaccurate and misleading. First, there is no such thing as typical reading performance at the 2.2 grade level. Second, computation of age and grade equivalents requires interpolation between obtained points on the graph so that scores are generated for an age or grade level that may not actually have been tested. Such a method of calculating age and grade equivalents also implies an even rate of development or change in the attribute being measured. Finally, age and grade norms are ordinal scales; as such, the distance between points on the scale is not equal, a reality that hinders the direct comparison or profiling of scores. Salvia and Ysseldyke (1991) provided a detailed discussion of the problems of age and grade equivalents; the appropriate sections of Aiken (1988) are also particularly noteworthy.

The Consumer's Guide Evaluative Criteria for Norms

Based upon our review of the measurement principles associated with test norms, we selected four specific areas to evaluate in the *Consumer's Guide*: normative scores, size of the normative group, demographic characteristics of the normative group, and recency of normative data. The criteria are reproduced below, followed by a brief rationale for their selection. The specific ways in which these criteria were applied by our reviewers in the actual *Consumer's Guide* rating process are detailed in the next chapter.

The reader will note that there are three criteria in every area. The first criterion illustrates the lowest or poorest technical quality; it represents unacceptable psychometric practice. The second criterion illustrates adequate technical quality; it represents acceptable psychometric practice. The third and final criterion illustrates the highest technical quality; it represents good psychometric practice.

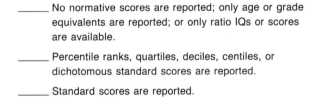

A. Normative Scores

_____ No normative scores are reported; only age or grade equivalents are reported; or only ratio IQs or scores are available.

_____ Percentile ranks, quartiles, deciles, centiles, or dichotomous standard scores are reported.

_____ Standard scores are reported.

The absence of normative scores or the exclusive use of raw scores, age equivalent scores, grade equivalent scores, or ratio scores, particularly ratio IQs, is not acceptable for norm-referenced tests. This is the lowest criterion. The use

of percentile ranks (and related scores) is deemed to be acceptable, and the use of standard scores is deemed to be good. The distinction between percentile ranks and standard scores is based on the versatility of the scores. Standard scores are not inherently any better than percentile ranks. However, they are interval data, a quality that makes them useful in more situations than percentile ranks.

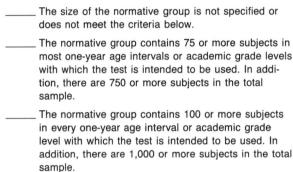

B. Size of the Normative Group

_____ The size of the normative group is not specified or does not meet the criteria below.

_____ The normative group contains 75 or more subjects in most one-year age intervals or academic grade levels with which the test is intended to be used. In addition, there are 750 or more subjects in the total sample.

_____ The normative group contains 100 or more subjects in every one-year age interval or academic grade level with which the test is intended to be used. In addition, there are 1,000 or more subjects in the total sample.

The optimum size of a normative group is at least 100 subjects in every age interval; this ensures sufficient dispersion for the calculation of percentile ranks and standard scores. The 1,000-subject criterion for the overall size of the normative group is a figure that we selected somewhat arbitrarily to ensure that there are sufficient subjects within the normative sample to represent all of the major demographic characteristics. The 75/750 criterion that is applied for the middle or acceptable level is based on a recognition that it is not always possible to have 100 subjects at each age interval or a total of 1,000 subjects in the sample. We reasoned that an average of 75 subjects usually would be adequate, so we settled on 75 subjects per age interval and 750 subjects overall as the minimum acceptable level. Any number of subjects under the 75/750 criterion, though, is unacceptable. Obviously, it is considered poor practice for a test author to omit any reference to the size of the normative sample.

C. Demographic Characteristics of the Normative Group

_____ The characteristics of the normative group are not specified or do not meet the criteria below.

_____ The characteristics of the normative group correspond approximately to the known characteristics of the specified population on three or four of the following variables: gender, domicile, parental education, parental occupation, geographic region, race, ethnicity, intelligence, socioeconomic status, or other relevant variables (specify: _____).

_____ The characteristics of the normative group correspond approximately to the known characteristics of the specified population on five or more of the following variables: gender, domicile, parental education, parental occupation, geographic region, race, ethnicity, intelligence, socioeconomic status, or other relevant variables (specify: _____).

The highest criterion is reserved for tests with normative samples that are representative of five or more important demographic characteristics. We arrived at this figure after reviewing the number of characteristics that could be identified and reported for a sample of school-aged subjects. We determined that three or four characteristics would be required at the middle, acceptable level because demographic characteristics are often interrelated; therefore, a sample that was representative across three or four variables was probably representative across most characteristics. However, anything less than three characteristics would not appear to be representative. Hence, the lowest criterion is assigned when the test manual fails to describe the normative group or can demonstrate representativeness on only one or two pertinent characteristics.

D. Recency of Normative Data

Normative data were gathered in

_____ 1975 or before.

_____ 1976–1985.

_____ 1986 or after.

The dates that were selected for the various recency criteria are based loosely on the frequency of census data collection as well as sociological estimates of what constitutes a generation of students in a school. When more than 15 years have passed, one can assume that a full generation of students has passed through school since normative data were collected; this is too long a period of time to assume that norms are still appropriate. Major demographic shifts will have occurred and educational practice will have been revised substantially during that period. Thus, our lowest criterion is set for norms developed in 1975 or before. Census data are estimated annually in this country, but they are actually collected every decade; we selected half of that period, 5 years, as the demarcation between good and acceptable practice.

RELIABILITY

Reliability is the degree to which a test is consistent in its scores or measurements. Knowledge about a test's reliability determines the degree of confidence that one can place in its results.

When examiners use unreliable tests, they get unstable results. Thus, if an unreliable test is used, students can be tested on one day and be "diagnosed" as having a particular deficiency. Testing on the next day might well produce normal results. The problem seems to have vanished. Of course, the problem did not really vanish. It may never have existed in the first place, or it could have been a false-positive by-product of the test's inadequate reliability.

Obviously such diagnoses are dubious and can be particularly damaging to students who receive or fail to receive needed services because they have been misdiagnosed. The use of unreliable tests also can cause considerable embarrassment to examiners who, on the basis of the initial examination, have informed teachers about the presence and seriousness of "the problems," planned remedial programs for the children, and scheduled interviews with their parents. Examiners can considerably lessen both of these consequences by choosing tests that have good reliability and therefore have little error associated with their scores.

The study of a test's reliability centers on estimating the amount of error variance associated with its scores. According to Anastasi (1988), this error can be related to such things as content sampling, time sampling, and interscorer differences. In this section we discuss each of these sources of error, the types of reliability that are used to estimate them, and the role of standard error of measurement. In addition, the manner in which the principles relating to reliability were operationalized into evaluative criteria is discussed.

Content Sampling Error (Internal Consistency Reliability)

Content sampling usually refers to internal consistency reliability, a measure of the interrelationship among test items. The purpose of a test is to measure a certain characteristic, ability, or content; the more the test's items relate to each other, the smaller the content sampling error will be. If the test items are unrelated to each other, they probably are measuring different qualities. Consequently the content sampling error would be great and the test's internal consistency reliability low. Common procedures for estimating internal consistency reliability are the split-half method, the Kuder-Richardson and coefficient Alpha formulas, and the immediate test-retest with alternate forms method.

Split-half procedure. The split-half procedure is one way to investigate the content sampling error or internal consistency reliability of a test. The test is administered one time to a sample of subjects. The items then are split into equivalent halves using some logical procedure such as a separation based on odd-even item numbers, upper half/lower half item numbers, random allocation of items into two halves, or Gutman's split-half procedure. The items are scored, sums for each half are computed, and the two totals are correlated. The resulting coefficient is an index of the reliability of each half-test. To gain an estimate of the reliability of the full-length test and to correct for the deflating influence of shortened test length, the Spearman-Brown correction formula is applied to the split-half coefficient.

Kuder-Richardson and coefficient Alpha formulas. Like the split-half procedure, the Kuder-Richardson method also is calculated using the scores from a single administration of a test. Theoretically, this method is the ultimate in "split-halving," for its results are equal to the mean of all possible split-half coefficients that could be calculated.

Instead of actually splitting the test into halves, this method involves applying one of several formulas to the test data. The most popular formula is the Kuder-Richardson Formula #20, which is based on the proportion of people passing each item and on the standard deviation of the total score. When done by hand, this method is tedious, so a computer usually is employed. The shorter and less accurate Kuder-Richardson Formula #21 sometimes is reported because it lends itself to hand calculations. In most cases, the coefficient that results from Formula #21 will be slightly smaller than that yielded by Formula #20.

Increasingly one reads that internal consistency was calculated using coefficient Alpha. This statistic is simply a more sophisticated generalization of Formula #20 that owes its popularity to the advent of computerized calculations.

Immediate test-retest with alternate forms. The use of alternate forms is another way of estimating content sampling error. To estimate internal consistency reliability with this technique, two equivalent forms of a test are given in immediate succession and the scores are correlated. Since the forms are equivalent, this method is not unlike the split-half procedure described earlier except that it requires two full-length tests.

Time Sampling Error (Stability Reliability)

Error due to time sampling refers to the extent to which a person's test performance is consistent or stable over a period of time. The importance of this kind of reliability in diagnostics is readily apparent. Unstable tests yield unstable results, and remedial programs or treatments designed on the basis of such results are likely to be misdirected or unnecessary. Stability reliability is typically estimated by the delayed test-retest method either using a single form of the test or using alternate forms. Because measures of a test's stability will always be confounded by the test's internal consistency, a few authors choose to extract the internal consistency coefficient from the obtained test-retest coefficient using the method described by Anastasi (1988).

Delayed test-retest with a single form. With this procedure a single test is given to a group of subjects; after a period of time, the same test is readministered to the same group of subjects, and the results are compared. The degree of similarity indicates the degree of stability reliability possessed by the test. The amount of time between the testings can vary from a few days to several months, 2 weeks being the most common practice. Though it is widely used, Anastasi (1988) asserts that for the large majority of psychological tests, the test-retest technique is inappropriate. She cites a variety of problems involving recall of items, practice, changes in the nature of the test situation due to retesting, and other factors. In addition, some tests measure content that presents special problems in the analysis of stability reliability. Tests of personality and other affective characteristics are an example. Anastasi (1988) noted that the content

> measured by personality tests . . . is more changeable over time than that measured by tests of ability. [This] fact complicates the determination of test reliability, since random temporal fluctuations in test performance are likely to become confused with broad systematic behavior changes. Even over relatively short intervals, it cannot be assumed that variations in test response are restricted to the test itself and do not characterize the area of nontest behavior under consideration. (p. 532)

Because of these problems, Anastasi recommended delayed test-retest with alternate forms.

Delayed test-retest with alternate forms. The best estimate of time sampling error requires the use of alternate forms. As we pointed out earlier, the reliability coefficient that results when the alternate form is given immediately following the first test is an estimate of error due to content sampling. When there is a delay between the administration of the two tests, the resulting coefficient estimates both content and time sampling error. Using this procedure, Anastasi (1988) estimated time sampling error by extracting the known or measured content sampling error of the two tests from the delayed alternate forms reliability coefficient. The actual interaction of time sampling and content sampling in this method cannot be determined precisely.

Occasionally a shortened version of a test will be developed. Correlating the abbreviated or short-form test with the original test may demonstrate the equivalency of the two tests, but they are not identical measures. For this reason, one cannot establish the stability reliability of the tests through the part test/whole test correlation.

Interscorer Differences Error (Scorer Reliability)

In addition to content and time sampling error, a third source of error is found in the variability with which individual examiners score a test. This variability often results when scorers are called upon to make subjective judgments about test performance, as when using projective tests of personality or speech articulation tests. It is less likely to occur on multiple choice tests or tests with only one correct answer designated. Scorer reliability usually is studied by having two or more examiners score the same test performance, tallying the results, and correlating or otherwise comparing the different examiners' scores.

Standard Error of Measurement

One of the primary reasons for determining a reliability coefficient is to estimate the test's standard error of measurement (SEM). This is done by inserting the coefficient into the formula $SEM = SD \sqrt{1 - r}$. In this formula SD refers to the standard deviation of the test score, and r refers to the test score's reliability coefficient. The resulting value is actually the standard deviation of the error distribution around a true score. As such, it sets the limits of confidence that an examiner can have in any one test score. For example, if a student scores 55 on a test that has less than perfect reliability (as they all do), and if we know that the SEM for the test is 3 points, then we can have confidence that 68% of the time the student's true score would be somewhere between 52 and 58. Reliable tests yield relatively small SEMs.

Consumer's Guide Evaluation Criteria for Test Reliability

Based upon our review of the measurement principles associated with a test's reliability, we decided to evaluate only two kinds of reliability in the Consumer's Guide: internal consistency reliability and stability reliability. Two kinds of reliability that were not evaluated are standard error of measurement and interscorer/interrater reliability. Standard error of measurement was not included because it is related to the value of an individual test score and because it is calculated directly from a set of reliability coefficients,

leading to the logical assumption that tests with adequate reliability coefficients also will have acceptable standard errors of measurement. Interscorer reliability is not evaluated because, while such differences do occur, scorer or rater error is a very small portion of the error variance of most of the norm-referenced tests reviewed for the Consumer's Guide. The administration and scoring procedures are so highly standardized on most of these tests that only a gross error by the examiner would make a significant difference.

The criteria used to evaluate both internal consistency and stability reliability are reproduced below, followed by a brief rationale for their selection. The specific ways in which these criteria were applied by our reviewers in the actual Consumer's Guide rating process are detailed in the next chapter.

The reader will note that, in both instances, three criteria were designated. The first criterion illustrates the lowest or poorest technical quality; it represents unacceptable psychometric practice. The second criterion illustrates adequate technical quality; it represents acceptable psychometric practice. The third criterion illustrates the highest technical quality; it represents good psychometric practice.

Reliability

A. Internal Consistency Reliability

Internal consistency reliability

_____ Is not reported; is below .80 at most ages; or is reported with no apparent controls for the effects of age.

_____ Is .80 or above at most ages when reported for two or more age intervals spanning no more than three years each; is .80–.89 for a single group when evidence is presented to demonstrate that the test is not significantly related to age; or is .80 or above when the effects of age are controlled statistically.

_____ Is .90 or above at most ages when reported for two or more age intervals spanning no more than three years each; or is .90 or above for a single group when evidence is presented to demonstrate that the test is not significantly related to age.

B. Stability Reliability

Stability reliability

_____ Is not reported; is below .80 at most ages; or is reported with no apparent controls for the effects of age.

_____ Is .80 or above at most ages when reported for two or more age intervals spanning no more than three years each; is .80–.89 for a single group when evidence is presented to demonstrate that the test is not significantly related to age; or is .80 or above when the effects of age are controlled statistically.

_____ Is .90 or above at most ages when reported for two or more age intervals spanning no more than three years each; or is .90 or above for a single group when evidence is presented to demonstrate that the test is not significantly related to age.

Kelley (1927), a pioneer in test construction, encouraged his colleagues to adopt a very high standard of reliability. He recommended .50 for tests that would be used to measure group achievement, .90 for tests used to measure differences in group performance, .94 for tests intended to measure individual achievement, and a near perfect .98 for tests used to measure differences among multiple performances by a single individual. Few tests that are reviewed in the *Consumer's Guide* could pass Kelley's standard, including those tests that enjoy both great popularity and reputations for statistical adequacy. In fact, Guilford (1956), Helmstadter (1964), and others have argued that these standards are much too rigorous for practical purposes. They argued for a less stringent minimum standard of .70 or .80; however, Guilford did advocate the .94 standard for tests used to discriminate among individuals, which again is a goal of many norm-referenced assessment devices used in the schools. Nunnally (1978) believed that reliability coefficients should reach the .90s before an examiner assumes that a test's results have value for making individual judgments; Aiken (1988) recommended .85 for this purpose. Salvia and Ysseldyke (1991) developed tripartite standards for tests that will be used to measure group performance (.60), tests that will be used for screening (.80), and tests that will be used to make diagnostic decisions about individual students (.90). Sattler (1988) contended that "for most tests of cognitive and special abilities, a reliability coefficient of .80 or higher is generally considered to be acceptable" (p. 25).

Our review of the literature led us to the conclusion that .80 is the minimum acceptable level of reliability for highly standardized, norm-referenced tests such as those reviewed in the *Consumer's Guide*. The more rigorous .90 is the preferred level.

VALIDITY

Validity refers to the extent to which the results of an evaluation procedure serve the particular uses for which they are intended. Sattler (1988) clarified this definition by stating that validity also refers to "the appropriateness with which inferences can be made on the basis of test results" (p. 23). Put another way, a test's results are valid when they measure the qualities or attributes that they are purported to measure.

In its *Standards for Educational and Psychological Tests*, the American Psychological Association (1985) suggested that test developers investigate three types of validity: content, criterion-related, and construct. This suggestion is echoed in the work of Gronlund and Linn (1990), Aiken (1988), Anastasi (1988), and Salvia and Ysseldyke (1991). In this section we discuss these three types of validity and the development of criteria for the *Consumer's Guide* to evaluate the validity of tests.

Content Validity

Content validity refers to the extent to which a particular domain or content is sampled adequately. Nunnally (1978) remarked that this type of validity is not "tested" but that it is "ensured" by carefully planning the procedures used during test construction and item selection and by establishing sensible criteria that will result in the retention of items that properly represent the intended domain. This selection process is based both on knowledge of the desired content and on the application of statistical item-analytic procedures that permit the identification of items that measure something in common.

Test developers use their knowledge of the domain to be tested to generate an initial body of items. Then they apply a variety of statistical procedures to evaluate the effectiveness of each item. This item analysis permits the developer to choose the good items and to discard those that are poor. Traditionally, two analyses are undertaken: item discrimination and item difficulty.

Item discrimination refers to "the degree to which an item discriminates correctly among examinees in the behavior that the test is designed to measure" (Anastasi, 1988, p. 200). The point-biserial correlation technique, by which each item is correlated with the total test score, is generally used to determine item discrimination, which is sometimes called item discriminating power or item validity.

Item difficulty is the percentage of children who pass an item. It is used to identify items that are too easy or too difficult to be particularly discriminating. Item difficulty percentages also are used to arrange items in easy-to-difficult order.

Studies of item discrimination and item difficulty are not the only empirical approaches that are available for selecting items. Today many researchers use Rasch-Wright procedures or factor analytic techniques to construct and select test items.

Sattler (1988) suggested that a test probably has good content validity if one can answer satisfactorily the following three questions:

1. Are the test questions appropriate test questions and does the test measure the domain of interest?

2. Does the test contain enough information to cover appropriately what it is supposed to measure?

3. What is the level of mastery at which the content is being assessed? (p. 30)

For some tests, such as a college final examination in world geography, content validity may be the only type of validity available or needed. For norm-referenced tests that will be used for diagnostic, screening, identification, and research purposes, content validity alone is usually insufficient.

Criterion-Related Validity

Studies of criterion-related validity examine the relationship of test scores to some criterion measure, such as a test, a diagnostic classification, or performance in a particular class or job. Two types of criterion-related validity are described in the measurement literature: predictive and concurrent.

In studies of predictive validity, the test being validated is used to estimate (or predict) some important form of future behavior that is external to the test. These studies are conducted over time. Predictive validity is of particular consequence to most measures of readiness or aptitude. It is important to know that a person who scored high on a clerical aptitude test subsequently obtained a good grade in a typing class or performed well on the job as a typist, or that a preschooler who scored low on a school readiness measure eventually required special services or experienced academic difficulties.

Concurrent validity is another form of criterion-related validity that often is studied by test developers. In this type of research, performance on one test is compared with contemporaneous performance on another test of the same construct or a similar ability. The criterion test itself must have demonstrated reliability and validity of its own if it is to be considered an acceptable criterion measure.

Often a new (and, one hopes, improved) test of an ability will be correlated with an older established test of the same or similar ability to provide evidence of criterion-related validity. Thus, a new IQ test might be correlated with the *Wechsler Intelligence Scale for Children–Third Edition*. For the purpose of demonstrating criterion-related validity, the tests need not be equivalent as long as they measure like abilities to some practical degree. The degree of similarity between the predictor test and the criterion test is reflected in the size of the validity coefficient, another specific use of the correlation coefficient.

Construct Validity

Construct validity refers to the extent to which test performance can be interpreted in terms of those psychological constructs that are identified as inherent to the test. Knowledge of these constructs allows one to formulate hypotheses about the use of the test's results. The testing of these hypotheses generates information that reflects on the test's construct validity. For example, a test that is supposed to measure a developmental ability should correlate with chronological age; the results of a test of reasoning ability should be different for groups known to differ in intellectual capacity; performance on tests of reading should bear some relationship to actual reading performance in school; and tests of anxiety should distinguish between people being treated for stress-related disorders and people not under treatment.

We conclude this section on validity by mentioning that authorities agree more on the definitions of the types of validity than they agree on which analyses and research designs relate to each type of validity. For example, Aiken (1988) and Anastasi (1988) accept item-test correlations as evidence of construct validity; Salvia and Ysseldyke (1988) do not. Most authorities agree that both criterion-related and construct validity can be studied by correlating the new test with other tests, but these sources are vague, confusing, and often conflicting when specifying the conditions under which the correlations reflect criterion-related validity and the conditions under which they reflect construct validity. In short, the discussions of validity are not as precise as those pertaining to reliability. Perhaps this is because the concept of validity is itself more abstract and, therefore, more difficult to explain. Anastasi (1988) put the case quite well: "content, criterion-related, and construct validation do not correspond to distinct or logically coordinate categories. On the contrary, construct validity is a comprehensive concept, which includes the other types" (pp. 152–153). This explains why one test author will report the results of a particular analysis (e.g., the correlation of a new achievement test with an older, established achievement test) as evidence of construct validity, while another author will report the same analysis as evidence of criterion-related validity.

In writing about the arbitrary classification of validity research into the categories of content, criterion-related, and construct validity, Anastasi (1984) pointed out that this tripartite division has helped to clarify our thinking about validation procedures but that it has provided some negative effects on testing practice. She made the following suggestion:

Validity should be built into the test from the outset, rather than being limited to the last stages of test development as in the traditional criterion-related validation. Typically, the validation process begins with the formulation of detailed trait definitions, derived from both psychological theory and prior research. Test items are then prepared to fit the trait definitions. Empirical item analyses follow, with the selection of the most effective (i.e., valid) items from the initial item pools. Other appropriate internal analyses may then be carried out, including factor analyses of item clusters or subtests. The final stage covers validation and cross-validation of various scores and interpretive combinations of scores through statistical analyses against external, real-life criteria. (p. 358)

Because we agree with Anastasi (1984) that test validation "represents essentially a gradual accumulation of data from many sources and by many methods" (p. 359), we did not attempt to organize the *Consumer's Guide* evaluation of test validity into its various types. Instead, we chose to emphasize the different designs that researchers use to study and demonstrate test validity.

As is the case with reliability studies, researchers who study validity often report their results as correlation coefficients, a statistic that represents the relationship between two variables. While there are no hard and fast rules about the interpretation of validity coefficients, a few general principles do exist. First, to be accepted as support for a test's validity, the coefficient must be statistically significant at or beyond the .05 level of confidence (Anastasi, 1988). Second, the coefficient needs to be of a reasonable size. Authorities seem to disagree on the magnitude that a significant validity coefficient has to reach in order to support a test's validity. Nunnally (1978) and Anastasi (1988) commented that under a few specified conditions significant coefficients as low as .20 or .30 can be useful in establishing the validity of a test's results. Other sources (e.g., Garrett, 1954) prefer .40. Of course, these criteria would be reversed in studies where negative relationships, or no relationships at all, were hypothesized.

Even though simple correlation is the more common technique used in studying validity, several other correlational techniques, such as factor analysis, multiple correlation, and regression, are employed widely. All of these correlational procedures contribute to the study of validity by providing answers to this question: To what is the test related?

Of course, not all validity data are derived from correlation. Some validity studies deal with questions like this: What kinds of groups can be distinguished on the basis of a test's results? These questions are concerned with matters of difference rather than relationships and use *t*-tests, Chi-squares, analyses of variance, and other noncorrelational statistics. Results that derive from such analyses often are reported as *t*s or *F*s rather than as coefficients. To be accepted as support for a test's validity, these values must be statistically significant at or beyond the .05 level.

Whether validity is studied by correlation or by tests of difference does not matter; they yield equally good data. Consider the following construct validity example.

Researchers may wish to study validity of a given test by investigating the influence of chronological age on its scores. Some researchers will test a large group of individuals who range widely in age. Correlating age with the test scores yields a validity coefficient of .60 ($p \leq .05$). Another piece of research also used a group of individuals who varied widely in age, but instead of correlating scores to age, the researchers divided their group into five subgroups, using age as the criterion for placement in a subgroup. Thus, Subgroup 1 was composed of the youngest members in the group, and Subgroup 5 had the oldest members. All individuals were given the test, and the average score for each subgroup was computed. The raw scores for the subgroups were tested for differences using analysis of variance; the resulting F was 15.44 ($p \leq .05$). This indicated that the subgroups made significantly different scores on the test. By consulting the averages of each subgroup, one can quickly determine that the older subgroup had higher average scores than the younger subgroup. The results of both approaches support the construct validity of the test being studied if test performance is hypothesized to be developmental or age-related.

Consumer's Guide Evaluative Criteria for Test Validity

Based upon our review of the measurement principles associated with validity, we decided not to divide the evaluation criteria into the traditional three areas of content, criterion-related, and construct validity. Instead, we decided simply to list the various types of research that typically are conducted to study the validity of a test score. This list is reproduced below, followed by a brief rationale for our evaluative criteria. The specific way in which this list was used by our reviewers in the actual *Consumer's Guide* rating process is detailed in the next chapter.

Validity

_____ Validity is not reported; validity studies are not acceptable in design; validity studies do not yield significant results as hypothesized; or validity is supported exclusively by nonempirical evidence of content validity.

_____ Validity is supported by studies that provide appropriate evidence that the test score

_____ is related as hypothesized to age or grade.

_____ correlates as hypothesized with measures of achievement.

_____ correlates as hypothesized with measures of aptitude/developmental abilities or general intelligence.

_____ correlates as hypothesized with measures of affect.

_____ produces hypothesized multiple correlation/regression results.

_____ has hypothesized factor structures.

_____ predicts appropriately over time.

_____ distinguishes between specified groups.

_____ intercorrelates as hypothesized with the test's other scores.

_____ has appropriate item-total correlations, item discriminating power, or evidence of another appropriate data-based approach to item selection.

_____ discriminates as hypothesized on the basis of gender, race, ethnicity, or other demographic variables.

_____ other (specify: _____).

Reviewers were asked to judge the adequacy of each research design reported in a test manual. They also were required to verify that the results of a particular study were significant. For instance, all research had to produce significant results, as hypothesized, at the .05 level or greater. In addition, correlational research had to produce coefficients that reached at least .35 in magnitude. In short, reviewers noted all of the studies reported in a test manual that were well designed and that produced significant, hypothesized results.

The criteria that we subsequently applied to evaluate the validity of a particular test score were based on the number of different types of validity research studies undertaken. We were not concerned with the number of validity studies reported but with the variety of research conducted. We established our criteria in this way because validity accrues over time and cannot be established conclusively by one or two studies, no matter how well designed. In addition, the three major types of validity (content, criterion-related, and construct) do not constitute discrete categories; a single study might satisfy the requirements for more than one type of validity.

We considered it to be unacceptable psychometric practice when no validity studies were reported, when flawed research designs were employed, when the results were not significant, or when only nonempirical evidence of validity was provided. Our criterion for adequate or acceptable psychometric practice was that at least three different types of well-designed validity research yielding significant, hypothesized results are reported. This figure is an arbitrary one that we believe reflects sufficient diversity in the accumulated validity evidence. The criterion for good psychometric practice was five or more different types of well-designed validity research that yielded significant, hypothesized results. Again, the figure was determined somewhat arbitrarily, but we believe it accurately reflects the diverse types of research that are characteristic of extremely well-built tests.

3

EVALUATING THE TECHNICAL CHARACTERISTICS OF TESTS

The object of the *Consumer's Guide* project was to operationalize theoretical principles of measurement so that objective, useful, and unbiased judgments could be made about the technical characteristics of individual test scores. This chapter describes the specific evaluation and scoring criteria that *Consumer's Guide* reviewers used when they were rating the technical adequacy of the various test scores included in this volume. Evaluative criteria for norms, reliability, and validity are discussed, and examples are provided to illustrate the specific ways in which the criteria were applied. The procedures used to generate the *Consumer's Guide* ratings also are described.

Readers should note that the discussion provided here does not contain any explanation or rationale for the criteria that were selected. Such theoretical information—including measurement issues, statistical procedures, and research designs as they relate to preferred practice in test construction—was discussed in the previous chapter. Only the application of the criteria is discussed here.

RATING TEST NORMS

The Norms section of the Reviewer Evaluation Form has four parts. They are Normative Scores, Size of the Normative Group, Demographic Characteristics of the Normative Group, and Recency of Normative Data. Each of these four components is reproduced below, followed by a discussion of the ways in which reviewers evaluated them.

A. Normative Scores

_____ No normative scores are reported; only age or grade equivalents are reported; or only ratio IQs or scores are available.

_____ Percentile ranks, quartiles, deciles, centiles, or dichotomous standard scores are reported.

_____ Standard scores are reported.

The lowest rating in this section, Unacceptable, is reserved for those tests that have no scores at all, that report only raw scores, or that convert raw scores into nonnormative scores. The nonnormative scores that we encountered most frequently were age equivalent scores, mental ages, grade equivalent scores, and ratio scores, particularly ratio IQs. For example, any intelligence quotient that is calculated by dividing a student's mental age by chronological age and multiplying the result by 100 is a ratio IQ and would be rated Unacceptable. When the raw scores for a reading test can only be converted to grade equivalents (e.g., a grade equivalent of 2.2), that score also is rated Unacceptable.

An Acceptable rating is awarded to two kinds of normative scores. The first are scores related to the percentage of scores above and below a specified point, including percentile ranks, centiles, deciles, and quartiles. Any test score that can be converted to percentile ranks and related scores is Acceptable. The second kind, called dichotomous standard scores, are scores that designate a cutoff point dividing the normative group into two parts, such as At Risk and Not At Risk. To qualify as a normative score, the cutoff for dichotomous standard scores must be derived statistically from the performance of a normative group. If the demarcation is determined intuitively or on the basis of clinical judgment, then the dichotomous score is not a normative score and is rated Unacceptable. For instance, if the test manual for a kindergarten screening test reports the mean and standard deviation of the normative group and then notes that any student who scores more than one standard deviation below the mean is considered to be At Risk for school failure, then the rating would be Acceptable. On the other hand, if this same test reported no scores for the normative group and simply stated that any student scoring 14 raw points or less is At Risk, then the rating would be Unacceptable.

Good ratings are given to standard scores. Standard scores are defined here as any type of normative score in which the raw score distribution has been normalized or transformed to a distribution with a predetermined mean and standard deviation. Examples of standard scores are z-scores, T-scores, scaled scores, stanines, deviation quotients, and normal curve equivalents. The Good rating also is given to composite standard scores that are formed by pooling standard scores from some combination of subtests. The Wechsler quotients are good examples of this.

Most tests report several types of scores. The rating is accorded to the highest level of score used. For instance, if the raw scores from a math test can be converted to grade equivalents and ratio IQs, then the rating is Unacceptable. If the raw scores can be converted to grade equivalents and percentile ranks, then the rating is Acceptable. If, however, the raw scores can be converted to grade equivalents, percentile ranks, and T-scores, then the rating is Good.

B. Size of the Normative Group

_____ The size of the normative group is not specified or does not meet the criteria below.

_____ The normative group contains 75 or more subjects in most one-year age intervals or academic grade levels with which the test is intended to be used. In addition, there are 750 or more subjects in the total sample.

_____ The normative group contains 100 or more subjects in every one-year age interval or academic grade level with which the test is intended to be used. In addition, there are 1,000 or more subjects in the total sample.

If the size of a test's normative group is not specified or if the size does not meet the stated criteria, then the test score in question receives an Unacceptable rating. For example, if the normative group for an early childhood screening test included 200 three-year-olds, 200 four-year-olds, and 200 five-year-olds, then the rating would be Unacceptable because the total sample size is under 750.

To earn an Acceptable rating, the normative group (a) must include 75 or more subjects in more than half of the one-year age intervals or academic grade levels with which the test is intended to be used and (b) also must include 750 or more subjects in the total group. For instance, if a test score is intended to be used in kindergarten through Grade 5, then in order to achieve an Acceptable rating the test's normative group must have at least 750 members overall, including at least 75 subjects in four or more of the six one-year intervals (i.e., kindergarten, Grade 1, Grade 2, Grade 3, Grade 4, and Grade 5). Let's take the previous example of the early childhood screening test. If the normative sample for that instrument included 200 children each at the 3-, 4-, 5-, and 6-year age levels, then the rating would be Acceptable. The total sample size is greater than 750 but less than 1,000, and it contains the requisite number of subjects per age interval.

The highest rating, Good, is reserved for very well built tests that satisfy more rigorous criteria. The normative groups for such tests must contain 100 or more subjects in *every* one-year age interval or academic grade level with which the test is intended to be used and also must include 1,000 or more subjects overall. To earn a Good evaluation, the normative sample of the test mentioned in the example above would need 1,000 or more members, including at least 100 kindergarteners, 100 first graders, 100 second graders, 100 third graders, 100 fourth graders, and 100 fifth graders. For instance, this description of the normative sample for the early childhood screening test would earn a Good rating: "The sample included 260 three-year-olds, 253 four-year-olds, 306 five-year-olds, and 277 six-year-olds." The following description, though, would merit an Acceptable rating because two of the age intervals fall below the 100-subject criterion: "The normative sample for this achievement battery included 80 first-grade and 80 second-grade students, and 150 students at each grade level from third through 12th grades."

Frequently test manuals specify the total normative population and the age range for the test, but fail to cite the number of subjects tested at each age. In these cases, the reviewers had to estimate by dividing the total number of subjects in the normative sample by the number of age or grade intervals spanned by the test. If the total sample size is under 750 or if the average number of subjects per year is below 75, then an Unacceptable rating is given. If the total sample size is 750 or larger and if the average is 75 or greater, than an Acceptable rating is given. A Good rating is never given when an estimate is required, *regardless* of the resulting average.

To illustrate the estimation procedure, let's use as an example a test that is intended to be administered to high school students in Grades 10 through 12. The test manual reports the total sample size to be 2,153 but fails to report the number of subjects in each grade. Dividing the total sample size (2,153) by the number of one-year grade intervals (3) yields an estimate of 718 subjects per grade. Since the overall size of the normative group exceeds the 750 criterion and the estimated number of subjects per grade exceeds the 75 criterion, an Acceptable rating would be given. Because estimation was required, however, the test is ineligible for a Good rating. The total sample size exceeded the necessary 1,000 members, but a reviewer can only estimate the number of students per age interval. It is possible, for example, that there were only 25 tenth graders in the normative group. This uncertainty and lack of specificity automatically removes the test from consideration for the Good category.

The size guidelines apply not only to national normative groups, but also to special normative groups. An achievement battery, for instance, may provide separate norms for boys and for girls. In such a case, there would be a *Consumer's Guide* rating for the boys' norms and a separate rating for the girls' norms. In order to be rated Acceptable, the normative sample of boys and the normative sample of girls *each* must include at least 750 subjects with 75 or more in most of the one-year age or grade intervals for which norms are reported. Likewise, each of the samples must include 1,000 or more subjects with at least 100 subjects in each one-year age interval in order to be rated Good. If an adaptive behavior inventory reports one set of norms based on the performance of students with mental retardation, another for students with emotional disturbance, and a third for students with hearing impairment, then the 75/750 or 100/1,000 size guidelines would be applied to each normative group individually (i.e., for the sample with mental retardation, for the sample with emotional disturbance, and for the sample with hearing impairment).

The only exception to these size guidelines is a test that extends well into the adult years—for instance, from 8-0 through 80-0 years. It is not reasonable to expect such a test to have one hundred 80-year-olds, one hundred 79-year-olds, one hundred 78-year-olds, and so on! These tests were not penalized in the *Consumer's Guide* ratings if they met the relevant criteria for the school-aged population and if they demonstrated that the age groupings employed for the adult population were derived through empirical means.

C. Demographic Characteristics of the Normative Group

_____ The characteristics of the normative group are not specified or do not meet the criteria below.

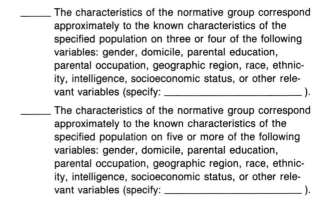

_____ The characteristics of the normative group correspond approximately to the known characteristics of the specified population on three or four of the following variables: gender, domicile, parental education, parental occupation, geographic region, race, ethnicity, intelligence, socioeconomic status, or other relevant variables (specify: _____).

_____ The characteristics of the normative group correspond approximately to the known characteristics of the specified population on five or more of the following variables: gender, domicile, parental education, parental occupation, geographic region, race, ethnicity, intelligence, socioeconomic status, or other relevant variables (specify: _____).

Unacceptable ratings are given when the test author neglects to describe any characteristics of the normative group or demonstrates that the normative group is representative of the specified reference population on only one or two variables. To earn the Acceptable rating, the author must provide evidence that the demographic characteristics of the normative group corresponded approximately to at least three or four of the known characteristics of the specified population. The Good rating is awarded to those test scores for which the normative groups are demonstrated to be representative of the specified population across five or more variables.

When evaluating this section, reviewers automatically compared the demographic characteristics of the normative group to the characteristics of the U.S. population *unless* the test author stated explicitly that the norms were representative of some other specified group. Ideally the test manual will include the known percentages of relevant demographic characteristics for the reference population and for the normative sample, but this is not always done. If the reference population is the U.S. population, then a test was not penalized if the manual failed to contain the national demographics; these data are well known and readily available. Some of the more widely reported demographic characteristics for the U.S. population as a whole and the U.S. school-aged population are given in Table 1. These figures were taken from the 1990 census projections published by the U.S. Department of Commerce's Bureau of the Census.

In a few instances, the test constructor indicated that the norms reported in the manual were representative of a population other than the U.S. population as a whole. Usually this was a group of individuals residing in a particular locality or geographic region ("The norms are based on students in California"; "The normative group is representative of students attending school in the Austin Independent School District") or a group of individuals composing a particular subsample ("Students in the normative group were legally blind and unable to use print as their

TABLE 1

DEMOGRAPHIC CHARACTERISTICS OF THE U.S. POPULATION[a]

Characteristics	Percentage of U.S. School-Aged Population	Percentage of U.S. Population
Gender		
Male	51.2	48.8
Female	48.8	51.2
Race		
Caucasoid	80.1	84.1
Negroid	15.7	12.4
Mongoloid	4.2	3.5
Ethnicity		
Anglo/European	70.4	75.8
Black American	14.1	11.9
Hispanic	10.6	7.9
Oriental/Pacific Islander	3.3	2.9
Native American/Eskimo/Aleut	1.1	0.8
All others	0.5	0.7
Principal Language Spoken in the Home[b]		
English	90.4	88.6
Spanish	6.2	5.0
French	0.5	0.8
German	0.4	0.9
Italian	0.3	0.9
Chinese dialects	0.2	0.3
Polish	0.1	0.5
Greek	0.1	0.2
Philippine dialects	0.1	0.3
Portuguese	0.1	0.2
Japanese	0.1	0.2
Korean	0.1	0.1
Vietnamese	0.1	0.1
All others	1.3	1.9
Geographic Region of Residence		
Northeast	18.7	20.2
North Central	24.4	23.9
South	35.5	35.0
West	21.4	20.9
Domicile		
Urban and suburban		77.5
Rural		22.5
Educational Attainment of Individuals 25–54 Years of Age[c]		
Completed 0–8 grades		5.9
Completed 1–3 years of high school		9.8
Graduated high school		40.3
Attended college or technical school		19.8
Graduated college		18.9
Completed postgraduate training		5.3

TABLE 1. Continued

Employment Status of Individuals in the Work Force[c]	
Unemployed	5.4
Resident armed forces	1.4
Managerial and professional services	23.7
Technical, sales, and administrative support	28.8
Service occupations	12.4
Precision production, craft, and repair	11.1
Operators, fabricators, and laborers	14.4
Farming, forestry, and fishing	2.8
Family Income[c]	
Under $5,000	4.4
$5,000–$9,999	7.3
$10,000–$14,999	9.1
$15,000–$24,999	18.7
$25,000–$34,999	17.5
$35,000–$49,999	20.2
$50,000 and over	22.8

[a]Unless otherwise noted, all figures are based on the 1990 census projections reported by the Bureau of the Census in *Statistical Abstract of the United States 1990*.
[b]Based on 1985 census projections.
[c]Based on 1988 census projections.

principal medium of instruction"; "The normative group consisted of students diagnosed as mentally retarded"; "The normative group is representative of students enrolled in first-year algebra classes"; "One normative group included only females and the other normative group included only males"). In these instances, credit for demographic conformity may be given only if descriptive statistics are supplied both for the designated reference population and for the normative sample. That is, the author of a test normed in California must provide a summary of the known demographic characteristics of California and must demonstrate that the normative sample is representative of the state population. Similarly, when male and female norms are provided, it is necessary to report the salient demographic characteristics of the male and female populations. It is not appropriate to expect a test consumer to know or to look up such obscure information.

The following description of a specialized normative sample would be rated Acceptable because it states the characteristics of the reference population (i.e., students with mental retardation) and it demonstrates equivalence on three relevant characteristics (i.e., gender, measured intelligence, and etiology of retardation): "The norms for this test are based on the performance of students with mental retardation. One would expect to find that 60–75% of this population is male; our sample was 59.8% male. The IQ range usually includes 92.4% with IQs 50–70 (our sample = 88.9%), 6.1% with IQs 20–49 (our sample = 10.7%), and

1.5% with IQs below 20 (our sample = 0.4%). The etiology of the retardation is organic in about 15–25% of the population (our sample = 14.1%) and is unknown in about 75–85% of the population (our sample = 85.8%)."

The characteristics most often used to establish national representativeness are gender, urban/suburban/rural residence, parental education or occupation, geographic region, race, ethnicity, and intelligence. Credit is given if the percentages reported in the test manual conform approximately to the known percentages reported in the relevant edition of the *Statistical Abstract of the United States* or if the normative sample is stratified according to these same variables. Determining whether the characteristics of the U.S. population and the characteristics of the normative sample were comparable required some judgment on the part of *Consumer's Guide* reviewers. In general, reviewers adhered to a rule of thumb that recognized plus or minus 5% as appropriate variation for larger demographic categories and plus or minus 1–2% for smaller categories. For instance, 23.9% of the U.S. population resides in the North Central census region; percentages of 19% to 29% reported for a test's normative group probably would have been accepted by reviewers. On the other hand, only 5.2% of all school-aged children are ethnically Oriental; therefore, a smaller range of about 1% to 5% Oriental ethnics within the normative sample would have been accepted as representative. This is an instance in which we had to rely heavily on the expertise, knowledge, and common sense of our review panel because no hard and fast rules could be devised to accommodate all possible cases.

This description of a normative sample would be rated Unacceptable because it fails to provide comparative percentages for the reference population and it claims representativeness on only one variable: "Students tested for the normative sample attended school in Chicago, Illinois; Austin, Texas; and Tempe, Arizona. There was an equal number of boys and girls in the group."

This description would be rated Acceptable: "Of the students in the normative group, 49.6% were male and 50.4% were female; 77.6% were white, 15.8% were black, and 6.6% were of other racial groups; and 18.3% resided in the Northeast census region, 22.4% in the North Central region, 38.2% in the South region, and 21.1% in the West region." The intended reference population is a national one, and the sample is representative across three important characteristics (i.e., gender, race, and geographic region). Had the description gone on to demonstrate that the ethnic makeup of the sample was representative and that the educational attainment of the students' parents approximated known percentages, the rating would have been raised to Good.

D. Recency of Normative Data

Normative data were gathered in

_____ 1975 or before.

_____ 1976–1985.

_____ 1986 or after.

This section is very easy to evaluate. Any test score normed in 1975 or before is Unacceptable. Normative dates from 1976 to 1985 are deemed to be Acceptable, and those from 1986 to the present garner Good ratings. If the manual did not specify when normative data were gathered, reviewers used the copyright date of the test. When normative data were gathered over a period of several years, the effective date used in the *Consumer's Guide* evaluation was the earliest year in which data were gathered. Occasionally a test author will show through a research study that norms collected earlier are still applicable. When this was done, the test received the appropriate rating for the year in which the equivalency study was conducted (e.g., a Good rating for equivalency studies conducted from 1986 on, an Acceptable rating for studies completed in the period 1976–1985, and an Unacceptable rating for equivalency research that took place prior to 1975).

To summarize, four aspects of a test's norms were evaluated in *Consumer's Guide* reviews: the normative scores, the

size of the normative group, the demographic characteristics of the normative group, and the recency of normative data. The evaluations for these subsections are combined to yield a Norms rating. If one or more of the four subsections receive an Unacceptable evaluation, then the Norms rating is Unacceptable. If the four subsections receive some combination of Acceptable and Good evaluations, then the Norms rating is Acceptable. If every one of the four subsections has a Good evaluation, then the Norms rating will be Good. Table 2 may be used to simplify the process of determining the Norms rating.

RATING TEST RELIABILITY

Two components of reliability were evaluated for the *Consumer's Guide*: internal consistency reliability and stability reliability. The criteria printed on the Reviewer Evaluation Form for each component are reproduced individually below, followed by a discussion of the ways in which reviewers evaluated them.

A. Internal Consistency Reliability

Internal consistency reliability

_____ Is not reported; is below .80 at most ages; or is reported with no apparent controls for the effects of age.

_____ Is .80 or above at most ages when reported for two or more age intervals spanning no more than three years each; is .80–.89 for a single group when evidence is presented to demonstrate that the test is not significantly related to age; or is .80 or above when the effects of age are controlled statistically.

_____ Is .90 or above at most ages when reported for two or more age intervals spanning no more than three years each; or is .90 or above for a single group when evidence is presented to demonstrate that the test is not significantly related to age.

Unacceptable ratings for this section were given in three instances: when no reliability studies are reported; when reliability studies are reported but the majority of the resulting coefficients failed either to achieve statistical significance or to reach .80 in magnitude; or when reliability studies are reported but no attempt is made to control the spuriously inflating effects of age or to demonstrate that age controls are not necessary because test performance is unrelated to age.

TABLE 2

DETERMINING THE NORMS RATING

Combined Ratings for Type of Score, Sample Size, Demographic Characteristics, and Recency	Descriptive Rating	Letter Rating
All Goods	Good	A
Goods and Acceptables	Acceptable	B
All Acceptables	Acceptable	B
Goods and Unacceptables	Unacceptable	F
Goods, Acceptables, and Unacceptables	Unacceptable	F
Acceptables and Unacceptables	Unacceptable	F
All Unacceptables	Unacceptable	F

For example, the coefficients Alpha for a reading test score are reported to be .65 for first-grade students, .81 for second-grade students, .76 for third-grade students, and .74 for fourth-grade students. The rating is Unacceptable because three of the four reported coefficients are below .80. If the authors of this same test reported a single split-half coefficient of .83 for students in Grades 1 through 4, the rating also would be Unacceptable because no attempt was made to control for the inflationary influence of age.

A test score was rated Acceptable when its internal consistency reliability coefficients were statistically significant and also met one of three additional criteria for magnitude: (a) The coefficients are .80 or greater for more than half of the age intervals studied, provided that two or more age intervals are included and that no age interval spans more than 3 years or grades; (b) the coefficients are .80 through .89 for a single group of subjects when evidence is presented to demonstrate that test performance is not significantly related to age; or (c) the coefficients are .80 or greater when age is controlled statistically through the use of partial correlation procedures, correlation of standard scores, and similar techniques.

For instance, if the internal consistency reliability of a score is reported to be .80 for 6- and 7-year-olds, .75 for 8- and 9-year-olds, .85 for 10- and 11-year-olds, and .86 for 12- and 13-year-olds, then the rating would be Acceptable. However, if the coefficients were .79, .75, .85, and .86 respectively, the rating would be Unacceptable because only half of the coefficients reach or exceed .80.

The following data concerning the total score from a behavior rating scale would earn an Acceptable rating for internal consistency reliability: "The Kuder-Richardson coefficient for this score is .86 for students ages 6-0 through 18-11 years. Since the score correlates .009 with age, it was deemed unnecessary to study reliability at individual age intervals."

This description also would earn an Acceptable rating because age is controlled statistically: "Using the split-half method, internal consistency reliability is estimated to be .86 for elementary students in Grades 1 through 6 and .84 for secondary students in Grades 7 through 12. The effects of age were partialed out of the coefficients."

Good ratings were granted to test scores when the reported coefficients were statistically significant and also met one of two criteria for magnitude: (a) The coefficients are .90 or greater in magnitude at more than half of the age intervals studied, provided that two or more age intervals are included and that no age interval span more than 3 years or grades; or (b) the coefficients are .90 or greater when evidence is presented to demonstrate that the test is not significantly related to age.

For example, if the internal consistency reliability of a score from a mathematics test is reported to be .90 for 6-year-olds, .91 for 8-year-olds, .95 for 10-year-olds, and .92 for 12-year-olds, then the rating would be Good. However, if the coefficients were .89, .88, .95, and .96 respectively, the rating would be Acceptable because half of the coefficients are in the .80s.

Internal consistency reliability sometimes is established through the immediate test-retest with alternate forms procedure. This description of such a study would merit a Good rating: "Form A and Form B of the test were given to one class of first graders, one class of third graders, and one class of fifth graders. The forms were given back-to-back, with no time intervening between administrations. The standard scores were correlated with the following results: .89, .95, and .96 respectively."

Authors sometimes cite the research of other professionals that attests to an instrument's reliability. This is a commendable practice. To receive credit for these data in the *Consumer's Guide* rating, the author had to provide sufficient information about the studies to enable reviewers to judge the appropriateness of sample size, subject characteristics, age controls, statistical analyses, and research design. If this information was not provided, then the studies were disregarded in the *Consumer's Guide* evaluations even when full bibliographic citations were included. This reflects our belief that consumers have the right to expect a test author to provide at least preliminary evidence of a test's reliability; they should not have to scour the literature to determine the basic psychometric adequacy of an instrument. A sufficient number of studies, whether independent studies or studies by the test author, must be explicated in detail in the manual.

For example, if the author simply states that "Dissertations by Adams (1982) and Jefferson (1983) yielded reliability coefficients of .93 and .89," the rating would be Unacceptable. Insufficient information is provided for the reader to know whether the study was properly designed, what type of coefficient was calculated, or even whether age controls were applied. However, the following statement is sufficiently detailed and the coefficients are of a magnitude to warrant an Acceptable rating: "Adams (1982) administered the test to all of the 54 students in two first-grade classes in the Santa Fe Independent School District. The resulting coefficient Alpha was .93. In a similar study, Jefferson (1983) computed a split-half coefficient of .89, corrected by the Spearman-Brown formula, based on the scores of 26 five-year-olds enrolled in a private kindergarten in Austin, Texas."

Tests that have been revised present a special set of problems. If the test was altered considerably in revision, then reliability studies conducted on previous editions of the test were not considered in the evaluation of the current edition. For example, if the length of a test was changed, if new items were created, if new formats were employed, or if new scoring procedures were applied, then the reliability of the revision must be established independently. However, if the test was basically unaltered in the course of revision, then reliability studies conducted with the earlier version could be applied to the revision *if* the author demonstrated empirically that the revision and the previous edition are equivalent. The reliability studies, of course, had to meet all of the evaluation criteria previously outlined in order to be considered.

This rule of equivalency was applied to alternate forms of tests, too. If the items of an alternate form of the test were identical to those on the original form, or if they contained items of the same type, content, and format, then credit for reliability of the alternate form or forms was given when the author demonstrated both the empirical equivalence of the forms and the reliability of the original form. If equivalence among the forms was not established, then reliability had to be determined for each form individually.

Some test authors report two or more sets of norms for the same instrument. For instance, an achievement test might have two sets of norms, one for boys and one for girls.

In such a case, the author must demonstrate the reliability of both sets of norms (i.e., reliability studies should be conducted for males and for females separately). If an adaptive behavior inventory includes norms for students with mental retardation, for students with emotional disturbance, and for students of normal intelligence, then reliability studies must be conducted for each of these three groups. Separate norms presumably are necessary because the groups in question perform quite differently from each other. Therefore, the psychometric properties of each set of norms must be established independently.

Some tests yield composite scores that are generated by combining subtest scores. For instance, a Reading Quotient might be computed by combining the standard scores from the Reading Vocabulary, Reading Comprehension, and Phonics subtests of a battery.

Ideally, a test author will establish reliability for all of the subtest scores and all of the composite scores that can be computed for a test. Unfortunately, some authors study the reliability of the subtest scores but neglect to do the same for the composite scores. Or they report reliability for the composites but not for the subtests.

In the first instance, when reliability data are available for subtests but not for composites, one can draw some logical inferences about the composite score from the available subtest data. It is reasonable to assume that the composite score is at least as reliable as its component subtest with the lowest reliability coefficient. Therefore, if the reliability coefficients associated with *all* of a composite score's constituent subtests or scales are .80 or higher and meet the stipulations for age control, then the reliability of the composite score should be rated Acceptable. The Good rating would be withheld because best practice dictates that the test author establish the reliability of every single score that is reported.

We applied the same reasoning to short-form tests that are built by combining scores from selected subtests. If all of the subtests had Acceptable or Good reliability, then the short-form composite score was rated Acceptable. Obviously, this procedure cannot be used to infer the reliability of a short form that contains selected items; in this situation, there is no way to draw helpful inferences from the available long-form data.

Let's use the hypothetical reading test described earlier. This test has a Reading Quotient that is a composite score computed by combining the standard scores from its Reading Vocabulary, Reading Comprehension, and Phonics subtests. Assume that the coefficients Alpha for second graders are .76, .83, and .85 for the three subtest scores. The Reading Quotient would be rated Unacceptable because one of the coefficients is below .80. If, however, the coefficients were .96, .93, and .95, then the Reading Quotient would be rated Acceptable for internal consistency reliability.

We encountered a different problem when reliability data were available for composite scores but not for subtest scores. Reviewers gave credit to the composite score based on the available reliability data. However, in the absence of reliability data, the subtest scores were rated Unacceptable. If no direct data are reported, then the only logical inference is that the subtests generally will be less reliable than the composites, but precisely how much less is unknown.

B. Stability Reliability

Stability reliability

_____ Is not reported; is below .80 at most ages; or is reported with no apparent controls for the effects of age.

_____ Is .80 or above at most ages when reported for two or more age intervals spanning no more than three years each; is .80–.89 for a single group when evidence is presented to demonstrate that the test is not significantly related to age; or is .80 or above when the effects of age are controlled statistically.

_____ Is .90 or above at most ages when reported for two or more age intervals spanning no more than three years each; or is .90 or above for a single group when evidence is presented to demonstrate that the test is not significantly related to age.

The evaluation criteria applied to studies of stability reliability are the same as those discussed previously for internal consistency reliability with regard to statistical significance, magnitude, and controls for the effects of age. That is, Good ratings were reserved for test scores with stability reliability coefficients of .90 or greater obtained by testing groups of students of approximately the same age. Acceptable ratings went to test scores with stability reliability coefficients of .80 or greater when age was controlled statistically or when groups of students of the same age were tested. Test scores with no coefficients reported, with coefficients below .80, or with coefficients uncontrolled for age received Unacceptable ratings.

In summary, a test's reliability was evaluated as two subsections on the Reviewer Evaluation Form: Internal Consistency Reliability and Stability Reliability. The evaluations accorded to the two subsections were combined to yield an overall Reliability rating. If both of these subsections received Unacceptable evaluations, then the Reliability rating was Unacceptable. If the two subsections received some combination of Unacceptable, Acceptable, and Good ratings, then Reliability was rated Acceptable. If both sections received Good evaluations, then the Reliability rating was Good. Table 3 may be used to simplify the determination of the Reliability rating.

RATING TEST VALIDITY

Unlike the previous two sections concerning norms and reliability, the Reviewer Evaluation Form section concerning the validity of a test score is not divided into subsections or categories. Because evidence of validity is something that accumulates over a period of time and because the commonly accepted types of validity—content, criterion-related, and construct—do not constitute discrete categories, we elected to evaluate validity using a list of the various types of research and research designs that may be undertaken to study validity. That list is reproduced below, followed by a discussion of the ways in which reviewers used the list as an evaluation tool.

Validity

_____ Validity is not reported; validity studies are not acceptable in design; validity studies do not yield significant results as hypothesized; or validity is supported exclusively by nonempirical evidence of content validity.

_____ Validity is supported by studies that provide appropriate evidence that the test score

_____ is related as hypothesized to age or grade.

_____ correlates as hypothesized with measures of achievement.

_____ correlates as hypothesized with measures of aptitude/developmental abilities or general intelligence.

_____ correlates as hypothesized with measures of affect.

_____ produces hypothesized multiple correlation/ regression results.

_____ has hypothesized factor structures.

_____ predicts appropriately over time.

_____ distinguishes between specified groups.

_____ intercorrelates as hypothesized with the test's other scores.

_____ has appropriate item-total correlations, item discriminating power, or evidence of another appropriate data-based approach to item selection.

_____ discriminates as hypothesized on the basis of gender, race, ethnicity, or other demographic variables.

_____ other (specify: _____).

Our reviewers were faced with three major decisions as they read the validity sections of various test manuals. The first was to determine whether the research design for a

TABLE 3

DETERMINING THE RELIABILITY RATING

Internal Consistency Rating	Stability Rating	Descriptive Rating	Letter Rating
Good	Good	Good	A
Good	Acceptable	Acceptable	B
Good	Unacceptable	Acceptable	B
Acceptable	Good	Acceptable	B
Acceptable	Acceptable	Acceptable	B
Acceptable	Unacceptable	Acceptable	B
Unacceptable	Good	Acceptable	B
Unacceptable	Acceptable	Acceptable	B
Unacceptable	Unacceptable	Unacceptable	F

particular study was appropriate. The test manual had to provide sufficient information concerning such things as the characteristics of the subjects, the procedures for data collection, and the nature of data analysis so that the reviewer could judge the adequacy and appropriateness of the research design.

The second decision that faced the *Consumer's Guide* reviewers was to determine whether the results of a particular validity study were significant. Reviewers accepted the .05 level of confidence as the significance criterion. This was applied both in studies where relationships were predicted and in studies where differences were predicted.

The simple correlation coefficient is probably the most common statistic used to study validity. Several other correlational statistics also are used, such as factor analysis, multiple correlation, and regression. All of these techniques are concerned with establishing what a particular test score is related to. In addition to statistical significance, correlation and intercorrelation coefficients cited as evidence of validity must reach or exceed .35 in magnitude.

To be accepted as evidence of validity, at least half of the correlation coefficients reported had to reach the stated criteria. If seven validity coefficients were reported, then at least four of them had to be statistically significant and greater than or equal to .35. If there were 20 coefficients reported and only 9 of them met the criteria for significance and magnitude, then credit was not given.

Of course, not all validity data are derived from correlation and other measures of relationship. Many validity studies are concerned with matters of difference rather than relationship. These studies usually employed *t*-tests, analyses of variance, multiple analyses of variance, Chi-square, and other noncorrelative statistics. To be accepted as support

for a score's validity, the resulting *t*s or *F*s had to be significant at least at the .05 level.

The third decision that reviewers faced was to determine whether the nature or direction of the reported results matched the hypotheses proposed by the test authors. Frankly, formal hypotheses were not always stated in test manuals; frequently they were implied by the manner in which the data were presented and discussed. In studies of relationship, the hypothesis might be that a positive relationship existed (e.g., "The test is developmental in nature and therefore test scores should be related positively and significantly to age"), that no relationship existed (e.g., "The test is not developmental in nature and therefore test scores should not correlate significantly with age"), or that a negative relationship existed (e.g., "This test yields a high score for students with emotional disturbance, and it was correlated with a test that yields a low score for students with emotional disturbance, so one would anticipate significant but negative correlation coefficients"). Similarly, studies of difference might hypothesize either the presence or absence of observed differences and might also hypothesize that a difference would favor one group over another (e.g., "On this test of reading, students with dyslexia will score lower than Title I students who, in turn, will score lower than normally achieving students").

In short, the task of the reviewers was to determine that the validity research reported in test manuals was well designed and yielded significant, hypothesized results. Although we structured broad guidelines for the reviewers, it was not possible to devise guidelines for every aspect of each piece of research they encountered. We relied heavily on their expertise, knowledge, and common sense. All of our reviewers were well qualified by their training and experience to evaluate the adequacy of research designs, to determine whether the results were significant, and to ensure that the results conformed to appropriate hypotheses.

Once reviewers determined that a particular set of data was acceptable, they checked the appropriate descriptive category on the list of research designs in the Validity section of the Reviewer Evaluation Form. A category of validity research is checked only one time. If, for instance, there were three studies all yielding acceptable correlations between a particular test score and the total scores from three different intelligence tests, then the reviewer checked the category "correlates as hypothesized with measures of aptitude/developmental abilities or general intelligence" only one time. If a score was appropriately correlated with an achievement test score, with actual grades in school, and with teacher judgment of reading ability, then the examiner checked only the category "correlates as hypothesized with measures of achievement." The checks are an indication of the different *types* of validity research undertaken, not the *number* of validity studies reported.

For the most part, the descriptive categories are self-explanatory. A few interpretive comments are in order, however.

The first category was checked when no validity studies were reported, when evidence of validity was flawed by negative findings or by a poor research design, or when the test's content validity was established through *nonempirical* means, such as the author's intuitive judgment that particular test items should be included. These categories do not contribute to the evaluation of a test score's validity. The remaining categories were checked when acceptable data were reported that conform to the category's description (e.g., data that establish the relationship of the test score to age, to aptitude, and so on).

The category concerning age or grade relationship was checked when there was some evidence of a connection between test performance and age. The relationship may be positive (which is the case with most measures of achievement or developmental abilities), negative (which might be hypothesized for measures of motor ability in elderly subjects), or neutral (which is often true of affective measures such as behavior checklists). Evidence of an age relationship usually is demonstrated by correlating raw scores with age or grade, by testing for mean differences among students of various ages or grades, by demonstrating that the mean raw scores reported in the normative tables become larger (or do not change) as age increases, or by demonstrating that the percentage of students passing a particular test item becomes greater (or does not change) as age increases.

The categories concerning relationships to achievement, aptitude, and affect were checked when the test author hypothesized the nature of such correlations and presented supporting evidence. Measures of achievement include scores from tests that conform to the definition of achievement in the *Consumer's Guide* Taxonomy, grades in school,

teacher evaluation of achievement, job performance, and other measures of skills that usually are acquired as a result of formal instruction. Measures of aptitude or developmental abilities include scores from tests that conform to the definition of aptitude in the Taxonomy, professional judgment of various developmental abilities, and other measures of abilities that usually are acquired developmentally or through incidental learning. Measures of affect include scores from tests that conform to the definition of affect in the Taxonomy, teacher evaluation of socioemotional development, sociometric information, peer nominations, and other measures of attitudes, interests, feelings, and behavior.

The next two categories concern multiple correlation, regression, and factor analysis. The hypothesized regression or factor structure must emerge from the data reported. Some authors factor analyze individual test items to build their tests or to confirm the organization of subtests or scales. In this instance, credit for factor analysis was given to all of the test scores that were built or confirmed by the factor analysis. Other authors do not factor individual test items, but instead factor subtest scores to verify the existence of specified composites, subtest clusters, constructs, or domains. In these cases, credit for factor analysis was not given to the individual subtest scores but to the composite, cluster, or total test scores.

The category concerning predictive studies was checked when evidence was presented to demonstrate that the test score accurately predicts hypothesized criterion variables over a specified period of time. For example, the author of a kindergarten screening test may demonstrate that students classified by their test scores as Not At Risk subsequently performed successfully in the first grade while those classified as At Risk experienced academic difficulty, were retained, or were placed in special and remedial education programs.

The next category, "distinguishes between specified groups," was checked when the test score was used effectively to discriminate among subjects or groups of subjects who exhibited (or did not exhibit) a particular criterion. For instance, the author of a reading test may demonstrate that children enrolled in remedial reading classes earn lower scores on the test than students in regular elementary classes. A test of aptitude should discriminate among groups of individuals who are gifted, normal, and who have mental retardation. An anxiety scale should produce different results for subjects known to suffer from anxiety disorders and those not similarly afflicted.

The intercorrelation category was checked when the various scores of a test were demonstrated to intercorrelate as hypothesized. For instance, if a test of spoken language has three subtests that intercorrelate to a significant degree, then one can conclude that the subtests are measuring a similar ability, presumably spoken language. Intercorrelations between composite or total scores and the subtest scores that constitute them were not accepted unless part-whole corrections were calculated. This is because there is a perfect correlation between the testing error of the composites and their components, which spuriously inflates intercorrelation coefficients.

The item analysis category was checked when there was an empirical basis, rather than a clinical or intuitive basis, for item selection. This might include traditional item analytic techniques such as item-total correlations and measures of item discriminating power, or newer procedures such as the Rasch-Wright method. If test items were selected through factor analytic means, then this category and the factor analysis category both were checked. However, if factor analysis was used after the fact simply to confirm earlier item selection and if no empirical procedures were used to select the items, then only the factor analysis category was checked.

Many test manuals provide evidence that the test results discriminate on the basis of particular demographic variables such as gender, race, ethnicity, linguistic competence, and so on. For instance, the authors of an achievement test might hypothesize that at the elementary school level, girls will score higher than boys. When hypotheses concerning the impact of such demographic variables on test performance are formulated and tested empirically, the final validity category was checked.

We could not list every conceivable type of validity study on the Reviewer Evaluation Form. The "other" category was provided for reviewers to check when they encountered those unique and less frequently used techniques. In reviewing the tests included in this edition of the *Consumer's Guide*, the reviewers did not find an occasion to list other evidence of validity. There were still some special instances to be considered when reviewing validity data.

When independent validity studies are cited in a test manual but published elsewhere, the author must provide sufficient information for reviewers to judge the appropriateness of the research design. If this information was not provided, the studies were not considered in *Consumer's Guide* evaluation, even when full bibliographic citations were included. If test authors want their readers to accept data as evidence of test validity, then they must provide a description of the conditions under which those data were gathered. The people buying and using the test should not have to review the literature to find this information. Studies cited in the manual were considered in the *Consumer's Guide* evaluation only if they were described in sufficient detail.

Tests that have undergone revision present a special set of problems to be considered. We applied the same rule of thumb here that was discussed previously in the section concerning test reliability. Namely, if the test changed considerably in revision—in length, type or content of items, formats, or scoring procedures—then validity studies conducted with the original or previous edition of the test were not considered in the review of the current edition. However, if the test was essentially unaltered in the course of

revision, then validity studies conducted with the earlier version were applied to the evaluation of the revision *if* the author demonstrated empirically that the revision and the previous edition are equivalent. Of course, the original validity studies had to conform to the evaluation criteria outlined earlier.

This rule of thumb concerning equivalency was applied to alternate forms of tests, too. If these tests had items identical to those on the original form or items of the same type, content, and format as those on the first form, then credit for validity of the alternate form or forms was given when the author demonstrated the empirical equivalence of the forms. If equivalence was not established, then validity had to be determined for each form individually.

If multiple norms were provided for the same instrument, then evidence of validity was required for each different set of norms. For instance, many adaptive behavior inventories provide norms for normal students and for students with mental retardation. Some tests also report separate norms for males and females. The presence of separate normative tables implies that the performance of the groups is *not* equivalent. In these instances, validity studies must be reported for each group. The adaptive behavior measures, for instance, must have studies demonstrating the validity of the instruments with subjects of normal intelligence and also with subjects of subnormal intelligence.

As we noted earlier in this chapter, some tests yield composite scores that are generated by combining subtest scores. In many instances, authors conduct studies to establish the validity of the constituent subtests but neglect to do the same for the composite scores. If *all* of the subtest scores that make up a composite score merited Validity ratings of Acceptable or Good, then the composite score was rated Acceptable by inference from the available subtest validity data. However, if any of the components of the composite were rated Unacceptable for Validity, then the composite also was rated Unacceptable. The Good rating was always withheld because inference, while a logical process, does not constitute ideal psychometric practice.

Conversely, if the author reported validity data only for the composite score and not for the scores that contribute to the composite, then the Unacceptable rating was given to the subtest scores. The only possible inference is that the constituent scores are likely to be less valid than the composite. We cannot accurately judge how much less.

After reviewers completed their analysis of validity studies and checked the appropriate descriptive categories on the Reviewer Evaluation Form, the number of check marks were added together to determine the Validity rating. The *Consumer's Guide* scoring criteria are based very simply on the number of different types of validity studies reported for a test score. This is a recognition of the fact that validity accrues over time and cannot be established conclusively by one or two studies, no matter how well designed. It is also a recognition that the three major types of validity (content, criterion-related, and construct) do not constitute discrete categories; a single study might satisfy the requirements for more than one type of validity.

An Unacceptable Validity rating was given to test scores when only the first two categories were checked—that is, when no studies were reported, when poorly designed studies were used, when the results were not significant, or when only nonempirical evidence of content validity was reported. Unacceptable ratings also were given to test scores when there were only one or two checks in the remaining categories describing well-designed studies with significant, hypothesized results.

If reviewers checked three or four different categories describing good validity research, then an Acceptable rating was awarded to the relevant test score. This was viewed as the minimum requirement for demonstrating the validity of a test score. Let's assume that reviewers credit a reading score with a developmental age relationship, correlation with two other reading scores (i.e., achievement), the ability to distinguish between readers with disabilities and normal readers, and empirical item selection. This evaluation would yield an Acceptable Validity rating based on the presence of four different types of well-designed validity research yielding significant, hypothesized results. However, if the test items were selected intuitively and if the authors correlated the reading score with two other reading scores, with actual grades in school, and with the teacher's evaluation of reading ability, then the Validity rating would be Unacceptable. The only evidence of validity associated with the test score is correlation with achievement measures.

Good ratings were bestowed on test scores whose validity was supported by five or more different types of research. The total score of a self-esteem inventory, for instance, might be validated by demonstrating that the score is not related to age, that it correlates as expected with a group-administered achievement test, that it is positively related to other measures of self-esteem, that it possesses hypothesized factor structures, that it distinguishes between children with emotional disturbances and normal children, that it intercorrelates with the test's other subtest scores, and that it was built through traditional empirical item analytic procedures. This score, credited with seven different types of validity research, would earn a Good rating.

Table 4 may be used to determine the Validity rating.

THE OVERALL RATING

This discussion outlines the methods that were used to combine the ratings for the Norms, Reliability, and Validity sections to determine a *Consumer's Guide* Overall Rating for

TABLE 4

DETERMINING THE VALIDITY RATING

Types of Empirical Research[a] Reported	Descriptive Rating	Letter Rating
>5	Good	A
5	Good	A
4	Acceptable	B
3	Acceptable	B
2	Unacceptable	F
1	Unacceptable	F
0	Unacceptable	F

[a]With significant, hypothesized results.

each test score that was reviewed. Three Overall Ratings were created. The lowest rating, designated by the letter *F*, indicates that the test score fails to meet minimum criteria for technical adequacy and therefore is Not Recommended. The middle rating, designated by the letter *B*, indicates that the test score satisfies minimum basic standards and is Recommended. The letter *A* represents the highest rating and was reserved for tests that are Highly Recommended.

If the Norms, Reliability, or Validity section received an Unacceptable rating, then the *Consumer's Guide* Overall Rating was Not Recommended, designated F. For instance, if a test score had a Good Norms rating, an Unacceptable Reliability rating, and an Acceptable Validity rating, then the Overall Rating was F, or Not Recommended. A test must, at the very least, have evidence of adequate norms, reliability, and validity before one can recommend its use.

If the evaluations accorded to these three components were any combination of Acceptable and Good, then the *Consumer's Guide* Overall Rating was Recommended, designated B. For example, if a test score's Norms, Reliability, and Validity ratings were all Acceptable, then the Overall Rating for the score was B, or Recommended. If its Norms and Validity were rated Good and its Reliability was rated Acceptable, then the Overall Rating was B, or Recommended. A consumer can be confident that any test score rated Recommended has met the minimum quality controls for psychometric adequacy.

If each of the three sections achieved a Good evaluation, then the *Consumer's Guide* Overall Rating was Highly Recommended, designated A. These scores were rare in the course of our reviews. Good test scores meet the very highest standards for technical quality in terms of norms, reliability, and validity and can be used with utmost confidence.

Table 5 may be used to convert the three section ratings to an Overall Rating.

TABLE 5

DETERMINING THE OVERALL RATING

Norms Rating	Reliability Rating	Validity Rating	Descriptive Rating	Letter Rating
Good	Good	Good	Highly Recommended	A
Good	Acceptable	Acceptable	Recommended	B
Good	Good	Acceptable	Recommended	B
Good	Acceptable	Good	Recommended	B
Acceptable	Good	Good	Recommended	B
Acceptable	Acceptable	Acceptable	Recommended	B
Acceptable	Good	Acceptable	Recommended	B
Acceptable	Acceptable	Good	Recommended	B
Good	Unacceptable	Unacceptable	Not Recommended	F
Good	Good	Unacceptable	Not Recommended	F
Good	Unacceptable	Good	Not Recommended	F
Acceptable	Unacceptable	Unacceptable	Not Recommended	F
Unacceptable	Unacceptable	Good	Not Recommended	F
Unacceptable	Acceptable	Acceptable	Not Recommended	F
Unacceptable	Good	Acceptable	Not Recommended	F
Unacceptable	Good	Unacceptable	Not Recommended	F
Unacceptable	Acceptable	Good	Not Recommended	F
Unacceptable	Unacceptable	Good	Not Recommended	F
Unacceptable	Unacceptable	Unacceptable	Not Recommended	F

4

DESCRIBING THE NONTECHNICAL CHARACTERISTICS OF TESTS

Appraisal personnel need to know that the tests they purchase and administer meet minimum psychometric standards and that the tests possess the very best technical characteristics of all the tests that are available. Still, this technical information, however valuable and necessary, is not the sole basis on which decisions to purchase and use tests are made. Nontechnical, descriptive information also must be considered. Variables such as the content area being measured, the administration and scoring procedures of the test, and the format requirements all have a distinct impact on the test selection process.

Nontechnical test attributes do not lend themselves to either qualitative or quantitative analysis; they must be considered on a test-by-test, subject-by-subject basis. A group-administered test is not inherently any better or any worse than an individually administered test. Nor is a test that requires one hour for administration necessarily superior to a test that requires only 15 minutes. The test situation dictates desired and undesired characteristics. For instance, no examiner will want to administer a highly complex, lengthy instrument—even one with the Highly Recommended (A) rating—to every student in a district-wide screening program. Other tests obviously are not satisfactory for sensorily or physically impaired students, students who can't read, or students who don't speak English.

Test users usually have certain requirements in mind before they select a test. The front side of the Reviewer Evaluation Form (Figure 1) was developed to provide the information that would meet these needs. The nontechnical, descriptive information that is provided for each test score reviewed in the *Consumer's Guide* is described briefly in this chapter, including the bibliographic citation and the taxonomic classification, as well as administration, scoring, examiner, and test format characteristics. The final section of the chapter summarizes the uses of this descriptive information.

BIBLIOGRAPHIC CITATION

A standard bibliographic citation was requested on the Reviewer Evaluation Form for each test score. This information is summarized in Appendix D, which contains a list of all the tests reviewed in the *Consumer's Guide*. The list is organized alphabetically by test name, followed by the publication date, the authors' names, and the test publisher. Publishers' addresses are given in Appendix E.

TAXONOMIC CLASSIFICATION

Tests reviewed in the *Consumer's Guide* evaluate a wide variety of aptitudes, abilities, content areas, and feelings. In order to describe these content areas conveniently and systematically, we developed a Taxonomy with four general domains: Achievement (1000), Aptitude (2000), Affect (3000), and General Intelligence (4000). These four domains are subdivided into 86 discrete categories or content areas, each of which is assigned a numerical code that was entered by the reviewer on the front page of the Reviewer Evaluation

Reviewer _____

CONSUMER'S GUIDE REVIEWER EVALUATION FORM

Test Name (Date of Publication) _____(_____)

Test Author(s) _____

Publisher, City, State _____

Test Score Being Reviewed _____

Taxonomy Classification _____

Administration and Scoring Characteristics

Administration: _____ Group or individual

_____ Individual only

Time required for administration: _____

Scores are interpreted in terms of:

_____ Age equivalents

_____ Grade equivalents

_____ Percentile ranks or related scores

_____ Standard scores

_____ Other (specify: _____)

Test may be administered to subjects in grades _____ through _____ or subjects ages _____ through _____ years.

Format Characteristics

_____ The respondent is not the target student but a third party such as a teacher, parent, or peer.

_____ The respondent is the target student, and the format requires the respondent to:

Input

_____ Listen

_____ Read print, including letters, words, and numbers

_____ Look at stimuli (pictures, objects)

_____ Other (specify: _____)

Output

_____ Make one-word responses

_____ Make multiple-word responses

_____ Manipulate objects

_____ Mark an answer sheet

_____ Point

_____ Draw

_____ Write print

_____ Other (specify: _____)

Examiner Characteristics

_____ The test is easily administered after reading the manual.

_____ Administration requires special training beyond familiarity with the test manual.

_____ Administration is restricted to examiners with specified certificates or licenses.

Determining the Overall Consumer's Guide Rating

Norms Rating _____

Reliability Rating _____

Validity Rating _____

Overall Rating _____

Figure 1. Front side of Reviewer Evaluation Form

Form. A fifth category, Unclassified Attributes (5000), was created for test scores that measure behaviors not encompassed by the four domains; an example is visual acuity. An outline of the Taxonomy is shown in Table 6.

Tests reviewed in the *Consumer's Guide* evaluate a wide variety of human mental endeavors, including various achievement abilities, aptitudes, and feelings. The four domains of the Taxonomy and the entries within each domain are defined in the following sections.

Achievement Domain

Achievement refers to all information and skills that are acquired as a result of formal instruction. Usually, but not necessarily, this instruction occurs in school. Achievement also includes abilities acquired through concerted self-study. The abilities in the achievement domain are rarely, if ever, acquired incidentally.

1000 Overall Achievement. Achievement includes academic skills such as reading, writing, and calculating; and specific occupational and daily living skills such as typing, operating a computer, cooking, or registering to vote. Scores assigned to the Overall Achievement category must include two or more specific achievement skills: basic information (1100), math (1200–1230), reading (1300–1340), science (1400), social studies (1500), writing (1600–1650), reference skills (1700), occupational skills (1800–1830), or adaptive behavior (1900–1930). For instance, the total score from an achievement battery that includes reading, writing, and arithmetic subtests would be assigned to the 1000 category.

1100 Basic Information. Basic or general information, as used here, refers to the understanding of facts that educated people usually know about everyday situations, events, and needs. This category includes such information as the fact that the U.S. Senate has 100 members, Lincoln's face is carved on Mount Rushmore, and the Normans invaded England in 1066 A.D. Although these facts may be acquired incidentally, they are more commonly learned in school or through self-directed study.

1200 Math, General. Overall math competence includes a variety of quantitative abilities such as arithmetic computation, mathematical reasoning skills, and knowledge of mathematical concepts or vocabulary. Scores that measure two or more of the following types of mathematical achievement are classified as Math, General (1200): math reasoning/problem solving (1210), math calculation (1220), or math vocabulary/concepts (1230).

1210 Math Reasoning/Problem Solving. Mathematical reasoning or problem solving is the ability to apply basic math concepts and arithmetic operations to the solution of word problems or to the deduction of abstract quantitative relationships.

1220 Math Calculation. Math calculation is the ability to perform basic arithmetic operations such as addition, subtraction, multiplication, and division.

1230 Math Vocabulary/Concepts. Test scores that measure math vocabulary or concepts require a subject to demonstrate knowledge of mathematical concepts without actually performing calculations or engaging in problem solving. For instance, the subject might be asked to explain how a thermometer and a ruler are alike, to tell what the symbol + means, or to define *divisor*.

1300 Reading, General. General reading ability requires mastery of a variety of reading skills, including print comprehension, word and letter recognition, alphabetic-phonetic knowledge, and oral reading rate. Scores assigned to this category must measure two or more of the following reading skills: reading comprehension (1310), word and letter recognition (1320), word and phonic analysis (1330), or reading rate (1340).

1310 Reading Comprehension. Reading comprehension is the ability to acquire information from print or to project meaning onto print. Included are the abilities to answer literal or inferential questions about the material read, to understand the meaning of words appearing in context or in isolation, to identify missing words in a passage, and to retell the plots and specific details of printed passages.

1320 Word and Letter Recognition. The recognition of words and letters usually is measured by having a person read aloud isolated words or graded word lists, name letters of the alphabet, identify words or letters by pointing to them, or read sentences or entire passages. Knowledge of the meaning or phonic attributes of the words or letters might be helpful in accomplishing the task, but only the ability to pronounce, say, or call them is scored.

1330 Word and Phonic Analysis. This category includes the ability to discriminate among letters and sound blends, associate sounds with letters, and analyze the phonetic and structural aspects of words and nonsense words.

1340 Reading Rate. Reading rate is the speed at which a person reads a written passage. It can be measured in both oral and silent reading.

1400 Science. While the term *science* actually refers to any knowledge that is the result of study or practice, its use in this Taxonomy is limited to those facts, principles, methods, and vocabulary that are associated with the natural sciences that are taught as part of the basic school curriculum such as physics, chemistry, biology, zoology, geology, and so on.

TABLE 6

CONSUMER'S GUIDE TAXONOMY

1000   ACHIEVEMENT

1000 Overall Achievement
1100 Basic Information
1200 Math, General
    1210   Math Reasoning/Problem Solving
    1220   Math Calculation
    1230   Math Vocabulary/Concepts
1300 Reading, General
    1310   Reading Comprehension
    1320   Word and Letter Recognition
    1330   Word and Phonic Analysis
    1340   Reading Rate
1400 Science
1500 Social Studies
1600 Writing, General
    1610   Writing Composition
    1620   Writing Conventions
    1630   Spelling
    1640   Penmanship
    1650   Writing Productivity
1700 Reference Skills
1800 Occupational Skills, General
    1810   Clerical Skills
    1820   Mechanical Skills
    1830   Other Occupational Skills
1900 Adaptive Behavior, General
    1910   Knowledge of Everyday Situations
    1920   Self-Help Skills
    1930   Other Adaptive Behaviors

2000   APTITUDE/DEVELOPMENTAL ABILITIES

2000 Overall Aptitude/Developmental Abilities
2100 Nonverbal Aptitude/Developmental Abilities, General
    2110   Nonverbal Cognition
    2120   Nonverbal Processing, Auditory Perception
    2130   Nonverbal Processing, Visual Perception
        2131 Visual Perception, Discrimination
        2132 Visual Perception, Visual-Motor Integration
        2133 Visual Perception, Memory
        2134 Visual Perception, Ocular Control
    2140   Nonverbal Processing, Haptic Perception
    2150   Nonverbal Processing, Gross Motor Abilities
        2151 Gross Motor Abilities, Balance/Posture
        2152 Gross Motor Abilities, Strength/Endurance
        2153 Gross Motor Abilities, Coordination
        2154 Other Gross Motor Abilities
2200 Verbal Aptitude/Developmental Abilities, General
    2210   Verbal Cognition, Reasoning
    2220   Verbal Cognition, Creativity

    2230   Verbal Cognition, Spoken Language
        2231 Spoken Language, Vocabulary
        2232 Spoken Language, Grammar
        2233 Spoken Language, Contextual Speech
    2240   Verbal Processing, Spoken Words
        2241 Spoken Words, Discrimination
        2242 Spoken Words, Memory
        2243 Spoken Words, Articulation
        2244 Other Spoken Words
    2250   Verbal Processing, Written Words

3000   AFFECT

3000 Overall Affect
3100 Anxiety
3200 Attitudes and Interests, General
    3210   Academic Attitudes and Interests
    3220   Occupational Attitudes and Interests
    3230   Other Attitudes and Interests
3300 Depression
3400 Interpersonal/Social Relations
3500 Opposition/Conduct Disorder
3600 Self-Abuse/Self-Destruction, General
    3610   Eating Disorders
    3620   Self-Injury
    3630   Substance Abuse, General
        3631 Alcohol Abuse
        3632 Other Substance Abuse
    3640   Suicide
    3650   Other Self-Abuse/Self-Destruction
3700 Self-Esteem, General
    3710   Cognitive Self-Esteem
    3720   Physical Self-Esteem
    3730   Social Self-Esteem
    3740   Other Self-Esteem
3800 Self-Regulation/Responsibility, General
    3810   Hyperactivity/Hypoactivity
    3820   Attention/Vigilance
    3830   Responsibility/Locus of Control
    3840   Other Self-Regulation/Responsibility
3900 Other Affective Characteristics

4000   GENERAL INTELLIGENCE

5000   UNCLASSIFIED ATTRIBUTES

1500 Social Studies. Social studies is synonymous with the term *social science* and includes the study of sociology, civics, anthropology, economics, psychology, history, and politics.

1600 Writing, General. Writing comprises several integrated skills, including the ability to compose, to write legibly, and to adhere to the rules of spelling, style, punctuation, and capitalization. Scores assigned to this category must measure two or more of the following writing skills: writing composition (1610), writing conventions (1620), spelling (1630), penmanship (1640), and productivity (1650).

1610 Writing Composition. Composition or conceptual writing refers to the ability to express ideas and feelings through writing. It includes such skills as the correct, functional use of sentences, sentence and paragraph structure, grammar, ideation, vocabulary, themes, and creativity.

1620 Writing Conventions. Writing conventions are the established rules that govern capitalization and punctuation.

1630 Spelling. Spelling, or orthography, is the use of letters to form words. Although spelling is usually associated with writing, it may be measured by both oral and written formats.

1640 Penmanship. Penmanship, also called handwriting, is the ability to write legibly. It refers to both cursive and manuscript forms of writing.

1650 Writing Productivity. Productivity refers to the generation of written material. It is typically evaluated through such measures as the total number of words or syllables written, without regard to penmanship, spelling, capitalization, or punctuation.

1700 Reference Skills. Reference skills involve the use of books and other materials to obtain specific information. They may include such things as understanding a title page, reading a table of contents, using dictionaries and reference sources, and reading maps, tables, and diagrams.

1800 Occupational Skills, General. Scores assigned to this category measure the skills required to pursue an occupation or vocation or to earn a living. To be assigned to this category a score must measure two or more of the following occupational skills: clerical skills (1810), mechanical skills (1820), or other occupational skills (1830).

1810 Clerical Skills. Tests of clerical skills measure competence in such areas as typewriting, filing, and shorthand.

1820 Mechanical Skills. Tests that measure specific mechanical skills or knowledge of mechanical principles are assigned to this category.

1830 Other Occupational Skills. Test scores that measure specific occupational skills other than clerical (1810) or mechanical skills (1820) are assigned to this category.

1900 Adaptive Behavior, General. Adaptive behavior encompasses the skills and knowledge required for practical everyday living. Appropriate scores will reflect adaptive behavior in areas such as community involvement and self-help skills. To be assigned to this category a score must measure two or more of the following skills: knowledge of everyday situations (1910), self-help skills (1920), or other adaptive behaviors (1930).

1910 Knowledge of Everyday Situations. Test scores that estimate a person's knowledge about various practical situations, events, and needs are assigned to this category of the Taxonomy. For the most part, these are nonacademic skills such as applying for a driver's license or registering to vote.

1920 Self-Help Skills. Self-help skills reflect those personal skills that contribute to day-to-day independence such as dressing, grooming, and eating.

1930 Other Adaptive Behaviors. Adaptive behaviors other than knowledge of everyday situations (1910) and self-help skills (1920) are assigned to this category.

Aptitude/Developmental Abilities Domain

Aptitude refers to natural capacity, potential, or ability. Most tests of intelligence and many tests of specific mental abilities can be considered to be measures of aptitude. Aptitudes generally are acquired through maturation, development, or incidental learning rather than as a consequence of systematic, planned, or formal instruction.

2000 Overall Aptitude/Developmental Abilities. Tests in this category must measure both of the aptitude categories: nonverbal aptitude/developmental abilities (2100–2154) and verbal aptitude/developmental abilities (2200–2250). The best single estimate of general aptitude will be the composite scores, usually intelligence quotients or standard scores, associated with multidimensional aptitude tests.

2100 Nonverbal Aptitude/Developmental Abilities, General. Test scores assigned to this category measure an individual's ability both to solve problems without using written or spoken words (cognition) and to understand the nonlinguistic properties of objects and sounds such as their form, structure, and intensity (processing). Simple verbal directions may be used to administer these tests as long as the subject matter being measured does not involve words in any critical way. Sometimes pantomime instructions and pointing responses are used to enhance the nonverbal nature of the test. Still, as English and English (1958) pointed out, "No test can be entirely free of verbal influence" (p. 581). To be assigned to this category, a score must measure two or more of the following aptitudes: nonverbal cognition (2110); nonverbal processing, auditory perception (2120); nonverbal processing, visual perception (2130–2134); nonverbal processing, haptic perception (2140); or nonverbal processing, gross motor abilities (2150–2154).

2110 Nonverbal Cognition. Test scores that measure problem solving, thinking, reasoning, creativity, or abstract abilities without the use of spoken or written language are assigned to this category.

2120 Nonverbal Processing, Auditory Perception. Test scores that measure sound discrimination, figure-ground perception, or memory of the intensity, pitch, or loudness of pure tones, isolated speech sounds (not words), or environmental noises are assigned to this category.

2130 Nonverbal Processing, Visual Perception. Tests that measure a variety of visual perceptions (discrimination, figure-ground, spatial relations, fine eye-hand coordination, closure, etc.) and memories related to the size, shape, or color of objects, drawings, or designs are placed in this taxonomic classification. To be assigned to this category, a score must measure two or more of the following aptitudes: visual perception, discrimination (2131); visual perception, visual-motor integration (2132); visual perception, memory (2133); or visual perception, ocular control (2134).

2131 Visual Perception, Discrimination. Visual discrimination is the ability to see differences in the physical properties of shapes, colors, designs, or objects.

2132 Visual Perception, Visual-Motor Integration. Visual-motor integration involves the ability to coordinate visual perceptions with fine motor responses. By far the most common testing format is to show people a geometric form or pattern and have them copy the stimulus by drawing it or reproducing it with manipulatives.

2133 Visual Perception, Memory. Scores of this type require a person to recall the physical properties of a stimulus after it has been removed and a period of time has elapsed. The test formats usually require a subject to reproduce a geometric pattern or to pick it out from a series of choices after the stimulus has been removed from view.

2134 Visual Perception, Ocular Control. Scores that measure a subject's ability to control the movement of the eye or that measure the dominance of one eye over the other are assigned to this category.

2140 Nonverbal Processing, Haptic Perception. Haptic perception refers to the sensation of touch and kinesthesia.

2150 Nonverbal Processing, Gross Motor Abilities. Test scores that reflect an individual's general motoric competence are included here. They represent the person's status on a variety of motor generalizations, including balance, dexterity, strength, ambulation, and gross motor coordination. Test scores assigned to this category must measure two or more of the following aptitudes: gross motor abilities, balance/posture (2151); gross motor abilities, strength/endurance (2152); gross motor abilities, coordination (2153); or other gross motor abilities (2154).

2151 Gross Motor Abilities, Balance/Posture. Test scores that measure equilibrium, bearing, or carriage are placed here.

2152 Gross Motor Abilities, Strength/Endurance. Test scores that measure strength, power, and endurance are assigned to this category.

2153 Gross Motor Abilities, Coordination. Tests of gross motor coordination are assigned to this category. They include such skills as running, catching, performing calisthenics, agility, and dexterity.

2154 Other Gross Motor Abilities. Test scores that measure gross motor abilities other than balance/posture (2151), strength/endurance (2152), and coordination (2153) are assigned here.

2200 Verbal Aptitude/Developmental Abilities, General. Test scores in this category of the Taxonomy use spoken or written words as an integral part of the content being measured. English and English (1958) noted that the term *verbal* refers to "words in any form: spoken, heard, seen, written, or thought" (p. 581). Words are the smallest linguistic unit that can stand alone. We have arbitrarily classified numerals and phonological elements as verbal because of their close relationship to words. A person's creativity, capacity for abstract thought, memory, and perceptual ability are all investigated by measuring proficiency in understanding or using words. To be assigned here, a score must measure two or more of the following aptitudes: verbal cognition, reasoning (2210); verbal cognition, creativity (2220); verbal cognition, spoken language (2230–2233); verbal processing, spoken words (2240–2244); or verbal processing, written words (2250).

2210 Verbal Cognition, Reasoning. Tests of verbal reasoning measure abstract problem solving involving words and word use. This includes such things as verbal analogies, riddles, and word association tasks.

2220 Verbal Cognition, Creativity. Test scores assigned here measure the capacity to use words to display divergent thinking, including the ability to see unique aspects of things and to make innovative responses.

2230 Verbal Cognition, Spoken Language. This category involves general linguistic ability, including oral aspects of semantics, syntax, and morphology. To be assigned to this category, a score must measure two or more of the following skills: spoken language, vocabulary (2231); spoken language, grammar (2232); or spoken language, contextual speech (2233).

2231 Spoken Language, Vocabulary. Tests of spoken vocabulary measure an individual's ability to understand the meaning of spoken words or to use spoken words appropriately.

2232 Spoken Language, Grammar. Spoken grammar is the ability to use and understand spoken grammar and syntax. Measures of word order, sentence structure, morphological elements, tense, and transformation would be assigned here.

2233 Spoken Language, Contextual Speech. This category includes measures of connected speech such as those that require subjects to tell a story or to answer questions about a story they have heard.

2240 Verbal Processing, Spoken Words. This category includes measures of verbal processing abilities that use spoken words but that do not require knowledge of the meaning of the words used. For instance, subjects may be asked to discriminate between pairs of phonemically similar words, to repeat a series of words or digits from memory, or to articulate words. To be assigned to this category, the score must measure two or more of the following skills: spoken words, discrimination (2241); spoken words, memory (2242); spoken words, articulation (2243); or other spoken words (2244).

2241 Spoken Words, Discrimination. Word discrimination is the ability to hear phonemic differences between spoken words. It usually is tested by saying a pair of phonemically similar words (*pear–bear*) and asking the subject whether the words are the same or different. Background noises may or may not be present as part of the testing format.

2242 Spoken Words, Memory. Test scores in this category measure the ability to repeat a series of unrelated words or digits that a subject has just heard.

2243 Spoken Words, Articulation. This category is reserved for test scores that measure the ability to produce individual speech sounds and to form them into spoken words.

2244 Other Spoken Words. All other processing tests that use words but that do not measure discrimination (2241), memory (2242), or articulation (2243) are assigned to this category.

2250 Verbal Processing, Written Words. Test scores placed in this category of the Taxonomy require a subject to see differences between written words and letters; to write series of unrelated words, letters, or digits from memory; or to recognize a whole written letter or word when only a fragment has been shown.

Affect Domain

Affect refers to behaviors, feelings, emotions, moods, attitudes, interests, values, traits of character or temperament, modes of conduct and adjustment, and social skills and interaction. Affective attributes may be associated with or directed toward oneself, toward other people, or toward inanimate objects. Personal affective characteristics principally involve the examination and knowledge of an individual's own actions, emotions, and motivations. Interpersonal affect also is of interest, particularly such things as social skills and the nature and importance of interactions with peers, family members, authority figures, and others in the community. Affective attributes are associated not only with people, but also may be associated with or directed toward institutions, ideas, and other objects (e.g., attitudes toward school, preference for pursuing a particular vocation, interest in music, and so on).

3000 Overall Affect. To be assigned to this category, a test score must yield information concerning two or more of the affective categories: anxiety (3100), attitudes and interests (3200–3230), depression (3300), interpersonal/social relations (3400), opposition/conduct disorder (3500), self-abuse/self-destruction (3600–3650), self-esteem (3700–3740), self-regulation/responsibility (3800–3840), or other affective characteristics (3900). Scores generated by global measures of personality and by broad-based behavior checklists and rating scales would be assigned to this category.

3100 Anxiety. Test scores assigned to this category assess anxiety—the complex emotional reactions associated with an individual's perception of threat. Anxiety may be a transitory reaction associated with a specific threatening situation or traumatic event, or it may be a typical response pattern to life experiences in general.

3200 Attitudes and Interests, General. Test scores in this category assess an individual's overall attitudes and interests. To be assigned here, a score must measure two or more of the following categories: academic attitudes and interests (3210), occupational attitudes and interests (3220), or other attitudes and interests (3230).

3210 Academic Attitudes and Interests. Test scores in this category measure attitudes and interests associated with school in general or with specific academic and intellectual pursuits.

3220 Occupational Attitudes and Interests. Test scores in this category measure attitudes and interests associated with work in general or with specific occupational and vocational pursuits.

3230 Other Attitudes and Interests. Test scores in this category measure specific attitudes and interests not associated with academic (3210) or occupational (3220) pursuits.

3300 Depression. Test scores that measure depression and feelings of emotional dejection are assigned to this category. Measures of conditions and syndromes such as unipolar and bipolar disorders, manic-depressive illness, and cyclothymic and dysthymic disorders are included here.

3400 Interpersonal/Social Relations. Test scores in this category are concerned with the nature and significance of an individual's relationships with other people. This category includes measures of such things as specific social skills; popularity; sociometric or social status; relationships with peers, coworkers, family members, authority figures, and others in the community; awareness of the actions, motivations, and emotions of other individuals; the ability to notice and make distinctions among people; and so on.

3500 Opposition/Conduct Disorder. Test scores in this category include measures of aggressive, hostile, contentious, rule-breaking, manipulative, or oppositional behaviors and feelings. Measures of conduct disorders and social maladjustment also would be assigned here.

3600 Self-Abuse/Self-Destruction, General. Diverse forms of self-harming behaviors and desires are observed. To be assigned to this category, a score must measure two or more of the following areas: eating disorders (3610), self-injury (3620), substance abuse (3630–3632), suicide (3640), or other self-abuse (3650).

3610 Eating Disorders. Tests assigned to this category measure unhealthy attitudes and behaviors with regard to food such as gross over- or undereating, bingeing, purging, and the eating of specific nonfood substances. Eating disorders include conditions such as anorexia nervosa, bulimia, and pica.

3620 Self-Injury. Test scores in this category measure a variety of self-harming behaviors and feelings, including such things as biting, hitting, pinching, and headbanging. Scores assigned here may measure actual behaviors or may be concerned with self-injurious desires, wishes, or fantasies.

3630 Substance Abuse, General. Substance abuse refers to significant psychological or behavioral impairments associated with the abuse of, dependence on, or addiction to psychoactive compounds. To be assigned to

this category, a score must measure both alcohol abuse (3631) and other substance abuse (3632).

3631 Alcohol Abuse. Scores assigned to this category are concerned with significant psychological or behavioral impairments associated with the abuse of, dependence on, or addiction to alcohol.

3632 Other Substance Abuse. Scores assigned to this category are concerned with significant psychological or behavioral impairments associated with the abuse of, dependence on, or addiction to psychoactive compounds other than alcohol, including barbiturates, tranquilizers, stimulants, hypnotics, and other mood- or mind-altering substances.

3640 Suicide. Measures of suicide risk, suicidal ideation, and potentially self-destructive behaviors and feelings are assigned to this category.

3650 Other Self-Abuse/Self-Destruction. Scores that measure specific self-harming behaviors and feelings other than eating disorders (3610), self-injury (3620), substance abuse (3630–3632), and suicide (3640) are assigned to this category.

3700 Self-Esteem, General. Test scores that describe the way that individuals perceive and value themselves and their own distinctive traits of mind, body, character, conduct, and temperament are assigned to this category. To be assigned here, a score must measure two or more of the following types of self-esteem: cognitive self-esteem (3710), physical self-esteem (3720), social self-esteem (3730), or other self-esteem (3740).

3710 Cognitive Self-Esteem. Measures of cognitive self-concept or self-esteem assess the awareness and personal evaluation of one's abilities and attributes in academic and intellectual pursuits. Scores assigned here evaluate perceptions of oneself pertaining to such things as intelligence, learning, school, education, academic skill, scholarly achievement, and intellectual prowess.

3720 Physical Self-Esteem. Measures of physical self-concept or self-esteem assess the awareness and personal evaluation of one's physical abilities and attributes. Scores assigned here evaluate perceptions of oneself pertaining to such things as bodily characteristics, anatomical features, attractiveness, strength, agility, and coordination.

3730 Social Self-Esteem. Measures of social self-concept or self-esteem assess the awareness and personal evaluation of one's social abilities and attributes. Scores assigned here evaluate perceptions of oneself pertaining to such things as peer popularity, confidence and skill in social situations, satisfaction in interpersonal relationships, and social status.

3740 Other Self-Esteem. All measures of specific types of self-concept or self-esteem other than cognitive self-esteem (3710), physical self-esteem (3720), and social self-esteem (3730) are assigned to this category.

3800 Self-Regulation/Responsibility, General. Self-regulation refers to the internal management of one's thoughts, feelings, and actions. To be assigned to this category, a score must measure two or more of the following categories: hyperactivity/hypoactivity (3810), attention/vigilance (3820), responsibility/locus of control (3830), or other self-regulation/responsibility (3840).

3810 Hyperactivity/Hypoactivity. Measures of activity level are assigned to this category. These may include hyperkinetic behaviors, hypo- or hyperactivity, impulsivity, lethargy, fidgetiness, and so on.

3820 Attention/Vigilance. Measures of the ability to sustain attention and effort are assigned to this category. These may include attention deficits (i.e., developmentally inappropriate inattention, failure to complete activities or remain on task, difficulty concentrating, distractibility, poor inhibitory control) and selective attention excesses (i.e., excessive attention to selected or limited aspects of a task or activity).

3830 Responsibility/Locus of Control. This category includes measures of one's ability or willingness to accept responsibility for one's own behavior and its consequences. Locus of control also is concerned with the degree to which people believe in their own capacity to influence the events in their lives rather than rejecting responsibility and blaming luck, fate, circumstance, or other people.

3840 Other Self-Regulation/Responsibility. Measures of specific self-monitoring or self-regulating behaviors other than hyperactivity/hypoactivity (3810), attention/vigilance (3820), and responsibility/locus of control (3830) are assigned to this category.

3900 Other Affective Characteristics. An almost infinite number of affective characteristics are measured through the use of norm-referenced tests. These include traits and personal attributes such as trustworthiness, autonomy, sexuality, satisfaction, conformity, temperament, hypochondriasis and somatic concerns, and so on. All scores that measure specific affective characteristics other than anxiety (3100), attitudes and interests (3200-3230), depression (3300), interpersonal/social relations (3400), opposition/conduct disorder (3500), self-abuse/self-destruction (3600-3650), self-esteem (3700-3740), and self-regulation/responsibility (3800-3840) are assigned to this category.

General Intelligence Domain

General Intelligence is the superordinate category or domain in the *Consumer's Guide* Taxonomy. General intelligence is a composite of one's affective characteristics, aptitude, and actual achievement.

4000 General Intelligence. Scores assigned to the General Intelligence category must include attributes from at least two of the three other domains: Achievement (1000-1930), Aptitude (2000-2250), or Affect (3000-3900).

The Taxonomy also is reproduced in tabular form in Appendix B. There each section of the Taxonomy is followed by a list of all the pertinent test scores that are reviewed in the *Consumer's Guide*. The Overall Rating of each score is given in the left-hand column preceding the score name. Scores with A ratings are listed first, followed by those with B ratings and then those with F ratings. This information is particularly valuable for individuals who use the *Consumer's Guide* to find an appropriate and well-built test that measures a specific content area.

For instance, a clinician may want to administer a test of arithmetic. The first step is to consult the Taxonomy to find the appropriate classification. Arithmetic is a learned skill that usually must be taught formally, so it will be found within the Achievement domain. There is an Achievement category called Math, General (1200), which has three subdivisions: Math Reasoning/Problem Solving (1210), Math Calculation (1220), and Math Vocabulary/Concepts (1230). Math Calculation is the appropriate Taxonomy category because it is defined as "the ability to perform basic arithmetic operations such as addition, subtraction, multiplication, and division."

Once the appropriate taxonomic classification has been identified, the clinician consults the list of tests that measure arithmetic. Under the taxonomic classification 1220 in Appendix B, there is an inventory of all the test scores evaluated in the *Consumer's Guide* that measure Math Calculation ability with their *Consumer's Guide* Overall Ratings. This allows the reader to eliminate from consideration those scores that are Not Recommended (designated by the letter F) and to focus on the ones that are Recommended (B) and Highly Recommended (A). The reader can then consult the alphabetic list in Appendix A to learn more about these tests.

ADMINISTRATION AND SCORING CHARACTERISTICS

The Reviewer Evaluation Form provides a great deal of information about how a test is administered and scored. Indications are given about the individual or group nature of the test administration, indicated by an I or G in the Administration column of the alphabetic table. The average time in minutes required for administration is also specified, along with the range of ages or grades of subjects with whom the test score may be used. If the test score can be converted into normative scores, these are listed on the Reviewer Evaluation Form, too. This information is summarized in the alphabetic list of tests in Appendix A to help examiners decide whether a particular test meets their needs.

EXAMINER CHARACTERISTICS

Another important characteristic to consider when selecting a test is the test examiner's qualifications. Some tests are restricted to examiners who hold particular professional licenses or certificates. In the alphabetic test list in Appendix A, these tests are classified as *restricted* (R) in the Examiner Qualifications column. Other tests require some *special training* (ST) before they can be used effectively. Still other tests can be *easily administered* (EA) and used with confidence by examiners who have taught themselves to use the instrument by reading the test manual and familiarizing themselves with the administration and scoring procedures. These requirements are identified on the front of the Reviewer Evaluation Form and in Appendix A.

TEST FORMAT CHARACTERISTICS

The format of a test is especially important when deciding whether the test is appropriate for a particular student. This information is recorded on the Reviewer Evaluation Form. It is also summarized in the alphabetic test list in Appendix A.

There are two broad categories of formats found among the tests reviewed for the *Consumer's Guide*. The first category includes tests that are not completed by the target students themselves but by a third party, usually by teachers, parents, or other adult respondents who know the student. Probably the best examples of this type of test are behavior rating scales or adaptive behavior inventories that ask a knowledgeable adult to rate or evaluate the observed behavior of a particular student. The formats of these tests are almost always of the paper-and-pencil or personal interview variety. This type of test is noted in the alphabetic list by a check in the Third Party column.

The vast majority of the tests reviewed in the *Consumer's Guide* fall into the second category. They are administered directly to a target student. For these tests, we have identified the specific behaviors required of a respondent. For

instance, the input format of a test may require a student to listen, to read print, or to look at various stimuli. The output or response format may take the form of speaking (either one-word or multiple-word responses), manipulating objects, marking an answer sheet, pointing, drawing, or writing. The necessary behaviors to receive test information (input) and to respond to test items (output) are designated by dots in the appropriate columns in the alphabetic test list in Appendix A.

Obviously, the nature of the test's format will be important when selecting a test that is appropriate for the target student. Certain formats will not be appropriate, for instance, for a student who is blind, a student with cerebral palsy, a student with limited English proficiency, or a student who cannot read.

USING THE NONTECHNICAL INFORMATION

Obviously an examiner must consider this nontechnical, descriptive information carefully in order to determine the appropriateness of a test for a specific student. For instance, does the test measure the desired content area? How much examiner expertise is required to administer the test? Will testing consume 15 minutes or several hours of the teacher's or school psychologist's time? Will a parent interview or a home visit be needed?

Knowledge about how test scores are reported is also important. For example, if a standard score is called for, the tester will want to avoid tests that generate only age or grade equivalents. The examiner also must be careful to select a test that has a suitable format for the student being tested. For instance, students with sensory impairments may be unable to see or hear particular stimuli, students with dyslexia may be unnecessarily penalized by tests that require subjects to read print, and students with motor impairments may require motor-free test formats.

Many professionals will want to use the *Consumer's Guide* reviews as the basis for selecting tests. These individuals are encouraged to begin the selection process by describing the content that they want to measure and then identifying the appropriate classification within the Taxonomy. They should make note of the tests listed at the end of the pertinent section of the taxonomic list in Appendix B that have A (Highly Recommended) or B (Recommended) ratings. Then they can consult the alphabetic list in Appendix A to learn more about the nontechnical characteristics of these particular tests or test scores.

By using the Taxonomy in Appendix B and the information in Appendix A in tandem, diagnosticians can ensure that their decision to purchase or to administer a test is an informed one. They know from the *Consumer's Guide* ratings that the tests they select are reliable, valid, and well normed. And they know from the descriptive information that these tests measure the intended content, have appropriate administration and response formats, and yield the desired type of normative score.

REFERENCES

Aiken, L. R. (1988). *Psychological testing and assessment* (6th ed.). Boston: Allyn & Bacon.

American Psychological Association. (1985). *Standards for educational and psychological tests.* Washington, DC: Author.

Anastasi, A. (1984). The K-ABC in historical and contemporary perspective. *The Journal of Special Education, 18*(3), 357–366.

Anastasi, A. (1988). *Psychological testing* (6th ed.). New York: Macmillan.

Anastasi, A. (1991). *Psychological testing* (7th ed.). New York: Macmillan.

Buros, O. K. (1983). *Tests in print III.* Lincoln: University of Nebraska Press.

Compton, C. (1984). *A guide to 75 tests for special education.* Belmont, CA: Fearon.

Conoley, J. C., & Kramer, J. J. (1989). *The tenth mental measurements yearbook.* Lincoln: University of Nebraska Press.

English, H. B., & English, A. C. (1958). *A comprehensive dictionary of psychological and psychoanalytical terms.* New York: David McKay.

Garrett, H. E. (1954). *Statistics in psychology and education.* New York: Longmans, Green.

Gronlund, N. E., & Linn, R. L. (1990). *Measurement and evaluation in teaching* (6th ed.). New York: Macmillan.

Guilford, J. P. (1956). *Fundamental statistics in psychology and education* (3rd ed.). New York: McGraw-Hill.

Helmstadter, G. C. (1964). *Principles of psychological measurement.* New York: Appleton-Century-Crofts.

International Reading Association Board of Directors. (1980, June). Board action. *Reading Today,* p. 1.

Kelley, T. L. (1927). *Interpretation of educational measurement.* Yonkers-on-Hudson, NY: World Press.

McLoughlin, J. A., & Lewis, R. B. (1990). *Assessing special students* (3rd ed.). Columbus, OH: Merrill.

Nunnally, J. S. (1978). *Psychometric theory.* New York: McGraw-Hill.

Salvia, J., & Ysseldyke, J. E. (1991). *Assessment* (5th ed.). Boston: Houghton Mifflin.

Sattler, J. M. (1988). *Assessment of children* (3rd ed.). San Diego: Author.

Statistical Abstract of the United States 1990. (1990). Washington, DC: U.S. Department of Commerce, Bureau of the Census.

Sweetland, R. C., & Keyser, D. J. (Eds.). (1991). *Tests: A comprehensive reference for assessments in psychology, education, and business.* Austin, TX: PRO-ED.

Wallace, G., & Larsen, S. C., & Elksnin, L. (1992). *Educational assessment of learning problems* (2nd ed.). Boston: Allyn & Bacon.

APPENDIX A

ALPHABETIC LISTING OF CONSUMER'S GUIDE TESTS

	Taxonomy code	Technical Characteristics										Ages/Grades for Intended Use	Nontechnical Characteristics																				
		Overall rating	Norms					Reliability			Val.		Admin.		Scores					Examiner qualifications	Test Formats												
																					Input					Output							
			Scores	Size	Demographics	Recency	Total	Internal consistency	Stability	Total	Total		Group/Individual	Testing time	Age equivalents	Grade equivalents	Percentile ranks	Standard scores	Other		Third Party	Listen	Read print	Look at stimuli	Other	Speak, minor	Speak, major	Manipulate objects	Mark answer sheet	Point	Draw	Write print	Other
AAMD ADAPTIVE BEHAVIOR SCALES (1969)																																	
Independent Functioning	1920	F	F	B	F	F	F	B	F	B	F	3-0/60+ yrs.	I	7					•[1]	EA	•		•						•				
Physical Development	2150	F	F	B	F	F	F	F	F	F	F	3-0/60+ yrs.	I	7					•[1]	EA	•		•						•				
Economic Activity	1930	F	F	B	F	F	F	F	F	F	F	3-0/60+ yrs.	I	7					•[1]	EA	•		•						•				
Language Development	4000	F	F	B	F	F	F	B	F	B	F	3-0/60+ yrs.	I	7					•[1]	EA	•		•						•				
Number and Time Concept	1230	F	F	B	F	F	F	F	F	F	F	3-0/60+ yrs.	I	7					•[1]	EA	•		•						•				
Occupation—Domestic	1830	F	F	B	F	F	F	B	F	B	F	3-0/60+ yrs.	I	7					•[1]	EA	•		•						•				
Occupation—General	1830	F	F	B	F	F	F	F	F	F	F	3-0/60+ yrs.	I	7					•[1]	EA	•		•						•				
Self-Direction	3830	F	F	B	F	F	F	F	F	F	F	3-0/60+ yrs.	I	7					•[1]	EA	•		•						•				
Responsibility	3830	F	F	B	F	F	F	F	F	F	F	3-0/60+ yrs.	I	7					•[1]	EA	•		•						•				
Socialization	3400	F	F	B	F	F	F	F	F	F	F	3-0/60+ yrs.	I	7					•[1]	EA	•		•						•				
Violent and Destructive Behavior	3500	F	F	B	F	F	F	F	F	F	F	3-0/60+ yrs.	I	7					•[1]	EA	•		•						•				
Antisocial Behavior	3500	F	F	B	F	F	F	B	F	B	F	3-0/60+ yrs.	I	7					•[1]	EA	•		•						•				
Rebellious Behavior	3500	F	F	B	F	F	F	F	F	F	F	3-0/60+ yrs.	I	7					•[1]	EA	•		•						•				
Untrustworthy Behavior	3830	F	F	B	F	F	F	F	F	F	F	3-0/60+ yrs.	I	7					•[1]	EA	•		•						•				
Withdrawal	3400	F	F	B	F	F	F	F	F	F	F	3-0/60+ yrs.	I	7					•[1]	EA	•		•						•				
Stereotyped Behavior and Odd Mannerisms	3900	F	F	B	F	F	F	F	F	F	F	3-0/60+ yrs.	I	7					•[1]	EA	•		•						•				
Inappropriate Interpersonal Manners	3400	F	F	B	F	F	F	F	F	F	F	3-0/60+ yrs.	I	7					•[1]	EA	•		•						•				
Unacceptable or Eccentric Habits	3900	F	F	B	F	F	F	F	F	F	F	3-0/60+ yrs.	I	7					•[1]	EA	•		•						•				
Unacceptable Vocal Habits	3900	F	F	B	F	F	F	F	F	F	F	3-0/60+ yrs.	I	7					•[1]	EA	•		•						•				
Self-Abusive Behavior	3620	F	F	B	F	F	F	F	F	F	F	3-0/60+ yrs.	I	7					•[1]	EA	•		•						•				
Hyperactive Tendencies	3810	F	F	B	F	F	F	F	F	F	F	3-0/60+ yrs.	I	7					•[1]	EA	•		•						•				
Sexually Aberrant Behavior	3900	F	F	B	F	F	F	F	F	F	F	3-0/60+ yrs.	I	7					•[1]	EA	•		•						•				
Psychological Disturbances	3900	F	F	B	F	F	F	F	F	F	F	3-0/60+ yrs.	I	7					•[1]	EA	•		•						•				
[1]Means used to estimate adaptive behavior level																																	
AAMD ADAPTIVE BEHAVIOR SCALES — PUBLIC SCHOOL VERSION — NORMAL NORMS (1974)																																	
Independent Living	1920	F	B	A	F	F	F	F	F	F	F	7-0/13-11 yrs.	I	7			•			EA	•		•						•				
Physical Development	2150	F	B	A	F	F	F	F	F	F	F	7-0/13-11 yrs.	I	7				•		EA	•		•						•				
Economic Activity	1930	F	B	A	F	F	F	F	F	F	F	7-0/13-11 yrs.	I	7			•			EA	•		•						•				

			Technical Characteristics										Nontechnical Characteristics																			
			Norms					Reliability			Val.	Ages/Grades for Intended Use	Admin.		Scores						Test Formats												
																						Input					Output							
	Taxonomy code	Overall rating	Scores	Size	Demographics	Recency	Total	Internal consistency	Stability	Total	Total		Group/Individual	Testing time	Age equivalents	Grade equivalents	Percentile ranks	Standard scores	Other	Examiner qualifications	Third Party	Listen	Read print	Look at stimuli	Other	Speak, minor	Speak, major	Manipulate objects	Mark answer sheet	Point	Draw	Write print	Other
AAMD ADAPTIVE BEHAVIOR SCALES — PUBLIC SCHOOL VERSION — NORMAL NORMS (1974) (cont.)																																	
Language Development	4000	F	B	A	F	F	F	F	F	F	F	7-0/13-11 yrs.	I	7			•			EA	•		•						•				
Numbers and Time	1230	F	B	A	F	F	F	F	F	F	F	7-0/13-11 yrs.	I	7			•			EA	•		•						•				
Domestic Activity	1830	F	B	A	F	F	F	F	F	F	F	7-0/13-11 yrs.	I	7			•			EA	•		•						•				
Vocational Activity	1830	F	B	A	F	F	F	F	F	F	F	7-0/13-11 yrs.	I	7			•			EA	•		•						•				
Self-Direction	3830	F	B	A	F	F	F	F	F	F	F	7-0/13-11 yrs.	I	7			•			EA	•		•						•				
Responsibility	3830	F	B	A	F	F	F	F	F	F	F	7-0/13-11 yrs.	I	7			•			EA	•		•						•				
Socialization	3400	F	B	A	F	F	F	F	F	F	F	7-0/13-11 yrs.	I	7			•			EA	•		•						•				
Violent and Destructive Behavior	3500	F	B	A	F	F	F	F	F	F	F	7-0/13-11 yrs.	I	7			•			EA	•		•						•				
Antisocial Behavior	3500	F	B	A	F	F	F	F	F	F	F	7-0/13-11 yrs.	I	7			•			EA	•		•						•				
Rebellious Behavior	3500	F	B	A	F	F	F	F	F	F	F	7-0/13-11 yrs.	I	7			•			EA	•		•						•				
Untrustworthy Behavior	3830	F	B	A	F	F	F	F	F	F	F	7-0/13-11 yrs.	I	7			•			EA	•		•						•				
Withdrawal	3400	F	B	A	F	F	F	F	F	F	F	7-0/13-11 yrs.	I	7			•			EA	•		•						•				
Stereotyped Behavior and Odd Mannerisms	3900	F	B	A	F	F	F	F	F	F	F	7-0/13-11 yrs.	I	7			•			EA	•		•						•				
Inappropriate Interpersonal Manners	3400	F	B	A	F	F	F	F	F	F	F	7-0/13-11 yrs.	I	7			•			EA	•		•						•				
Unacceptable Vocal Habits	3900	F	B	A	F	F	F	F	F	F	F	7-0/13-11 yrs.	I	7			•			EA	•		•						•				
Unacceptable or Eccentric Habits	3900	F	B	A	F	F	F	F	F	F	F	7-0/13-11 yrs.	I	7			•			EA	•		•						•				
Self-Abusive Behavior	3620	F	B	A	F	F	F	F	F	F	F	7-0/13-11 yrs.	I	7			•			EA	•		•						•				
Hyperactive Tendencies	3810	F	B	A	F	F	F	F	F	F	F	7-0/13-11 yrs.	I	7			•			EA	•		•						•				
Sexually Aberrant Behavior	3900	F	B	A	F	F	F	F	F	F	F	7-0/13-11 yrs.	I	7			•			EA	•		•						•				
Psychological Disturbances	3900	F	B	A	F	F	F	F	F	F	F	7-0/13-11 yrs.	I	7			•			EA	•		•						•				
AAMD ADAPTIVE BEHAVIOR SCALES — PUBLIC SCHOOL VERSION — SPECIAL NORMS[1] (1974)																																	
Independent Living	1920	F	B	F	F	F	F	F	F	F	F	7-0/13-11 yrs.	I	7			•			EA	•		•						•				
Physical Development	2150	F	B	F	F	F	F	F	F	F	F	7-0/13-11 yrs.	I	7			•			EA	•		•						•				
Economic Activity	1930	F	B	F	F	F	F	F	F	F	F	7-0/13-11 yrs.	I	7			•			EA	•		•						•				
Language Development	4000	F	B	F	F	F	F	F	F	F	F	7-0/13-11 yrs.	I	7			•			EA	•		•						•				
Numbers and Time	1230	F	B	F	F	F	F	F	F	F	F	7-0/13-11 yrs.	I	7			•			EA	•		•						•				
Domestic Activity	1830	F	B	F	F	F	F	F	F	F	F	7-0/13-11 yrs.	I	7			•			EA	•		•						•				

[1]Constitutes four groups: EMR, TMR, EH$_1$, and EH$_2$

		Technical Characteristics										Nontechnical Characteristics																						
		Norms					Reliability			Val.	Ages/Grades for Intended Use	Admin.		Scores							Test Formats												
																					Input					Output							
Taxonomy code	Overall rating	Scores	Size	Demographics	Recency	Total	Internal consistency	Stability	Total	Total		Group/Individual	Testing time	Age equivalents	Grade equivalents	Percentile ranks	Standard scores	Other	Examiner qualifications	Third Party	Listen	Read print	Look at stimuli	Other	Speak, minor	Speak, major	Manipulate objects	Mark answer sheet	Point	Draw	Write print	Other
AAMD ADAPTIVE BEHAVIOR SCALES — PUBLIC SCHOOL VERSION — SPECIAL NORMS[1] (1974) (cont.)																																
Vocational Activity	1830	F	B	F	F	F	F	F	F	F	F	7-0/13-11 yrs.	I	7			•			EA	•		•						•				
Self-Direction	3830	F	B	F	F	F	F	F	F	F	F	7-0/13-11 yrs.	I	7			•			EA	•		•						•				
Responsibility	3830	F	B	F	F	F	F	F	F	F	F	7-0/13-11 yrs.	I	7			•			EA	•		•						•				
Socialization	3400	F	B	F	F	F	F	F	F	F	F	7-0/13-11 yrs.	I	7			•			EA	•		•						•				
Violent and Destructive Behavior	3500	F	B	F	F	F	F	F	F	F	F	7-0/13-11 yrs.	I	7			•			EA	•		•						•				
Antisocial Behavior	3500	F	B	F	F	F	F	F	F	F	F	7-0/13-11 yrs.	I	7			•			EA	•		•						•				
Rebellious Behavior	3500	F	B	F	F	F	F	F	F	F	F	7-0/13-11 yrs.	I	7			•			EA	•		•						•				
Untrustworthy Behavior	3830	F	B	F	F	F	F	F	F	F	F	7-0/13-11 yrs.	I	7			•			EA	•		•						•				
Withdrawal	3400	F	B	F	F	F	F	F	F	F	F	7-0/13-11 yrs.	I	7			•			EA	•		•						•				
Stereotyped Behavior and Odd Mannerisms	3900	F	B	F	F	F	F	F	F	F	F	7-0/13-11 yrs.	I	7			•			EA	•		•						•				
Inappropriate Interpersonal Manners	3400	F	B	F	F	F	F	F	F	F	F	7-0/13-11 yrs.	I	7			•			EA	•		•						•				
Unacceptable Vocal Habits	3900	F	B	F	F	F	F	F	F	F	F	7-0/13-11 yrs.	I	7			•			EA	•		•						•				
Unacceptable or Eccentric Habits	3900	F	B	F	F	F	F	F	F	F	F	7-0/13-11 yrs.	I	7			•			EA	•		•						•				
Self-Abusive Behavior	3620	F	B	F	F	F	F	F	F	F	F	7-0/13-11 yrs.	I	7			•			EA	•		•						•				
Hyperactive Tendencies	3810	F	B	F	F	F	F	F	F	F	F	7-0/13-11 yrs.	I	7			•			EA	•		•						•				
Sexually Aberrant Behavior	3900	F	B	F	F	F	F	F	F	F	F	7-0/13-11 yrs.	I	7			•			EA	•		•						•				
Psychological Disturbances	3900	F	B	F	F	F	F	F	F	F	F	7-0/13-11 yrs.	I	7			•			EA	•		•						•				

[1]Constitutes four groups: EMR, TMR, EH_1, and EH_2

AAMD ADAPTIVE BEHAVIOR SCALES — SCHOOL EDITION — NORMAL NORMS (1981)																																
Factor 1: Personal Self-Sufficiency	1920	F	A	A	F	B	F	F	F	F	F	3-0/16-5 yrs.	I	45				•		EA	•		•						•				
Factor 2: Community Self-Sufficiency	1000	F	A	A	F	B	F	B	F	B	F	3-0/16-5 yrs.	I	45				•		EA	•		•						•				
Factor 3: Personal-Social Responsibility	1920	F	A	A	F	B	F	B	F	B	F	3-0/16-5 yrs.	I	45				•		EA	•		•						•				
Factor 4: Social Adjustment	3400	F	A	A	F	B	F	A	F	B	F	3-0/16-5 yrs.	I	45				•		EA	•		•						•				
Factor 5: Personal Adjustment	3000	F	A	A	F	B	F	F	F	F	F	3-0/16-5 yrs.	I	45				•		EA	•		•						•				
Independent Functioning	1920	F	B	A	F	B	F	F	F	F	F	3-0/16-5 yrs.	I	7			•			EA	•		•						•				
Physical Development	2150	F	B	A	F	B	F	F	F	F	F	3-0/16-5 yrs.	I	7			•			EA	•		•						•				
Economic Activity	1930	F	B	A	F	B	F	F	F	F	F	3-0/16-5 yrs.	I	7			•			EA	•		•						•				
Language Development	4000	F	B	A	F	B	F	F	F	F	F	3-0/16-5 yrs.	I	7			•			EA	•		•						•				

	Taxonomy code	Overall rating	Norms: Scores	Size	Demographics	Recency	Total	Reliability: Internal consistency	Stability	Total	Val. Total	Ages/Grades for Intended Use	Group/Individual	Testing time	Age equivalents	Grade equivalents	Percentile ranks	Standard scores	Other	Examiner qualifications	Third Party	Listen	Read print	Look at stimuli	Other	Speak, minor	Speak, major	Manipulate objects	Mark answer sheet	Point	Draw	Write print	Other
AAMD ADAPTIVE BEHAVIOR SCALES — SCHOOL EDITION — NORMAL NORMS (1981) (cont.)																																	
Numbers and Time	1230	F	B	A	F	B	F	F	F	F	F	3-0/16-5 yrs.	I	7			•			EA	•		•						•				
Prevocational Activity	1830	F	B	A	F	B	F	F	F	F	F	3-0/16-5 yrs.	I	7			•			EA	•		•						•				
Self-Direction	3830	F	B	A	F	B	F	F	F	F	F	3-0/16-5 yrs.	I	7			•			EA	•		•						•				
Responsibility	3830	F	B	A	F	B	F	F	F	F	F	3-0/16-5 yrs.	I	7			•			EA	•		•						•				
Socialization	3400	F	B	A	F	B	F	F	F	F	F	3-0/16-5 yrs.	I	7			•			EA	•		•						•				
Aggressiveness	3500	F	B	A	F	B	F	F	F	F	F	3-0/16-5 yrs.	I	7			•			EA	•		•						•				
Antisocial vs. Social Behavior	3400	F	B	A	F	B	F	F	F	F	F	3-0/16-5 yrs.	I	7			•			EA	•		•						•				
Rebelliousness	3500	F	B	A	F	B	F	F	F	F	F	3-0/16-5 yrs.	I	7			•			EA	•		•						•				
Trustworthiness	3830	F	B	A	F	B	F	F	F	F	F	3-0/16-5 yrs.	I	7			•			EA	•		•						•				
Withdrawal vs. Involvement	3400	F	B	A	F	B	F	F	F	F	F	3-0/16-5 yrs.	I	7			•			EA	•		•						•				
Mannerisms	3900	F	B	A	F	B	F	F	F	F	F	3-0/16-5 yrs.	I	7			•			EA	•		•						•				
Interpersonal Manners	3400	F	B	A	F	B	F	F	F	F	F	3-0/16-5 yrs.	I	7			•			EA	•		•						•				
Acceptability of Vocal Habits	3900	F	B	A	F	B	F	F	F	F	F	3-0/16-5 yrs.	I	7			•			EA	•		•						•				
Acceptability of Habits	3900	F	B	A	F	B	F	F	F	F	F	3-0/16-5 yrs.	I	7			•			EA	•		•						•				
Activity Level	3810	F	B	A	F	B	F	F	F	F	F	3-0/16-5 yrs.	I	7			•			EA	•		•						•				
Symptomatic Behavior	3100	F	B	A	F	B	F	F	F	F	F	3-0/16-5 yrs.	I	7			•			EA	•		•						•				
AAMD ADAPTIVE BEHAVIOR SCALES — SCHOOL EDITION — SPECIAL NORMS[1] (1981)																																	
Factor 1: Personal Self-Sufficiency	1920	F	A	B	F	B	F	B	F	B	F	3-6[2]/17-5 yrs.	I	45				•		EA	•		•						•				
Factor 2: Community Self-Sufficiency	1000	F	A	B	F	B	F	B	F	B	F	3-6[2]/17-5 yrs.	I	45				•		EA	•		•						•				
Factor 3: Personal-Social Responsibility	1920	F	A	B	F	B	F	B	F	B	F	3-6[2]/17-5 yrs.	I	45				•		EA	•		•						•				
Factor 4: Social Adjustment	3400	F	A	B	F	B	F	A	F	B	F	3-6[2]/17-5 yrs.	I	45				•		EA	•		•						•				
Factor 5: Personal Adjustment	3000	F	A	B	F	B	F	F	F	F	F	3-6[2]/17-5 yrs.	I	45				•		EA	•		•						•				
Independent Functioning	1920	F	B	B	F	B	F	F	F	F	F	3-6[2]/17-5 yrs.	I	7			•			EA	•		•						•				
Physical Development	2150	F	B	B	F	B	F	F	F	F	F	3-6[2]/17-5 yrs.	I	7			•			EA	•		•						•				
Economic Activity	1930	F	B	B	F	B	F	F	F	F	F	3-6[2]/17-5 yrs.	I	7			•			EA	•		•						•				
Language Development	4000	F	B	B	F	B	F	F	F	F	F	3-6[2]/17-5 yrs.	I	7			•			EA	•		•						•				
Numbers and Time	1230	F	B	B	F	B	F	F	F	F	F	3-6[2]/17-5 yrs.	I	7			•			EA	•		•						•				

[1]Includes EMR and TMR; [2]EMR begins at age 7-6

			Technical Characteristics									Nontechnical Characteristics																					
			Norms					Reliability		Val.	Ages/Grades for Intended Use	Admin.		Scores							Test Formats												
																					Input					Output							
	Taxonomy code	Overall rating	Scores	Size	Demographics	Recency	Total	Internal consistency	Stability	Total	Total		Group/Individual	Testing time	Age equivalents	Grade equivalents	Percentile ranks	Standard scores	Other	Examiner qualifications	Third Party	Listen	Read print	Look at stimuli	Other	Speak, minor	Speak, major	Manipulate objects	Mark answer sheet	Point	Draw	Write print	Other
AAMD ADAPTIVE BEHAVIOR SCALES — SCHOOL EDITION — SPECIAL NORMS¹ (1981) (cont.)																																	
Prevocational Activity	1830	F	B	B	F	B	F	F	F	F	F	3-6²/17-5 yrs.	I	7				•		EA	•		•						•				
Self-Direction	3830	F	B	B	F	B	F	F	F	F	F	3-6²/17-5 yrs.	I	7				•		EA	•		•						•				
Responsibility	3830	F	B	B	F	B	F	F	F	F	F	3-6²/17-5 yrs.	I	7				•		EA	•		•						•				
Socialization	3400	F	B	B	F	B	F	F	F	F	F	3-6²/17-5 yrs.	I	7				•		EA	•		•						•				
Aggressiveness	3500	F	B	B	F	B	F	F	F	F	F	3-6²/17-5 yrs.	I	7				•		EA	•		•						•				
Antisocial vs. Social Behavior	3400	F	B	B	F	B	F	F	F	F	F	3-6²/17-5 yrs.	I	7				•		EA	•		•						•				
Rebelliousness	3500	F	B	B	F	B	F	F	F	F	F	3-6²/17-5 yrs.	I	7				•		EA	•		•						•				
Trustworthiness	3830	F	B	B	F	B	F	F	F	F	F	3-6²/17-5 yrs.	I	7				•		EA	•		•						•				
Withdrawal vs. Involvement	3400	F	B	B	F	B	F	F	F	F	F	3-6²/17-5 yrs.	I	7				•		EA	•		•						•				
Mannerisms	3900	F	B	B	F	B	F	F	F	F	F	3-6²/17-5 yrs.	I	7				•		EA	•		•						•				
Interpersonal Manners	3400	F	B	B	F	B	F	F	F	F	F	3-6²/17-5 yrs.	I	7				•		EA	•		•						•				
Acceptability of Vocal Habits	3900	F	B	B	F	B	F	F	F	F	F	3-6²/17-5 yrs.	I	7				•		EA	•		•						•				
Acceptability of Habits	3900	F	B	B	F	B	F	F	F	F	F	3-6²/17-5 yrs.	I	7				•		EA	•		•						•				
Activity Level	3810	F	B	B	F	B	F	F	F	F	F	3-6²/17-5 yrs.	I	7				•		EA	•		•						•				
Symptomatic Behavior	3100	F	B	B	F	B	F	F	F	F	F	3-6²/17-5 yrs.	I	7				•		EA	•		•						•				

¹Includes EMR and TMR; ²EMR begins at age 7-6

ABERRANT BEHAVIOR CHECKLIST (1986)																																	
Irritability	3900	F	B	F	F	B	F	F	F	F	F	5-0/51 + yrs.	I	5					•¹	EA	•		•						•				
Lethargy	3810	F	B	F	F	B	F	F	F	F	F	5-0/51 + yrs.	I	5					•¹	EA	•		•						•				
Stereotypy	3900	F	B	F	F	B	F	F	F	F	F	5-0/51 + yrs.	I	5					•¹	EA	•		•						•				
Hyperactivity	3810	F	B	F	F	B	F	F	F	F	F	5-0/41 + yrs.	I	5					•¹	EA	•		•						•				
Inappropriate Speech	3900	F	B	F	F	B	F	F	F	F	F	5-0/41 + yrs.	I	5					•¹	EA	•		•						•				

¹Means and standard deviations provided

ADAPTIVE BEHAVIOR INVENTORY — NORMAL NORMS (1986)																																	
Total Score — Long Form	4000	B	A	B	A	A	B	A	B	B	A	5-0/18-11 yrs.	I	22			•	•		EA	•		•						•				
Total Score — Short Form	4000	B	A	B	A	A	B	A	B	B	A	5-0/18-11 yrs.	I	7			•	•		EA	•		•						•				
Self-Care Skills	1920	B	A	B	A	A	B	A	B	B	A	5-0/18-11 yrs.	I	7			•	•		EA	•		•						•				
Communication Skills	4000	B	A	B	A	A	B	A	B	B	A	5-0/18-11 yrs.	I	7			•	•		EA	•		•						•				
Social Skills	3400	B	A	B	A	A	B	A	B	B	A	5-0/18-11 yrs.	I	7			•	•		EA	•		•						•				

	Taxonomy code	Overall rating	Scores	Size	Demographics	Recency	Total	Internal consistency	Stability	Total	Total (Val)	Ages/Grades for Intended Use	Group/Individual	Testing time	Age equivalents	Grade equivalents	Percentile ranks	Standard scores	Other	Examiner qualifications	Third Party	Listen	Read print	Look at stimuli	Other	Speak, minor	Speak, major	Manipulate objects	Mark answer sheet	Point	Draw	Write print	Other
ADAPTIVE BEHAVIOR INVENTORY — NORMAL NORMS (1986) (cont.)																																	
Academic Skills	1000	B	A	B	A	A	B	A	B	B	A	5-0/18-11 yrs.	I	7			•	•		EA	•		•						•				
Occupational Skills	1800	B	A	B	A	A	B	A	B	B	A	5-0/18-11 yrs.	I	7			•	•		EA	•		•						•				
ADAPTIVE BEHAVIOR INVENTORY — RETARDED NORMS (1986)																																	
Total Score — Long Form	4000	B	A	B	A	A	B	A	B	B	A	6-0/18-11 yrs.	I	22			•	•		EA	•		•						•				
Total Score — Short Form	4000	B	A	B	A	A	B	A	B	B	A	6-0/18-11 yrs.	I	7			•	•		EA	•		•						•				
Self-Care Skills	1920	B	A	B	A	A	B	A	B	B	A	6-0/18-11 yrs.	I	7			•	•		EA	•		•						•				
Communication Skills	4000	B	A	B	A	A	B	A	B	B	A	6-0/18-11 yrs.	I	7			•	•		EA	•		•						•				
Social Skills	3400	B	A	B	A	A	B	A	B	B	A	6-0/18-11 yrs.	I	7			•	•		EA	•		•						•				
Academic Skills	1000	B	A	B	A	A	B	A	B	B	A	6-0/18-11 yrs.	I	7			•	•		EA	•		•						•				
Occupational Skills	1800	B	A	B	A	A	B	A	B	B	A	6-0/18-11 yrs.	I	7			•	•		EA	•		•						•				
ADD-H COMPREHENSIVE TEACHER'S RATING SCALE (1988)																																	
Attention	3820	F	B	F	F	A	F	A	F	B	A	gr. K–5	I	15				•		EA	•		•						•				
Hyperactivity	3810	F	B	F	F	A	F	A	B	B	B	gr. K–5	I	15				•		EA	•		•						•				
Social Skills	3400	F	B	F	F	A	F	A	B	B	B	gr. K–5	I	15				•		EA	•		•						•				
Oppositional	3500	F	B	F	F	A	F	A	B	B	B	gr. K–5	I	15				•		EA	•		•						•				
ADOLESCENT DRINKING INDEX (1989)																																	
Total Score	3000	F	B	F	F	F	F	F	F	F	F	12-0/17-11 yrs.	I	10				•		EA	•		•						•				
Self-Medicated Drinking	3631	F	B	F	F	F	F	F	F	F	F	12-0/17-11 yrs.	I	10				•		EA	•		•						•				
Rebellious Behavior	3500	F	B	F	F	F	F	F	F	F	F	12-0/17-11 yrs.	I	10				•		EA	•		•						•				
THE ALPHA TEST OF PHONOLOGY (1986)																																	
Total Processes	2243	F	A	B	F	A	F	F	A	B	F	3-0/8-11 yrs.	I	30			•	•		ST	•		•			•							
Consonant Deletion	2243	F	A	B	F	A	F	F	A	B	F	3-0/8-11 yrs.	I	30			•	•		ST	•		•			•							
Syllable Deletion	2243	F	A	B	F	A	F	F	B	B	F	3-0/8-11 yrs.	I	30			•	•		ST	•		•			•							
Stridency Deletion	2243	F	A	B	F	A	F	F	A	B	F	3-0/8-11 yrs.	I	30			•	•		ST	•		•			•							
Stopping	2243	F	A	B	F	A	F	F	B	B	F	3-0/8-11 yrs.	I	30			•	•		ST	•		•			•							
Fronting	2243	F	A	B	F	A	F	F	A	B	F	3-0/8-11 yrs.	I	30			•	•		ST	•		•			•							
Backing	2243	F	A	B	F	A	F	F	A	B	F	3-0/8-11 yrs.	I	30			•	•		ST	•		•			•							
Alveolarization	2243	F	A	B	F	A	F	F	A	B	F	3-0/8-11 yrs.	I	30			•	•		ST	•		•			•							
Labialization	2243	F	A	B	F	A	F	F	A	B	F	3-0/8-11 yrs.	I	30			•	•		ST	•		•			•							

	Taxonomy code	Overall rating	Scores	Size	Demographics	Recency	Total (Norms)	Internal consistency	Stability	Total (Rel.)	Total (Val.)	Ages/Grades for Intended Use	Group/Individual	Testing time	Age equivalents	Grade equivalents	Percentile ranks	Standard scores	Other	Examiner qualifications	Third Party	Listen	Read print	Look at stimuli	Other	Speak, minor	Speak, major	Manipulate objects	Mark answer sheet	Point	Draw	Write print	Other
THE ALPHA TEST OF PHONOLOGY (1986) (cont.)																																	
Affrication	2243	F	A	B	F	A	F	F	A	B	F	3-0/8-11 yrs.	I	30			•	•		ST		•		•			•						
Deaffrication	2243	F	A	B	F	A	F	F	A	B	F	3-0/8-11 yrs.	I	30			•	•		ST		•		•			•						
Voicing Change	2243	F	A	B	F	A	F	F	A	B	F	3-0/8-11 yrs.	I	30			•	•		ST		•		•			•						
Gliding	2243	F	A	B	F	A	F	F	A	B	F	3-0/8-11 yrs.	I	30			•	•		ST		•		•			•						
Vowelization	2243	F	A	B	F	A	F	F	A	B	F	3-0/8-11 yrs.	I	30			•	•		ST		•		•			•						
Cluster Reduction	2243	F	A	B	F	A	F	F	B	B	F	3-0/8-11 yrs.	I	30			•	•		ST		•		•			•						
Cluster Substitution	2243	F	A	B	F	A	F	F	A	B	F	3-0/8-11 yrs.	I	30			•	•		ST		•		•			•						
ANALYSIS OF THE LANGUAGE OF LEARNING (1987)																																	
Total	2200	F	A	A	F	A	F	F	B	B	B	4-0/9-11 yrs.	I	35	•		•	•		EA		•		•		•	•				•		
Defining Concepts	2231	F	A	A	F	A	F	F	B	B	A	4-0/9-11 yrs.	I	5	•		•	•		EA		•				•							
Generating Concept Examples	2231	F	A	A	F	A	F	F	F	F	A	4-0/9-11 yrs.	I	5	•		•	•		EA		•				•	•						
Recognizing Concepts	2231	F	A	A	F	A	F	F	F	F	A	4-0/9-11 yrs.	I	5	•		•	•		EA		•								•			
Segmenting Sentences	2244	F	A	A	F	A	F	F	F	F	B	4-0/9-11 yrs.	I	5	•		•	•		EA		•		•		•				•			
Generating Words	2244	F	A	A	F	A	F	F	B	B	A	4-0/9-11 yrs.	I	5	•		•	•		EA		•				•							
Segmenting Words	2244	F	A	A	F	A	F	F	F	F	B	4-0/9-11 yrs.	I	5	•		•	•		EA		•		•		•				•			
Repairing Sentences	2230	F	A	A	F	A	F	F	B	B	A	4-0/9-11 yrs.	I	5	•		•	•		EA		•				•							
ARIZONA ARTICULATION PROFICIENCY SCALE, SECOND EDITION (1977)																																	
Total Score	2243	F	A	A	F	A	F	B	F	B	F	1-6/13-11 yrs.	G	20	•		•	•		EA		•	•	•		•	•						
ASSESSING SEMANTIC SKILLS THROUGH EVERYDAY THEMES (1988)																																	
Total Test	2231	F	A	A	F	A	F	F	A	B	B	3-0/9-11 yrs.	I	30	•		•	•		EA		•		•			•						
Total Receptive	2231	F	A	A	F	A	F	F	B	B	B	3-0/9-11 yrs.	I	30	•		•	•		EA		•		•						•			
Total Expressive	2231	F	A	A	F	A	F	F	A	B	B	3-0/9-11 yrs.	I	30	•		•	•		EA		•		•			•						
Identifying Labels	2231	F	A	A	F	A	F	F	F	F	A	3-0/9-11 yrs.	I	30	•		•	•		EA		•		•						•			
Identifying Categories	2231	F	A	A	F	A	F	F	F	F	A	3-0/9-11 yrs.	I	30	•		•	•		EA		•		•						•			
Identifying Attributes	2231	F	A	A	F	A	F	F	F	F	A	3-0/9-11 yrs.	I	30	•		•	•		EA		•		•						•			
Identifying Functions	2231	F	A	A	F	A	F	F	F	F	A	3-0/9-11 yrs.	I	30	•		•	•		EA		•		•						•			
Identifying Definitions	2231	F	A	A	F	A	F	F	F	F	A	3-0/9-11 yrs.	I	30	•		•	•		EA		•		•						•			
Stating Labels	2231	F	A	A	F	A	F	F	B	B	A	3-0/9-11 yrs.	I	30	•		•	•		EA		•		•			•						
Stating Categories	2231	F	A	A	F	A	F	F	B	B	A	3-0/9-11 yrs.	I	30	•		•	•		EA		•		•			•						

	Taxonomy code	Overall rating	Norms: Scores	Norms: Size	Norms: Demographics	Norms: Recency	Norms: Total	Rel: Internal consistency	Rel: Stability	Rel: Total	Val. Total	Ages/Grades for Intended Use	Group/Individual	Testing time	Age equivalents	Grade equivalents	Percentile ranks	Standard scores	Scores: Other	Examiner qualifications	Third Party	Listen	Read print	Look at stimuli	Input: Other	Speak, minor	Speak, major	Manipulate objects	Mark answer sheet	Point	Draw	Write print	Output: Other
ASSESSING SEMANTIC SKILLS THROUGH EVERYDAY THEMES (1988) (cont.)																																	
Stating Attributes	2231	F	A	A	F	A	F	F	F	F	A	3-0/9-11 yrs.	I	30	•		•	•		EA	•		•				•						
Stating Functions	2231	F	A	A	F	A	F	F	F	F	A	3-0/9-11 yrs.	I	30	•		•	•		EA	•		•				•						
Stating Definitions	2231	F	A	A	F	A	F	F	F	F	A	3-0/9-11 yrs.	I	30	•		•	•		EA	•		•				•						
AUDITORY DISCRIMINATION TEST — REVISED (1973)																																	
Total	2241	F	B	F	F	F	F	F	F	F	B	5-0/8-11 yrs.	I	7					•¹	EA	•									•			

¹Rating scale

	Taxonomy code	Overall rating	Norms: Scores	Norms: Size	Norms: Demographics	Norms: Recency	Norms: Total	Rel: Internal consistency	Rel: Stability	Rel: Total	Val. Total	Ages/Grades for Intended Use	Group/Individual	Testing time	Age equivalents	Grade equivalents	Percentile ranks	Standard scores	Scores: Other	Examiner qualifications	Third Party	Listen	Read print	Look at stimuli	Input: Other	Speak, minor	Speak, major	Manipulate objects	Mark answer sheet	Point	Draw	Write print	Output: Other
AUDITORY-VISUAL, SINGLE-WORD PICTURE VOCABULARY TEST — ADOLESCENT (1986)																																	
Total	2231	F	A	F	F	A	F	B	F	B	B	12-0/16-11 yrs.	I	7	•		•	•		EA	•		•							•		•	
BANKSON-BERNTHAL TEST OF PHONOLOGY (1990)																																	
Phonological Process Composite	2243	F	A	A	F	A	F	A	B	B	B	3-0/9-11 yrs.	I	15			•	•		EA	•		•				•						
Consonants Composite	2243	F	A	A	F	A	F	A	F	B	B	3-0/9-11 yrs.	I	15			•	•		EA	•		•				•						
Word Inventory	2231	F	A	A	F	A	F	A	B	B	F	3-0/9-11 yrs.	I	15			•	•		EA	•		•				•						
BANKSON LANGUAGE SCREENING TEST (1977)																																	
Total	2000	F	B	F	F	B	F	F	F	F	F	4-1/8-0 yrs.	I	22				•		EA	•		•			•	•			•			
BASIC ACHIEVEMENT SKILLS INDIVIDUAL SCREENER (1983)																																	
Mathematics	1200	B	A	A	B	B	B	A	B	B	B	gr. 1–12	I	22	•	•	•	•		EA	•	•	•									•	
Reading	1300	B	A	A	B	B	B	A	A	A	B	gr. 1–12	I	22	•	•	•	•		EA	•	•	•			•	•			•			
Spelling	1630	B	A	A	B	B	B	A	A	A	B	gr. 1–12	I	22	•	•	•	•		EA	•											•	
Writing	1600	F	F	F	F	B	F	F	F	F	F	gr. 3–8	I	7					•¹	EA	•											•	

¹Above Average, Average, Below Average

	Taxonomy code	Overall rating	Norms: Scores	Norms: Size	Norms: Demographics	Norms: Recency	Norms: Total	Rel: Internal consistency	Rel: Stability	Rel: Total	Val. Total	Ages/Grades for Intended Use	Group/Individual	Testing time	Age equivalents	Grade equivalents	Percentile ranks	Standard scores	Scores: Other	Examiner qualifications	Third Party	Listen	Read print	Look at stimuli	Input: Other	Speak, minor	Speak, major	Manipulate objects	Mark answer sheet	Point	Draw	Write print	Output: Other
BASIC SCHOOL SKILLS INVENTORY — DIAGNOSTIC (1983)																																	
Total Score	4000	F	A	B	B	B	B	A	F	B	F	4-0/7-5 yrs.	I	22			•	•		EA	•¹		•							•			
Daily Living Skills	1900	F	A	B	B	B	B	B	F	B	F	4-0/7-5 yrs.	I	7			•	•		EA	•¹		•							•			
Spoken Language	2230	F	A	B	B	B	B	A	F	B	F	4-0/7-5 yrs.	I	7			•	•		EA	•¹		•							•			
Reading	1300	F	A	B	B	B	B	A	F	B	F	4-0/7-5 yrs.	I	7			•	•		EA	•¹		•							•			
Writing	1600	F	A	B	B	B	B	B	F	B	F	4-0/7-5 yrs.	I	7			•	•		EA	•¹		•							•			
Mathematics	1200	F	A	B	B	B	B	B	F	B	F	4-0/7-5 yrs.	I	7			•	•		EA	•¹		•							•			
Classroom Behavior	3000	F	A	B	B	B	B	A	F	B	F	4-0/7-5 yrs.	I	7			•	•	•	EA	•¹		•							•			

¹Teacher rates student abilities or administers items if abilities are unknown

			Technical Characteristics									Nontechnical Characteristics																				
			Norms					Reliability			Val.	Ages/Grades for Intended Use	Admin.		Scores							Test Formats										
																					Input					Output						
	Taxonomy code	Overall rating	Scores	Size	Demographics	Recency	Total	Internal consistency	Stability	Total	Total		Group/Individual	Testing time	Age equivalents	Grade equivalents	Percentile ranks	Standard scores	Other	Examiner qualifications	Third Party	Listen	Read print	Look at stimuli	Other	Speak, minor	Speak, major	Manipulate objects	Mark answer sheet	Point	Draw	Write print	Other
BECK DEPRESSION INVENTORY (1987)																																	
Total	3300	F	B	F	F	F	F	F	F	F	B	13-0+ yrs.	G	15					•[1]	EA		•							•				
												[1]Cutoff scores provided																					
BECK HOPELESSNESS SCALE (1988)																																	
Total	3900	F	F	F	F	B	F	A	F	B	A	17+ yrs.	G	10					•[1]	EA		•							•				
												[1]Clinical cutoffs for raw scores provided																					
BEHAVIOR DIMENSIONS RATING SCALE (1989)																																	
Total	3000	F	A	F/B[1]	F	A	F	A	F	B	F	gr. K–11	I	30				•		EA	•		•						•				
Aggressive/Acting Out	3500	F	A	F/B[1]	F	A	F	A	F	B	F	gr. K–11	I	30				•		EA	•		•						•				
Irresponsible/Inattentive	3800	F	A	F/B[1]	F	A	F	A	F	B	F	gr. K–11	I	30				•		EA	•		•						•				
Socially Withdrawn	3400	F	A	F/B[1]	F	A	F	A	F	B	F	gr. K–11	I	30				•		EA	•		•						•				
Fearful/Anxious	3100	F	A	F/B[1]	F	A	F	A	F	B	F	gr. K–11	I	30				•		EA	•		•						•				
												[1]Rating for Female Norms appears first, Male Norms second																					
BEHAVIOR EVALUATION SCALE (1983)																																	
Behavior Quotient	3000	B	A	B	B	B	B	B	B	B	B	gr. K–12	I	22				•		EA	•		•						•				
Learning Problems	3000	B	A	B	B	B	B	B	B	B	A	gr. K–12	I	22				•		EA	•		•						•				
Interpersonal Difficulties	3400	B	A	B	B	B	B	B	B	B	A	gr. K–12	I	22				•		EA	•		•						•				
Inappropriate Behavior	3000	B	A	B	B	B	B	B	B	B	A	gr. K–12	I	22				•		EA	•		•						•				
Unhappiness/Depression	3300	B	A	B	B	B	B	B	B	B	B	gr. K–12	I	22				•		EA	•		•						•				
Physical Symptoms/Fears	3100	B	A	B	B	B	B	B	B	B	B	gr. K–12	I	22				•		EA	•		•						•				
BEHAVIOR EVALUATION SCALE–2 (1990)																																	
Total	3000	B	A	A	B	A	B	A	A	A	B	gr. K–12	I	20			•	•		EA	•		•						•				
Learning Problems	3000	B	A	A	B	A	B	A	A	A	A	gr. K–12	I	20			•	•		EA	•		•						•				
Interpersonal Difficulties	3400	B	A	A	B	A	B	A	A	A	A	gr. K–12	I	20			•	•		EA	•		•						•				
Inappropriate Behavior	3000	B	A	A	B	A	B	A	A	A	A	gr. K–12	I	20			•	•		EA	•		•						•				
Unhappiness/Depression	3300	B	A	A	B	A	B	B	A	B	A	13-0 yrs.	I	20			•	•		EA	•		•						•				
Physical Symptoms/Fears	3100	B	A	A	B	A	B	F	A	B	A	gr. K–12	I	20			•	•		EA	•		•						•				
BEHAVIOR RATING PROFILE (1983)																																	
Student Rating Scales-Home	3000	B	A	B	B	B	B	B	F	B	B	6-6/18-6 yrs.	I	7			•	•		EA			•						•				
Student Rating Scales-School	3000	B	A	B	B	B	B	B	B	B	B	6-6/18-6 yrs.	I	7			•	•		EA			•						•				

		Norms					Reliability			Val.			Admin.		Scores						Input				Output							
Taxonomy code	Overall rating	Scores	Size	Demographics	Recency	Total	Internal consistency	Stability	Total	Total	Ages/Grades for Intended Use	Group/Individual	Testing time	Age equivalents	Grade equivalents	Percentile ranks	Standard scores	Other	Examiner qualifications	Third Party	Listen	Read print	Look at stimuli	Other	Speak, minor	Speak, major	Manipulate objects	Mark answer sheet	Point	Draw	Write print	Other
BEHAVIOR RATING PROFILE (1983) (cont.)																																
Student Rating Scales-Peer 3400	B	A	B	B	B	B	B	B	B	B	6-6/18-6 yrs.	I	7			•	•		EA			•						•				
Teacher Rating Scale 3000	F	A	B	F	B	F	A	B	B	B	6-6/18-6 yrs.	I	7			•	•		EA	•		•						•				
Parent Rating Scale 3000	F	A	B	F	B	F	B	B	B	B	6-6/18-6 yrs.	I	7			•	•		EA	•		•						•				
Sociogram 3400	F	A	A[1]	A[1]	A[1]	A[1]	F	F	F	F	6-6/18-6 yrs.	I	7			•	•		EA	•	•											•

[1]Sociogram normed on class sample; thus, sample is own population

		Norms					Reliability			Val.			Admin.		Scores						Input				Output							
Taxonomy code	Overall rating	Scores	Size	Demographics	Recency	Total	Internal consistency	Stability	Total	Total	Ages/Grades for Intended Use	Group/Individual	Testing time	Age equivalents	Grade equivalents	Percentile ranks	Standard scores	Other	Examiner qualifications	Third Party	Listen	Read print	Look at stimuli	Other	Speak, minor	Speak, major	Manipulate objects	Mark answer sheet	Point	Draw	Write print	Other
BEHAVIOR RATING PROFILE, SECOND EDITION (1990)																																
Student Rating Scales-Home 3000	B	A	B	A	B	B	B	F	B	A	6-6/18-6 yrs.	G	20			•	•		EA			•						•				
Student Rating Scales-School 3000	B	A	B	A	B	B	B	B	B	A	6-6/18-6 yrs.	G	20			•	•		EA			•						•				
Student Rating Scales-Peer 3400	B	A	B	A	B	B	B	B	B	A	6-6/18-6 yrs.	G	20			•	•		EA			•						•				
Teacher Rating Scale 3000	B	A	B	A	B	B	A	A	A	A	6-6/18-6 yrs.	I	15			•	•		EA	•		•						•				
Parent Rating Scale 3000	B	A	B	B	B	B	B	B	B	A	6-6/18-6 yrs.	I	15			•	•		EA	•		•						•				
Sociogram 3400	F	A	A[1]	A[1]	A[1]	A[1]	F	F	F	F	6-6/18-6 yrs.	G	20			•	•		EA	•	•											•

[1]Sociogram is normed on a class sample which is the entire population

		Norms					Reliability			Val.			Admin.		Scores						Input				Output							
Taxonomy code	Overall rating	Scores	Size	Demographics	Recency	Total	Internal consistency	Stability	Total	Total	Ages/Grades for Intended Use	Group/Individual	Testing time	Age equivalents	Grade equivalents	Percentile ranks	Standard scores	Other	Examiner qualifications	Third Party	Listen	Read print	Look at stimuli	Other	Speak, minor	Speak, major	Manipulate objects	Mark answer sheet	Point	Draw	Write print	Other
THE BENDER GESTALT TEST FOR YOUNG CHILDREN (1975)																																
Total 2132	F	B	B	F	F	F	F	F	F	B	5-0/11-11 yrs.	G	22	•		•			ST	•			•							•		
BODER TEST OF READING AND SPELLING PATTERNS (1982)																																
Reading 1320	F	F	F	F	F	F	F	F	F	B	gr. K–Adult	I	45	•	•			•[1]	EA	•		•				•					•	

[1]Ratio quotient

		Norms					Reliability			Val.			Admin.		Scores						Input				Output							
Taxonomy code	Overall rating	Scores	Size	Demographics	Recency	Total	Internal consistency	Stability	Total	Total	Ages/Grades for Intended Use	Group/Individual	Testing time	Age equivalents	Grade equivalents	Percentile ranks	Standard scores	Other	Examiner qualifications	Third Party	Listen	Read print	Look at stimuli	Other	Speak, minor	Speak, major	Manipulate objects	Mark answer sheet	Point	Draw	Write print	Other
BOEHM TEST OF BASIC CONCEPTS — REVISED (1986)																																
Total 2231	F	A	A	F	A	F	F	F	F	B	gr. K–2	G	22			•	•		EA	•			•					•				
BRUININKS-OSERETSKY TEST OF MOTOR PROFICIENCY (1978)																																
Battery Composite 2100	F	A	B	F	B	F	F	B	B	B	4-6/14-5 yrs.	I	60+	•		•	•		EA	•			•				•			•		•[1]
Gross Motor Composite 2150	F	A	B	F	B	F	F	B	B	B	4-6/14-5 yrs.	I	22				•		EA	•			•									•[2]
Fine Motor Composite 2132	F	A	B	F	B	F	F	B	B	B	4-6/14-5 yrs.	I	22				•		EA	•			•				•			•		•[3]
Short Form 2100	F	A	B	F	B	F	F	B	B	B	4-6/14-5 yrs.	I	7			•	•		EA	•			•				•			•		•[4]
Running Speed and Agility 2154	F	A	B	F	B	F	F	F	F	B	4-6/14-5 yrs.	I	7	•		•	•		EA	•												•[5]
Balance 2151	F	A	B	F	B	F	F	F	F	B	4-6/14-5 yrs.	I	7	•		•	•		EA	•			•									•[6]
Bilateral Coordination 2153	F	A	B	F	B	F	F	B	B	B	4-6/14-5 yrs.	I	7	•		•	•		EA	•			•									•[7]

[1]Various gross and fine motor skills; [2]gross and fine motor responses; [3]cut with scissors, stop falling object with hand; [4]various gross and fine motor skills; [5]runs; [6]stand/walk; [7]gesture movements

	Taxonomy code	Overall rating	Norms: Scores	Size	Demographics	Recency	Total	Reliability: Internal consistency	Stability	Total	Val. Total	Ages/Grades for Intended Use	Admin. Group/Individual	Testing time	Scores: Age equivalents	Grade equivalents	Percentile ranks	Standard scores	Other	Examiner qualifications	Input: Third Party	Listen	Read print	Look at stimuli	Other	Output: Speak, minor	Speak, major	Manipulate objects	Mark answer sheet	Point	Draw	Write print	Other

BRUININKS-OSERETSKY TEST OF MOTOR PROFICIENCY (1978) (cont.)

	Taxonomy	Overall	Scores	Size	Demog.	Recency	Total	IntCons	Stab	Total	Val	Ages/Grades	G/I	Time	AgeEq	GradeEq	PctRanks	StdScores	Other	Exam	ThirdParty	Listen	ReadPrint	LookStim	Other	SpkMin	SpkMaj	Manip	MarkAns	Point	Draw	WritePrint	Other
Strength	2152	F	A	B	F	B	F	F	B	B	B	4-6/14-5 yrs.	I	7	•		•	•		EA	•			•									•8
Upper-Limb Coordination	2153	F	A	B	F	B	F	F	F	F	B	4-6/14-5 yrs.	I	7	•		•	•		EA	•			•									•9
Response Speed	2132	F	A	B	F	B	F	F	F	F	B	4-6/14-5 yrs.	I	7	•		•	•		EA	•			•									•
Visual-Motor Control	2132	F	A	B	F	B	F	F	F	F	B	4-6/14-5 yrs.	I	7	•		•	•		EA	•												•10
Upper-Limb Speed and Dexterity	2132	F	A	B	F	B	F	F	B	B	B	4-6/14-5 yrs.	I	7	•		•	•		EA	•			•					•			•	

8Jump, movements; 9catch; 10scissor cutting

BURKS' BEHAVIOR RATING SCALES (1977)

	Taxonomy	Overall	Scores	Size	Demog.	Recency	Total	IntCons	Stab	Total	Val	Ages/Grades	G/I	Time	AgeEq	GradeEq	PctRanks	StdScores	Other	Exam	ThirdParty	Listen	ReadPrint	LookStim	Other	SpkMin	SpkMaj	Manip	MarkAns	Point	Draw	WritePrint	Other
Excessive Self-Blame	3830	F	F	F	F	B	F	F	F	F	F	Unspecified	I	20					•1	EA	•		•						•				
Excessive Anxiety	3100	F	F	F	F	B	F	F	F	F	F	Unspecified	I	20					•1	EA	•		•						•				
Excessive Withdrawal	3400	F	F	F	F	B	F	F	F	F	F	Unspecified	I	20					•1	EA	•		•						•				
Excessive Dependency	3830	F	F	F	F	B	F	F	F	F	F	Unspecified	I	20					•1	EA	•		•						•				
Poor Ego Strength	3900	F	F	F	F	B	F	F	F	F	B	Unspecified	I	20					•1	EA	•		•						•				
Poor Physical Strength	3720	F	F	F	F	B	F	F	F	F	F	Unspecified	I	20					•1	EA	•		•						•				
Poor Coordination	3720	F	F	F	F	B	F	F	F	F	B	Unspecified	I	20					•1	EA	•		•						•				
Poor Intellectuality	3710	F	F	F	F	B	F	F	F	F	F	Unspecified	I	20					•1	EA	•		•						•				
Poor Academics	3710	F	F	F	F	B	F	F	F	F	B	Unspecified	I	20					•1	EA	•		•						•				
Poor Attention	3820	F	F	F	F	B	F	F	F	F	B	Unspecified	I	20					•1	EA	•		•						•				
Poor Impulse Control	3840	F	F	F	F	B	F	F	F	F	B	Unspecified	I	20					•1	EA	•		•						•				
Poor Reality Contact	3900	F	F	F	F	B	F	F	F	F	B	Unspecified	I	20					•1	EA	•		•						•				
Poor Sense of Identity	3700	F	F	F	F	B	F	F	F	F	F	Unspecified	I	20					•1	EA	•		•						•				
Excessive Suffering	3900	F	F	F	F	B	F	F	F	F	F	Unspecified	I	20					•1	EA	•		•						•				
Poor Anger Control	3830	F	F	F	F	B	F	F	F	F	B	Unspecified	I	20					•1	EA	•		•						•				
Excessive Sense of Persecution	3900	F	F	F	F	B	F	F	F	F	B	Unspecified	I	20					•1	EA	•		•						•				
Excessive Aggressiveness	3500	F	F	F	F	B	F	F	F	F	F	Unspecified	I	20					•1	EA	•		•						•				
Excessive Resistance	3500	F	F	F	F	B	F	F	F	F	B	Unspecified	I	20					•1	EA	•		•						•				
Poor Social Conformity	3400	F	F	F	F	B	F	F	F	F	F	Unspecified	I	20					•1	EA	•		•						•				

1Raw scores and clinical scores only

		Technical Characteristics									Nontechnical Characteristics																						
		Norms					Reliability			Val.	Ages/Grades for Intended Use	Admin.		Scores							Test Formats											
																						Input				Output							
	Taxonomy code	Overall rating	Scores	Size	Demographics	Recency	Total	Internal consistency	Stability	Total	Total		Group/Individual	Testing time	Age equivalents	Grade equivalents	Percentile ranks	Standard scores	Other	Examiner qualifications	Third Party	Listen	Read print	Look at stimuli	Other	Speak, minor	Speak, major	Manipulate objects	Mark answer sheet	Point	Draw	Write print	Other
CANFIELD LEARNING STYLES INVENTORY (1988)[1]																																	
Peer	3400	F	A	B/F[2]	F	B	F	F	F	F	F	Jr. High–Adult	G	40			•	•		EA			•						•				
Organization	3830	F	A	B/F[2]	F	B	F	F	F	F	F	Jr. High–Adult	G	40			•	•		EA			•						•				
Goal Setting	3900	F	A	B/F[2]	F	B	F	F	F	F	F	Jr. High–Adult	G	40			•	•		EA			•						•				
Competition	3400	F	A	B/F[2]	F	B	F	F	F	F	F	Jr. High–Adult	G	40			•	•		EA			•						•				
Instructor	3400	F	A	B/F[2]	F	B	F	F	F	F	F	Jr. High–Adult	G	40			•	•		EA			•						•				
Detail	3820	F	A	B/F[2]	F	B	F	F	F	F	F	Jr. High–Adult	G	40			•	•		EA			•						•				
Independence	3830	F	A	B/F[2]	F	B	F	F	F	F	F	Jr. High–Adult	G	40			•	•		EA			•						•				
Authority	3830	F	A	B/F[2]	F	B	F	F	F	F	F	Jr. High–Adult	G	40			•	•		EA			•						•				
Numeric	3900	F	A	B/F[2]	F	B	F	F	F	F	F	Jr. High–Adult	G	40			•	•		EA			•						•				
Qualitative	3900	F	A	B/F[2]	F	B	F	F	F	F	F	Jr. High–Adult	G	40			•	•		EA			•						•				
Inanimate	3900	F	A	B/F[2]	F	B	F	F	F	F	F	Jr. High–Adult	G	40			•	•		EA			•						•				
People	3400	F	A	B/F[2]	F	B	F	F	F	F	F	Jr. High–Adult	G	40			•	•		EA			•						•				
Listening	3900	F	A	B/F[2]	F	B	F	F	F	F	F	Jr. High–Adult	G	40			•	•		EA			•						•				
Reading	3900	F	A	B/F[2]	F	B	F	F	F	F	F	Jr. High–Adult	G	40			•	•		EA			•						•				
Iconic	3900	F	A	B/F[2]	F	B	F	F	F	F	F	Jr. High–Adult	G	40			•	•		EA			•						•				
Direct Experience	3900	F	A	B/F[2]	F	B	F	F	F	F	F	Jr. High–Adult	G	40			•	•		EA			•						•				
A Expectation	3900	F	A	B/F[2]	F	B	F	F	F	F	F	Jr. High–Adult	G	40			•	•		EA			•						•				
B Expectation	3900	F	A	B/F[2]	F	B	F	F	F	F	F	Jr. High–Adult	G	40			•	•		EA			•						•				
C Expectation	3900	F	A	B/F[2]	F	B	F	F	F	F	F	Jr. High–Adult	G	40			•	•		EA			•						•				
D Expectation	3900	F	A	B/F[2]	F	B	F	F	F	F	F	Jr. High–Adult	G	40			•	•		EA			•						•				
Total Expectation	3900	F	A	B/F[2]	F	B	F	F	F	F	F	Jr. High–Adult	G	40			•	•		EA			•						•				

[1]Ratings for Forms A, B, C, D are the same except where indicated; [2]rating for Form A is first, for forms B, C, and D second

CAREER DECISION-MAKING SYSTEM (1982)																																	
Crafts	3220	F	B	A	F	B	F	A	F	B	F	gr. 7–12 +	G	7			•			EA	•	•							•				
Scientific	3220	F	B	A	F	B	F	A	B	B	F	gr. 7–12 +	G	7			•			EA	•	•							•				
The Arts	3220	F	B	A	F	B	F	A	F	B	F	gr. 7–12 +	G	7			•			EA	•	•							•				
Social	3220	F	B	A	F	B	F	A	B	B	F	gr. 7–12 +	G	7			•			EA	•	•							•				
Business	3220	F	B	A	F	B	F	B	B	B	F	gr. 7–12 +	G	7			•			EA	•	•							•				
Clerical	3220	F	B	A	F	B	F	B	B	B	F	gr. 7–12 +	G	7			•			EA	•	•							•				

			Technical Characteristics									Ages/Grades for Intended Use	Nontechnical Characteristics																					
				Norms				Reliability			Val.		Admin.		Scores							Input					Output							
	Taxonomy code	Overall rating	Scores	Size	Demographics	Recency	Total	Internal consistency	Stability	Total	Total		Group/Individual	Testing time	Age equivalents	Grade equivalents	Percentile ranks	Standard scores	Other	Examiner qualifications	Third Party	Listen	Read print	Look at stimuli	Other	Speak, minor	Speak, major	Manipulate objects	Mark answer sheet	Point	Draw	Write print	Other
CAREER MATURITY INVENTORY (1978)																																	
Attitude Scale A-1	3220	F	A	B	F	B	F	F	F	F	B	gr. 6–12	G	22			•	•		EA		•	•						•				
Attitude Scale A-2 Screening Form	3220	F	A	B	F	B	F	F	F	F	B	gr. 6–12	G	22			•	•		EA		•	•						•				
Attitude Scale B-2 Counseling Form-Decisiveness	3220	F	A	B	F	B	F	F	F	F	F	gr. 6–12	G	22			•	•		EA		•	•						•				
Attitude Scale B-2 Counseling Form-Involvement	3220	F	A	B	F	B	F	F	F	F	F	gr. 6–12	G	22			•	•		EA		•	•						•				
Attitude Scale B-2 Counseling Form-Independence	3220	F	A	B	F	B	F	F	F	F	F	gr. 6–12	G	22			•	•		EA		•	•						•				
Attitude Scale B-2 Counseling Form-Orientation	3220	F	A	B	F	B	F	F	F	F	F	gr. 6–12	G	22			•	•		EA		•	•						•				
Attitude Scale B-2 Counseling Form-Compromise	3220	F	A	B	F	B	F	F	F	F	F	gr. 6–12	G	22			•	•		EA		•	•						•				
Competence Test Part 1 Self Appraisal	3700	F	A	B	F	B	F	F	F	F	B	gr. 6–12	G	22			•	•		EA		•	•						•				
Competence Test Part 2 Occupational Information	1100	F	A	B	F	B	F	B	F	B	B	gr. 6–12	G	22			•	•		EA		•	•						•				
Competence Test Part 3 Goal Selection	3220	F	A	B	F	B	F	B	F	B	B	gr. 6–12	G	22			•	•		EA		•	•						•				
Competence Test Part 4 Planning	1800	F	A	B	F	B	F	B	F	B	B	gr. 6–12	G	22			•	•		EA		•	•						•				
Competence Test Part 5 Problem Solving	2210	F	A	B	F	B	F	F	F	F	B	gr. 6–12	G	22			•	•		EA		•	•						•				
CARROW AUDITORY-VISUAL ABILITIES TEST (1981)																																	
Total	2000	F	A	A	F	B	F	F	F	F	B	4-0/10-11 yrs.	I	60+			•	•		EA		•		•		•	•			•	•		
Visual Battery	2000	F	A	A	F	B	F	F	F	F	B	4-0/10-11 yrs.	I	60+			•	•		EA		•		•						•	•		
Auditory Battery	2200	F	A	A	F	B	F	F	F	F	B	4-0/10-11 yrs.	I	60+			•	•		EA		•		•		•	•			•	•		
General Visual Memory	2130	F	A	A	F	B	F	F	F	F	B	4-0/10-11 yrs.	I	60+			•	•		EA		•		•						•	•		
General Auditory Memory	2120	F	A	A	F	B	F	F	F	F	B	4-0/10-11 yrs.	I	60+			•	•		EA		•		•		•	•			•	•		
Auditory Memory for Sequence	2100	F	A	A	F	B	F	F	F	F	B	4-0/10-11 yrs.	I	60+			•	•		EA		•		•		•	•			•	•		
Auditory Memory for Unrelated Stimuli	2100	F	A	A	F	B	F	F	F	F	B	4-0/10-11 yrs.	I	60+			•	•		EA		•		•		•	•			•	•		
Short-Term Memory Span	2100	F	A	A	F	B	F	F	F	F	B	4-0/10-11 yrs.	I	60+			•	•		EA		•		•		•	•			•	•		
Auditory Discrimination	2100	F	A	A	F	B	F	F	F	F	F	4-0/10-11 yrs.	I	60+			•	•		EA		•		•		•	•			•	•		
General Reproduction	2130	F	A	A	F	B	F	F	F	F	F	4-0/10-11 yrs.	I	60+			•	•		EA		•		•		•	•			•	•		
Graphic Reproduction of Visual Stimuli	2130	F	A	A	F	B	F	F	F	F	F	4-0/10-11 yrs.	I	60+			•	•		EA		•		•		•	•			•	•		
Verbal Reproduction of Auditory Stimuli	2000	F	A	A	F	B	F	F	F	F	F	4-0/10-11 yrs.	I	60+			•	•		EA		•		•		•	•			•	•		
Response by Indication, Auditory Stimuli	2120	F	A	A	F	B	F	F	F	F	F	4-0/10-11 yrs.	I	60+			•	•		EA		•		•		•	•			•	•		
Grammatical Organization	2000	F	A	A	F	B	F	F	F	F	B	4-0/10-11 yrs.	I	60+			•	•		EA		•		•		•	•			•	•		
General Visual Processing	2000	F	A	A	F	B	F	F	F	F	F	4-0/10-11 yrs.	I	60+			•	•		EA		•		•						•	•		
Perceptual-Cognitive Integration	2000	F	A	A	F	B	F	F	F	F	F	4-0/10-11 yrs.	I	60+			•	•		EA		•		•		•	•			•	•		

CARROW AUDITORY-VISUAL ABILITIES TEST (1981) (cont.)

	Taxonomy code	Overall rating	Scores	Size	Demographics	Recency	Total	Internal consistency	Stability	Total	Total (Val.)	Ages/Grades for Intended Use	Group/Individual	Testing time	Age equivalents	Grade equivalents	Percentile ranks	Standard scores	Other	Examiner qualifications	Third Party	Listen	Read print	Look at stimuli	Other	Speak, minor	Speak, major	Manipulate objects	Mark answer sheet	Point	Draw	Write print	Other
Visual Discrimination Matching	2131	F	A	A	F	B	F	F	F	F	B	4-0/10-11 yrs.	I	60+			•	•		EA		•		•						•			
Visual Discrimination Memory	2133	F	A	A	F	B	F	F	F	F	B	4-0/10-11 yrs.	I	60+			•	•		EA		•		•						•			
Visual-Motor Copying	2132	F	A	A	F	B	F	F	F	F	B	4-0/10-11 yrs.	I	60+			•	•		EA		•		•								•	
Visual-Motor Memory	2133	F	A	A	F	B	F	F	F	F	B	4-0/10-11 yrs.	I	60+			•	•		EA		•		•						•			
Motor Speed	2132	F	A	A	F	B	F	F	F	F	F	4-0/10-11 yrs.	I	60+			•	•		EA		•		•							•		
Picture Memory	2231	F	A	A	F	B	F	F	F	F	B	4-0/10-11 yrs.	I	60+			•	•		EA		•		•						•			
Picture Sequence Selection	2231	F	A	A	F	B	F	F	F	F	B	4-0/10-11 yrs.	I	60+			•	•		EA		•		•						•			
Digit Repetition Forward	2242	F	A	A	F	B	F	F	F	F	B	4-0/10-11 yrs.	I	60+			•	•		EA				•		•							
Digit Repetition Backward	2242	F	A	A	F	B	F	F	F	F	B	4-0/10-11 yrs.	I	60+			•	•		EA				•		•							
Sentence Repetition	2232	F	A	A	F	B	F	F	F	F	B	4-0/10-11 yrs.	I	60+			•	•		EA		•		•		•							
Word Repetition	2242	F	A	A	F	B	F	F	F	F	B	4-0/10-11 yrs.	I	60+			•	•		EA		•		•		•							
Auditory Blending	2244	F	A	A	F	B	F	F	F	F	F	4-0/10-11 yrs.	I	60+			•	•		EA		•		•				•					
Entry Test	2000	F	B	A	F	B	F	F	F	F	B	4-0/10-11 yrs.	I	60+					•¹	EA		•		•		•	•			•	•		

¹Cutoff scores provided

CARROW ELICITED LANGUAGE INVENTORY (1974)

	Taxonomy code	Overall rating	Scores	Size	Demographics	Recency	Total	Internal consistency	Stability	Total	Total (Val.)	Ages/Grades for Intended Use	Group/Individual	Testing time	Age equivalents	Grade equivalents	Percentile ranks	Standard scores	Other	Examiner qualifications	Third Party	Listen	Read print	Look at stimuli	Other	Speak, minor	Speak, major	Manipulate objects	Mark answer sheet	Point	Draw	Write print	Other
Total	2232	F	A	F	F	F	F	F	F	F	F	3-0/7-11 yrs.	I	7			•	•		EA		•				•							
Articles	2232	F	B	F	F	F	F	F	F	F	F	3-0/7-11 yrs.	I	7				•		EA		•				•							
Adjectives	2232	F	B	F	F	F	F	F	F	F	F	3-0/7-11 yrs.	I	7				•		EA		•				•							
Nouns	2232	F	B	F	F	F	F	F	F	F	F	3-0/7-11 yrs.	I	7				•		EA		•				•							
Noun Plurals	2232	F	B	F	F	F	F	F	F	F	F	3-0/7-11 yrs.	I	7				•		EA		•				•							
Pronouns	2232	F	B	F	F	F	F	F	F	F	F	3-0/7-11 yrs.	I	7				•		EA		•				•							
Verbs	2232	F	B	F	F	F	F	F	F	F	F	3-0/7-11 yrs.	I	7				•		EA		•				•							
Negatives	2232	F	B	F	F	F	F	F	F	F	F	3-0/7-11 yrs.	I	7				•		EA		•				•							
Contractions	2232	F	B	F	F	F	F	F	F	F	F	3-0/7-11 yrs.	I	7				•		EA		•				•							
Adverbs	2232	F	B	F	F	F	F	F	F	F	F	3-0/7-11 yrs.	I	7				•		EA		•				•							
Prepositions	2232	F	B	F	F	F	F	F	F	F	F	3-0/7-11 yrs.	I	7				•		EA		•				•							
Demonstratives	2232	F	B	F	F	F	F	F	F	F	F	3-0/7-11 yrs.	I	7				•		EA		•				•							
Conjunctions	2232	F	B	F	F	F	F	F	F	F	F	3-0/7-11 yrs.	I	7				•		EA		•				•							

			Technical Characteristics									Nontechnical Characteristics																			
			Norms					Reliability			Val.		Admin.		Scores						Input					Output						
	Taxonomy code	Overall rating	Scores	Size	Demographics	Recency	Total	Internal consistency	Stability	Total	Total	Ages/Grades for Intended Use	Group/Individual	Testing time	Age equivalents	Grade equivalents	Percentile ranks	Standard scores	Other	Examiner qualifications	Third Party	Listen	Read print	Look at stimuli	Other	Speak, minor	Speak, major	Manipulate objects	Mark answer sheet	Point	Draw	Write print	Other

THE CHILDHOOD AUTISM RATING SCALE (1988)

Total	3000	F	F	B	F	A	F	F	F	F	F	Unspecified	I	20					•[1]	EA	•		•						•				•[2]

[1]Clinical cutoff scores only; [2]various observed behaviors, including eye contact, motor skills, social behaviors, etc.

CHILDREN'S APPERCEPTIVE STORY-TELLING TEST (1989)

Adaptive Factor	3000	B	A	B	A	A	B	B	F	B	B	6-0/13-11 yrs.	I	40			•			ST	•		•				•						
Nonadaptive Factor	3000	B	A	B	A	A	B	B	F	B	B	6-0/13-11 yrs.	I	40			•			ST	•		•				•						
Immature Factor	3840	B	A	B	A	A	B	B	F	B	B	6-0/13-11 yrs.	I	40			•			ST	•		•				•						
Uninvested Factor	3900	B	A	B	A	A	B	B	F	B	B	6-0/13-11 yrs.	I	40			•			ST	•		•				•						
Instrumentality	3900	B	A	B	A	A	B	B	F	B	B	6-0/13-11 yrs.	I	40			•			ST	•		•				•						
Interpersonal Cooperation	3400	F	A	B	A	A	B	F	F	F	B	6-0/13-11 yrs.	I	40			•			ST	•		•				•						
Affiliation	3400	F	A	B	A	A	B	F	F	F	B	6-0/13-11 yrs.	I	40			•			ST	•		•				•						
Positive Affect	3000	F	A	B	A	A	B	F	F	F	F	6-0/13-11 yrs.	I	40			•			ST	•		•				•						
Inadequacy	3100	F	A	B	A	A	B	F	F	F	F	6-0/13-11 yrs.	I	40			•			ST	•		•				•						
Alienation	3400	F	A	B	A	A	B	F	F	F	F	6-0/13-11 yrs.	I	40			•			ST	•		•				•						
Interpersonal Conflict	3400	F	A	B	A	A	B	F	F	F	F	6-0/13-11 yrs.	I	40			•			ST	•		•				•						
Limits	3840	F	A	B	A	A	B	F	F	F	F	6-0/13-11 yrs.	I	40			•			ST	•		•				•						
Negative Affect	3000	F	A	B	A	A	B	F	F	F	F	6-0/13-11 yrs.	I	40			•			ST	•		•				•						
Positive Preoperational	3000	F	A	B	A	A	B	B	F	B	F	6-0/13-11 yrs.	I	40			•			ST	•		•				•						
Positive Operational	3000	B	A	B	A	A	B	B	F	B	B	6-0/13-11 yrs.	I	40			•			ST	•		•				•						
Refusal	3900	B	A	B	A	A	B	B	F	B	B	6-0/13-11 yrs.	I	40			•			ST	•		•				•						
Unresolved	3900	F	A	B	A	A	B	B	F	B	F	6-0/13-11 yrs.	I	40			•			ST	•		•				•						
Negative Preoperational	3000	F	A	B	A	A	B	B	F	B	F	6-0/13-11 yrs.	I	40			•			ST	•		•				•						
Negative Operational	3000	F	A	B	A	A	B	F	F	F	F	6-0/13-11 yrs.	I	40			•			ST	•		•				•						

CHILDREN'S AUDITORY VERBAL LEARNING TEST (1990)

Immediate Memory Span	2242	F	A	F	F	A	F	F	F	F	F	6-6/12-11 yrs.	I	30	•	•				EA	•					•	•						
Level of Learning	2242	F	A	F	F	A	F	F	F	F	F	6-6/12-11 yrs.	I	30	•	•				EA	•					•	•						
Immediate Recall	2242	F	A	F	F	A	F	F	F	F	F	6-6/12-11 yrs.	I	30	•	•				EA	•					•	•						
Delayed Recall	2242	F	A	F	F	A	F	F	F	F	F	6-6/12-11 yrs.	I	30	•	•				EA	•					•	•						
Recognition Accuracy	2242	F	A	F	F	A	F	F	F	F	F	6-6/12-11 yrs.	I	30	•	•				EA	•					•	•						
Total Intrusions	2242	F	A	F	F	A	F	F	F	F	F	6-6/12-11 yrs.	I	30	•	•				EA	•					•	•						

	Taxonomy code	Overall rating	Scores	Size	Demographics	Recency	Total	Internal consistency	Stability	Total	Total (Val.)	Ages/Grades for Intended Use	Group/Individual	Testing time	Age equivalents	Grade equivalents	Percentile ranks	Standard scores	Other	Examiner qualifications	Third Party	Listen	Read print	Look at stimuli	Other	Speak, minor	Speak, major	Manipulate objects	Mark answer sheet	Point	Draw	Write print	Other
THE CHILDREN'S VERSION OF THE FAMILY ENVIRONMENT SCALE (1984)																																	
Cohesion	3400	F	A	F	F	B	F	F	F	F	F	5-0/12-11 yrs.	G	10				•		EA		•	•						•				
Expressiveness	3900	F	A	F	F	B	F	F	F	F	F	5-0/12-11 yrs.	G	10				•		EA		•	•						•				
Conflict	3400	F	A	F	F	B	F	F	F	F	F	5-0/12-11 yrs.	G	10				•		EA		•	•						•				
Independence	3830	F	A	F	F	B	F	F	F	F	F	5-0/12-11 yrs.	G	10				•		EA		•	•						•				
Achievement Orientation	3900	F	A	F	F	B	F	F	F	F	F	5-0/12-11 yrs.	G	10				•		EA		•	•						•				
Intellectual-Cultural Orientation	3900	F	A	F	F	B	F	F	F	F	F	5-0/12-11 yrs.	G	10				•		EA		•	•						•				
Active-Recreational Orientation	3900	F	A	F	F	B	F	F	F	F	F	5-0/12-11 yrs.	G	10				•		EA		•	•						•				
Moral-Religious Emphasis	3900	F	A	F	F	B	F	F	F	F	F	5-0/12-11 yrs.	G	10				•		EA		•	•						•				
Organization	3400	F	A	F	F	B	F	F	F	F	F	5-0/12-11 yrs.	G	10				•		EA		•	•						•				
Control	3840	F	A	F	F	B	F	F	F	F	F	5-0/12-11 yrs.	G	10				•		EA		•	•						•				
CLARK-MADISON TEST OF ORAL LANGUAGE (1986)																																	
Total	2230	F	B	F	F	B	F	F	A	B	B	4-0/8-11 yrs.	I	22	•				•[1]	EA	•		•			•							

¹Means and standard deviations with age curve

	Taxonomy code	Overall rating	Scores	Size	Demographics	Recency	Total	Internal consistency	Stability	Total	Total (Val.)	Ages/Grades for Intended Use	Group/Individual	Testing time	Age equivalents	Grade equivalents	Percentile ranks	Standard scores	Other	Examiner qualifications	Third Party	Listen	Read print	Look at stimuli	Other	Speak, minor	Speak, major	Manipulate objects	Mark answer sheet	Point	Draw	Write print	Other
CLINICAL EVALUATION OF LANGUAGE FUNCTIONS — DIAGNOSTIC TEST (1983)																																	
Processing	2230	B	A	B	B	B	B	F	B	B	B	gr. K–12	I	45	•		•	•		EA	•		•	•						•			
Production	2230	B	A	B	B	B	B	F	B	B	B	gr. K–12	I	45	•		•	•		EA	•		•	•		•	•						
Processing Word and Sentence Structures	2232	B	A	B	B	B	B	F	B	B	B	gr. K–12	I	7			•	•		EA	•									•			
Processing Word Classes	2231	B	A	B	B	B	B	F	B	B	B	gr. K–12	I	7			•	•		EA	•					•							
Processing Linguistic Concepts	2230	B	A	B	B	B	B	F	B	B	B	gr. K–12	I	7			•	•		EA	•		•							•			
Processing Relationships and Ambiguities	2230	F	A	B	B	B	B	F	F	F	B	gr. K–12	I	7			•	•		EA	•					•							
Processing Oral Directions	2230	F	A	B	B	B	B	F	F	F	B	gr. K–12	I	7			•	•		EA	•		•							•			
Processing Spoken Paragraphs	2230	B	A	B	B	B	B	F	B	B	B	gr. K–12	I	7			•	•		EA	•					•							
Producing Word Series-Accuracy	2231	F	A	B	B	B	B	F	F	F	B	gr. K–12	I	7			•	•		EA	•						•						
Producing Word Series-Time	2231	B	A	B	B	B	B	F	B	B	B	gr. K–12	I	7			•	•		EA	•						•						
Producing Names on Confrontation-Accuracy	2231	B	A	B	B	B	B	F	B	B	B	gr. K–12	I	7			•	•		EA	•		•			•							
Producing Names on Confrontation-Time	2231	B	A	B	B	B	B	F	B	B	B	gr. K–12	I	7			•	•		EA	•		•			•							
Producing Word Associations	2231	F	A	B	B	B	B	F	F	F	B	gr. K–12	I	7			•	•		EA						•							
Producing Model Sentences	2232	B	A	B	B	B	B	F	B	B	B	gr. K–12	I	7			•	•		EA	•					•	•						
Producing Formulated Sentences	2230	B	A	B	B	B	B	F	B	B	B	gr. K–12	I	7			•	•		EA	•						•						

CLINICAL EVALUATION OF LANGUAGE FUNCTIONS — DIAGNOSTIC TEST (1983) (cont.)

	Taxonomy code	Overall rating	Scores	Size	Demographics	Recency	Total	Internal consistency	Stability	Total	Val. Total	Ages/Grades for Intended Use	Group/Individual	Testing time	Age equivalents	Grade equivalents	Percentile ranks	Standard scores	Other	Examiner qualifications	Third Party	Listen	Read print	Look at stimuli	Other	Speak, minor	Speak, major	Manipulate objects	Mark answer sheet	Point	Draw	Write print	Other
Processing Speech Sounds	2241	F	A	B	B	B	B	F	B	B	F	gr. K–12	I	7			•	•		EA		•				•							
Producing Speech Sounds	2243	F	A	B	B	B	B	F	B	B	F	gr. K–12	I	7			•	•		EA		•		•		•							

CLINICAL EVALUATION OF LANGUAGE FUNCTIONS — SCREENING TEST — ADVANCED LEVEL (1983)

	Taxonomy code	Overall rating	Scores	Size	Demographics	Recency	Total	Internal consistency	Stability	Total	Val. Total	Ages/Grades for Intended Use	Group/Individual	Testing time	Age equivalents	Grade equivalents	Percentile ranks	Standard scores	Other	Examiner qualifications	Third Party	Listen	Read print	Look at stimuli	Other	Speak, minor	Speak, major	Manipulate objects	Mark answer sheet	Point	Draw	Write print	Other
Total	2200	B	A	B	B	B	B	B	F	B	B	gr. 5–12	I	22	•		•	•		EA		•				•	•			•			•[1]
Processing Items	2200	F	A	B	B	B	B	B	F	F	B	gr. 5–12	I	7	•		•	•		EA		•								•			•[1]
Production Items	2200	F	A	B	B	B	B	B	F	F	B	gr. 5–12	I	7	•		•	•		EA		•				•	•						

¹Touch body parts, do body movements

CLINICAL EVALUATION OF LANGUAGE FUNCTIONS — SCREENING TEST — ELEMENTARY LEVEL (1983)

	Taxonomy code	Overall rating	Scores	Size	Demographics	Recency	Total	Internal consistency	Stability	Total	Val. Total	Ages/Grades for Intended Use	Group/Individual	Testing time	Age equivalents	Grade equivalents	Percentile ranks	Standard scores	Other	Examiner qualifications	Third Party	Listen	Read print	Look at stimuli	Other	Speak, minor	Speak, major	Manipulate objects	Mark answer sheet	Point	Draw	Write print	Other
Total	2200	B	A	B	B	B	B	B	F	B	B	gr. K–5	I	22	•		•	•		EA		•		•		•	•			•			
Processing Items	2200	F	A	B	B	B	B	B	F	F	B	gr. K–5	I	7	•		•	•		EA		•		•						•			
Production Items	2200	F	A	B	B	B	B	B	F	F	B	gr. K–5	I	7	•		•	•		EA		•		•		•	•						

¹Touch body parts, do body movements

CLINICAL EVALUATION OF LANGUAGE FUNDAMENTALS — REVISED (1987)

	Taxonomy code	Overall rating	Scores	Size	Demographics	Recency	Total	Internal consistency	Stability	Total	Val. Total	Ages/Grades for Intended Use	Group/Individual	Testing time	Age equivalents	Grade equivalents	Percentile ranks	Standard scores	Other	Examiner qualifications	Third Party	Listen	Read print	Look at stimuli	Other	Speak, minor	Speak, major	Manipulate objects	Mark answer sheet	Point	Draw	Write print	Other
Total Language	2200	B	A	B	B	A	B	B	F	B	B	8-0/16-11 yrs.	I	48	•			•		EA		•		•		•				•			
Receptive Language	2200	B	A	B	B	A	B	B	F	B	B	8-0/16-11 yrs.	I	20				•		EA		•		•		•				•			
Expressive Language	2230	B	A	B	B	A	B	B	F	B	B	8-0/16-11 yrs.	I	28				•		EA		•		•		•							
Oral Directions	2231	F	A	B	B	A	B	F	F	F	B	8-0/16-11 yrs.	I	7				•		EA		•		•						•			
Word Classes	2210	B	A	B	B	A	B	B	F	B	B	8-0/16-11 yrs.	I	7				•		EA		•								•			
Semantic Relationships	2231	B	A	B	B	A	B	B	F	B	B	8-0/16-11 yrs.	I	7				•		EA		•						•					
Formulated Sentences	2231	B	A	B	B	A	B	B	F	B	B	8-0/16-11 yrs.	I	9				•		EA		•		•			•						
Recalling Sentences	2232	B	A	B	B	A	B	B	F	B	B	8-0/16-11 yrs.	I	9				•		EA		•				•							
Sentence Assembly	2232	B	A	B	B	A	B	B	F	B	B	8-0/16-11 yrs.	I	9				•		EA		•				•							
Total Language	2230	B	A	B	B	A	B	B	F	B	B	5-0/7-11 yrs.	I	42	•			•		EA		•										•	
Receptive Language	2230	B	A	B	B	A	B	B	F	B	B	5-0/7-11 yrs.	I	16				•		EA		•		•									
Expressive Language	2230	B	A	B	B	A	B	B	F	B	B	5-0/7-11 yrs.	I	27				•		EA		•		•				•	•				
Linguistic Concepts	2231	B	A	B	B	A	B	B	F	B	B	5-0/7-11 yrs.	I	5				•		EA		•								•			
Sentence Structure	2232	B	A	B	B	A	B	B	F	B	B	5-0/7-11 yrs.	I	5				•		EA		•		•						•			
Oral Directions	2231	F	A	B	B	A	B	F	F	F	B	5-0/7-11 yrs.	I	5				•		EA		•		•						•			
Word Structure	2232	B	A	B	B	A	B	B	F	B	B	5-0/7-11 yrs.	I	9				•		EA		•				•							

CLINICAL EVALUATION OF LANGUAGE FUNDAMENTALS — REVISED (1987) (cont.)

	Taxonomy code	Overall rating	Scores (Norms)	Size	Demographics	Recency	Total (Norms)	Internal consistency	Stability	Total (Rel.)	Val. Total	Ages/Grades for Intended Use	Group/Individual	Testing time	Age equivalents	Grade equivalents	Percentile ranks	Standard scores	Other (Scores)	Examiner qualifications	Third Party	Listen	Read print	Look at stimuli	Other (Input)	Speak, minor	Speak, major	Manipulate objects	Mark answer sheet	Point	Draw	Write print	Other (Output)
Formulated Sentences	2231	**B**	A	B	B	A	B	B	F	B	B	5-0/7-11 yrs.	I	9				•		EA		•		•			•						
Recalling Sentences	2232	**B**	A	B	B	A	B	B	F	B	B	5-0/7-11 yrs.	I	9				•		EA		•					•						

CLINICAL EVALUATION OF LANGUAGE FUNDAMENTALS — REVISED SCREENING TEST (1989)

	Taxonomy code	Overall rating	Scores (Norms)	Size	Demographics	Recency	Total (Norms)	Internal consistency	Stability	Total (Rel.)	Val. Total	Ages/Grades for Intended Use	Group/Individual	Testing time	Age equivalents	Grade equivalents	Percentile ranks	Standard scores	Other (Scores)	Examiner qualifications	Third Party	Listen	Read print	Look at stimuli	Other (Input)	Speak, minor	Speak, major	Manipulate objects	Mark answer sheet	Point	Draw	Write print	Other (Output)
Total	2230	**B**	B	A	B	A	B	F	B	B	B	5-0/16-11 yrs.	I	15					•[1]	EA		•	•	•		•	•			•			

[1]Raw score means and standard deviations provided

COGNITIVE LEVELS TEST (1988)

	Taxonomy code	Overall rating	Scores (Norms)	Size	Demographics	Recency	Total (Norms)	Internal consistency	Stability	Total (Rel.)	Val. Total	Ages/Grades for Intended Use	Group/Individual	Testing time	Age equivalents	Grade equivalents	Percentile ranks	Standard scores	Other (Scores)	Examiner qualifications	Third Party	Listen	Read print	Look at stimuli	Other (Input)	Speak, minor	Speak, major	Manipulate objects	Mark answer sheet	Point	Draw	Write print	Other (Output)
Verbal Reasoning	2210	**F**	A	B	F	A	F	A	F	B	F	5-0/21-11 yrs.	I	10	•		•	•		EA		•		•		•	•						
Abstract Reasoning	2110	**F**	A	B	F	A	F	B	F	B	F	5-0/21-11 yrs.	I	10	•		•	•		EA		•		•		•				•	•		•[1]
Quantitative Reasoning	1200	**F**	A	B	F	A	F	A	F	B	F	5-0/21-11 yrs.	I	10	•		•	•		EA		•		•		•	•				•		•[1]
Memory	2000	**F**	A	B	F	A	F	B	F	B	F	5-0/21-11 yrs.	I	10	•		•	•		EA		•		•		•							•[1]
Abstract Quantitative Reasoning	4000	**F**	A	B	F	A	F	A	F	B	F	5-0/21-11 yrs.	I	10	•		•	•		EA		•		•		•				•	•		•[1]
Rapid Cognitive Index	4000	**F**	A	B	F	A	F	A	F	B	F	5-0/21-11 yrs.	I	30	•		•	•		EA		•		•		•	•			•	•		•[1]
Best g Index	4000	**F**	A	B	F	A	F	A	F	B	F	5-0/21-11 yrs.	I	30	•		•	•		EA		•		•		•	•			•	•		•[1]
Cognitive Index	4000	**F**	A	B	F	A	F	A	B	B	F	5-0/21-11 yrs.	I	60+	•		•	•		EA		•		•		•	•			•	•		•[1]

[1]Various motor responses

COLUMBIA MENTAL MATURITY SCALE (1972)

	Taxonomy code	Overall rating	Scores (Norms)	Size	Demographics	Recency	Total (Norms)	Internal consistency	Stability	Total (Rel.)	Val. Total	Ages/Grades for Intended Use	Group/Individual	Testing time	Age equivalents	Grade equivalents	Percentile ranks	Standard scores	Other (Scores)	Examiner qualifications	Third Party	Listen	Read print	Look at stimuli	Other (Input)	Speak, minor	Speak, major	Manipulate objects	Mark answer sheet	Point	Draw	Write print	Other (Output)
Total	2110	**F**	A	A	A	F	F	B	B	B	B	3-6/10-11 yrs.	I	22	•		•			EA		•		•						•			

COMMUNICATION ABILITIES DIAGNOSTIC TEST (1990)

	Taxonomy code	Overall rating	Scores (Norms)	Size	Demographics	Recency	Total (Norms)	Internal consistency	Stability	Total (Rel.)	Val. Total	Ages/Grades for Intended Use	Group/Individual	Testing time	Age equivalents	Grade equivalents	Percentile ranks	Standard scores	Other (Scores)	Examiner qualifications	Third Party	Listen	Read print	Look at stimuli	Other (Input)	Speak, minor	Speak, major	Manipulate objects	Mark answer sheet	Point	Draw	Write print	Other (Output)
Total Language	2230	**F**	A	B	F	A	F	A	F	B	B	3-0/9-11 yrs.	I	45			•	•		EA		•		•		•	•						
Semantics	2231	**F**	A	B	F	A	F	B	F	B	A	3-0/9-11 yrs.	I	9			•	•		EA		•		•		•	•						
Syntax	2232	**F**	A	B	F	A	F	F	F	F	B	3-0/9-11 yrs.	I	9			•	•		EA		•		•		•	•						
Pragmatics	2230	**F**	A	B	F	A	F	B	F	B	A	3-0/9-11 yrs.	I	9			•	•		EA		•		•		•	•						
Language Comprehension	2230	**F**	A	B	F	A	F	F	F	F	F	3-0/9-11 yrs.	I	9			•	•		EA		•		•		•	•						
Language Expression	2230	**F**	A	B	F	A	F	A	B	B	F	3-0/9-11 yrs.	I	9			•	•		EA		•		•		•	•						

COMPREHENSIVE BEHAVIOR RATING SCALE FOR CHILDREN (1990)

	Taxonomy code	Overall rating	Scores (Norms)	Size	Demographics	Recency	Total (Norms)	Internal consistency	Stability	Total (Rel.)	Val. Total	Ages/Grades for Intended Use	Group/Individual	Testing time	Age equivalents	Grade equivalents	Percentile ranks	Standard scores	Other (Scores)	Examiner qualifications	Third Party	Listen	Read print	Look at stimuli	Other (Input)	Speak, minor	Speak, major	Manipulate objects	Mark answer sheet	Point	Draw	Write print	Other (Output)
Inattention-Disorganization	3800	**F**	A	A/B/B[1]	F	A	F	A	F	B	B/F/F[1]	6-0/14-11 yrs.	I	20			•	•		EA	•		•						•				
Reading Problems	1300	**F**	A	A/B/B[1]	F	A	F	A	F	B	B/F/F[1]	6-0/14-11 yrs.	I	20			•	•		EA	•		•						•				
Cognitive Deficits	4000	**F**	A	A/B/B[1]	F	A	F	A	F	B	B/F/F[1]	6-0/14-11 yrs.	I	20			•	•		EA	•		•						•				
Oppositional-Conduct Disorders	3500	**F**	A	A/B/B[1]	F	A	F	A	F	B	A/F/F[1]	6-0/14-11 yrs.	I	20			•	•		EA	•		•						•				

	Taxonomy code	Overall rating	Scores	Size	Demographics	Recency	Total	Internal consistency	Stability	Total	Total	Ages/Grades for Intended Use	Group/Individual	Testing time	Age equivalents	Grade equivalents	Percentile ranks	Standard scores	Other	Examiner qualifications	Third Party	Listen	Read print	Look at stimuli	Other	Speak, minor	Speak, major	Manipulate objects	Mark answer sheet	Point	Draw	Write print	Other

COMPREHENSIVE BEHAVIOR RATING SCALE FOR CHILDREN (1990) (cont.)

	Taxonomy code	Overall rating	Scores	Size	Demographics	Recency	Total	Internal consistency	Stability	Total	Total	Ages/Grades for Intended Use	Group/Individual	Testing time	Age eq.	Grade eq.	Percentile ranks	Standard scores	Other	Examiner qual.	Third Party	Listen	Read print	Look at stimuli	Other	Speak, minor	Speak, major	Manipulate objects	Mark answer sheet	Point	Draw	Write print	Other
Motor Hyperactivity	3810	F	A	A/B/B[1]	F	A	F	B	F	B	B/F/F[1]	6-0/14-11 yrs.	I	20			•	•		EA	•		•						•				
Anxiety	3100	F	A	A/B/B[1]	F	A	F	B	F	B	B/F/F[1]	6-0/14-11 yrs.	I	20			•	•		EA	•		•						•				
Sluggish Tempo	3810	F	A	A/B/B[1]	F	A	F	A	F	B	B/F/F[1]	6-0/14-11 yrs.	I	20			•	•		EA	•		•						•				
Daydreaming	3840	F	A	A/B/B[1]	F	A	F	A	F	B	B/F/F[1]	6-0/14-11 yrs.	I	20			•	•		EA	•		•						•				
Social Competence	3400	F	A	A/B/B[1]	F	A	F	B	F	B	B/F/F[1]	6-0/14-11 yrs.	I	20			•	•		EA	•		•						•				

[1]Rating for Total Population Norms appears first, Male Norms second, and Female Norms third

COMPREHENSIVE TEST OF VISUAL FUNCTIONING (1990)

	Taxonomy code	Overall rating	Scores	Size	Demographics	Recency	Total	Internal consistency	Stability	Total	Total	Ages/Grades for Intended Use	Group/Individual	Testing time	Age eq.	Grade eq.	Percentile ranks	Standard scores	Other	Examiner qual.	Third Party	Listen	Read print	Look at stimuli	Other	Speak, minor	Speak, major	Manipulate objects	Mark answer sheet	Point	Draw	Write print	Other
Total	4000	F	A	F	F	A	F	F	F	F	F	8-0/16-11 yrs.	I	60 +				•		EA	•	•	•		•			•		•	•		•[1]
Visual Acuity	5000	F	A	F	F	A	F	F	F	F	F	8-0/16-11 yrs.	I	5				•		EA	•		•		•								
Visual Processing/ Figure Ground	2131	F	A	F	F	A	F	F	F	F	F	8-0/16-11 yrs.	I	5				•		EA	•		•		•								
Visual Tracking	2134	F	A	F	F	A	F	F	F	F	F	8-0/16-11 yrs.	I	5				•		EA	•		•										•[1]
Reading Word Analysis	1320	F	A	F	F	A	F	F	F	F	F	8-0/16-11 yrs.	I	5				•		EA	•	•			•								
Visual/Letter Recognition	1320	F	A	F	F	A	F	F	F	F	F	8-0/16-11 yrs.	I	5				•		EA	•	•			•								
Visual/Writing Integration	1600	F	A	F	F	A	F	F	F	F	F	8-0/16-11 yrs.	I	5				•		EA	•		•									•	
Nonverbal Visual Closure	2131	F	A	F	F	A	F	F	F	F	F	8-0/16-11 yrs.	I	5				•		EA	•		•		•								
Nonverbal Visual Reasoning/Memory	2110	F	A	F	F	A	F	F	F	F	F	8-0/16-11 yrs.	I	5				•		EA	•		•					•					
Spatial Orientation/ Memory/Motor	2133	F	A	F	F	A	F	F	F	F	F	8-0/16-11 yrs.	I	5				•		EA	•		•					•					
Spatial Orientation/Motor	2132	F	A	F	F	A	F	F	F	F	F	8-0/16-11 yrs.	I	5				•		EA	•										•		
Visual Design/Motor	2132	F	A	F	F	A	F	F	F	F	F	8-0/16-11 yrs.	I	5				•		EA	•		•								•		
Visual Design/ Memory/Motor	2133	F	A	F	F	A	F	F	F	F	F	8-0/16-11 yrs.	I	5				•		EA	•		•								•		

[1]Various motor responses

COMPUTER APTITUDE, LITERACY, AND INTEREST PROFILE (1984)

	Taxonomy code	Overall rating	Scores	Size	Demographics	Recency	Total	Internal consistency	Stability	Total	Total	Ages/Grades for Intended Use	Group/Individual	Testing time	Age eq.	Grade eq.	Percentile ranks	Standard scores	Other	Examiner qual.	Third Party	Listen	Read print	Look at stimuli	Other	Speak, minor	Speak, major	Manipulate objects	Mark answer sheet	Point	Draw	Write print	Other
Total	4000	F	A	B	F	B	F	F	B	B	B	12-0/60-11 yrs.	G	60 +				•		EA	•	•	•						•			•	
Estimation	1220	F	A	B	F	B	F	F	F	F	B	12-0/60-11 yrs.	G	7				•		EA	•		•								•	
Graphic Patterns	2110	F	A	B	F	B	F	B	B	B	B	12-0/60-11 yrs.	G	7				•		EA	•		•					•				
Logical Structures	2000	F	A	B	F	B	F	A	F	B	B	12-0/60-11 yrs.	G	7				•		EA	•	•						•				
Series	2000	F	A	B	F	B	F	A	B	B	B	12-0/60-11 yrs.	G	7				•		EA	•	•						•				
Interest-Male	3220	F	A	B	F	B	F	F	F	F	B	12-0/60-11 yrs.	G	7				•		EA	•	•						•				

			Technical Characteristics									Nontechnical Characteristics																					
			Norms					Reliability			Val.		Admin.		Scores						Test Formats												
																					Input					Output							
	Taxonomy code	Overall rating	Scores	Size	Demographics	Recency	Total	Internal consistency	Stability	Total	Total	Ages/Grades for Intended Use	Group/Individual	Testing time	Age equivalents	Grade equivalents	Percentile ranks	Standard scores	Other	Examiner qualifications	Third Party	Listen	Read print	Look at stimuli	Other	Speak, minor	Speak, major	Manipulate objects	Mark answer sheet	Point	Draw	Write print	Other
COMPUTER APTITUDE, LITERACY, AND INTEREST PROFILE (1984) (cont.)																																	
Interest-Female	3220	F	A	B	F	B	F	F	F	F	B	12-0/60-11 yrs.	G	7				•		EA		•	•						•				
Literacy	1100	F	A	B	F	B	F	A	B	B	B	12-0/60-11 yrs.	G	7				•		EA		•	•						•				
CONNERS' PARENT RATING SCALES — 48 (1990)																																	
Conduct Problem	3500	F	A	F	F	B	F	F	F	F	F	3-0/17-11 yrs.	I	15				•		EA	•		•						•				
Learning Problem	1000	F	A	F	F	B	F	F	F	F	F	3-0/17-11 yrs.	I	15				•		EA	•		•						•				
Psychosomatic	3100	F	A	F	F	B	F	F	F	F	F	3-0/17-11 yrs.	I	15				•		EA	•		•						•				
Impulsive-Hyperactive	3800	F	A	F	F	B	F	F	F	F	F	3-0/17-11 yrs.	I	15				•		EA	•		•						•				
Anxiety	3100	F	A	F	F	B	F	F	F	F	F	3-0/17-11 yrs.	I	15				•		EA	•		•						•				
Hyperactivity Index	3810	F	A	F	F	B	F	F	F	F	F	3-0/17-11 yrs.	I	15				•		EA	•		•						•				
CONNERS' PARENT RATING SCALES — 93 (1990)																																	
Conduct Disorder	3500	F	A	F	F	F	F	F	F	F	F	6-0/14-11 yrs.	I	20				•		EA	•		•						•				
Anxious-Shy	3100	F	A	F	F	F	F	F	F	F	F	6-0/14-11 yrs.	I	20				•		EA	•		•						•				
Restless-Disorganized	3840	F	A	F	F	F	F	F	F	F	F	6-0/14-11 yrs.	I	20				•		EA	•		•						•				
Learning Problem	1000	F	A	F	F	F	F	F	F	F	F	6-0/14-11 yrs.	I	20				•		EA	•		•						•				
Psychosomatic	3100	F	A	F	F	F	F	F	F	F	F	6-0/14-11 yrs.	I	20				•		EA	•		•						•				
Obsessive-Compulsive	3900	F	A	F	F	F	F	F	F	F	F	6-0/14-11 yrs.	I	20				•		EA	•		•						•				
Antisocial	3500	F	A	F	F	F	F	F	F	F	F	6-0/14-11 yrs.	I	20				•		EA	•		•						•				
Hyperactive-Immature	3800	F	A	F	F	F	F	F	F	F	F	6-0/14-11 yrs.	I	20				•		EA	•		•						•				
Hyperactivity Index	3810	F	A	F	F	F	F	F	F	F	F	6-0/14-11 yrs.	I	20				•		EA	•		•						•				
CONNERS' TEACHER RATING SCALES — 28 (1990)																																	
Conduct Problem	3500	F	A	F	F	B	F	F	F	F	F	3-0/17-11 yrs.	I	15				•		EA	•		•						•				
Hyperactivity	3810	F	A	F	F	B	F	F	F	F	F	3-0/17-11 yrs.	I	15				•		EA	•		•						•				
Inattentive-Passive	3820	F	A	F	F	B	F	F	F	F	F	3-0/17-11 yrs.	I	15				•		EA	•		•						•				
Hyperactivity Index	3810	F	A	F	F	B	F	F	F	F	F	3-0/17-11 yrs.	I	15				•		EA	•		•						•				
CONNERS' TEACHER RATING SCALES — 39 (1990)																																	
Hyperactivity	3810	F	A	B	F	F	F	F	F	F	F	4-0/12-11 yrs.	I	20				•		EA	•		•						•				
Conduct Problem	3500	F	A	B	F	F	F	F	F	F	F	4-0/12-11 yrs.	I	20				•		EA	•		•						•				
Emotional-Overindulgent	3900	F	A	B	F	F	F	F	F	F	F	4-0/12-11 yrs.	I	20				•		EA	•		•						•				
Anxious-Passive	3100	F	A	B	F	F	F	F	F	F	F	4-0/12-11 yrs.	I	20				•		EA	•		•						•				

		Technical Characteristics										Ages/Grades for Intended Use	Nontechnical Characteristics																				
			Norms					Reliability			Val.		Admin.		Scores					Examiner qual.	Input					Output							
	Taxonomy code	Overall rating	Scores	Size	Demographics	Recency	Total	Internal consistency	Stability	Total	Total		Group/Individual	Testing time	Age equivalents	Grade equivalents	Percentile ranks	Standard scores	Other	Examiner qualifications	Third Party	Listen	Read print	Look at stimuli	Other	Speak, minor	Speak, major	Manipulate objects	Mark answer sheet	Point	Draw	Write print	Other
CONNERS' TEACHER RATING SCALES — 39 (1990) (cont.)																																	
Asocial	3400	F	A	B	F	F	F	F	F	F	F	4-0/12-11 yrs.	I	20				•		EA	•		•						•				
Daydream-Attention Problem	3800	F	A	B	F	F	F	F	F	F	F	4-0/12-11 yrs.	I	20				•		EA	•		•						•				
Hyperactivity Index	3810	F	A	B	F	F	F	F	F	F	F	4-0/12-11 yrs.	I	20				•		EA	•		•						•				
CULTURE FAIR INTELLIGENCE TESTS (1973)																																	
Total Test Scale 2	2110	F	A	A	F	F	F	B	B	B	B	7-6/Adult yrs.	G	22				•		EA	•			•					•				
Short Form Scale 2	2110	F	A	A	F	F	F	F	F	F	F	7-6/Adult yrs.	G	7				•		EA	•			•					•				
Total Test Scale 3	2110	F	A	A	F	F	F	F	F	F	B	13-0/Adult yrs.	G	22				•		EA	•			•					•				
Short Form Scale 3	2110	F	A	A	F	F	F	F	F	F	F	13-0/Adult yrs.	G	7				•		EA	•			•					•				
CULTURE-FREE SELF-ESTEEM INVENTORIES FOR CHILDREN AND ADULTS (1981)																																	
Total	3700	F	F	F	F	B	F	F	B	B	A	gr. 3–9	G	22			•	•		EA			•						•				
General	3700	F	F	F	F	B	F	F	F	F	F	gr. 3–9	G	22			•	•		EA			•						•				
Social	3730	F	F	F	F	B	F	F	F	F	F	gr. 3–9	G	22			•	•		EA			•						•				
Academics	3710	F	F	F	F	B	F	F	F	F	F	gr. 3–9	G	22			•	•		EA			•						•				
Parents	3700	F	F	F	F	B	F	F	F	F	F	gr. 3–9	G	22			•	•		EA			•						•				
DETROIT TESTS OF LEARNING APTITUDE, SECOND EDITION (1985)																																	
General Intelligence Quotient	2000	B	A	B	A	B	B	A	B	B	B	6-0/17-11 yrs.	I	60+				•		EA	•	•	•			•	•			•	•	•	
Verbal Quotient	2000	B	A	B	A	B	B	A	B	B	B	6-0/17-11 yrs.	I	45				•		EA	•	•	•			•	•					•	
Nonverbal Quotient	2000	B	A	B	A	B	B	A	B	B	B	6-0/17-11 yrs.	I	45				•		EA	•	•	•							•	•	•	
Conceptual Quotient	2000	B	A	B	A	B	B	A	B	B	B	6-0/17-11 yrs.	I	45				•		EA	•	•	•			•	•			•	•		
Structural Quotient	2000	B	A	B	A	B	B	A	B	B	B	6-0/17-11 yrs.	I	45				•		EA	•	•	•							•	•		
Motor-Enhanced Quotient	2000	B	A	B	A	B	B	A	B	B	B	6-0/17-11 yrs.	I	45				•		EA	•	•	•								•	•	
Motor-Reduced Quotient	2000	B	A	B	A	B	B	A	B	B	B	6-0/17-11 yrs.	I	45				•		EA	•	•	•			•	•			•			
Attention-Enhanced Quotient	2000	B	A	B	A	B	B	A	B	B	B	6-0/17-11 yrs.	I	45				•		EA	•	•	•				•				•	•	
Attention-Reduced Quotient	2000	B	A	B	A	B	B	A	B	B	B	6-0/17-11 yrs.	I	45				•		EA	•	•	•			•	•			•			
Word Opposites	2231	B	A	B	A	B	B	B	B	B	A	6-0/17-11 yrs.	I	7			•	•		EA	•					•							
Sentence Imitation	2232	B	A	B	A	B	B	B	B	B	A	6-0/17-11 yrs.	I	7			•	•		EA	•						•						
Oral Directions	2000	F	A	B	A	B	F	F	F	F	A	6-0/17-11 yrs.	I	7			•	•		EA	•									•			
Word Sequences	2242	B	A	B	A	B	B	B	B	B	A	6-0/17-11 yrs.	I	7			•	•		EA	•						•						
Story Construction	2233	B	A	B	A	B	B	B	B	B	A	6-0/17-11 yrs.	I	7			•	•		EA	•		•				•						

| | | | Technical Characteristics | | | | | | | | | Nontechnical Characteristics | | | | | | | | | | | | | | | | | | | | | | |
| | | | Norms | | | | | Reliability | | | Val. | Ages/Grades for Intended Use | Admin. | | Scores | | | | | | Input | | | | | Output | | | | | | | |
	Taxonomy code	Overall rating	Scores	Size	Demographics	Recency	Total	Internal consistency	Stability	Total	Total		Group/Individual	Testing time	Age equivalents	Grade equivalents	Percentile ranks	Standard scores	Other	Examiner qualifications	Third Party	Listen	Read print	Look at stimuli	Other	Speak, minor	Speak, major	Manipulate objects	Mark answer sheet	Point	Draw	Write print	Other
DETROIT TESTS OF LEARNING APTITUDE, SECOND EDITION (1985) (cont.)																																	
Design Reproduction	2132	B	A	B	A	B	B	A	B	B	A	6-0/17-11 yrs.	I	7			•	•		EA		•		•							•		
Object Sequences	2133	B	A	B	A	B	B	A	F	B	A	6-0/17-11 yrs.	I	7			•	•		EA		•		•								•	
Symbolic Relations	2110	B	A	B	A	B	B	B	B	B	A	6-0/17-11 yrs.	I	7			•	•		EA		•		•						•			
Conceptual Matching	2110	F	A	B	A	B	B	F	F	F	B	6-0/17-11 yrs.	I	7			•	•		EA		•		•						•			
Word Fragments	2250	B	A	B	A	B	B	A	B	B	A	6-0/17-11 yrs.	I	7			•	•		EA		•	•			•							
Letter Sequences	2250	B	A	B	A	B	B	B	F	B	A	6-0/17-11 yrs.	I	7			•	•		EA		•	•									•	
DETROIT TESTS OF LEARNING APTITUDE, THIRD EDITION (1991)																																	
General Mental Ability	4000	B	A	A	A	B	B	A	A	A	A	8-0/17-11 yrs.	I	60+			•	•		EA		•		•		•	•	•		•	•		
Verbal Composite	4000	B	A	A	A	B	B	A	A	A	A	8-0/17-11 yrs.	I	60+			•	•		EA		•		•		•							
Nonverbal Composite	2000	B	A	A	A	B	B	A	B	B	A	8-0/17-11 yrs.	I	60+			•	•		EA		•		•						•	•		
Attention-Enhanced Composite	2000	B	A	A	A	B	B	A	A	A	A	8-0/17-11 yrs.	I	60+			•	•		EA		•		•		•	•			•			
Attention-Reduced Composite	4000	B	A	A	A	B	B	A	A	A	A	8-0/17-11 yrs.	I	60+			•	•		EA		•		•		•				•			
Motor-Enhanced Composite	2000	B	A	A	A	B	B	A	B	B	A	8-0/17-11 yrs.	I	60+			•	•		EA		•		•							•		
Motor-Reduced Composite	4000	B	A	A	A	B	B	A	A	A	A	8-0/17-11 yrs.	I	60+			•	•		EA		•		•		•	•				•		
Fluid Intelligence	2100	B	A	A	A	B	B	A	B	B	A	8-0/17-11 yrs.	I	60+			•	•		EA		•		•				•		•	•		
Crystallized Intelligence	4000	B	A	A	A	B	B	A	B	B	A	8-0/17-11 yrs.	I	60+			•	•		EA		•		•		•	•			•			
Associative Level	2000	B	A	A	A	B	B	A	A	A	A	8-0/17-11 yrs.	I	60+			•	•		EA		•		•		•	•				•		
Cognitive Level	4000	B	A	A	A	B	B	A	B	B	A	8-0/17-11 yrs.	I	60+			•	•		EA		•		•			•			•			
Simultaneous Processing	2000	B	A	A	A	B	B	A	A	A	A	8-0/17-11 yrs.	I	60+			•	•		EA		•		•						•	•		
Successive Processing	2000	B	A	A	A	B	B	A	B	B	A	8-0/17-11 yrs.	I	60+			•	•		EA		•		•			•	•					
Verbal Scale	4000	B	A	A	A	B	B	A	A	A	A	8-0/17-11 yrs.	I	60+			•	•		EA		•		•		•	•						
Performance Scale	2000	B	A	A	A	B	B	A	B	B	A	8-0/17-11 yrs.	I	60+			•	•		EA		•		•				•		•	•		
Word Opposites	2231	B	A	A	A	B	B	A	A	A	A	8-0/17-11 yrs.	I	10	•		•	•		EA		•				•							
Design Sequences	2132	B	A	A	A	A	A	A	F	B	A	8-0/17-11 yrs.	I	10	•		•	•		EA		•		•				•					
Sentence Imitation	2232	B	A	A	A	B	B	B	A	B	A	8-0/17-11 yrs.	I	10	•		•	•		EA		•				•							
Reversed Letters	2242	B	A	A	A	A	A	A	B	B	A	8-0/17-11 yrs.	I	10	•		•	•		EA		•				•							
Story Construction	2233	B	A	A	A	B	B	B	A	B	B	8-0/17-11 yrs.	I	10	•		•	•		EA		•		•		•							
Design Reproduction	2132	B	A	A	A	B	B	A	B	B	A	8-0/17-11 yrs.	I	10	•		•	•		EA		•		•								•	
Basic Information	1100	B	A	A	A	A	A	B	A	B	A	8-0/17-11 yrs.	I	10	•		•	•		EA		•				•							

			Technical Characteristics									Nontechnical Characteristics																						
			Norms					Reliability			Val.		Admin.		Scores						Test Formats — Input					Test Formats — Output							
	Taxonomy code	Overall rating	Scores	Size	Demographics	Recency	Total	Internal consistency	Stability	Total	Total	Ages/Grades for Intended Use	Group/Individual	Testing time	Age equivalents	Grade equivalents	Percentile ranks	Standard scores	Other	Examiner qualifications	Third Party	Listen	Read print	Look at stimuli	Other	Speak, minor	Speak, major	Manipulate objects	Mark answer sheet	Point	Draw	Write print	Other
DETROIT TESTS OF LEARNING APTITUDE, THIRD EDITION (1991) (cont.)																																	
Symbolic Relations	2110	B	A	A	A	A	A	B	B	B	A	8-0/17-11 yrs.	I	10	•		•	•		EA	•			•						•			
Word Sequences	2242	B	A	A	A	B	B	B	B	B	A	8-0/17-11 yrs.	I	10	•		•	•		EA	•						•						
Story Sequences	2233	B	A	A	A	A	A	B	F	B	B	8-0/17-11 yrs.	I	10	•		•	•		EA	•			•				•					
Picture Fragments	2131	B	A	A	A	A	A	F	B	B	B	8-0/17-11 yrs.	I	10	•		•	•		EA	•			•		•							
DETROIT TESTS OF LEARNING APTITUDE — ADULT (1991)																																	
General Mental Ability	4000	B	A	B	A	A	B	A	B	B	B	16-0/79-11 yrs.	I	60+			•	•		EA	•	•	•			•	•	•		•	•	•	
Optimal Composite	5000	B	A	B	A	A	B	A	B	B	B	16-0/79-11 yrs.	I	40			•	•		EA													
Verbal Composite	4000	B	A	B	A	A	B	A	B	B	B	16-0/79-11 yrs.	I	60			•	•		EA	•					•	•					•	
Nonverbal Composite	4000	B	A	B	A	A	B	A	B	B	B	16-0/79-11 yrs.	I	60			•	•		EA	•	•	•			•		•		•	•		
Attention-Enhanced Composite	2000	B	A	B	A	A	B	A	B	B	B	16-0/79-11 yrs.	I	50			•	•		EA	•		•			•		•		•	•		
Attention-Reduced Composite	4000	B	A	B	A	A	B	A	B	B	B	16-0/79-11 yrs.	I	60+			•	•		EA	•	•	•			•	•		•				
Motor-Enhanced Composite	2000	B	A	B	A	A	B	A	B	B	B	16-0/79-11 yrs.	I	50			•	•		EA	•		•				•			•	•		
Motor-Reduced Composite	4000	B	A	B	A	A	B	A	B	B	B	16-0/79-11 yrs.	I	60+			•	•		EA	•	•	•			•	•		•				
Fluid Intelligence	2100	B	A	B	A	A	B	A	B	B	B	16-0/79-11 yrs.	I	40			•	•		EA	•			•				•		•	•		
Crystallized Intelligence	4000	B	A	B	A	A	B	A	B	B	B	16-0/79-11 yrs.	I	60+			•	•		EA	•	•	•			•	•					•	
Simultaneous Processing	4000	B	A	B	A	A	B	A	B	B	B	16-0/79-11 yrs.	I	60+			•	•		EA	•		•			•	•		•		•	•	
Successive Processing	2000	B	A	B	A	A	B	A	F	B	B	16-0/79-11 yrs.	I	40			•	•		EA	•		•			•	•					•	
Associative Level	2000	B	A	B	A	A	B	A	B	B	B	16-0/79-11 yrs.	I	60			•	•		EA	•		•			•	•			•	•		
Cognitive Level	4000	B	A	B	A	A	B	A	B	B	B	16-0/79-11 yrs.	I	60			•	•		EA	•	•	•			•	•		•				
Verbal Scale	4000	B	A	B	A	A	B	A	B	B	B	16-0/79-11 yrs.	I	60			•	•		EA	•					•	•					•	
Performance Scale	4000	B	A	B	A	A	B	A	B	B	B	16-0/79-11 yrs.	I	60			•	•		EA	•	•	•			•		•		•	•		
Word Opposites	2231	B	A	B	A	A	B	B	B	B	A	16-0/79-11 yrs.	I	10			•	•		EA	•					•							
Story Sequences	2110	B	A	B	A	A	B	B	F	B	B	16-0/79-11 yrs.	I	10			•	•		EA	•		•					•					
Reversed Letters	2242	B	A	B	A	A	B	B	B	B	A	16-0/79-11 yrs.	I	10			•	•		EA	•											•	
Mathematical Problems	1210	B	A	B	A	A	B	B	B	B	A	16-0/79-11 yrs.	I	10			•	•		EA	•							•					
Design Sequences	2132	B	A	B	A	A	B	A	F	B	B	16-0/79-11 yrs.	I	10			•	•		EA	•		•					•					
Basic Information	1100	B	A	B	A	A	B	B	B	B	A	16-0/79-11 yrs.	I	10			•	•		EA	•							•					
Quantitative Relations	1220	B	A	B	A	A	B	B	B	B	A	16-0/79-11 yrs.	I	10			•	•		EA	•	•				•							
Word Sequences	2242	B	A	B	A	A	B	B	B	B	A	16-0/79-11 yrs.	I	10			•	•		EA	•						•						

		Technical Characteristics										Ages/Grades for Intended Use	Nontechnical Characteristics																				
			Norms					Reliability			Val.		Admin.		Scores						Test Formats		Input			Output							
	Taxonomy code	Overall rating	Scores	Size	Demographics	Recency	Total	Internal consistency	Stability	Total	Total		Group/Individual	Testing time	Age equivalents	Grade equivalents	Percentile ranks	Standard scores	Other	Examiner qualifications	Third Party	Listen	Read print	Look at stimuli	Other	Speak, minor	Speak, major	Manipulate objects	Mark answer sheet	Point	Draw	Write print	Other
DETROIT TESTS OF LEARNING APTITUDE — ADULT (1991) (cont.)																																	
Design Reproduction	2132	B	A	B	A	A	B	A	B	B	A	16-0/79-11 yrs.	I	10			•	•		EA		•		•						•			
Symbolic Relations	2110	B	A	B	A	A	B	B	B	B	A	16-0/79-11 yrs.	I	10			•	•		EA		•		•						•			
Form Assembly	2110	B	A	B	A	A	B	F	B	B	B	16-0/79-11 yrs.	I	20			•	•		EA		•		•				•					
Sentence Imitation	2232	B	A	B	A	A	B	B	B	B	A	16-0/79-11 yrs.	I	10			•	•		EA		•					•						
DETROIT TESTS OF LEARNING APTITUDE — PRIMARY (1986)																																	
General Intelligence Quotient	2000	B	A	B	A	A	B	A	B	B	A	3-6/9-11 yrs.	I	45			•	•		EA		•		•		•	•			•	•	•	•[1]
Verbal Quotient	2200	B	A	B	A	A	B	A	B	B	A	3-6/9-11 yrs.	I	45			•	•		EA		•		•			•			•			
Nonverbal Quotient	2100	B	A	B	A	A	B	A	B	B	A	3-6/9-11 yrs.	I	45			•	•		EA		•		•						•	•	•	•[1]
Conceptual Quotient	2000	B	A	B	A	A	B	A	B	B	A	3-6/9-11 yrs.	I	45			•	•		EA		•		•		•	•			•	•		•[1]
Structural Quotient	2000	B	A	B	A	A	B	A	F	B	A	3-6/9-11 yrs.	I	45			•	•		EA		•		•		•	•			•	•		•[1]
Attention-Enhanced Quotient	2000	B	A	B	A	A	B	A	B	B	A	3-6/9-11 yrs.	I	45			•	•		EA		•		•			•						
Attention-Reduced Quotient	2000	B	A	B	A	A	B	A	B	B	A	3-6/9-11 yrs.	I	45			•	•		EA		•		•		•	•			•	•		•[1]
Motor-Enhanced Quotient	2000	B	A	B	A	A	B	A	B	B	A	3-6/9-11 yrs.	I	45			•	•		EA		•		•						•	•	•	•[1]
Motor-Reduced Quotient	2000	B	A	B	A	A	B	A	B	B	A	3-6/9-11 yrs.	I	45			•	•		EA		•		•		•	•			•			•[1]

[1]Imitate motor patterns

DETROIT TESTS OF LEARNING APTITUDE — PRIMARY, SECOND EDITION (1991)																																	
General Mental Ability	2000	B	A	A	A	B	B	A	A	A	A	3-0/9-11 yrs.	I	30	•		•	•		EA		•	•	•		•	•			•	•	•	•[1]
Verbal	2200	B	A	A	A	B	B	A	A	A	A	3-0/9-11 yrs.	I	30	•		•	•		EA		•		•		•	•						
Nonverbal	2100	B	A	A	A	B	B	B	A	B	A	3-0/9-11 yrs.	I	30	•		•	•		EA		•	•	•						•	•	•	•[1]
Attention-Enhanced	2000	B	A	A	A	B	B	A	B	B	A	3-0/9-11 yrs.	I	30	•		•	•		EA		•	•	•			•			•	•		•[1]
Attention-Reduced	2000	B	A	A	A	B	B	A	A	A	A	3-0/9-11 yrs.	I	30	•		•	•		EA		•		•		•				•	•		
Motor-Enhanced	2000	B	A	A	A	B	B	B	A	B	A	3-0/9-11 yrs.	I	30	•		•	•		EA		•	•	•						•	•	•	•[1]
Motor-Reduced	2000	B	A	A	A	B	B	A	A	A	A	3-0/9-11 yrs.	I	30	•		•	•		EA		•		•		•	•			•			

[1]Imitate motor patterns

DEVELOPMENTAL INDICATORS FOR THE ASSESSMENT OF LEARNING — REVISED (1990)																																	
Total	2000	B	A	A	B	B	B	B	B	B	A	2-0/5-11 yrs.	G	30			•	•		EA		•		•		•	•	•		•	•	•	•[1]
Motor Area	2100	F	A	A	B	B	B	F	F	F	F	2-0/5-11 yrs.	G	10			•	•		EA		•		•				•		•	•		•[1]
Concepts Area	2200	F	A	A	B	B	B	F	B	F	F	2-0/5-11 yrs.	G	10			•	•		EA		•		•		•	•	•					

[1]Various motor responses

			Technical Characteristics — Norms					Reliability			Val.	Nontechnical Characteristics	Admin.		Scores					Examiner qualifications	Input					Output							
	Taxonomy code	Overall rating	Scores	Size	Demographics	Recency	Total	Internal consistency	Stability	Total	Total	Ages/Grades for Intended Use	Group/Individual	Testing time	Age equivalents	Grade equivalents	Percentile ranks	Standard scores	Other		Third Party	Listen	Read print	Look at stimuli	Other	Speak, minor	Speak, major	Manipulate objects	Mark answer sheet	Point	Draw	Write print	Other
DEVELOPMENTAL INDICATORS FOR THE ASSESSMENT OF LEARNING — REVISED (1990) (cont.)																																	
Language Area	2230	**F**	A	A	B	B	B	F	F	F	F	2-0/5-11 yrs.	G	10			•	•		EA	•		•			•	•						•[1]

[1]Various motor responses

DEVELOPMENTAL PROFILE II (1986)																																	
IQ Equivalence	4000	**F**	F	A	F	B	F	F	F	F	F	Birth/7-11 yrs.	I	30	•[1]					EA	•	•					•						
Physical	2150	**F**	B	A	F	B	F	F	F	F	F	Birth/7-11 yrs.	I	6	•			•[2]		EA	•	•					•						
Self-Help	1920	**F**	B	A	F	B	F	F	F	F	F	Birth/7-11 yrs.	I	6	•			•[2]		EA	•	•					•						
Social	3000	**F**	B	A	F	B	F	F	F	F	F	Birth/7-11 yrs.	I	6	•			•[2]		EA	•	•					•						
Academic	2000	**F**	B	A	F	B	F	F	F	F	F	Birth/7-11 yrs.	I	6	•			•[2]		EA	•	•					•						
Communication	4000	**F**	B	A	F	B	F	F	F	F	F	Birth/7-11 yrs.	I	6	•			•[2]		EA	•	•					•						

[1]Ratio IQ; [2]dichotomous standard scores

DEVELOPMENTAL TEST OF VISUAL-MOTOR INTEGRATION (1982)																																	
Total Score	2132	**F**	A	A	B	B	B	F	F	F	B	4-0/14-0 yrs.[1]	G	22	•		•	•		EA	•			•							•		

[1]Qualitative norms for as low as 28 weeks; authors note the 13–14 yr. norms serve for older age groups

DEVELOPMENTAL TEST OF VISUAL PERCEPTION (1966)																																	
Perceptual Quotient	2130	**F**	A	A	F	F	F	B	F	B	F	3-0/9-11 yrs.	G	45			•	•		EA	•			•							•		
Eye-Hand Coordination	2132	**F**	A	A	F	F	F	F	F	F	F	3-0/9-11 yrs.	G	7	•			•		EA	•			•							•		
Figure Ground	2131	**F**	A	A	F	F	F	A	F	B	F	3-0/9-11 yrs.	G	7	•			•		EA	•			•							•		
Constancy of Shape	2131	**F**	A	A	F	F	F	F	F	F	F	3-0/9-11 yrs.	G	7	•			•		EA	•			•							•		
Position in Space	2131	**F**	A	A	F	F	F	F	F	F	F	3-0/9-11 yrs.	G	7	•			•		EA	•			•							•		
Spatial Relations	2132	**F**	A	A	F	F	F	F	F	F	F	3-0/9-11 yrs.	G	7	•			•		EA	•			•							•		

DEVEREUX ADOLESCENT BEHAVIOR RATING SCALE (1967)[1]																																	
Unethical Behavior	3830	**F**	B	F	F	F	F	F	F	F	F	13-0/18-11 yrs.	I	7				•[2]		EA	•		•							•			
Defiant-Resistive	3500	**F**	B	F	F	F	F	F	F	F	F	13-0/18-11 yrs.	I	7				•[2]		EA	•		•							•			
Domineering-Sadistic	3400	**F**	B	F	F	F	F	F	F	F	F	13-0/18-11 yrs.	I	7				•[2]		EA	•		•							•			
Heterosexual Interest	3400	**F**	B	F	F	F	F	F	F	F	F	13-0/18-11 yrs.	I	7				•[2]		EA	•		•							•			
Hyperactive-Expansive	3810	**F**	B	F	F	F	F	F	F	F	F	13-0/18-11 yrs.	I	7				•[2]		EA	•		•							•			
Poor Emotional Control	3840	**F**	B	F	F	F	F	F	F	F	F	13-0/18-11 yrs.	I	7				•[2]		EA	•		•							•			
Need Approval, Dependency	3400	**F**	B	F	F	F	F	F	F	F	F	13-0/18-11 yrs.	I	7				•[2]		EA	•		•							•			

[1]Ratings apply to normal and special populations; [2]means and standard deviations

		Norms: Scores	Norms: Size	Norms: Demographics	Norms: Recency	Norms: Total	Rel.: Internal consistency	Rel.: Stability	Rel.: Total	Val.: Total	Ages/Grades for Intended Use	Group/Individual	Testing time	Age equivalents	Grade equivalents	Percentile ranks	Standard scores	Other	Examiner qualifications	Third Party	Listen	Read print	Look at stimuli	Other	Speak, minor	Speak, major	Manipulate objects	Mark answer sheet	Point	Draw	Write print	Other
DEVEREUX ADOLESCENT BEHAVIOR RATING SCALE (1967)[1] (cont.)																																
Emotional Distance · 3900	F	B	F	F	F	F	F	F	F	F	13-0/18-11 yrs.	I	7					•[2]	EA	•		•						•				
Physical Inferiority/Timidity · 4000	F	B	F	F	F	F	F	F	F	F	13-0/18-11 yrs.	I	7					•[2]	EA	•		•						•				
Schizoid Withdrawal · 3900	F	B	F	F	F	F	F	F	F	F	13-0/18-11 yrs.	I	7					•[2]	EA	•		•						•				
Bizarre Speech and Cognition · 2230	F	B	F	F	F	F	F	F	F	F	13-0/18-11 yrs.	I	7					•[2]	EA	•		•						•				
Bizarre Action · 3840	F	B	F	F	F	F	F	F	F	F	13-0/18-11 yrs.	I	7					•[2]	EA	•		•						•				
Inability to Delay · 3840	F	B	F	F	F	F	F	F	F	F	13-0/18-11 yrs.	I	7					•[2]	EA	•		•						•				
Paranoid Thinking · 3900	F	B	F	F	F	F	F	F	F	F	13-0/18-11 yrs.	I	7					•[2]	EA	•		•						•				
Anxious Self-Blame · 3100	F	B	F	F	F	F	F	F	F	F	13-0/18-11 yrs.	I	7					•[2]	EA	•		•						•				

[1]Ratings apply to normal and special populations; [2]means and standard deviations

DEVEREUX CHILD BEHAVIOR RATING SCALE (1966)[1]																																
Distractibility · 3820	F	B	F	F	F	F	F	F	F	F	8-0/12-11 yrs.	I	7					•[2]	EA	•		•						•				
Poor Self-Care · 1920	F	B	F	F	F	F	F	F	F	F	8-0/12-11 yrs.	I	7					•[2]	EA	•		•						•				
Pathological Use of Senses · 3900	F	B	F	F	F	F	F	F	F	F	8-0/12-11 yrs.	I	7					•[2]	EA	•		•						•				
Emotional Detachment · 3900	F	B	F	F	F	F	F	F	F	F	8-0/12-11 yrs.	I	7					•[2]	EA	•		•						•				
Social Isolation · 3400	F	B	F	F	F	F	F	F	F	F	8-0/12-11 yrs.	I	7					•[2]	EA	•		•						•				
Poor Coordination and Body Tonus · 2150	F	B	F	F	F	F	F	F	F	F	8-0/12-11 yrs.	I	7					•[2]	EA	•		•						•				
Incontinence · 1920	F	B	F	F	F	F	F	F	F	F	8-0/12-11 yrs.	I	7					•[2]	EA	•		•						•				
Messiness, Sloppiness · 1920	F	B	F	F	F	F	F	F	F	F	8-0/12-11 yrs.	I	7					•[2]	EA	•		•						•				
Inadequate Need for Independence · 3830	F	B	F	F	F	F	F	F	F	F	8-0/12-11 yrs.	I	7					•[2]	EA	•		•						•				
Unresponsiveness to Stimulation · 3810	F	B	F	F	F	F	F	F	F	F	8-0/12-11 yrs.	I	7					•[2]	EA	•		•						•				
Proneness to Emotional Upset · 3840	F	B	F	F	F	F	F	F	F	F	8-0/12-11 yrs.	I	7					•[2]	EA	•		•						•				
Need for Adult Contact · 3400	F	B	F	F	F	F	F	F	F	F	8-0/12-11 yrs.	I	7					•[2]	EA	•		•						•				
Anxious-Fearful Ideation · 3100	F	B	F	F	F	F	F	F	F	F	8-0/12-11 yrs.	I	7					•[2]	EA	•		•						•				
"Impulse" Ideation · 3840	F	B	F	F	F	F	F	F	F	F	8-0/12-11 yrs.	I	7					•[2]	EA	•		•						•				
Inability to Delay · 3840	F	B	F	F	F	F	F	F	F	F	8-0/12-11 yrs.	I	7					•[2]	EA	•		•						•				
Social Integration · 3400	F	B	F	F	F	F	F	F	F	F	8-0/12-11 yrs.	I	7					•[2]	EA	•		•						•				

[1]Ratings apply to normal and special populations; [2]means and standard deviations

		Technical Characteristics — Norms					Reliability			Val.	Ages/Grades for Intended Use	Admin.		Scores						Test Formats												
Taxonomy code	Overall rating	Scores	Size	Demographics	Recency	Total	Internal consistency	Stability	Total	Total		Group/Individual	Testing time	Age equivalents	Grade equivalents	Percentile ranks	Standard scores	Other	Examiner qualifications	Third Party	Listen	Read print	Look at stimuli	Other	Speak, minor	Speak, major	Manipulate objects	Mark answer sheet	Point	Draw	Write print	Other
DEVEREUX ELEMENTARY SCHOOL BEHAVIOR RATING SCALE II (1982)[1]																																
Work Organization — 3830	F	B	F	F	B	F	F	F	F	B	gr. K–6	I	7					•[2]	EA	•		•						•				
Creative Initiative/Involvement — 2220	F	B	F	F	B	F	F	F	F	F	gr. K–6	I	7					•[2]	EA	•		•						•				
Positive Toward Teacher — 3210	F	B	F	F	B	F	F	F	F	F	gr. K–6	I	7					•[2]	EA	•		•						•				
Need for Direction in Work — 3830	F	B	F	F	B	F	F	F	F	B	gr. K–6	I	7					•[2]	EA	•		•						•				
Socially Withdrawn — 3400	F	B	F	F	B	F	F	F	F	F	gr. K–6	I	7					•[2]	EA	•		•						•				
Failure Anxiety — 3100	F	B	F	F	B	F	F	F	F	F	gr. K–6	I	7					•[2]	EA	•		•						•				
Impatience — 3820	F	B	F	F	B	F	F	F	F	B	gr. K–6	I	7					•[2]	EA	•		•						•				
Irrelevant Thinking/Talk — 3810	F	B	F	F	B	F	F	F	F	F	gr. K–6	I	7					•[2]	EA	•		•						•				
Blaming — 3830	F	B	F	F	B	F	F	F	F	F	gr. K–6	I	7					•[2]	EA	•		•						•				
Negative-Aggressive — 3500	F	B	F	F	B	F	F	F	F	F	gr. K–6	I	7					•[2]	EA	•		•						•				
Perseverance — 3820	F	B	F	F	B	F	F	F	F	B	gr. K–6	I	7					•[2]	EA	•		•						•				
Peer Cooperation — 3400	F	B	F	F	B	F	F	F	F	F	gr. K–6	I	7					•[2]	EA	•		•						•				
Confusion — 3900	F	B	F	F	B	F	F	F	F	B	gr. K–6	I	7					•[2]	EA	•		•						•				
Inattention — 3820	F	B	F	F	B	F	F	F	F	B	gr. K–6	I	7					•[2]	EA	•		•						•				

[1]Ratings apply to normal and special populations; [2]standard score units similar to Z-scores

DIAGNOSTIC ACHIEVEMENT BATTERY (1984)																																
Total Achievement — 4000	F	A	B	F	B	F	F	B	B	B	6-0/14-11 yrs.	I	60+				•		EA		•	•	•		•	•			•		•	
Listening — 2230	F	A	B	F	B	F	A	B	B	B	6-0/14-11 yrs.	I	22				•		EA		•				•	•						
Speaking — 2230	F	A	B	F	B	F	B	B	B	B	6-0/14-11 yrs.	I	22				•		EA		•				•	•						
Reading — 1300	F	A	B	F	B	F	A	B	B	B	6-0/14-11 yrs.	I	45				•		EA		•				•	•						
Writing — 1600	F	A	B	F	B	F	F	B	B	B	6-0/14-11 yrs.	I	45				•		EA		•	•	•								•	
Applied Mathematics — 1200	F	A	B	F	B	F	A	B	B	B	6-0/14-11 yrs.	I	22				•		EA		•	•	•		•				•		•	
Spoken Language — 2230	F	A	B	F	B	F	B	B	B	B	6-0/14-11 yrs.	I	45				•		EA						•	•						
Written Language — 1000	F	A	B	F	B	F	F	B	B	B	6-0/14-11 yrs.	I	45				•		EA		•	•	•		•	•					•	
Story Comprehension — 2233	F	A	B	F	B	F	B	B	B	A	6-0/14-11 yrs.	I	7	•	•				EA		•								•			
Characteristics — 2231	F	A	B	F	B	F	B	B	B	A	6-0/14-11 yrs.	I	7	•	•				EA		•				•							
Synonyms — 2231	F	A	B	F	B	F	F	B	B	A	6-0/14-11 yrs.	I	7	•	•				EA		•				•							
Grammatic Completion — 2232	F	A	B	F	B	F	B	B	B	A	6-0/14-11 yrs.	I	7	•	•				EA		•				•							
Alphabet/Word Knowledge — 1320	F	A	B	F	B	F	A	B	B	A	6-0/14-11 yrs.	I	7	•	•				EA		•	•			•							

			Technical Characteristics									Nontechnical Characteristics																					
			Norms					Reliability			Val.	Ages/Grades for Intended Use	Admin.		Scores						Test Formats												
																					Input					Output							
	Taxonomy code	Overall rating	Scores	Size	Demographics	Recency	Total	Internal consistency	Stability	Total	Total		Group/Individual	Testing time	Age equivalents	Grade equivalents	Percentile ranks	Standard scores	Other	Examiner qualifications	Third Party	Listen	Read print	Look at stimuli	Other	Speak, minor	Speak, major	Manipulate objects	Mark answer sheet	Point	Draw	Write print	Other
DIAGNOSTIC ACHIEVEMENT BATTERY (1984) (cont.)																																	
Reading Comprehension	1310	F	A	B	F	B	F	B	B	B	A	6-0/14-11 yrs.	I	7			•	•		EA		•	•			•	•						
Capitalization	1620	F	A	B	F	B	F	F	B	B	B	6-0/14-11 yrs.	I	7			•	•		EA		•	•									•	
Punctuation	1620	F	A	B	F	B	F	F	B	B	B	6-0/14-11 yrs.	I	7			•	•		EA		•	•									•	
Spelling	1630	F	A	B	F	B	F	B	B	B	A	6-0/14-11 yrs.	I	7			•	•		EA		•										•	
Written Vocabulary	1610	F	A	B	F	B	F	F	B	B	B	6-0/14-11 yrs.	I	22			•	•		EA		•		•								•	
Math Reasoning	1210	F	A	B	F	B	F	A	B	B	A	6-0/14-11 yrs.	I	22			•	•		EA		•	•									•	
Math Calculation	1220	F	A	B	F	B	F	A	B	B	A	6-0/14-11 yrs.	I	7			•	•		EA		•		•		•				•			
DIAGNOSTIC ACHIEVEMENT BATTERY, SECOND EDITION (1990)																																	
Total Achievement	4000	B	A	B	A	B	B	A	B	B	B	6-0/14-11 yrs.	I	60 +				•		EA		•	•	•		•	•			•		•	
Listening	2230	B	A	B	A	B	B	A	B	B	B	6-0/14-11 yrs.	I	30				•		EA		•				•							
Speaking	2230	B	A	B	A	B	B	A	B	B	B	6-0/14-11 yrs.	I	20				•		EA		•				•							
Reading	1300	B	A	B	A	B	B	A	B	B	B	6-0/14-11 yrs.	I	30				•		EA		•	•			•	•			•			
Writing	1600	B	A	B	A	B	B	A	B	B	B	6-0/14-11 yrs.	I	30				•		EA		•	•	•								•	
Math	1200	B	A	B	A	B	B	B	B	B	B	6-0/14-11 yrs.	I	35				•		EA		•	•	•		•	•		•	•		•	
Spoken Language	2230	B	A	B	A	B	B	A	B	B	B	6-0/14-11 yrs.	I	50				•		EA		•				•							
Written Language	1000	B	A	B	A	B	B	A	B	B	B	6-0/14-11 yrs.	I	60				•		EA		•	•	•		•	•			•		•	
Story Comprehension	2233	B	A	B	A	B	B	A	B	B	A	6-0/14-11 yrs.	I	20	•	•	•	•		EA		•				•	•						
Characteristics	2231	B	A	B	A	B	B	B	B	B	A	6-0/14-11 yrs.	I	10	•	•	•	•		EA		•				•							
Synonyms	2231	B	A	B	A	B	B	B	B	B	B	6-0/14-11 yrs.	I	10	•	•	•	•		EA		•				•							
Grammatic Completion	2232	B	A	B	A	B	B	A	B	B	A	6-0/14-11 yrs.	I	10	•	•	•	•		EA		•				•							
Alphabet/Word Knowledge	1320	B	A	B	A	B	B	A	B	B	A	6-0/14-11 yrs.	I	10	•	•	•	•		EA		•	•	•		•				•			
Reading Comprehension	1310	B	A	B	A	A	B	A	B	B	A	6-0/14-11 yrs.	I	20	•	•	•	•		EA		•	•			•	•					•	
Capitalization	1620	B	A	B	A	A	B	A	F	B	A	6-0/14-11 yrs.	I	20	•	•	•	•		EA		•	•										
Punctuation	1620	B	A	B	A	B	A	A	F	B	A	6-0/14-11 yrs.	I	20	•	•	•	•		EA		•	•									•	
Spelling	1630	B	A	B	A	B	B	B	B	B	A	6-0/14-11 yrs.	I	10	•	•	•	•		EA		•										•	
Writing Composition	1610	F	A	B	A	A	B	F	F	F	B	6-0/14-11 yrs.	I	20	•	•	•	•		EA		•		•								•	
Math Reasoning	1210	B	A	B	A	B	B	B	B	B	A	6-0/14-11 yrs.	I	15	•	•	•	•		EA		•				•	•			•			
Calculation	1220	B	A	B	A	B	B	B	B	B	A	6-0/14-11 yrs.	I	20	•	•	•	•		EA		•	•			•						•	

			Technical Characteristics — Norms					Reliability			Val.	Nontechnical Characteristics	Admin.		Scores						Test Formats — Input					Output							
	Taxonomy code	Overall rating	Scores	Size	Demographics	Recency	Total	Internal consistency	Stability	Total	Total	Ages/Grades for Intended Use	Group/Individual	Testing time	Age equivalents	Grade equivalents	Percentile ranks	Standard scores	Other	Examiner qualifications	Third Party	Listen	Read print	Look at stimuli	Other	Speak, minor	Speak, major	Manipulate objects	Mark answer sheet	Point	Draw	Write print	Other
DIAGNOSTIC ACHIEVEMENT TEST FOR ADOLESCENTS (1986)																																	
Overall Achievement	1000	B	A	B	A	A	B	A	B	B	B	12-0/18-11 yrs.	I	60+			•	•		EA	•	•	•			•	•					•	
Achievement Screener	1000	B	A	B	A	A	B	A	B	B	B	12-0/18-11 yrs.	I	22			•	•		EA	•	•				•						•	
Reading	1300	B	A	B	A	A	B	A	B	B	B	12-0/18-11 yrs.	I	22			•	•		EA	•	•				•	•						
Mathematics	1200	B	A	B	A	A	B	A	B	B	B	12-0/18-11 yrs.	I	22			•	•		EA	•	•										•	
Writing	1600	B	A	B	A	A	B	A	B	B	B	12-0/18-11 yrs.	I	22			•	•		EA	•			•								•	
Word Identification	1320	B	A	B	A	A	B	A	B	B	A	12-0/18-11 yrs.	I	7			•	•		EA	•	•				•							
Reading Comprehension	1310	B	A	B	A	A	B	A	F	B	A	12-0/18-11 yrs.	I	7			•	•		EA	•	•					•						
Math Calculation	1220	B	A	B	A	A	B	A	B	B	A	12-0/18-11 yrs.	I	7			•	•		EA	•	•										•	
Math Problem Solving	1210	B	A	B	A	A	B	A	B	B	A	12-0/18-11 yrs.	I	7			•	•		EA	•											•	
Spelling	1630	B	A	B	A	A	B	A	B	B	A	12-0/18-11 yrs.	I	7			•	•		EA	•											•	
Writing Compostion	1610	F	A	B	A	A	B	F	F	F	F	12-0/18-11 yrs.	I	7			•	•		EA	•			•								•	
Science	1400	B	A	B	A	A	B	A	B	B	A	12-0/18-11 yrs.	I	7			•	•		EA	•						•						
Social Studies	1500	B	A	B	A	A	B	A	B	B	A	12-0/18-11 yrs.	I	7			•	•		EA	•						•						
Reference Skills	1700	B	A	B	A	A	B	A	F	B	A	12-0/18-11 yrs.	I	7			•	•		EA	•	•					•						
DIAGNOSTIC ANALYSIS OF READING ERRORS (1979)																																	
Correct Score	1630	F	A	F	F	B	F	F	B	B	B	gr. 7-12[1]	G	22	•	•	•			EA	•	•							•				

¹Community college norms also provided

DIAGNOSTIC READING SCALES (1981)																																	
Instructional Level	1300	F	F	F	F	F	F	F	B	B	F	gr. 1-7	I	22	•					EA			•			•	•						
Independent Level	1310	F	F	F	F	F	F	F	F	F	F	gr. 1-7	I	22	•					EA			•				•						
Potential Level	2230	F	F	F	F	F	F	F	F	F	F	gr. 1-7	I	22	•					EA		•					•						
DIAGNOSTIC SCREENING TEST: ACHIEVEMENT (1977)																																	
Total	1000	F	B	A	F	B	F	B	F	B	B	gr. 1-12	G	20			•	•		EA	•	•							•				
Practical Knowledge	1100	F	F	A	F	B	F	F	F	F	F	gr. 1-12	G	5			•			EA	•	•							•				
Science	1400	F	B	A	F	B	F	F	F	F	F	gr. 1-12	G	5			•	•		EA	•	•							•				
Social Studies	1500	F	B	A	F	B	F	F	F	F	F	gr. 1-12	G	5			•	•		EA	•	•							•				
Literature & the Arts	5000	F	B	A	F	B	F	F	F	F	F	gr. 1-12	G	5			•	•		EA	•	•							•				

	Taxonomy code	Overall rating	Norms: Scores	Norms: Size	Norms: Demographics	Norms: Recency	Norms: Total	Reliability: Internal consistency	Reliability: Stability	Reliability: Total	Val: Total	Ages/Grades for Intended Use	Admin: Group/Individual	Admin: Testing time	Scores: Age equivalents	Scores: Grade equivalents	Scores: Percentile ranks	Scores: Standard scores	Scores: Other	Examiner qualifications	Third Party	Input: Listen	Input: Read print	Input: Look at stimuli	Input: Other	Output: Speak, minor	Output: Speak, major	Output: Manipulate objects	Output: Mark answer sheet	Output: Point	Output: Draw	Output: Write print	Output: Other
DIAGNOSTIC SCREENING TEST: LANGUAGE, SECOND EDITION (1980)																																	
Total Test	1600	F	A	A	F	B	F	B	F	B	F	gr. 1–12	G	20	•	•	•			EA		•	•						•				
Formal Knowledge	1600	F	F	A	F	B	F	F	F	F	F	gr. 1–12	G	10	•					EA		•	•						•				
Applied Knowledge	1600	F	F	A	F	B	F	F	F	F	F	gr. 1–12	G	10	•					EA		•	•						•				
Punctuation	1620	F	A	A	F	B	F	F	F	F	F	gr. 1–12	G	4		•	•			EA		•	•						•				
Spelling Rules	1630	F	A	A	F	B	F	F	F	F	F	gr. 1–12	G	4		•	•			EA		•	•						•				
Sentence Structure	1610	F	A	A	F	B	F	F	F	F	F	gr. 1–12	G	4		•	•			EA		•	•						•				
Grammar	1610	F	A	A	F	B	F	F	F	F	F	gr. 1–12	G	4		•	•			EA		•	•						•				
Capitalization	1620	F	A	A	F	B	F	F	F	F	F	gr. 1–12	G	4		•	•			EA		•	•						•				
DIAGNOSTIC SCREENING TEST: MATH, THIRD EDITION (1980)																																	
Total Basic	1220	F	A	F	F	B	F	F	F	F	F	6-1/16-7 yrs.	G	30	•	•	•			EA		•	•	•					•			•	
Total Specialized	1200	F	A	F	F	B	F	F	F	F	F	6-1/16-7 yrs.	G	30	•	•	•			EA		•	•	•					•			•	
Addition	1220	F	A	F	F	B	F	F	F	F	F	6-1/16-7 yrs.	G	30	•	•	•			EA		•	•	•					•			•	
Subtraction	1220	F	A	F	F	B	F	F	F	F	F	6-1/16-7 yrs.	G	30	•	•	•			EA		•	•	•					•			•	
Multiplication	1220	F	A	F	F	B	F	F	F	F	F	6-1/16-7 yrs.	G	30	•	•	•			EA		•	•	•					•			•	
Division	1220	F	A	F	F	B	F	F	F	F	F	6-1/16-7 yrs.	G	30	•	•	•			EA		•	•	•					•			•	
Process	1220	F	A	F	F	B	F	F	F	F	F	6-1/16-7 yrs.	G	30	•	•	•			EA		•	•	•					•			•	
Sequencing	1220	F	A	F	F	B	F	F	F	F	F	6-1/16-7 yrs.	G	30	•	•	•			EA		•	•	•					•			•	
Simple Computation	1220	F	A	F	F	B	F	F	F	F	F	6-1/16-7 yrs.	G	30	•	•	•			EA		•	•	•					•			•	
Complex Computation	1220	F	A	F	F	B	F	F	F	F	F	6-1/16-7 yrs.	G	30	•	•	•			EA		•	•	•					•			•	
Special Manipulations	1220	F	A	F	F	B	F	F	F	F	F	6-1/16-7 yrs.	G	30	•	•	•			EA		•	•	•					•			•	
Use of Zero	1220	F	A	F	F	B	F	F	F	F	F	6-1/16-7 yrs.	G	30	•	•	•			EA		•	•	•					•			•	
Decimals	1220	F	A	F	F	B	F	F	F	F	F	6-1/16-7 yrs.	G	30	•	•	•			EA		•	•	•					•			•	
Simple Fractions	1220	F	A	F	F	B	F	F	F	F	F	6-1/16-7 yrs.	G	30	•	•	•			EA		•	•	•					•			•	
Manipulation in Fractions	1220	F	A	F	F	B	F	F	F	F	F	6-1/16-7 yrs.	G	30	•	•	•			EA		•	•	•					•			•	
Money	1200	F	B	F	F	B	F	F	F	F	F	6-1/16-7 yrs.	G	30	•	•				EA		•	•	•					•			•	
Time	1200	F	B	F	F	B	F	F	F	F	F	6-1/16-7 yrs.	G	30	•	•				EA		•	•	•					•			•	
Percent	1200	F	B	F	F	B	F	F	F	F	F	6-1/16-7 yrs.	G	30	•	•				EA		•	•	•					•			•	
U.S. Measure	1200	F	B	F	F	B	F	F	F	F	F	6-1/16-7 yrs.	G	30	•	•				EA		•	•	•					•			•	
Metric	1200	F	B	F	F	B	F	F	F	F	F	6-1/16-7 yrs.	G	30	•	•				EA		•	•	•					•			•	

			Technical Characteristics								Nontechnical Characteristics																						
			Norms					Reliability			Val.	Ages/Grades for Intended Use	Admin.		Scores						Input					Output							
	Taxonomy code	Overall rating	Scores	Size	Demographics	Recency	Total	Internal consistency	Stability	Total	Total		Group/Individual	Testing time	Age equivalents	Grade equivalents	Percentile ranks	Standard scores	Other	Examiner qualifications	Third Party	Listen	Read print	Look at stimuli	Other	Speak, minor	Speak, major	Manipulate objects	Mark answer sheet	Point	Draw	Write print	Other
DIAGNOSTIC SCREENING TEST: READING, THIRD EDITION (1982)																																	
Phonics Total	1320	F	F	B	F	B	F	A	F	B	F	gr. 1–12	I	30	•					EA	•	•				•	•						
Sight Total	1320	F	F	B	F	B	F	A	F	B	F	gr. 1–12	I	30	•					EA	•	•				•	•						
Passage Comprehension	1310	F	F	B	F	B	F	B	F	B	F	gr. 1–12	I	30	•					EA	•	•				•	•						
Word Reading	1320	F	A	B	F	B	F	F	F	F	F	gr. 1–12	I	30	•	•	•			EA	•	•				•	•						
DIAGNOSTIC SCREENING TEST: SPELLING, THIRD EDITION (1982)																																	
Total Spelling	1630	F	A	B	F	B	F	A	F	B	F	gr. 1–12	I	10	•	•	•			EA	•											•	
Phonics Spelling	1630	F	A	B	F	B	F	A	F	B	F	gr. 1–12	I	10	•	•	•			EA	•											•	
Sight Spelling	1630	F	A	B	F	B	F	A	F	B	F	gr. 1–12	I	10	•	•	•			EA	•											•	
DIAGNOSTIC SPELLING POTENTIAL TEST (1982)																																	
Spelling	1630	F	A	F	F	B	F	F	F	F	B	7-0/Adult yrs.	G	7	•	•	•			EA	•											•	
Sight Word Recognition	1320	F	A	F	F	B	F	B	F	B	B	7-0/Adult yrs.	I	7	•	•	•			EA	•	•				•							
Phonetic Word Recognition	1330	F	A	F	F	B	F	B	F	B	B	7-0/Adult yrs.	I	7	•	•	•			EA	•	•				•							
Visual Recognition	1630	F	A	F	F	B	F	B	F	B	B	7-0/Adult yrs.	G	7	•	•	•			EA	•	•								•			
Auditory-Visual Recognition	1630	F	A	F	F	B	F	B	F	B	B	7-0/Adult yrs.	G	7	•	•	•			EA	•	•								•			
DIFFERENTIAL TEST OF CONDUCT AND EMOTIONAL PROBLEMS (1990)																																	
Conduct Problem	3500	F	B	A	F	A	F	F	F	F	B	gr. K–12	G	20					•¹	EA	•		•						•				
Emotional Disturbance	3000	F	B	A	F	A	F	F	F	F	B	gr. K–12	G	20					•¹	EA	•		•						•				

¹Means and standard deviations provided

	Taxonomy code	Overall rating	Scores	Size	Demographics	Recency	Total	Internal consistency	Stability	Total	Total	Ages/Grades	Group/Individual	Testing time	Age equivalents	Grade equivalents	Percentile ranks	Standard scores	Other	Examiner qualifications	Third Party	Listen	Read print	Look at stimuli	Other	Speak, minor	Speak, major	Manipulate objects	Mark answer sheet	Point	Draw	Write print	Other
DRAW A PERSON (1991)																																	
Total	3000	F	A	A	F	A	F	F	F	F	F	6-0/17-11 yrs.	G	15				•		EA	•										•		
EMOTIONAL & BEHAVIOR PROBLEM SCALE (1987)																																	
Total	4000	F	A	B	F	A	F	F	F	F	F	4-6/21-11 yrs.	I	20		•				EA	•		•						•				
Social Aggression/ Conduct Disorder	3500	F	A	B	F	A	F	F	F	F	F	4-6/21-11 yrs.	I	20		•	•			EA	•		•						•				
Social-Emotional Withdrawal/Depression	3300	F	A	B	F	A	F	F	F	F	F	4-6/21-11 yrs.	I	20		•	•			EA	•		•						•				
Learning/Comprehension Disorder	1000	F	A	B	F	A	F	F	F	F	F	4-6/21-11 yrs.	I	20		•	•			EA	•		•						•				
Avoidance/ Unresponsiveness	3400	F	A	B	F	A	F	F	F	F	F	4-6/21-11 yrs.	I	20		•	•			EA	•		•						•				
Aggressive/ Self-Destructive	3620	F	A	B	F	A	F	F	F	F	F	4-6/21-11 yrs.	I	20		•	•			EA	•		•						•				

| | | | Norms | | | | | Reliability | | | Val. | | Admin. | | Scores | | | | | | | Input | | | | Output | | | | | | | |
	Taxonomy code	Overall rating	Scores	Size	Demographics	Recency	Total	Internal consistency	Stability	Total	Total	Ages/Grades for Intended Use	Group/Individual	Testing time	Age equivalents	Grade equivalents	Percentile ranks	Standard scores	Other	Examiner qualifications	Third Party	Listen	Read print	Look at stimuli	Other	Speak, minor	Speak, major	Manipulate objects	Mark answer sheet	Point	Draw	Write print	Other
ENDLER MULTIDIMENSIONAL ANXIETY SCALES (1991)																																	
Perception Scales:																																	
Total	3100	F	A	F	F	A	F	F	F	F	F	15-0/65-11 yrs.	G	10			•	•		EA			•							•			
State Scales:																																	
Total	3100	F	A	F	F	A	F	A	F	B	A	15-0/65-11 yrs.	G	10			•	•		EA			•							•			
Cognitive-Worry	3100	F	A	F	F	A	F	B	F	B	A	15-0/65-11 yrs.	G	10			•	•		EA			•							•			
Autonomic-Emotional	3100	F	A	F	F	A	F	B	F	B	A	15-0/65-11 yrs.	G	10			•	•		EA			•							•			
Trait Scales:																																	
Social Evaluation	3100	F	A	F	F	A	F	A	F	B	B	15-0/65-11 yrs.	G	25			•	•		EA			•							•			
Ambiguous	3100	F	A	F	F	A	F	A	F	B	B	15-0/65-11 yrs.	G	25			•	•		EA			•							•			
Physical Danger	3100	F	A	F	F	A	F	A	F	B	B	15-0/65-11 yrs.	G	25			•	•		EA			•							•			
Daily Routines	3100	F	A	F	F	A	F	B	F	B	B	15-0/65-11 yrs.	G	25			•	•		EA			•							•			
EXPRESSIVE ONE-WORD PICTURE VOCABULARY TEST (1979)																																	
Total	2231	F	A	A	F	B	F	A	F	B	F	2-0/11-11 yrs.	I	7	•		•	•		EA		•		•		•							
EXPRESSIVE ONE-WORD PICTURE VOCABULARY TEST (REVISED) (1990)																																	
Total	2231	F	A	B	F	A	F	B	F	B	B	2-0/11-11 yrs.	I	15	•		•	•		EA		•		•		•							
EXPRESSIVE ONE-WORD PICTURE VOCABULARY TEST — UPPER EXTENSION (1983)																																	
Total	2231	F	A	F	F	B	F	A	F	B	B	12-0/15-11 yrs.	G	7	•		•	•		EA		•		•		•							
FAMILY APPERCEPTION TEST (1991)																																	
Total Dysfunctional Index	3000	F	F	F	F	A	F	F	F	F	F	6-0/15-11 yrs.	I	30					•[1]	ST		•		•			•						

[1]Raw scores only

| | | | Norms | | | | | Reliability | | | Val. | | Admin. | | Scores | | | | | | | Input | | | | Output | | | | | | | |
	Taxonomy code	Overall rating	Scores	Size	Demographics	Recency	Total	Internal consistency	Stability	Total	Total	Ages/Grades for Intended Use	Group/Individual	Testing time	Age equivalents	Grade equivalents	Percentile ranks	Standard scores	Other	Examiner qualifications	Third Party	Listen	Read print	Look at stimuli	Other	Speak, minor	Speak, major	Manipulate objects	Mark answer sheet	Point	Draw	Write print	Other
FLUHARTY PRESCHOOL SPEECH AND LANGUAGE SCREENING TEST (1978)																																	
Identification	2231	F	B	B	F	F	F	F	F	F	F	2-0/6-11 yrs.	I	5					•[1]	EA		•		•		•							
Articulation	2243	F	B	B	F	F	F	F	F	F	F	2-0/6-11 yrs.	I	5					•[1]	EA		•		•		•							
Comprehension	2230	F	B	B	F	F	F	F	F	F	F	2-0/6-11 yrs.	I	5					•[1]	EA		•		•				•					•[2]
Repetition	2232	F	B	B	F	F	F	F	F	F	F	2-0/6-11 yrs.	I	5					•[1]	EA		•		•			•						

[1]Cutoff scores provided; [2]various motor responses

| | | | Norms | | | | | Reliability | | | Val. | | Admin. | | Scores | | | | | | | Input | | | | Output | | | | | | | |
	Taxonomy code	Overall rating	Scores	Size	Demographics	Recency	Total	Internal consistency	Stability	Total	Total	Ages/Grades for Intended Use	Group/Individual	Testing time	Age equivalents	Grade equivalents	Percentile ranks	Standard scores	Other	Examiner qualifications	Third Party	Listen	Read print	Look at stimuli	Other	Speak, minor	Speak, major	Manipulate objects	Mark answer sheet	Point	Draw	Write print	Other
FORMAL READING INVENTORY (1986)																																	
Silent Reading Quotient	1310	B	A	B	B	A	B	A	F	B	A	6-6/17-11 yrs.	G	45			•	•		EA		•	•							•			

	Taxonomy code	Overall rating	Norms: Scores	Size	Demographics	Recency	Total	Reliability: Internal consistency	Stability	Total	Val.: Total	Ages/Grades for Intended Use	Admin.: Group/Individual	Testing time	Scores: Age equivalents	Grade equivalents	Percentile ranks	Standard scores	Other	Examiner qualifications	Input: Third Party	Listen	Read print	Look at stimuli	Other	Output: Speak, minor	Speak, major	Manipulate objects	Mark answer sheet	Point	Draw	Write print	Other
THE GIFTED EVALUATION SCALE (1987)																																	
Total	4000	F	A	B	F	A	F	F	F	F	F	4-6/19-11 yrs.	I	20			•	•		EA			•						•				
Intellectual	4000	F	A	B	F	A	F	F	F	F	F	4-6/19-11 yrs.	I	20				•		EA			•						•				
Creativity	4000	F	A	B	F	A	F	F	F	F	F	4-6/19-11 yrs.	I	20				•		EA			•						•				
Academic Aptitude	4000	F	A	B	F	A	F	F	F	F	F	4-6/19-11 yrs.	I	20				•		EA			•						•				
Leadership Ability	4000	F	A	B	F	A	F	F	F	F	F	4-6/19-11 yrs.	I	20				•		EA			•						•				
Performing and Visual Arts	4000	F	A	B	F	A	F	F	F	F	F	4-6/19-11 yrs.	I	20				•		EA			•						•				
GILMORE ORAL READING TEST (1968)																																	
Accuracy	1320	F	A	A	F	F	F	B	B	B	F	gr. 1–8	I	22	•	•	•		•¹	EA		•	•				•						
Comprehension	1310	F	A	A	F	F	F	F	F	F	F	gr. 1–8	I	22	•	•	•		•¹	EA		•	•				•						
Rate	1340	F	F	A	F	F	F	F	F	F	F	gr. 1–8	I	22	•	•	•		•¹	EA		•	•				•						

¹Performance ratings

	Taxonomy code	Overall rating	Scores	Size	Demographics	Recency	Total	Internal consistency	Stability	Total	Total	Ages/Grades for Intended Use	Group/Individual	Testing time	Age equivalents	Grade equivalents	Percentile ranks	Standard scores	Other	Examiner qualifications	Third Party	Listen	Read print	Look at stimuli	Other	Speak, minor	Speak, major	Manipulate objects	Mark answer sheet	Point	Draw	Write print	Other
GOLDMAN-FRISTOE TEST OF ARTICULATION (1972)																																	
Sounds-in-Words	2243	F	B	B	F	F	F	F	B	B	F	2-0/16-11 yrs.	I	7			•			ST		•		•		•							
Sounds-in-Sentences	2243	F	F	F	F	F	F	F	B	B	F	2-0/16-11 yrs.	I	7					•¹	ST		•	•			•							
Stimulability	2243	F	B	A	F	F	F	F	F	F	F	2-0/16-11 yrs.	I	7			•			ST		•		•		•							

¹Error classification

GOLDMAN-FRISTOE TEST OF ARTICULATION (1986)																																	
Sounds-in-Words	2243	F	B	F	F	A	F	F	F	F	F	6-0/16-11 yrs.	I	15			•			ST		•		•		•	•						
Sounds-in-Sentences	2243	F	F	F	F	A	F	F	F	F	F	6-0/16-11 yrs.	I	15					•¹	ST		•	•			•							
Stimulability	2243	F	B	F	F	A	F	F	F	F	F	6-0/16-11 yrs.	I	15			•			ST		•		•		•	•						

¹Raw scores only

GOLDMAN-FRISTOE-WOODCOCK AUDITORY SKILLS TEST BATTERY (1976)																																	
Selective Attention	2231	F	B	B	F	B	F	F	F	F	F	3-0/80-11 yrs.	G	10	•		•	•		EA		•		•						•			
Diagnostic Discrimination	2241	F	B	B	F	B	F	F	F	F	F	3-0/80-11 yrs.	G	10	•		•	•		EA		•		•						•			
Recognition Memory	2242	F	B	B	F	B	F	A	F	B	F	3-0/80-11 yrs.	G	10	•		•	•		EA		•						•					
Memory for Content	2242	F	B	B	F	B	F	F	F	F	B	3-0/80-11 yrs.	G	10	•		•	•		EA		•		•						•			
Memory for Sequence	2242	F	B	B	F	B	F	A	F	B	B	3-0/80-11 yrs.	G	10	•		•	•		EA		•		•					•				
Sound Mimicry	2243	F	B	B	F	B	F	A	F	B	F	3-0/80-11 yrs.	G	10	•		•	•		EA		•						•					
Sound Recognition	2244	F	B	B	F	B	F	B	F	B	B	3-0/80-11 yrs.	G	10	•		•	•		EA		•						•					

	Taxonomy code	Overall rating	Norms: Scores	Size	Demographics	Recency	Total	Reliability: Internal consistency	Stability	Total	Val. Total	Ages/Grades for Intended Use	Group/Individual	Testing time	Age equivalents	Grade equivalents	Percentile ranks	Standard scores	Other	Examiner qualifications	Third Party	Listen	Read print	Look at stimuli	Other	Speak, minor	Speak, major	Manipulate objects	Mark answer sheet	Point	Draw	Write print	Other
GOLDMAN-FRISTOE-WOODCOCK AUDITORY SKILLS TEST BATTERY (1976) (cont.)																																
Sound Analysis	2244	F	B	B	F	B	F	B	F	B	B	3-0/80-11 yrs.	G	10	•		•	•		EA		•				•							
Sound Blending	2244	F	B	B	F	B	F	A	F	B	B	3-0/80-11 yrs.	G	10	•		•	•		EA		•				•							
Sound-Symbol Association	1330	F	B	B	F	B	F	B	F	B	F	3-0/80-11 yrs.	G	10	•		•	•		EA		•		•								•	
Reading of Symbols	1330	F	B	B	F	B	F	A	F	B	F	3-0/80-11 yrs.	G	10	•		•	•		EA		•	•			•							
Spelling of Sounds	1330	F	B	B	F	B	F	A	F	B	F	3-0/80-11 yrs.	G	10	•		•	•		EA		•				•							•
GOLDMAN-FRISTOE-WOODCOCK TEST OF AUDITORY DISCRIMINATION (1970)																																
Quiet Subtest	2241	F	A	F	F	F	F	B	B	B	B	3-8/Adult yrs.	I	22			•	•		EA		•		•						•			
Noise Subtest	2241	F	A	F	F	F	F	F	B	B	B	3-8/Adult yrs.	I	22			•	•		EA		•		•						•			
GRAY ORAL READING TEST (1967)																																
Total Passage Score	1300	F	F	F	F	F	F	A	F	B	F	gr. 1–12	I	22		•				EA		•	•	•[1]			•						

[1]Pictures provided for primary stories only

GRAY ORAL READING TESTS — REVISED (1986)																																
Oral Reading Quotient	1300	B	A	B	A	A	B	A	F	B	B	7-0/17-11 yrs.	I	22	•	•	•			EA		•	•			•							
Passage Score	1300	B	A	B	A	A	B	B	F	B	A	7-0/17-11 yrs.	I	22	•	•	•			EA		•	•			•							
Comprehension Score	1310	B	A	B	A	A	B	A	F	B	A	7-0/17-11 yrs.	I	22	•	•	•			EA		•	•			•							
HAHNEMANN ELEMENTARY SCHOOL BEHAVIOR RATING SCALE (1975)																																
Originality	2200	F	B	B	F	F	F	F	F	F	F	gr. 1–6	I	22				•[1]		EA	•		•						•				
Independent Learning	3830	F	B	B	F	F	F	F	F	F	F	gr. 1–6	I	22				•[1]		EA	•		•						•				
Involvement	3400	F	B	B	F	F	F	F	F	F	F	gr. 1–6	I	22				•[1]		EA	•		•						•				
Productive with Peers	3400	F	B	B	F	F	F	F	F	F	F	gr. 1–6	I	22				•[1]		EA	•		•						•				
Intellectual Dependency with Peers	3400	F	B	B	F	F	F	F	F	F	F	gr. 1–6	I	22				•[1]		EA	•		•						•				
Failure Anxiety	3100	F	B	B	F	F	F	F	F	F	F	gr. 1–6	I	22				•[1]		EA	•		•						•				
Unreflectiveness	3820	F	B	B	F	F	F	F	F	F	F	gr. 1–6	I	22				•[1]		EA	•		•						•				
Irrelevant Talk	3810	F	B	B	F	F	F	F	F	F	F	gr. 1–6	I	22				•[1]		EA	•		•						•				
Disruptive Social Involvement	3400	F	B	B	F	F	F	F	F	F	F	gr. 1–6	I	22				•[1]		EA	•		•						•				
Negative Feelings	3900	F	B	B	F	F	F	F	F	F	F	gr. 1–6	I	22				•[1]		EA	•		•						•				
Holding Back/Withdrawn	3400	F	B	B	F	F	F	F	F	F	F	gr. 1–6	I	22				•[1]		EA	•		•						•				
Critical-Competitive	3400	F	B	B	F	F	F	F	F	F	F	gr. 1–6	I	22				•[1]		EA	•		•						•				

[1] ± 1 Standard deviation cutoff score

	Taxonomy code	Overall rating	Norms: Scores	Size	Demographics	Recency	Total	Reliability: Internal consistency	Stability	Total	Val. Total	Ages/Grades for Intended Use	Group/Individual	Testing time	Age equivalents	Grade equivalents	Percentile ranks	Standard scores	Other	Examiner qualifications	Third Party	Listen	Read print	Look at stimuli	Other	Speak, minor	Speak, major	Manipulate objects	Mark answer sheet	Point	Draw	Write print	Other
HAHNEMANN ELEMENTARY SCHOOL BEHAVIOR RATING SCALE (1975) (cont.)																																	
Blaming	3830	F	B	B	F	F	F	F	F	F	F	gr. 1–6	I	22					•[1]	EA	•		•						•				
Approach to Teacher	3210	F	B	B	F	F	F	F	F	F	F	gr. 1–6	I	22					•[1]	EA	•		•						•				

[1] ± 1 Standard deviation cutoff score

	Taxonomy code	Overall rating	Norms: Scores	Size	Demographics	Recency	Total	Reliability: Internal consistency	Stability	Total	Val. Total	Ages/Grades for Intended Use	Group/Individual	Testing time	Age equivalents	Grade equivalents	Percentile ranks	Standard scores	Other	Examiner qualifications	Third Party	Listen	Read print	Look at stimuli	Other	Speak, minor	Speak, major	Manipulate objects	Mark answer sheet	Point	Draw	Write print	Other
HAHNEMANN HIGH SCHOOL BEHAVIOR RATING SCALE (1971)																																	
Reasoning Ability	2210	F	B	B	F	F	F	F	F	F	F	12-0/19-11 yrs.	I	7					•[1]	EA	•		•						•				
Originality	2220	F	B	B	F	F	F	F	F	F	F	12-0/19-11 yrs.	I	7					•[1]	EA	•		•						•				
Verbal Interaction	3400	F	B	B	F	F	F	F	F	F	F	12-0/19-11 yrs.	I	7					•[1]	EA	•		•						•				
Rapport with Teacher	3400	F	B	B	F	F	F	F	F	F	F	12-0/19-11 yrs.	I	7					•[1]	EA	•		•						•				
Anxious Producer	3100	F	B	B	F	F	F	F	F	F	F	12-0/19-11 yrs.	I	7					•[1]	EA	•		•						•				
General Anxiety	3100	F	B	B	F	F	F	F	F	F	F	12-0/19-11 yrs.	I	7					•[1]	EA	•		•						•				
Quiet-Withdrawn	3400	F	B	B	F	F	F	F	F	F	F	12-0/19-11 yrs.	I	7					•[1]	EA	•		•						•				
Poor Work Habits	3830	F	B	B	F	F	F	F	F	F	F	12-0/19-11 yrs.	I	7					•[1]	EA	•		•						•				
Lack of Intellectual Independence	3830	F	B	B	F	F	F	F	F	F	F	12-0/19-11 yrs.	I	7					•[1]	EA	•		•						•				
Dogmatic-Inflexible	3900	F	B	B	F	F	F	F	F	F	F	12-0/19-11 yrs.	I	7					•[1]	EA	•		•						•				
Verbal Negativism	3900	F	B	B	F	F	F	F	F	F	F	12-0/19-11 yrs.	I	7					•[1]	EA	•		•						•				
Disturbance-Restlessness	3810	F	B	B	F	F	F	F	F	F	F	12-0/19-11 yrs.	I	7					•[1]	EA	•		•						•				
Expressed Inability	3210	F	B	B	F	F	F	F	F	F	F	12-0/19-11 yrs.	I	7					•[1]	EA	•		•						•				

[1] ± 1 Standard deviation cutoff score

	Taxonomy code	Overall rating	Norms: Scores	Size	Demographics	Recency	Total	Reliability: Internal consistency	Stability	Total	Val. Total	Ages/Grades for Intended Use	Group/Individual	Testing time	Age equivalents	Grade equivalents	Percentile ranks	Standard scores	Other	Examiner qualifications	Third Party	Listen	Read print	Look at stimuli	Other	Speak, minor	Speak, major	Manipulate objects	Mark answer sheet	Point	Draw	Write print	Other
HOUSTON TEST OF LANGUAGE DEVELOPMENT — REVISED (1978)																																	
Total	2230	F	F	F	F	F	F	F	F	F	F	0-6/6-11 yrs.	I	22	•					EA	•		•			•	•	•		•	•		•[1]

[1] Multiple types of responses (e.g., smiling, cooing, following instructions)

	Taxonomy code	Overall rating	Norms: Scores	Size	Demographics	Recency	Total	Reliability: Internal consistency	Stability	Total	Val. Total	Ages/Grades for Intended Use	Group/Individual	Testing time	Age equivalents	Grade equivalents	Percentile ranks	Standard scores	Other	Examiner qualifications	Third Party	Listen	Read print	Look at stimuli	Other	Speak, minor	Speak, major	Manipulate objects	Mark answer sheet	Point	Draw	Write print	Other
HUMAN FIGURES DRAWING TEST (1986)																																	
Total Score	2110	B	A	A	B	A	B	B	B	B	B	5-0/10-11 yrs.	G	7			•	•		EA	•										•		

	Taxonomy code	Overall rating	Norms: Scores	Size	Demographics	Recency	Total	Reliability: Internal consistency	Stability	Total	Val. Total	Ages/Grades for Intended Use	Group/Individual	Testing time	Age equivalents	Grade equivalents	Percentile ranks	Standard scores	Other	Examiner qualifications	Third Party	Listen	Read print	Look at stimuli	Other	Speak, minor	Speak, major	Manipulate objects	Mark answer sheet	Point	Draw	Write print	Other
ILLINOIS TEST OF PSYCHOLINGUISTIC ABILITIES (1968)																																	
Composite	2000	F	A	B	B	F	F	A	B	B	B	2-4/10-3 yrs.	I	60+	•			•		ST	•		•			•	•	•		•			•[1]
Auditory Reception	2231	F	A	B	B	F	F	A	F	B	F	2-4/10-3 yrs.	I	7	•			•		ST	•					•							
Visual Reception	2110	F	A	B	B	F	F	A	F	B	F	2-4/10-3 yrs.	I	7	•			•		ST	•			•						•			
Auditory Association	2210	F	A	B	B	F	F	A	F	B	F	2-4/10-3 yrs.	I	7	•			•		ST	•					•							

[1] Gesture

	Taxonomy code	Overall rating	Technical Characteristics — Norms: Scores	Size	Demographics	Recency	Total	Reliability: Internal consistency	Stability	Total	Val.: Total	Ages/Grades for Intended Use	Admin.: Group/Individual	Testing time	Scores: Age equivalents	Grade equivalents	Percentile ranks	Standard scores	Other	Examiner qualifications	Input: Third Party	Listen	Read print	Look at stimuli	Other	Output: Speak, minor	Speak, major	Manipulate objects	Mark answer sheet	Point	Draw	Write print	Other
ILLINOIS TEST OF PSYCHOLINGUISTIC ABILITIES (1968) (cont.)																																	
Visual Association	2110	F	A	B	B	F	F	B	F	B	F	2-4/10-3 yrs.	I	7	•			•		ST	•			•							•		
Verbal Expression	2231	F	A	B	B	F	F	B	F	B	F	2-4/10-3 yrs.	I	7	•			•		ST	•			•			•						
Manual Expression	2110	F	A	B	B	F	F	B	F	B	F	2-4/10-3 yrs.	I	7	•			•		ST	•			•									•1
Grammatic Closure	2232	F	A	B	B	F	F	B	F	B	F	2-4/10-3 yrs.	I	7	•			•		ST	•			•		•							
Auditory Closure	2244	F	A	B	B	F	F	F	F	F	F	2-4/10-3 yrs.	I	7	•			•		ST	•					•							
Sound Blending	2244	F	A	B	B	F	F	B	F	B	F	2-4/10-3 yrs.	I	7	•			•		ST	•			•		•							
Visual Closure	2131	F	A	B	B	F	F	F	F	F	F	2-4/10-3 yrs.	I	7	•			•		ST	•			•							•		
Auditory Sequential Memory	2242	F	A	B	B	F	F	B	B	B	F	2-4/10-3 yrs.	I	7	•			•		ST	•							•					
Visual Sequential Memory	2133	F	A	B	B	F	F	B	F	B	F	2-4/10-3 yrs.	I	7	•			•		ST	•			•				•					

1Gesture

	Taxonomy code	Overall rating	Scores	Size	Demographics	Recency	Total	Internal consistency	Stability	Total	Total	Ages/Grades	Group/Individual	Testing time	Age equivalents	Grade equivalents	Percentile ranks	Standard scores	Other	Examiner qualifications	Third Party	Listen	Read print	Look at stimuli	Other	Speak, minor	Speak, major	Manipulate objects	Mark answer sheet	Point	Draw	Write print	Other
INDEX OF PERSONALITY CHARACTERISTICS (1988)																																	
Total Test	3000	B	A	A	A	A	A	B	B	B	A	8-0/17-11 yrs.	G	45			•	•		EA	•	•							•				
Academic Scale	3000	B	A	A	A	A	A	B	B	B	A	8-0/17-11 yrs.	G	45			•	•		EA	•	•							•				
Nonacademic Scale	3000	B	A	A	A	A	A	B	B	B	A	8-0/17-11 yrs.	G	45			•	•		EA	•	•							•				
Perception of Self Scale	3700	B	A	A	A	A	A	B	B	B	A	8-0/17-11 yrs.	G	45			•	•		EA	•	•							•				
Perception of Others Scale	3400	B	A	A	A	A	A	B	B	B	A	8-0/17-11 yrs.	G	45			•	•		EA	•	•							•				
Acting In Scale	3000	B	A	A	A	A	A	B	B	B	A	8-0/17-11 yrs.	G	45			•	•		EA	•	•							•				
Acting Out Scale	3500	B	A	A	A	A	A	B	B	B	A	8-0/17-11 yrs.	G	45			•	•		EA	•	•							•				
Internal Locus of Control Scale	3830	B	A	A	A	A	A	B	B	B	A	8-0/17-11 yrs.	G	45			•	•		EA	•	•							•				
External Locus of Control Scale	3830	B	A	A	A	A	A	B	B	B	A	8-0/17-11 yrs.	G	45			•	•		EA	•	•							•				

	Taxonomy code	Overall rating	Scores	Size	Demographics	Recency	Total	Internal consistency	Stability	Total	Total	Ages/Grades	Group/Individual	Testing time	Age equivalents	Grade equivalents	Percentile ranks	Standard scores	Other	Examiner qualifications	Third Party	Listen	Read print	Look at stimuli	Other	Speak, minor	Speak, major	Manipulate objects	Mark answer sheet	Point	Draw	Write print	Other
INVENTORY FOR CLIENT & AGENCY PLANNING (1986)																																	
Broad Independence	4000	B	A	B	B	A	B	B	A	B	A	0-1/40+ yrs.	I	30	•		•	•	•1	EA	•		•						•				
Motor Skills	2100	F	A	B	B	A	B	F	F	F	A	0-1/40+ yrs.	I	5	•		•	•	•1	EA	•		•						•				
Social & Communication Skills	3400	F	A	B	B	A	B	F	F	F	A	0-1/40+ yrs.	I	5	•		•	•	•1	EA	•		•						•				
Personal Living Skills	1900	B	A	B	B	A	B	F	B	B	A	0-1/40+ yrs.	I	5	•		•	•	•1	EA	•		•						•				
Community Living Skills	1930	B	A	B	B	A	B	F	B	B	A	0-1/40+ yrs.	I	5	•		•	•	•1	EA	•		•						•				

1Instructional range provided

| | | | Technical Characteristics | | | | | | | | | Nontechnical Characteristics | | | | | | | | | | | | | | | | | | | | | | |
| | | | Norms | | | | | Reliability | | | Val. | | Admin. | | Scores | | | | | | Test Formats (Input) | | | | | Test Formats (Output) | | | | | | | |
	Taxonomy code	Overall rating	Scores	Size	Demographics	Recency	Total	Internal consistency	Stability	Total	Total	Ages/Grades for Intended Use	Group/Individual	Testing time	Age equivalents	Grade equivalents	Percentile ranks	Standard scores	Other	Examiner qualifications	Third Party	Listen	Read print	Look at stimuli	Other	Speak, minor	Speak, major	Manipulate objects	Mark answer sheet	Point	Draw	Write print	Other
JORDAN LEFT-RIGHT REVERSAL TEST (1980)																																	
Level I Total	2131	F	B	F	F	B	F	F	B	B	F	5-0/12-11 yrs.	G	22	•		•			EA		•	•								•		
Level II Total	2131	F	B	F	F	B	F	F	A	B	F	9-0/12-11 yrs.	G	22	•		•			EA		•	•								•		
JORDAN LEFT-RIGHT REVERSAL TEST, 1990 EDITION (1990)																																	
Level I Total	2131	F	B	B	F	A	F	F	A	B	F	5-0/12-11 yrs.	G	20	•		•			EA			•						•				
Level II Total	1310	F	B	B	F	A	F	F	A	B	F	9-0/12-11 yrs.	G	20	•		•			EA			•						•				
KAUFMAN ASSESSMENT BATTERY FOR CHILDREN (1983)																																	
Mental Processing	2000	B	A	A	A	B	B	A	B	B	A	2-0/12-5 yrs.	I	45			•	•		R		•		•		•	•	•		•			•1
Sequential Processing	2000	B	A	A	A	B	B	B	B	B	A	2-0/12-5 yrs.	I	45			•	•		R		•		•			•			•			•1
Simultaneous Processing	2000	B	A	A	A	B	B	B	B	B	A	2-0/12-5 yrs.	I	22			•	•		R		•		•			•			•			
Nonverbal Scale	2100	B	A	A	A	B	B	A	B	B	A	4-0/12-5 yrs.	I	45			•	•		R		•		•				•		•			•1
Achievement Scale	4000	B	A	A	A	B	B	A	A	A	A	2-0/12-5 yrs.	I	45			•	•		R		•	•	•		•							•2
Hand Movements	2133	F	A	A	A	B	B	F	F	F	A	2-0/12-5 yrs.	I	7	•		•	•		R		•		•									•1
Number Recall	2242	B	A	A	A	B	B	B	B	B	A	2-0/12-5 yrs.	I	7	•		•	•		R		•						•					
Word Order	2242	B	A	A	A	B	B	B	F	B	A	4-0/12-5 yrs.	I	7	•		•	•		R		•								•			
Magic Window	2131	F	A	A	A	B	B	F	F	F	A	2-6/4-11 yrs.	I	7	•		•	•		R		•		•		•							
Face Recognition	2133	F	A	A	A	B	B	F	F	F	A	2-6/4-11 yrs.	I	7	•		•	•		R		•		•						•			
Gestalt Closure	2000	B	A	A	A	B	B	F	B	B	A	2-0/12-5 yrs.	I	7	•		•	•		R		•		•		•							
Triangles	2132	B	A	A	A	B	B	B	F	B	A	4-0/12-5 yrs.	I	7	•		•	•		R		•		•				•					
Matrix Analogies	2110	B	A	A	A	B	B	B	F	B	A	5-0/12-5 yrs.	I	7	•		•	•		R		•		•						•			
Spatial Memory	2133	B	A	A	A	B	B	B	F	B	A	5-0/12-5 yrs.	I	7	•		•	•		R		•		•						•			
Photo Series	2110	B	A	A	A	B	B	B	B	B	A	6-0/12-5 yrs.	I	7	•		•	•		R		•		•				•					
Expressive Vocabulary	2231	B	A	A	A	B	B	B	B	B	A	2-6/4-11 yrs.	I	7	•		•	•		R		•		•		•							
Faces and Places	1100	B	A	A	A	B	B	B	A	B	A	2-0/12-5 yrs.	I	7	•		•	•		R		•		•		•							
Arithmetic	1200	B	A	A	A	B	B	B	B	B	A	3-0/12-5 yrs.	I	7	•		•	•		R		•		•		•							
Riddles	2231	B	A	A	A	B	B	B	B	B	A	3-0/12-5 yrs.	I	7	•		•	•		R		•				•							
Reading/Decoding	1320	A	A	A	A	B	B	A	A	A	A	5-0/12-5 yrs.	I	7	•	•	•	•		R		•	•			•							
Reading/Understanding	1310	A	A	A	A	B	B	A	A	A	A	7-0/12-5 yrs.	I	7	•	•	•	•		R		•	•										•2

¹Gesture; ²gestures and physical responses

	Taxonomy code	Overall rating	Scores	Size	Demographics	Recency	Total	Internal consistency	Stability	Total	Total (Val.)	Ages/Grades for Intended Use	Group/Individual	Testing time	Age equivalents	Grade equivalents	Percentile ranks	Standard scores	Other	Examiner qualifications	Third Party	Listen	Read print	Look at stimuli	Other	Speak, minor	Speak, major	Manipulate objects	Mark answer sheet	Point	Draw	Write print	Other
KAUFMAN BRIEF INTELLIGENCE TEST (1990)																																	
Total	2000	**B**	A	B	B	A	B	A	A	A	B	4-0/90-11 yrs.	I	20			•	•		EA		•		•		•	•			•			
Vocabulary	2231	**B**	A	B	B	A	B	A	A	A	A	4-0/90-11 yrs.	I	10			•	•		EA		•		•		•	•						
Matrices	2110	**B**	A	B	B	A	B	B	B	B	A	4-0/90-11 yrs.	I	10			•	•		EA		•		•						•			
KAUFMAN TEST OF EDUCATIONAL ACHIEVEMENT — BRIEF FORM (1985)																																	
Battery Composite	1000	**F**	A	F	A	B	F	A	A	A	A	gr. 1–12	I	22	•	•	•	•		EA		•	•	•		•						•	•[1]
Mathematics	1200	**F**	A	F	A	B	F	B	B	B	A	gr. 1–12	I	7	•	•	•	•		EA		•	•	•		•						•	
Reading	1300	**F**	A	F	A	B	F	B	B	B	A	gr. 1–12	I	7	•	•	•	•		EA		•	•			•	•						•[1]
Spelling	1630	**F**	A	F	A	B	F	B	B	B	B	gr. 1–12	I	7	•	•	•	•		EA		•										•	•[2]

¹Physical response; ²can respond orally if unable to write

	Taxonomy code	Overall rating	Scores	Size	Demographics	Recency	Total	Internal consistency	Stability	Total	Total (Val.)	Ages/Grades for Intended Use	Group/Individual	Testing time	Age equivalents	Grade equivalents	Percentile ranks	Standard scores	Other	Examiner qualifications	Third Party	Listen	Read print	Look at stimuli	Other	Speak, minor	Speak, major	Manipulate objects	Mark answer sheet	Point	Draw	Write print	Other
KAUFMAN TEST OF EDUCATIONAL ACHIEVEMENT — COMPREHENSIVE FORM (1985)																																	
Battery Composite	1000	**B**	A	B/A¹	A	B	B	A	A	A	A	gr. 1-12	I	60+	•	•	•	•		EA		•	•	•		•	•					•	•[2]
Mathematics Composite	1200	**B**	A	B/A¹	A	B	B	A	B	B	A	gr. 1-12	I	22	•	•	•	•		EA		•	•	•		•						•	
Reading Composite	1300	**B**	A	B/A¹	A	B	B	A	B	B	A	gr. 1–12	I	22	•	•	•	•		EA		•	•	•		•	•						•[2]
Mathematics Applications	1210	**B**	A	B/A¹	A	B	B	A	A	A	A	gr. 1-12	I	7	•	•	•	•		EA		•	•	•		•							
Reading Decoding	1320	**B**	A	B/A¹	A	B	B	A	A	A	A	gr. 1-12	I	7	•	•	•	•		EA		•	•			•							
Spelling	1630	**B**	A	B/A¹	A	B	B	A	B	B	A	gr. 1-12	I	7	•	•	•	•		EA		•										•	
Reading Comprehension	1310	**B**	A	B/A¹	A	B	B	A	A	A	A	gr. 1–12	I	7	•	•	•	•		EA		•	•							•			•[2]
Mathematics Computation	1220	**B**	A	B/A¹	A	B	B	A	B	B	A	gr. 1–12	I	7	•	•	•	•		EA		•	•									•	

¹Fall norms appear first; Spring norms follow; ²physical responses

	Taxonomy code	Overall rating	Scores	Size	Demographics	Recency	Total	Internal consistency	Stability	Total	Total (Val.)	Ages/Grades for Intended Use	Group/Individual	Testing time	Age equivalents	Grade equivalents	Percentile ranks	Standard scores	Other	Examiner qualifications	Third Party	Listen	Read print	Look at stimuli	Other	Speak, minor	Speak, major	Manipulate objects	Mark answer sheet	Point	Draw	Write print	Other
KEYMATH DIAGNOSTIC ARITHMETIC TEST (1971)																																	
Total	1200	**F**	F	B	F	F	F	A	A	A	F	gr. K–8	I	45	•					EA		•	•	•		•	•			•		•	
Numeration	1210	**F**	F	B	F	F	F	F	F	F	F	gr. K–8	I	7	•					EA		•	•	•		•	•					•	
Fractions	1210	**F**	F	B	F	F	F	F	F	F	F	gr. K–8	I	7	•					EA		•	•	•		•	•						
Geometry and Symbols	1210	**F**	F	B	F	F	F	F	F	F	F	gr. K–8	I	7	•					EA		•	•	•		•				•			
Addition	1220	**F**	F	B	F	F	F	F	F	F	F	gr. K–8	I	7	•					EA		•	•	•		•						•	
Subtraction	1220	**F**	F	B	F	F	F	F	F	F	F	gr. K–8	I	7	•					EA		•	•	•		•						•	
Multiplication	1220	**F**	F	B	F	F	F	F	F	F	F	gr. K–8	I	7	•					EA		•	•			•						•	
Division	1220	**F**	F	B	F	F	F	F	F	F	F	gr. K–8	I	7	•					EA		•	•	•		•						•	
Mental Computation	1220	**F**	F	B	F	F	F	B	F	B	F	gr. K–8	I	7	•					EA		•				•							

			Technical Characteristics									Nontechnical Characteristics																					
			Norms					Reliability			Val.		Admin.		Scores						Test Formats											
																					Input					Output							
Test / Subtest	Taxonomy code	Overall rating	Scores	Size	Demographics	Recency	Total	Internal consistency	Stability	Total	Total	Ages/Grades for Intended Use	Group/Individual	Testing time	Age equivalents	Grade equivalents	Percentile ranks	Standard scores	Other	Examiner qualifications	Third Party	Listen	Read print	Look at stimuli	Other	Speak, minor	Speak, major	Manipulate objects	Mark answer sheet	Point	Draw	Write print	Other
KEYMATH DIAGNOSTIC ARITHMETIC TEST (1971) (cont.)																																	
Numerical Reasoning	1220	F	F	B	F	F	F	F	F	F	F	gr. K–8	I	7		•				EA		•		•		•							
Word Problems	1210	F	F	B	F	F	F	F	F	F	F	gr. K–8	I	7		•				EA		•	•	•		•							
Missing Problems	1210	F	F	B	F	F	F	F	F	F	F	gr. K–8	I	7		•				EA		•	•	•				•					
Money	1210	F	F	B	F	F	F	F	F	F	F	gr. K–8	I	7		•				EA		•	•	•		•	•			•			
Measurement	1210	F	F	B	F	F	F	B	F	B	F	gr. K–8	I	7		•				EA		•	•	•		•	•						
Time	1210	F	F	B	F	F	F	F	F	F	F	gr. K–8	I	7		•				EA		•	•	•		•	•						
KEYMATH — REVISED (1988)																																	
Total Test	1200	B	A	A	A	A	A	A	B	B	B	5-0/13-11 yrs.	I	45	•	•	•	•		EA		•	•	•		•				•		•	
Basic Concepts Area	1210	B	A	A	A	A	A	A	F	B	B	5-0/13-11 yrs.	I	22	•	•	•	•		EA		•	•	•		•				•		•	
Operations Area	1220	B	A	A	A	A	A	B	B	B	B	5-0/13-11 yrs.	I	45	•	•	•	•		EA		•	•	•		•						•	
Applications Area	1210	B	A	A	A	A	A	B	B	B	B	5-0/13-11 yrs.	I	45	•	•	•	•		EA		•	•	•		•	•			•			
Numeration	1210	B	A	A	A	A	A	B	F	B	B	5-0/13-11 yrs.	I	7			•	•		EA		•	•	•		•						•	
Rational Numbers	1210	B	A	A	A	A	A	B	F	B	B	5-0/13-11 yrs.	I	7			•	•		EA		•	•	•		•							
Geometry	1210	B	A	A	A	A	A	B	F	B	B	5-0/13-11 yrs.	I	7			•	•		EA		•	•	•		•					•		
Addition	1220	F	A	A	A	A	A	F	F	F	B	5-0/13-11 yrs.	I	7			•	•		EA		•	•	•		•						•	
Subtraction	1220	B	A	A	A	A	A	B	F	B	B	5-0/13-11 yrs.	I	7			•	•		EA		•	•	•		•						•	
Multiplication	1220	F	A	A	A	A	A	F	F	F	B	5-0/13-11 yrs.	I	7			•	•		EA		•	•	•		•						•	
Division	1220	B	A	A	A	A	A	B	F	B	B	5-0/13-11 yrs.	I	7			•	•		EA		•	•	•		•						•	
Mental Computation	1220	B	A	A	A	A	A	B	F	B	B	5-0/13-11 yrs.	I	7			•	•		EA		•				•							
Measurement	1210	B	A	A	A	A	A	B	F	B	B	5-0/13-11 yrs.	I	7			•	•		EA		•	•	•		•	•						
Time and Money	1210	B	A	A	A	A	A	B	F	B	B	5-0/13-11 yrs.	I	7			•	•		EA		•	•	•		•	•			•			
Estimation	1210	F	A	A	A	A	A	F	F	F	B	5-0/13-11 yrs.	I	7			•	•		EA		•	•	•		•	•						
Interpreting Data	1210	B	A	A	A	A	A	B	F	B	B	5-0/13-11 yrs.	I	7			•	•		EA		•	•	•		•	•						
Problem Solving	1210	B	A	A	A	A	A	B	F	B	B	5-0/13-11 yrs.	I	7			•	•		EA		•	•	•		•	•						
KINDERGARTEN LANGUAGE SCREENING TEST (1983)																																	
Total	2230	F	B	F	F	B	F	F	B	B	B	4-0/6-11 yrs.	I	7	•		•			EA		•		•		•	•	•		•			
KINDERGARTEN READINESS TEST (1988)																																	
Total	4000	F	F	B	F	B	F	F	F	F	F	4-0/6-11 yrs.	I	20					•¹	EA		•	•	•						•		•	•

¹Cutoff scores provided

Taxonomy code	Overall rating	Norms: Scores	Norms: Size	Norms: Demographics	Norms: Recency	Norms: Total	Reliability: Internal consistency	Reliability: Stability	Reliability: Total	Val: Total	Ages/Grades for Intended Use	Group/Individual	Testing time	Scores: Age equivalents	Scores: Grade equivalents	Scores: Percentile ranks	Scores: Standard scores	Scores: Other	Examiner qualifications	Input: Third Party	Input: Listen	Input: Read print	Input: Look at stimuli	Input: Other	Output: Speak, minor	Output: Speak, major	Output: Manipulate objects	Output: Mark answer sheet	Output: Point	Output: Draw	Output: Write print	Output: Other
KOHN PROBLEM CHECKLIST/KOHN SOCIAL COMPETENCE SCALE (1988)																																
KPC Apathy-Withdrawal — 3400	F	A	F	F	A	F	F	F	F	B	3-0/6-11 yrs.	I	10				•		EA		•							•				
KPC Anger-Defiance — 3500	F	A	F	F	A	F	F	F	F	B	3-0/6-11 yrs.	I	10				•		EA		•							•				
KSC Apathy-Withdrawal — 3400	F	A	F	F	A	F	F	F	F	B	3-0/6-11 yrs.	I	10				•		EA		•							•				
KSC Anger-Defiance — 3500	F	A	F	F	A	F	F	F	F	B	3-0/6-11 yrs.	I	10				•		EA		•							•				
LANGUAGE PROCESSING TEST (1985)																																
Total — 2200	F	A	B	F	B	F	A	F	B	F	5-0/11-11 yrs.	I	30	•		•	•		EA		•				•	•						
Associations — 2210	F	A	B	F	B	F	F	F	F	B	5-0/11-11 yrs.	I	5	•		•	•		EA		•				•							
Categorization — 2210	F	A	B	F	B	F	F	F	F	B	5-0/11-11 yrs.	I	5	•		•	•		EA		•						•					
Similarities — 2210	F	A	B	F	B	F	B	B	B	B	5-0/11-11 yrs.	I	5	•		•	•		EA		•						•					
Differences — 2210	F	A	B	F	B	F	B	B	B	B	5-0/11-11 yrs.	I	5	•		•	•		EA		•						•					
Multiple Meanings — 2231	F	A	B	F	B	F	B	B	B	B	5-0/11-11 yrs.	I	5	•		•	•		EA		•						•					
Attributes — 2231	F	A	B	F	B	F	A	B	B	F	5-0/11-11 yrs.	I	5	•		•	•		EA		•						•					
THE LEARNING DISABILITY EVALUATION SCALE (1983)																																
Learning Quotient — 4000	F	A	B	B	B	B	F	F	F	F	4-6/19-0 yrs.	I	20				•		EA	•		•						•				
Listening — 2230	F	A	B	B	B	B	F	F	F	B	4-6/19-0 yrs.	I	20				•		EA	•		•						•				
Thinking — 1100	F	A	B	B	B	B	F	F	F	B	4-6/19-0 yrs.	I	20				•		EA	•		•						•				
Speaking — 2230	F	A	B	B	B	B	F	F	F	B	4-6/19-0 yrs.	I	20				•		EA	•		•						•				
Reading — 1300	F	A	B	B	B	B	F	F	F	B	4-6/19-0 yrs.	I	20				•		EA	•		•						•				
Writing — 1600	F	A	B	B	B	B	F	F	F	F	4-6/19-0 yrs.	I	20				•		EA	•		•						•				
Spelling — 1630	F	A	B	B	B	B	F	F	F	B	4-6/19-0 yrs.	I	20				•		EA	•		•						•				
Mathematical Calculations — 1220	F	A	B	B	B	B	F	F	F	B	4-6/19-0 yrs.	I	20				•		EA	•		•						•				
LEARNING DISABILITY RATING PROCEDURE (1981)																																
Total — 4000	F	B	F	F	B	F	F	F	F	F	gr. 1–12	I	7					•¹	EA	•		•						•				

¹Cutoff scores based on means and standard deviations

Taxonomy code	Overall rating	Norms: Scores	Norms: Size	Norms: Demographics	Norms: Recency	Norms: Total	Reliability: Internal consistency	Reliability: Stability	Reliability: Total	Val: Total	Ages/Grades for Intended Use	Group/Individual	Testing time	Scores: Age equivalents	Scores: Grade equivalents	Scores: Percentile ranks	Scores: Standard scores	Scores: Other	Examiner qualifications	Input: Third Party	Input: Listen	Input: Read print	Input: Look at stimuli	Input: Other	Output: Speak, minor	Output: Speak, major	Output: Manipulate objects	Output: Mark answer sheet	Output: Point	Output: Draw	Output: Write print	Output: Other
LEARNING EFFICIENCY TEST (1981)																																
Visual Memory Ordered Immediate Recall — 2133	F	A	F	F	B	F	F	B	B	F	6-0/17-11 yrs.	I	7			•	•		EA	•		•						•				
Visual Memory Ordered Short Term Recall — 2133	F	A	F	F	B	F	F	B	B	F	6-0/17-11 yrs.	I	7			•	•		EA	•		•						•				
Visual Memory Ordered Long Term Recall — 2133	F	A	F	F	B	F	F	B	B	F	6-0/17-11 yrs.	I	7			•	•		EA	•		•						•				
Visual Memory Unordered Immediate Recall — 2133	F	A	F	F	B	F	F	B	B	F	6-0/17-11 yrs.	I	7			•	•		EA	•		•						•				

		Technical Characteristics										Nontechnical Characteristics																					
		Norms					Reliability			Val.		Admin.		Scores						Test Formats — Input					Test Formats — Output							
Taxonomy code	Overall rating	Scores	Size	Demographics	Recency	Total	Internal consistency	Stability	Total	Total	Ages/Grades for Intended Use	Group/Individual	Testing time	Age equivalents	Grade equivalents	Percentile ranks	Standard scores	Other	Examiner qualifications	Third Party	Listen	Read print	Look at stimuli	Other	Speak, minor	Speak, major	Manipulate objects	Mark answer sheet	Point	Draw	Write print	Other

LEARNING EFFICIENCY TEST (1981) (cont.)

Test	Taxonomy code	Overall rating	Scores	Size	Demographics	Recency	Total	Internal consistency	Stability	Total	Val. Total	Ages/Grades	Group/Ind.	Testing time	Age eq.	Grade eq.	Percentile ranks	Standard scores	Other	Examiner qual.	Third Party	Listen	Read print	Look at stimuli	Other	Speak, minor	Speak, major	Manipulate objects	Mark answer sheet	Point	Draw	Write print	Other
Visual Memory Unordered Short Term Recall	2133	F	A	F	F	B	F	F	B	B	F	6-0/17-11 yrs.	I	7			•	•		EA		•	•							•			
Visual Memory Unordered Long Term Recall	2133	F	A	F	F	B	F	F	B	B	F	6-0/17-11 yrs.	I	7			•	•		EA		•	•							•			
Auditory Memory Ordered Immediate Recall	2242	F	A	F	F	B	F	F	B	B	F	6-0/17-11 yrs.	I	7			•	•		EA		•								•			
Auditory Memory Ordered Short Term Recall	2242	F	A	F	F	B	F	F	B	B	F	6-0/17-11 yrs.	I	7			•	•		EA		•								•			
Auditory Memory Ordered Long Term Recall	2242	F	A	F	F	B	F	F	B	B	F	6-0/17-11 yrs.	I	7			•	•		EA		•								•			
Auditory Memory Unordered Immediate Recall	2242	F	A	F	F	B	F	F	B	B	F	6-0/17-11 yrs.	I	7			•	•		EA		•								•			
Auditory Memory Unordered Short Term Recall	2242	F	A	F	F	B	F	F	B	B	F	6-0/17-11 yrs.	I	7			•	•		EA		•								•			
Auditory Memory Unordered Long Term Recall	2242	F	A	F	F	B	F	F	B	B	F	6-0/17-11 yrs.	I	7			•	•		EA		•								•			

THE LEITER INTERNATIONAL PERFORMANCE SCALE HANDBOOK (1982)

Test	Taxonomy code	Overall rating	Scores	Size	Demographics	Recency	Total	Internal consistency	Stability	Total	Val. Total	Ages/Grades	Group/Ind.	Testing time	Age eq.	Grade eq.	Percentile ranks	Standard scores	Other	Examiner qual.	Third Party	Listen	Read print	Look at stimuli	Other	Speak, minor	Speak, major	Manipulate objects	Mark answer sheet	Point	Draw	Write print	Other
Total	2100	F	F	F	F	F	F	F	B	B	B	2-0/13-0 yrs.	I	60+	•				•[1]	EA		•		•				•					

[1]Ratio IQ

LINDAMOOD AUDITORY CONCEPTUALIZATION TEST (1971)

Test	Taxonomy code	Overall rating	Scores	Size	Demographics	Recency	Total	Internal consistency	Stability	Total	Val. Total	Ages/Grades	Group/Ind.	Testing time	Age eq.	Grade eq.	Percentile ranks	Standard scores	Other	Examiner qual.	Third Party	Listen	Read print	Look at stimuli	Other	Speak, minor	Speak, major	Manipulate objects	Mark answer sheet	Point	Draw	Write print	Other
Total	2241	F	F	F	F	F	F	F	F	F	F	3-0/Adult yrs.	I	45					•[1]	EA		•		•		•		•					

[1]Recommended minimum scores

LURIA-NEBRASKA NEUROPSYCHOLOGICAL BATTERY: CHILDREN'S REVISION (1987)

Test	Taxonomy code	Overall rating	Scores	Size	Demographics	Recency	Total	Internal consistency	Stability	Total	Val. Total	Ages/Grades	Group/Ind.	Testing time	Age eq.	Grade eq.	Percentile ranks	Standard scores	Other	Examiner qual.	Third Party	Listen	Read print	Look at stimuli	Other	Speak, minor	Speak, major	Manipulate objects	Mark answer sheet	Point	Draw	Write print	Other
C1	2140	F	A	F	F	B	F	F	F	F	F	8-0/12-11 yrs.	I	60+				•		ST		•		•							•		•[1]
C2	2120	F	A	F	F	B	F	F	F	F	F	8-0/12-11 yrs.	I	60+				•		ST		•						•					•[1,2]
C3	2140	F	A	F	F	B	F	F	F	F	B	8-0/12-11 yrs.	I	60+				•		ST		•		•									•[1]
C4	2131	F	A	F	F	B	F	F	F	F	B	8-0/12-11 yrs.	I	60+				•		ST		•						•					
C5	2230	F	A	F	F	B	F	F	F	F	B	8-0/12-11 yrs.	I	60+				•		ST		•						•				•	
C6	2230	F	A	F	F	B	F	F	F	F	B	8-0/12-11 yrs.	I	60+				•		ST		•						•					
C7	1600	F	A	F	F	B	F	F	F	F	B	8-0/12-11 yrs.	I	60+				•		ST		•		•								•	
C8	1320	F	A	F	F	B	F	F	F	F	B	8-0/12-11 yrs.	I	60+				•		ST		•	•			•	•						
C9	1200	F	A	F	F	B	F	F	F	F	B	8-0/12-11 yrs.	I	60+				•		ST		•	•			•						•	
C10	1300	F	A	F	F	B	F	F	F	F	B	8-0/12-11 yrs.	I	60+				•		ST		•		•						•			
C11	4000	F	A	F	F	B	F	F	F	F	B	8-0/12-11 yrs.	I	60+				•		ST		•		•		•	•						
O1	1630	F	A	F	F	B	F	F	F	F	F	8-0/12-11 yrs.	I	60+				•		ST		•		•								•	
O2	1640	F	A	F	F	B	F	F	F	F	F	8-0/12-11 yrs.	I	60+				•		ST		•		•								•	

[1]Various motor responses; [2]singing

	Taxonomy code	Overall rating	Norms Scores	Size	Demographics	Recency	Total	Reliability Internal consistency	Stability	Total	Val. Total	Ages/Grades for Intended Use	Group/Individual	Testing time	Age equivalents	Grade equivalents	Percentile ranks	Standard scores	Other	Examiner qualifications	Third Party	Listen	Read print	Look at stimuli	Other	Speak, minor	Speak, major	Manipulate objects	Mark answer sheet	Point	Draw	Write print	Other
LURIA-NEBRASKA NEUROPSYCHOLOGICAL BATTERY: CHILDREN'S REVISION (1987) (cont.)																																	
S1	2100	F	A	F	F	B	F	F	F	F	F	8-0/12-11 yrs.	I	60+				•		ST		•		•	•	•						•		•[1]
S2	2100	F	A	F	F	B	F	F	F	F	F	8-0/12-11 yrs.	I	60+				•		ST		•		•	•	•						•		•[1]
S3	2100	F	A	F	F	B	F	F	F	F	F	8-0/12-11 yrs.	I	60+				•		ST		•		•	•	•								•[1]
F1	4000	F	A	F	F	B	F	F	F	F	F	8-0/12-11 yrs.	I	60+				•		ST		•	•	•			•	•			•	•	
F2	2140	F	A	F	F	B	F	F	F	F	F	8-0/12-11 yrs.	I	60+				•		ST		•	•	•			•	•			•	•	•[1]
F3	2153	F	A	F	F	B	F	F	F	F	F	8-0/12-11 yrs.	I	60+				•		ST		•		•								•		•[1]
F4	2132	F	A	F	F	B	F	F	F	F	F	8-0/12-11 yrs.	I	60+				•		ST		•		•								•		•[1]
F5	2132	F	A	F	F	B	F	F	F	F	F	8-0/12-11 yrs.	I	60+				•		ST		•		•								•		•[1]
F6	2120	F	A	F	F	B	F	F	F	F	F	8-0/12-11 yrs.	I	60+				•		ST		•		•								•		•[1]
F7	2140	F	A	F	F	B	F	F	F	F	F	8-0/12-11 yrs.	I	60+				•		ST		•						•						•[1,2]
F8	2240	F	A	F	F	B	F	F	F	F	F	8-0/12-11 yrs.	I	60+				•		ST		•												•[1]
F9	2240	F	A	F	F	B	F	F	F	F	F	8-0/12-11 yrs.	I	60+				•		ST		•							•				•	
F10	2240	F	A	F	F	B	F	F	F	F	F	8-0/12-11 yrs.	I	60+				•		ST		•								•				
F11	2210	F	A	F	F	B	F	F	F	F	F	8-0/12-11 yrs.	I	60+				•		ST		•		•			•	•						
												[1]Various motor responses; [2]singing																						
MATRIX ANALOGIES TEST — EXPANDED FORM (1985)																																	
Total	2110	F	A	A	F	B	F	A	F	B	B	5-0/17-11 yrs.	I	48	•		•			EA		•		•						•			
Pattern Completion	2110	F	A	A	F	B	F	F	F	F	F	5-0/17-11 yrs.	I	12			•			EA		•		•						•			
Reasoning by Analogy	2110	F	A	A	F	B	F	F	F	F	F	5-0/17-11 yrs.	I	12			•			EA		•		•						•			
Serial Reasoning	2110	F	A	A	F	B	F	B	F	B	F	5-0/17-11 yrs.	I	12			•			EA		•		•						•			
Spatial Visualization	2110	F	A	A	F	B	F	B	F	B	F	5-0/17-11 yrs.	I	12			•			EA		•		•						•			
MATRIX ANALOGIES TEST — SHORT FORM (1985)																																	
Total	2110	B	A	A	B	B	B	B	F	B	B	5-0/17-11 yrs.	G	25	•		•	•		EA		•		•					•				
McCARTHY SCALES OF CHILDREN'S ABILITIES (1972)																																	
General Cognitive Index	4000	F	A	A	A	F	F	A	A	A	B	2-6/8-5 yrs.	I	45	•		•	•		EA		•		•		•	•	•		•	•		•[2]
Verbal	2200	F	A	A	A	F	F	B	B	B	B	2-6/8-5 yrs.	I	7	•		•	•		EA		•		•		•	•			•			
Perceptual-Performance	2100	F	A	A	A	F	F	B	F	B	B	2-6/8-5 yrs.	I	7	•		•	•		EA		•		•				•		•	•		
Quantitative	4000	F	A	A	A	F	F	B	B	B	B	2-6/8-5 yrs.	I	7	•		•	•		EA		•		•						•	•		
												[1]Tapping; [2]performing motor tasks																						

		Technical Characteristics									Ages/Grades for Intended Use	Nontechnical Characteristics																					
		Overall rating	Norms					Reliability			Val.		Admin.		Scores					Examiner qualifications	Test Formats												
																					Input					Output							
	Taxonomy code	Overall rating	Scores	Size	Demographics	Recency	Total	Internal consistency	Stability	Total	Total		Group/Individual	Testing time	Age equivalents	Grade equivalents	Percentile ranks	Standard scores	Other	Examiner qualifications	Third Party	Listen	Read print	Look at stimuli	Other	Speak, minor	Speak, major	Manipulate objects	Mark answer sheet	Point	Draw	Write print	Other
McCARTHY SCALES OF CHILDREN'S ABILITIES (1972) (cont.)																																	
Memory	2000	F	A	A	A	F	F	F	B	B	B	2-6/8-5 yrs.	I	7	•		•	•		EA	•			•		•	•						•1
Motor	2100	F	A	A	A	F	F	B	F	B	F	2-6/8-5 yrs.	I	7	•		•	•		EA	•			•				•				•	•2
1Tapping; 2performing motor tasks																																	
MEASUREMENT OF LANGUAGE DEVELOPMENT (1975)																																	
Receptive	2232	F	B	A	F	F	F	B	F	B	A	3-0/7-11 yrs.	I	7			•			EA	•			•						•			
Expressive	2232	F	B	A	F	F	F	B	F	B	A	3-0/7-11 yrs.	I	7			•			EA	•			•			•						
MERRILL LANGUAGE SCREENING TEST (1980)																																	
Total Score	2230	F	B	A	F	B	F	B	F	B	F	5-4/8-11 yrs.	•	10			•			EA	•							•					
MILLER ASSESSMENT FOR PRESCHOOLERS (1988)																																	
Total	2000	F	B	A	F	B	F	F	F	F	B	2-9/5-8 yrs.	I	30			•			EA	•			•		•	•	•		•			•1
Foundations	2000	F	B	A	F	B	F	F	F	F	F	2-9/5-8 yrs.	I	30			•			EA				•		•	•	•		•			
Coordination	2153	F	B	A	F	B	F	F	F	F	F	2-9/5-8 yrs.	I	30			•			EA				•		•	•	•					•1
Verbal	2200	F	B	A	F	B	F	F	F	F	F	2-9/5-8 yrs.	I	30			•			EA	•			•		•	•						
Non-verbal	2100	F	B	A	F	B	F	F	F	F	F	2-9/5-8 yrs.	I	30			•			EA				•				•					•1
Complex Tasks	2000	F	B	A	F	B	F	F	F	F	F	2-9/5-8 yrs.	I	30			•			EA	•			•		•	•	•		•			
1Variety of motor responses																																	
MILLER-YODER LANGUAGE COMPREHENSION TEST — CLINICAL EDITION (1984)																																	
Total	2232	F	F	F	F	F	F	F	F	F	F	3-0/8-11 yrs.	I	7	•					EA	•			•						•			
MINNESOTA PERCEPTO-DIAGNOSTIC TEST (1982)																																	
Total	2132	F	A	B	F	B	F	F	F	F	F	5-0/20-11 yrs.	G	7	•			•		EA	•			•							•		
MOTOR-FREE VISUAL PERCEPTION TEST (1972)																																	
Total	2130	F	A	B	F	F	F	B	B	B	B	4-0/8-11 yrs.	I	7	•			•		EA	•			•						•			
MULTISCORE DEPRESSION INVENTORY (1986)																																	
Full Scale	4000	F	A	F	F	A	F	F	F	F	B	gr. 7–Adult	G	30			•	•		EA			•						•				
Short Form	4000	F	A	F	F	A	F	F	F	F	B	gr. 7–Adult	G	30			•	•		EA			•						•				
Low Energy Level	3810	F	A	F	F	A	F	F	F	F	B	gr. 7–Adult	G	30			•	•		EA			•						•				
Cognitive Difficulty	2000	F	A	F	F	A	F	F	F	F	B	gr. 7–Adult	G	30			•	•		EA			•						•				
Guilt	3900	F	A	F	F	A	F	F	F	F	B	gr. 7–Adult	G	30			•	•		EA			•						•				
Low Self-Esteem	3700	F	A	F	F	A	F	F	F	F	B	gr. 7–Adult	G	30			•	•		EA			•						•				

	Taxonomy code	Overall rating	Scores	Size	Demographics	Recency	Total	Internal consistency	Stability	Total	Total (Val.)	Ages/Grades for Intended Use	Group/Individual	Testing time	Age equivalents	Grade equivalents	Percentile ranks	Standard scores	Other	Examiner qualifications	Third Party	Listen	Read print	Look at stimuli	Other	Speak, minor	Speak, major	Manipulate objects	Mark answer sheet	Point	Draw	Write print	Other
MULTISCORE DEPRESSION INVENTORY (1986) (cont.)																																	
Social Introversion	3400	F	A	F	F	A	F	F	F	F	B	gr. 7–Adult	G	30			•	•		EA			•						•				
Pessimism	3900	F	A	F	F	A	F	F	F	F	B	gr. 7–Adult	G	30			•	•		EA			•						•				
Irritability	3900	F	A	F	F	A	F	F	F	F	B	gr. 7–Adult	G	30			•	•		EA			•						•				
Sad Mood	3300	F	A	F	F	A	F	F	F	F	B	gr. 7–Adult	G	30			•	•		EA			•						•				
Instrumental Helplessness	3840	F	A	F	F	A	F	F	F	F	B	gr. 7–Adult	G	30			•	•		EA			•						•				
Learned Helplessness	3840	F	A	F	F	A	F	F	F	F	B	gr. 7–Adult	G	30			•	•		EA			•						•				
NONVERBAL TEST OF COGNITIVE SKILLS (1981)																																	
Cognitive Skills Index	2100	F	B	F	F	B	F	B	F	B	F	gr. K–7	I	45	•		•		•¹	EA				•²				•		•	•		•³

¹Ratio IQ; ²examiner pantomines; ³fold paper, tap cubes

	Taxonomy code	Overall rating	Scores	Size	Demographics	Recency	Total	Internal consistency	Stability	Total	Total (Val.)	Ages/Grades for Intended Use	Group/Individual	Testing time	Age equivalents	Grade equivalents	Percentile ranks	Standard scores	Other	Examiner qualifications	Third Party	Listen	Read print	Look at stimuli	Other	Speak, minor	Speak, major	Manipulate objects	Mark answer sheet	Point	Draw	Write print	Other
NORMATIVE ADAPTIVE BEHAVIOR CHECKLIST (1986)																																	
Total Test	4000	F	A	A	F	B	F	A	F	B	F	1-0/21-11 yrs.	I	22	•		•	•		EA	•		•						•				
Self-Help	1920	F	A	A	F	B	F	A	F	B	F	1-0/21-0 yrs.	I	22				•		EA	•		•						•				
Home Living	1910	F	A	A	F	B	F	B	F	B	F	1-0/21-0 yrs.	I	22				•		EA	•		•						•				
Independent Living	1910	F	A	A	F	B	F	F	F	F	F	1-0/21-0 yrs.	I	22				•		EA	•		•						•				
Social Skills	3400	F	A	A	F	B	F	B	F	B	F	1-0/21-0 yrs.	I	22				•		EA	•		•						•				
Sensory Motor	2130	F	A	A	F	B	F	A	F	B	F	1-0/21-0 yrs.	I	22				•		EA	•		•						•				
Language/Concepts	2231	F	A	A	F	B	F	A	F	B	F	1-0/21-0 yrs.	I	22				•		EA	•		•						•				
NORTHWESTERN SYNTAX SCREENING TEST (1971)																																	
Receptive	2232	F	B	F	F	F	F	F	F	F	F	3-0/7-11 yrs.	I	7			•			EA		•		•						•			
Expressive	2232	F	B	F	F	F	F	F	F	F	F	3-0/7-11 yrs.	I	7			•			EA		•		•			•						
OCCUPATIONAL APTITUDE SURVEY AND INTEREST SCHEDULE — APTITUDE SURVEY — FEMALE NORMS (1983)																																	
General Ability	4000	F	A	F	F	B	F	F	F	F	F	gr. 8–12	G	22			•	•		EA	•	•	•						•				
Vocabulary	1320	F	A	F	F	B	F	F	F	F	F	gr. 8–12	G	7			•	•		EA	•	•							•				
Computation	1220	F	A	F	F	B	F	F	F	F	F	gr. 8–12	G	7			•	•		EA	•								•				
Spatial Relations	2110	F	A	F	F	B	F	F	F	F	F	gr. 8–12	G	7			•	•		EA	•			•					•				
Word Comparison	2131	F	A	F	F	B	F	F	F	F	F	gr. 8–12	G	7			•	•		EA	•			•					•				
Making Marks	2132	F	A	F	F	B	F	F	F	F	F	gr. 8–12	G	7			•	•		EA	•								•				

	Taxonomy code	Overall rating	Scores	Size	Demographics	Recency	Total	Internal consistency	Stability	Total	Total (Val)	Ages/Grades for Intended Use	Group/Individual	Testing time	Age equivalents	Grade equivalents	Percentile ranks	Standard scores	Other	Examiner qualifications	Third Party	Listen	Read print	Look at stimuli	Other	Speak, minor	Speak, major	Manipulate objects	Mark answer sheet	Point	Draw	Write print	Other
OCCUPATIONAL APTITUDE SURVEY AND INTEREST SCHEDULE — APTITUDE SURVEY — MALE NORMS (1983)
General Ability	4000	F	A	F	F	B	F	F	F	F	F	gr. 8–12	G	22			•	•		EA		•	•	•					•				
Vocabulary	1320	F	A	F	F	B	F	F	F	F	F	gr. 8–12	G	7			•	•		EA		•	•						•				
Computation	1220	F	A	F	F	B	F	F	F	F	F	gr. 8–12	G	7			•	•		EA		•	•						•				
Spatial Relations	2110	F	A	F	F	B	F	F	F	F	F	gr. 8–12	G	7			•	•		EA		•		•					•				
Word Comparison	2131	F	A	F	F	B	F	F	F	F	F	gr. 8–12	G	7			•	•		EA		•		•					•				
Making Marks	2132	F	A	F	F	B	F	F	F	F	F	gr. 8–12	G	7			•	•		EA		•		•					•				
OCCUPATIONAL APTITUDE SURVEY AND INTEREST SCHEDULE — INTEREST SCHEDULE — FEMALE NORMS (1983)
Artistic	3220	F	A	F	F	B	F	F	F	F	F	gr. 8–12	G	45			•	•		EA			•						•				
Scientific	3220	F	A	F	F	B	F	F	F	F	F	gr. 8–12	G	45			•	•		EA			•						•				
Nature	3220	F	A	F	F	B	F	F	F	F	F	gr. 8–12	G	45			•	•		EA			•						•				
Protective	3220	F	A	F	F	B	F	F	F	F	F	gr. 8–12	G	45			•	•		EA			•						•				
Mechanical	3220	F	A	F	F	B	F	F	F	F	F	gr. 8–12	G	45			•	•		EA			•						•				
Industrial	3220	F	A	F	F	B	F	F	F	F	F	gr. 8–12	G	45			•	•		EA			•						•				
Business Detail	3220	F	A	F	F	B	F	F	F	F	F	gr. 8–12	G	45			•	•		EA			•						•				
Selling	3220	F	A	F	F	B	F	F	F	F	F	gr. 8–12	G	45			•	•		EA			•						•				
Accommodating	3220	F	A	F	F	B	F	F	F	F	F	gr. 8–12	G	45			•	•		EA			•						•				
Humanitarian	3220	F	A	F	F	B	F	F	F	F	F	gr. 8–12	G	45			•	•		EA			•						•				
Leading-Influencing	3220	F	A	F	F	B	F	F	F	F	F	gr. 8–12	G	45			•	•		EA			•						•				
Physical Performing	3220	F	A	F	F	B	F	F	F	F	F	gr. 8–12	G	45			•	•		EA			•						•				
OCCUPATIONAL APTITUDE SURVEY AND INTEREST SCHEDULE — INTEREST SCHEDULE — MALE NORMS (1983)
Artistic	3220	F	A	F	F	B	F	F	F	F	F	gr. 8–12	G	45			•	•		EA			•						•				
Scientific	3220	F	A	F	F	B	F	F	F	F	F	gr. 8–12	G	45			•	•		EA			•						•				
Nature	3220	F	A	F	F	B	F	F	F	F	F	gr. 8–12	G	45			•	•		EA			•						•				
Protective	3220	F	A	F	F	B	F	F	F	F	F	gr. 8–12	G	45			•	•		EA			•						•				
Mechanical	3220	F	A	F	F	B	F	F	F	F	F	gr. 8–12	G	45			•	•		EA			•						•				
Industrial	3220	F	A	F	F	B	F	F	F	F	F	gr. 8–12	G	45			•	•		EA			•						•				
Business Detail	3220	F	A	F	F	B	F	F	F	F	F	gr. 8–12	G	45			•	•		EA			•						•				
Selling	3220	F	A	F	F	B	F	F	F	F	F	gr. 8–12	G	45			•	•		EA			•						•				
Accommodating	3220	F	A	F	F	B	F	F	F	F	F	gr. 8–12	G	45			•	•		EA			•						•				

	Taxonomy code	Overall rating	Scores	Size	Demographics	Recency	Total	Internal consistency	Stability	Total	Total (Val.)	Ages/Grades for Intended Use	Group/Individual	Testing time	Age equivalents	Grade equivalents	Percentile ranks	Standard scores	Other	Examiner qualifications	Third Party	Listen	Read print	Look at stimuli	Other	Speak, minor	Speak, major	Manipulate objects	Mark answer sheet	Point	Draw	Write print	Other
OCCUPATIONAL APTITUDE SURVEY AND INTEREST SCHEDULE — INTEREST SCHEDULE — MALE NORMS (1983) (cont.)																																	
Humanitarian	3220	F	A	F	F	B	F	F	F	F	F	gr. 8–12	G	45			•	•		EA			•						•				
Leading-Influencing	3220	F	A	F	F	B	F	F	F	F	F	gr. 8–12	G	45			•	•		EA			•						•				
Physical Performing	3220	F	A	F	F	B	F	F	F	F	F	gr. 8–12	G	45			•	•		EA			•						•				
OCCUPATIONAL APTITUDE SURVEY AND INTEREST SCHEDULE — APTITUDE SURVEY — SECOND EDITION (1991)																																	
General Ability	4000	B	A	A	B	A	A	A	B	B	B	gr. 8–12	G	21			•	•		EA		•	•						•				
Vocabulary	1310	B	A	A	B	A	A	B	B	B	A	gr. 8–12	G	9			•	•		EA		•	•						•				
Computation	1220	B	A	A	B	A	A	B	A	B	A	gr. 8–12	G	12			•	•		EA		•	•						•				
Spatial Relations	2110	B	A	A	B	A	A	F	B	B	A	gr. 8–12	G	8			•	•		EA		•	•	•					•				
Word Comparison	2250	B	A	A	B	A	A	A	F	B	B	gr. 8–12	G	5			•	•		EA		•	•						•				
Making Marks	2132	B	A	A	B	A	A	B	A	B	B	gr. 8–12	G	1			•	•		EA		•							•				
OCCUPATIONAL APTITUDE SURVEY AND INTEREST SCHEDULE — INTEREST SCHEDULE — SECOND EDITION (1991)																																	
Artistic	3220	B	A	A	B	B	B	B	A	B	B	gr. 8–12	G	30			•	•		EA			•						•				
Scientific	3220	B	A	A	B	B	B	B	F	B	B	gr. 8–12	G	30			•	•		EA			•						•				
Nature	3220	B	A	A	B	B	B	A	F	B	B	gr. 8–12	G	30			•	•		EA			•						•				
Protective	3220	B	A	A	B	B	B	A	B	B	B	gr. 8–12	G	30			•	•		EA			•						•				
Mechanical	3220	B	A	A	B	B	B	B	F	B	B	gr. 8–12	G	30			•	•		EA			•						•				
Industrial	3220	B	A	A	B	B	B	B	F	B	B	gr. 8–12	G	30			•	•		EA			•						•				
Business Detail	3220	B	A	A	B	B	B	B	F	B	B	gr. 8–12	G	30			•	•		EA			•						•				
Selling	3220	B	A	A	B	B	B	B	F	B	B	gr. 8–12	G	30			•	•		EA			•						•				
Accommodating	3220	B	A	A	B	B	B	B	F	B	B	gr. 8–12	G	30			•	•		EA			•						•				
Humanitarian	3220	B	A	A	B	B	B	B	F	B	B	gr. 8–12	G	30			•	•		EA			•						•				
Leading-Influencing	3220	B	A	A	B	B	B	B	B	B	B	gr. 8–12	G	30			•	•		EA			•						•				
Physical Performing	3220	B	A	A	B	B	B	B	F	B	B	gr. 8–12	G	30			•	•		EA			•						•				
PARENT RATING OF STUDENT BEHAVIOR (1987)																																	
Total	4000	F	A	F	F	A	F	F	F	F	F	gr. K–12	I	15				•		EA	•		•						•				
Social Responsibility	3900	F	A	F	F	A	F	F	F	F	F	gr. K–12	I	15				•		EA	•		•						•				
Self-Care	1900	F	A	F	F	A	F	F	F	F	F	gr. K–12	I	15				•		EA	•		•						•				
Personal Independence	4000	F	A	F	F	A	F	F	F	F	F	gr. K–12	I	15				•		EA	•		•						•				

			Technical Characteristics								Nontechnical Characteristics																							
			Norms					Reliability		Val.	Ages/Grades for Intended Use	Admin.		Scores						Test Formats — Input					Output							
	Taxonomy code	Overall rating	Scores	Size	Demographics	Recency	Total	Internal consistency	Stability	Total	Total		Group/Individual	Testing time	Age equivalents	Grade equivalents	Percentile ranks	Standard scores	Other	Examiner qualifications	Third Party	Listen	Read print	Look at stimuli	Other	Speak, minor	Speak, major	Manipulate objects	Mark answer sheet	Point	Draw	Write print	Other
PEABODY INDIVIDUAL ACHIEVEMENT TEST (1970)																																	
Total Test	1000	**F**	A	A	A	F	F	F	B	B	B	gr. K–12	I	45	•	•	•	•		EA		•	•	•						•			
Mathematics	1200	**F**	A	A	A	F	F	F	F	F	B	gr. K–12	I	7	•	•	•	•		EA		•	•	•						•			
Reading Recognition	1320	**F**	A	A	A	F	F	F	B	B	B	gr. K–12	I	7	•	•	•	•		EA		•	•	•		•				•			
Reading Comprehension	1310	**F**	A	A	A	F	F	F	F	F	B	gr. K–12	I	7	•	•	•	•		EA		•	•	•						•			
Spelling	1630	**F**	A	A	A	F	F	F	F	F	B	gr. K–12	I	7	•	•	•	•		EA		•	•	•						•			
General Information	1100	**F**	A	A	A	F	F	F	F	F	B	gr. K–12	I	7	•	•	•	•		EA		•				•	•						
PEABODY INDIVIDUAL ACHIEVEMENT TEST — REVISED (1989)																																	
Total Test	1000	**B**	A	B	B	A	B	A	B	B	A	gr. K–12	I	60+	•	•	•	•		EA		•	•	•		•	•			•		•	
Total Reading	1300	**B**	A	B	B	A	B	A	A	A	A	gr. K–12	I	20	•	•	•	•		EA		•	•	•		•				•			
Written Language Composite	1600	**F**	A	B	B	A	B	A	F	B	F	gr. K–12	I	30				•		EA		•	•	•						•		•	
General Information	1100	**B**	A	B	B	A	B	A	A	A	A	gr. K–12	I	10	•	•	•	•		EA		•				•	•						
Reading Recognition	1320	**B**	A	B	B	A	B	A	A	A	A	gr. K–12	I	10	•	•	•	•		EA		•	•			•							
Reading Comprehension	1310	**B**	A	B	B	A	B	A	B	B	A	gr. K–12	I	10	•	•	•	•		EA		•	•							•			
Mathematics	1200	**B**	A	B	B	A	B	A	B	B	A	gr. K–12	I	10	•	•	•	•		EA		•	•	•						•			
Spelling	1630	**B**	A	B	B	A	B	A	B	B	A	gr. K–12	I	10	•	•	•	•		EA		•	•							•			
Written Expression I	1600	**F**	A	B	B	A	B	F	F	F	F	gr. K–1	I	10				•		EA		•	•									•	
Written Expression II	1600	**F**	A	B	B	A	B	B	F	B	F	gr. 2–12	I	20				•		EA		•		•								•	
PEABODY PICTURE VOCABULARY TEST (1965)																																	
Total Score	2231	**F**	A	A	F	F	F	F	F	F	A	2-3/18-5 yrs.	I	7	•		•	•		EA		•		•						•			
PEABODY PICTURE VOCABULARY TEST — REVISED (1981)																																	
Total Score	2231	**B**	A	A	A	B	B	B	F	B	B	2-6/40-11 yrs.	I	7	•		•	•		EA		•		•						•			
PERSONAL EXPERIENCE INVENTORY (1989)[1]																																	
Personal Involvement with Chemicals	3630	**F/F**	A/A	B/F	F/F	A/A	F/F	A/A	F/B	B/B	B/B	gr. 7–12	G	45				•		EA		•							•				
Effects from Drug Use	3630	**F/F**	A/A	B/F	F/F	A/A	F/F	A/B	F/B	B/B	B/B	gr. 7–12	G	45				•		EA		•							•				
Social Benefits of Drug Use	3630	**F/F**	A/A	B/F	F/F	A/A	F/F	B/B	F/F	B/B	B/B	gr. 7–12	G	45				•		EA		•							•				
Personal Consequences of Drug Use	3630	**F/F**	A/A	B/F	F/F	A/A	F/F	B/B	B/F	B/B	B/B	gr. 7–12	G	45				•		EA		•							•				
Polydrug Use	3630	**F/F**	A/A	B/F	F/F	A/A	F/F	B/B	A/F	B/B	B/B	gr. 7–12	G	45				•		EA		•							•				
Psychological Benefits of Drug Use	3630	**F/F**	A/A	B/F	F/F	A/A	F/F	A/B	F/F	B/B	B/B	gr. 7–12	G	45				•		EA		•							•				

[1]Rating for dependency group appears first, for high school group second

	Taxonomy code	Overall rating	Scores	Size	Demographics	Recency	Total	Internal consistency	Stability	Total	Val. Total	Ages/Grades for Intended Use	Group/Individual	Testing time	Age equivalents	Grade equivalents	Percentile ranks	Standard scores	Other	Examiner qualifications	Third Party	Listen	Read print	Look at stimuli	Other	Speak, minor	Speak, major	Manipulate objects	Mark answer sheet	Point	Draw	Write print	Other
PERSONAL EXPERIENCE INVENTORY (1989)[1] (cont.)																																	
Transitional Drug Use	3630	F/F	A/A	B/F	F/F	A/A	F/F	A/B	A/F	A/B	B/B	gr. 7–12	G	45				•		EA			•						•				
Preoccupation with Drugs	3630	F/F	A/A	B/F	F/F	A/A	F/F	A/B	F/F	B/B	B/B	gr. 7–12	G	45				•		EA			•						•				
Loss of Control	3630	F/F	A/A	B/F	F/F	A/A	F/F	B/F	F/F	B/F	B/B	gr. 7–12	G	45				•		EA			•						•				
Negative Self-Image	3700	F/F	A/A	B/F	F/F	A/A	F/F	B/F	F/B	B/B	B/B	gr. 7–12	G	45				•		EA			•						•				
Psychological Disturbance	3000	F/F	A/A	B/F	F/F	A/A	F/F	B/F	F/F	B/F	B/B	gr. 7–12	G	45				•		EA			•						•				
Social Isolation	3400	F/F	A/A	B/F	F/F	A/A	F/F	F/F	F/B	F/B	B/B	gr. 7–12	G	45				•		EA			•						•				
Uncontrolled	3800	F/F	A/A	B/F	F/F	A/A	F/F	B/B	F/B	B/B	B/B	gr. 7–12	G	45				•		EA			•						•				
Rejecting Conventions	3400	F/F	A/A	B/F	F/F	A/A	F/F	F/F	F/B	F/B	B/B	gr. 7–12	G	45				•		EA			•						•				
Deviant Behavior	3000	F/F	A/A	B/F	F/F	A/A	F/F	F/F	F/B	F/B	B/B	gr. 7–12	G	45				•		EA			•						•				
Absence of Goals	3800	F/F	A/A	B/F	F/F	A/A	F/F	B/B	F/F	B/B	B/B	gr. 7–12	G	45				•		EA			•						•				
Spiritual Isolation	3400	F/F	A/A	B/F	F/F	A/A	F/F	B/B	F/A	B/B	B/B	gr. 7–12	G	45				•		EA			•						•				
Peer Chemical Environment	3630	F/F	A/A	B/F	F/F	A/A	F/F	B/B	F/F	B/B	B/B	gr. 7–12	G	45				•		EA			•						•				
Sibling Chemical Use	3630	F/F	A/A	B/F	F/F	A/A	F/F	B/F	B/B	B/B	B/B	gr. 7–12	G	45				•		EA			•						•				
Family Pathology	3400	F/F	A/A	B/F	F/F	A/A	F/F	B/B	B/B	B/B	B/B	gr. 7–12	G	45				•		EA			•						•				
Family Estrangement	3400	F/F	A/A	B/F	F/F	A/A	F/F	B/B	F/B	B/B	B/B	gr. 7–12	G	45				•		EA			•						•				

[1]Rating for dependency group appears first, for high school group second

	Taxonomy code	Overall rating	Scores	Size	Demographics	Recency	Total	Internal consistency	Stability	Total	Val. Total	Ages/Grades for Intended Use	Group/Individual	Testing time	Age equivalents	Grade equivalents	Percentile ranks	Standard scores	Other	Examiner qualifications	Third Party	Listen	Read print	Look at stimuli	Other	Speak, minor	Speak, major	Manipulate objects	Mark answer sheet	Point	Draw	Write print	Other
PICTORIAL TEST OF INTELLIGENCE (1964)																																	
Deviation Quotient	4000	F	A	A	A	F	F	A	A	A	B	2-10/8-6 yrs.	I	45	•		•	•		EA	•		•							•			
Short Form	4000	F	A	A	A	F	F	B	F	B	F	2-10/8-6 yrs.	I	22	•		•	•		EA	•		•							•			
Picture Vocabulary	2231	F	A	A	A	F	F	F	F	F	B	2-10/8-6 yrs.	I	7	•		•	•		EA	•		•							•			
Form Discrimination	2131	F	A	A	A	F	F	F	F	F	B	2-10/8-6 yrs.	I	7	•		•	•		EA	•		•							•			
Information-Comprehension	2231	F	A	A	A	F	F	F	F	F	B	2-10/8-6 yrs.	I	7	•		•	•		EA	•		•							•			
Size and Number	1210	F	A	A	A	F	F	F	F	F	B	2-10/8-6 yrs.	I	7	•		•	•		EA	•		•							•			
Similarities	2210	F	A	A	A	F	F	F	F	F	B	2-10/8-6 yrs.	I	7	•		•	•		EA	•		•							•			
Immediate Recall	2133	F	A	A	A	F	F	F	F	F	B	2-10/8-6 yrs.	I	7	•		•	•		EA	•		•							•			
PIERS-HARRIS CHILDREN'S SELF-CONCEPT SCALE (1969)																																	
Total Score	3700	F	A	B	F	F	F	B	F	B	F	gr. 4–12	G	22			•	•		EA	•	•							•				

		Technical Characteristics											Nontechnical Characteristics																			
		Norms					Reliability			Val.		Admin.		Scores							Test Formats										
																					Input					Output						
Taxonomy code	Overall rating	Scores	Size	Demographics	Recency	Total	Internal consistency	Stability	Total	Total	Ages/Grades for Intended Use	Group/Individual	Testing time	Age equivalents	Grade equivalents	Percentile ranks	Standard scores	Other	Examiner qualifications	Third Party	Listen	Read print	Look at stimuli	Other	Speak, minor	Speak, major	Manipulate objects	Mark answer sheet	Point	Draw	Write print	Other
PIERS-HARRIS CHILDREN'S SELF-CONCEPT SCALE — REVISED MANUAL 1984 (1984)																																
Total Score — 3700	F	A	B	F	F	F	B	F	B	B	8-0/18-11 yrs.	G	22			•	•		EA	•	•							•				
Behavior — 3740	F	A	B	F	F	F	B	F	B	F	8-0/18-11 yrs.	G	22			•	•		EA	•	•							•				
Intellectual and School Status — 3710	F	A	B	F	F	F	F	F	F	F	8-0/18-11 yrs.	G	22			•	•		EA	•	•							•				
Physical Appearance and Attributes — 3720	F	A	B	F	F	F	F	F	F	F	8-0/18-11 yrs.	G	22			•	•		EA	•	•							•				
Anxiety — 3100	F	A	B	F	F	F	F	F	F	F	8-0/18-11 yrs.	G	22			•	•		EA	•	•							•				
Popularity — 3730	F	A	B	F	F	F	F	F	F	F	8-0/18-11 yrs.	G	22			•	•		EA	•	•							•				
Happiness and Satisfaction — 3740	F	A	B	F	F	F	F	F	F	F	8-0/18-11 yrs.	G	22			•	•		EA	•	•							•				
PRESCRIPTIVE READING PERFORMANCE TEST (1978)																																
Total — 1320	F	F	B	F	B	F	F	F	F	F	Pre-reading–Adult	I	15	•					EA	•	•								•			
PRIMARY VISUAL MOTOR TEST — NORMAL NORMS (1970)																																
Total — 2132	F	B	F	F	F	F	F	B	B	F	4-0/8-11 yrs.	I	45					•¹	EA	•			•							•		
PRIMARY VISUAL MOTOR TEST — RETARDED NORMS (1970)																																
Total — 2132	F	B	F	F	F	F	F	B	B	F	4-0/8-11 yrs.	I	45					•¹	EA	•			•							•		
PSYCHOLINGUISTIC RATING SCALE (1982)																																
Total — 2000	F	A	F	F	B	F	A	F	B	F	gr. K–8.9	I	60 +		•				EA	•		•						•				
Symbolic — 2000	F	A	F	F	B	F	A	F	B	F	gr. K–8.9	I	30		•				EA	•		•						•				
Nonsymbolic — 2000	F	A	F	F	B	F	A	F	B	F	gr. K–8.9	I	20		•				EA	•		•						•				
Auditory — 2200	F	A	F	F	B	F	A	F	B	F	gr. K–8.9	I	50		•				EA	•		•						•				
Visual — 2000	F	A	F	F	B	F	A	F	B	F	gr. K–8.9	I	50		•				EA	•		•						•				
Reception — 2000	F	A	F	F	B	F	A	F	B	F	gr. K–8.9	I	20		•				EA	•		•						•				
Association — 2000	F	A	F	F	B	F	A	F	B	F	gr. K–8.9	I	20		•				EA	•		•						•				
Expression — 2000	F	A	F	F	B	F	A	F	B	F	gr. K–8.9	I	20		•				EA	•		•						•				
Memory — 2000	F	A	F	F	B	F	A	F	B	F	gr. K–8.9	I	20		•				EA	•		•						•				
Closure — 2000	F	A	F	F	B	F	A	F	B	F	gr. K–8.9	I	20		•				EA	•		•						•				
Auditory Reception — 2200	F	A	F	F	B	F	A	F	B	F	gr. K–8.9	I	10		•				EA	•		•						•				
Auditory Association — 2200	F	A	F	F	B	F	A	F	B	F	gr. K–8.9	I	10		•				EA	•		•						•				
Auditory Memory — 2242	F	A	F	F	B	F	A	F	B	F	gr. K–8.9	I	10		•				EA	•		•						•				

¹Raw score means and standard deviations

	Taxonomy code	Overall rating	Norms: Scores	Norms: Size	Norms: Demographics	Norms: Recency	Norms: Total	Rel.: Internal consistency	Rel.: Stability	Rel.: Total	Val.: Total	Ages/Grades for Intended Use	Group/Individual	Testing time	Age equivalents	Grade equivalents	Percentile ranks	Standard scores	Other	Examiner qualifications	Third Party	Listen	Read print	Look at stimuli	Other (input)	Speak, minor	Speak, major	Manipulate objects	Mark answer sheet	Point	Draw	Write print	Other (output)
PSYCHOLINGUISTIC RATING SCALE (1982) (cont.)																																	
Auditory Closure	2200	F	A	F	F	B	F	A	F	B	F	gr. K–8.9	I	10				•		EA	•		•						•				
Verbal Expression	2230	F	A	F	F	B	F	A	F	B	F	gr. K–8.9	I	10				•		EA	•		•						•				
Visual Reception	2230	F	A	F	F	B	F	A	F	B	F	gr. K–8.9	I	10				•		EA	•		•						•				
Visual Association	2230	F	A	F	F	B	F	A	F	B	F	gr. K–8.9	I	10				•		EA	•		•						•				
Visual Memory	2133	F	A	F	F	B	F	A	F	B	F	gr. K–8.9	I	10				•		EA	•		•						•				
Visual Closure	2130	F	A	F	F	B	F	A	F	B	F	gr. K–8.9	I	10				•		EA	•		•						•				
Manual Expression	2100	F	A	F	F	B	F	A	F	B	F	gr. K–8.9	I	10				•		EA	•		•						•				
THE PUPIL RATING SCALE — REVISED (1981)																																	
Total Scale	4000	F	B	B	F	F	F	F	F	F	B	gr. K–6	I	10					•¹	EA	•		•						•				
Total Verbal	2230	F	B	B	F	F	F	F	F	F	B	gr. K–6	I	5					•¹	EA	•		•						•				
Total Nonverbal	4000	F	B	B	F	F	F	F	F	F	B	gr. K–6	I	5					•¹	EA	•		•						•				
Auditory Comprehension	2230	F	B	B	F	F	F	F	F	F	B	gr. K–6	I	2					•¹	EA	•		•						•				
Spoken Language	2230	F	B	B	F	F	F	F	F	F	B	gr. K–6	I	2					•¹	EA	•		•						•				
Orientation	2000	F	B	B	F	F	F	F	F	F	B	gr. K–6	I	2					•¹	EA	•		•						•				
Motor Coordination	2150	F	B	B	F	F	F	F	F	F	B	gr. K–6	I	2					•¹	EA	•		•						•				
Personal-Social Behavior	3000	F	B	B	F	F	F	F	F	F	B	gr. K–6	I	2					•¹	EA	•		•						•				

¹Raw score means and standard deviations provided

	Taxonomy code	Overall rating	Norms: Scores	Norms: Size	Norms: Demographics	Norms: Recency	Norms: Total	Rel.: Internal consistency	Rel.: Stability	Rel.: Total	Val.: Total	Ages/Grades for Intended Use	Group/Individual	Testing time	Age equivalents	Grade equivalents	Percentile ranks	Standard scores	Other	Examiner qualifications	Third Party	Listen	Read print	Look at stimuli	Other (input)	Speak, minor	Speak, major	Manipulate objects	Mark answer sheet	Point	Draw	Write print	Other (output)
THE PURDUE PERCEPTUAL-MOTOR SURVEY (1966)																																	
Total	2000	F	B	F	F	F	F	F	F	F	F	gr. 1–4	I	30					•¹	EA		•		•						•	•		•²
Walking Board	2153	F	B	F	F	F	F	F	F	F	F	gr. 1–4	I	3					•¹	EA		•		•									•²
Jumping	2153	F	B	F	F	F	F	F	F	F	F	gr. 1–4	I	3					•¹	EA		•											•²
Identification of Body Parts	2231	F	B	F	F	F	F	F	F	F	F	gr. 1–4	I	3					•¹	EA		•								•			
Imitation of Movement	2132	F	B	F	F	F	F	F	F	F	F	gr. 1–4	I	3					•¹	EA		•		•									•²
Obstacle Course	2153	F	B	F	F	F	F	F	F	F	F	gr. 1–4	I	3					•¹	EA		•											•²
Kraus-Weber	2152	F	B	F	F	F	F	F	F	F	F	gr. 1–4	I	3					•¹	EA		•											•²
Angels-in-the-Snow	2153	F	B	F	F	F	F	F	F	F	F	gr. 1–4	I	3					•¹	EA		•		•									•²
Chalkboard	2132	F	B	F	F	F	F	F	F	F	F	gr. 1–4	I	3					•¹	EA		•									•		
Rhythmic Writing	2132	F	B	F	F	F	F	F	F	F	F	gr. 1–4	I	3					•¹	EA		•		•								•	

¹Raw score means and standard deviations provided; ²multiple motor responses required

| | Taxonomy code | Overall rating | Norms | | | | | Reliability | | | Val. | Ages/Grades for Intended Use | Group/Individual | Testing time | Scores | | | | | Examiner qualifications | Input | | | | | Output | | | | | | | |
			Scores	Size	Demographics	Recency	Total	Internal consistency	Stability	Total	Total				Age equivalents	Grade equivalents	Percentile ranks	Standard scores	Other		Third Party	Listen	Read print	Look at stimuli	Other	Speak, minor	Speak, major	Manipulate objects	Mark answer sheet	Point	Draw	Write print	Other
THE PURDUE PERCEPTUAL-MOTOR SURVEY (1966) (cont.)																																	
Ocular Control	2134	F	B	F	F	F	F	F	F	F	F	gr. 1–4	I	3					•1	EA		•		•									•2
Visual Achievement Forms	2132	F	B	F	F	F	F	F	F	F	F	gr. 1–4	I	3					•1	EA		•		•							•		
1Raw score means and standard deviations provided; 2multiple motor responses required																																	
QUICK-SCORE ACHIEVEMENT TEST (1987)																																	
General Achievement Quotient	1000	B	A	A	B	A	B	A	B	B	B	7-0/17-11 yrs.	I	45			•			EA	•	•				•	•					•	
Writing	1600	B	A	A	B	A	B	B/A1	B	B	A	7-0/17-11 yrs.	I	7			•	•		EA		•										•	
Arithmetic	1220	B	A	A	B	A	B	B/A1	B	B	A	7-0/17-11 yrs.	I	7			•	•		EA		•	•									•	
Reading	1320	B	A	A	B	A	B	A	B	B	A	7-0/17-11 yrs.	I	7			•	•		EA		•	•			•							
Facts	1100	F/B1	A	A	B	A	B	F/B1	F	F/B1	A	7-0/17-11 yrs.	I	7			•	•		EA		•						•					
1Form A appears first, Form B second																																	
THE QUICK TEST (1962)																																	
Total	2231	F	A	F	F	F	F	B	F	B	B	1-6/19-11 yrs.	I	22			•			EA		•		•						•			
RECEPTIVE ONE-WORD PICTURE VOCABULARY TEST (1985)																																	
Total	2231	F	A	B	F	B	F	A	F	B	F	2-0/11-11yrs.	I	7	•		•	•		EA		•		•						•			
RESPONSIBILITY AND INDEPENDENCE SCALE FOR ADOLESCENTS (1990)																																	
Adaptive Behavior Total	1900	B	A	A	B	A	B	A	A	A	A	12-0/19-11 yrs.	I	40			•	•		EA	•	•		•		•							
Responsibility	1900	B	A	A	B	A	B	A	A	A	A	12-0/19-11 yrs.	I	40			•	•		EA	•	•		•		•							
Independence	1900	B	A	A	B	A	B	A	A	A	A	12-0/19-11 yrs.	I	40			•	•		EA	•	•		•		•							
REYNELL DEVELOPMENTAL LANGUAGE SCALES, U.S. EDITION (1990)																																	
Verbal Comprehension	2230	F	A	F	F	A	F	B	F	B	A	1-0/6-11 yrs.	I	30	•		•	•		EA		•		•						•			
Expressive Language	2230	F	A	F	F	A	F	B	F	B	A	1-0/6-11 yrs.	I	30	•		•	•		EA		•		•		•	•						
REYNOLDS ADOLESCENT DEPRESSION SCALE (1987)																																	
Total	3300	B/F1	B	A	B/F1	A	B/F1	A	F	B	A/F1	gr. 7–12	G	15			•			EA			•						•				
1Rating for Total Norm group appears first, for Male and Female Norms second																																	
REYNOLDS CHILD DEPRESSION SCALE (1989)																																	
Total Score	3300	F	B	A	F	A	F	B/A1	B	B	A	gr. 3–6	G	15			•			EA			•						•				
1Rating for Male Norms appears first, Female Norms second																																	

		Technical Characteristics										Ages/Grades for Intended Use	Nontechnical Characteristics																			
			Norms					Reliability			Val.		Admin.		Scores							Test Formats											
																						Input					Output						
	Taxonomy code	Overall rating	Scores	Size	Demographics	Recency	Total	Internal consistency	Stability	Total	Total		Group/Individual	Testing time	Age equivalents	Grade equivalents	Percentile ranks	Standard scores	Other	Examiner qualifications	Third Party	Listen	Read print	Look at stimuli	Other	Speak, minor	Speak, major	Manipulate objects	Mark answer sheet	Point	Draw	Write print	Other

RHODE ISLAND TEST OF LANGUAGE STRUCTURE — HEARING IMPAIRED NORMS (1983)

Total	2232	F	A	F	F	B	F	F	F	F	B	5-0/Adult yrs.	I	45			•	•		ST				•	•[1]					•			

...derstand sign language

RHODE ISLAND TEST OF LANGUAGE ~~~~ (1983)

Total	2232	F	A	F									I	45			•	•		EA	•		•							•			

ROBERTS APPERCEPTION TEST ~~~

Reliance on Others	3400	F	A										I	22				•		ST	•		•							•			
Support-Other	3400	F	A										I	22				•		ST	•		•							•			
Support-Child	3400	F											I	22				•		ST	•		•							•			
Limit Setting	3840	F											I	22				•		ST	•		•							•			
Problem Identification	3000	F								5-11 yrs.			I	22				•		ST	•		•							•			
Resolution 1	3900									15-11 yrs.			I	22				•		ST	•		•							•			
Resolution 2	3900									0/15-11 yrs.			I	22				•		ST	•		•							•			
Resolution 3	390									6-0/15-11 yrs.			I	22				•		ST	•		•							•			
Anxiety	3									6-0/15-11 yrs.			I	22				•		ST	•		•							•			
Aggression										6-0/15-11 yrs.			I	22				•		ST	•		•							•			
Depression										6-0/15-11 yrs.			I	22				•		ST	•		•							•			
Rejection											F	6-0/15-11 yrs.	I	22				•		ST	•		•							•			
Unresolved											F	6-0/15-11 yrs.	I	22				•		ST	•		•							•			

SCALES OF INDEPENDENT ~~~

Broad Independence										B	B	0-3/44-11 yrs.	I	45	•		•	•		EA	•		•							•			
General Maladaptive Behavior										B	F	0-3/44-11 yrs.	I	7				•		EA	•		•							•			
Short Form Scale	4000									B	B	0-3/44-11 yrs.	I	7	•		•	•		EA	•		•							•			
Early Development Scale	1920	F	A	B	B	B	B		F	B	F	0-3/2-5 yrs.	I	7	•		•	•		EA	•		•							•			
Motor Skills	2150	B	A	B	B	B	B	B	B	B	B	0-3/44-11 yrs.	I	7	•		•	•		EA	•		•							•			
Social Interaction and Communication Skills	4000	B	A	B	B	B	B	B	B	B	B	0-3/44-11 yrs.	I	7	•		•	•		EA	•		•							•			
Personal Living Skills	1900	B	A	B	B	B	B	A	B	B	B	0-3/44-11 yrs.	I	7	•		•	•		EA	•		•							•			
Community Living Skills	1900	B	A	B	B	B	B	A	B	B	B	0-3/44-11 yrs.	I	7	•		•	•		EA	•		•							•			
Internalized Maladaptive Behavior	3000	F	A	B	B	B	B	F	B	B	F	0-3/44-11 yrs.	I	7	•		•	•		EA	•		•							•			
Asocial Maladaptive Behavior	3500	F	A	B	B	B	B	F	F	F	F	0-3/44-11 yrs.	I	7	•		•	•		EA	•		•							•			

| | | | Technical Characteristics | | | | | | | | | Nontechnical Characteristics | | | | | | | | | | | | | | | | | | | | | | |
| | | | Norms | | | | | Reliability | | | Val. | | Admin. | | Scores | | | | | | Input | | | | | Output | | | | | | | |
	Taxonomy code	Overall rating	Scores	Size	Demographics	Recency	Total	Internal consistency	Stability	Total	Total	Ages/Grades for Intended Use	Group/Individual	Testing time	Age equivalents	Grade equivalents	Percentile ranks	Standard scores	Other	Examiner qualifications	Third Party	Listen	Read print	Look at stimuli	Other	Speak, minor	Speak, major	Manipulate objects	Mark answer sheet	Point	Draw	Write print	Other
SCALES OF INDEPENDENT BEHAVIOR (1985) (cont.)																																	
Externalized Maladaptive Behavior	3500	F	A	B	B	B	B	F	B	B	F	0-3/44-11 yrs.	I	7	•		•	•		EA	•		•						•				
Gross Motor	2150	B	A	B	B	B	B	F	B	B	B	0-3/44-11 yrs.	I	7	•		•	•		EA	•		•						•				
Fine Motor	2154	F	A	B	B	B	B	F	F	F	B	0-3/44-11 yrs.	I	7	•		•	•		EA	•		•						•				
Social Interaction	3400	F	A	B	B	B	B	F	F	F	B	0-3/44-11 yrs.	I	7	•		•	•		EA	•		•						•				
Language Comprehension	2230	B	A	B	B	B	B	B	B	B	B	0-3/44-11 yrs.	I	7	•		•	•		EA	•		•						•				
Language Expression	2230	B	A	B	B	B	B	F	B	B	B	0-3/44-11 yrs.	I	7	•		•	•		EA	•		•						•				
Eating and Meal Preparation	1920	B	A	B	B	B	B	F	B	B	B	0-3/44-11 yrs.	I	7	•		•	•		EA	•		•						•				
Toileting	1920	B	A	B	B	B	B	F	B	B	B	0-3/44-11 yrs.	I	7	•		•	•		EA	•		•						•				
Dressing	1920	B	A	B	B	B	B	B	F	B	B	0-3/44-11 yrs.	I	7	•		•	•		EA	•		•						•				
Personal Self-Care	1920	F	A	B	B	B	B	F	F	F	B	0-3/44-11 yrs.	I	7	•		•	•		EA	•		•						•				
Domestic Skills	1920	B	A	B	B	B	B	B	F	B	B	0-3/44-11 yrs.	I	7	•		•	•		EA	•		•						•				
Time and Punctuality	1920	F	A	B	B	B	B	F	F	F	B	0-3/44-11 yrs.	I	7	•		•	•		EA	•		•						•				
Money and Value	1920	F	A	B	B	B	B	F	B	B	B	0-3/44-11 yrs.	I	7	•		•	•		EA	•		•						•				
Work Skills	3220	B	A	B	B	B	B	B	B	B	B	0-3/44-11 yrs.	I	7	•		•	•		EA	•		•						•				
Home/Community Orientation	1920	B	A	B	B	B	B	F	B	B	B	0-3/44-11 yrs.	I	7	•		•	•		EA	•		•						•				
Hurtful to Self	3620	F	A	B	B	B	B	F	B	B	F	0-3/44-11 yrs.	I	7	•		•	•		EA	•		•						•				
Unusual or Repetitive Habits	3900	F	A	B	B	B	B	F	F	F	F	0-3/44-11 yrs.	I	7	•		•	•		EA	•		•						•				
Withdrawal or Inattentive Behavior	3820	F	A	B	B	B	B	F	F	F	F	0-3/44-11 yrs.	I	7	•		•	•		EA	•		•						•				
Socially Offensive Behavior	3400	F	A	B	B	B	B	F	F	F	F	0-3/44-11 yrs.	I	7	•		•	•		EA	•		•						•				
Uncooperative Behavior	3500	F	A	B	B	B	B	F	F	F	F	0-3/44-11 yrs.	I	7	•		•	•		EA	•		•						•				
Hurtful to Others	3500	F	A	B	B	B	B	F	B	B	F	0-3/44-11 yrs.	I	7	•		•	•		EA	•		•						•				
Destructive to Property	3500	F	A	B	B	B	B	F	B	B	F	0-3/44-11 yrs.	I	7	•		•	•		EA	•		•						•				
Disruptive Behavior	3500	F	A	B	B	B	B	F	F	F	F	0-3/44-11 yrs.	I	7	•		•	•		EA	•		•						•				
SCHOLASTIC ABILITIES TEST FOR ADULTS (1991)																																	
Scholastic Abilities	4000	B	A	B	B	A	B	A	A	A	A	16-0/79-11 yrs.	G	60+			•			EA		•	•	•		•			•	•		•	
General Aptitude	4000	B	A	B	B	A	B	A	A	A	B	16-0/79-11 yrs.	G	35			•			EA		•	•	•		•				•		•	
Total Achievement	1000	B	A	B	B	A	B	A	A	A	B	16-0/79-11 yrs.	G	60+			•			EA												•	
Verbal	4000	B	A	B	B	A	B	A	A	A	A	16-0/79-11 yrs.	G	60+			•			EA		•	•	•		•			•			•	
Quantitative	4000	B	A	B	B	A	B	A	A	A	A	16-0/79-11 yrs.	G	50			•			EA		•	•	•						•		•	

SCHOLASTIC ABILITIES TEST FOR ADULTS (1991) (cont.)

	Taxonomy code	Overall rating	Norms: Scores	Norms: Size	Norms: Demographics	Norms: Recency	Norms: Total	Reliability: Internal consistency	Reliability: Stability	Reliability: Total	Val.: Total	Ages/Grades for Intended Use	Admin.: Group/Individual	Admin.: Testing time	Scores: Age equivalents	Scores: Grade equivalents	Scores: Percentile ranks	Scores: Standard scores	Scores: Other	Examiner qualifications	Input: Third Party	Input: Listen	Input: Read print	Input: Look at stimuli	Input: Other	Output: Speak, minor	Output: Speak, major	Output: Manipulate objects	Output: Mark answer sheet	Output: Point	Output: Draw	Output: Write print	Output: Other
Reading	1310	B	A	B	B	A	B	A	A	A	B	16-0/79-11 yrs.	G	25				•		EA		•	•						•				
Mathematics	1200	B	A	B	B	A	B	A	A	A	B	16-0/79-11 yrs.	G	25				•		EA		•	•									•	
Writing	1600	B	A	B	B	A	B	A	A	A	B	16-0/79-11 yrs.	G	35				•		EA		•	•	•								•	
Achievement Screener	1000	B	A	B	B	A	B	A	A	A	B	16-0/79-11 yrs.	G	40				•		EA		•	•						•			•	
Verbal Reasoning	2210	B	A	B	B	A	B	B	A	B	A	16-0/79-11 yrs.	G	10			•	•		EA		•				•							
Nonverbal Reasoning	2110	B	A	B	B	A	B	B	F	B	A	16-0/79-11 yrs.	G	10			•	•		EA		•		•						•			
Quantitative Reasoning	1210	B	A	B	B	A	B	B	A	B	A	16-0/79-11 yrs.	G	15			•	•		EA		•	•									•	
Reading Vocabulary	1310	B	A	B	B	A	B	B	A	B	A	16-0/79-11 yrs.	G	10			•	•		EA		•	•						•				
Reading Comprehension	1310	B	A	B	B	A	B	A	F	B	A	16-0/79-11 yrs.	G	15			•	•		EA		•	•						•				
Math Calculation	1220	B	A	B	B	A	B	A	A	A	B	16-0/79-11 yrs.	G	10			•	•		EA		•	•									•	
Math Application	1210	B	A	B	B	A	B	B	A	B	A	16-0/79-11 yrs.	G	15			•	•		EA		•	•							•		•	
Writing Mechanics	1600	B	A	B	B	A	B	A	A	A	A	16-0/79-11 yrs.	G	20			•	•		EA		•	•										
Writing Composition	1600	B	A	B	B	A	B	A	F	B	A	16-0/79-11 yrs.	G	15			•	•		EA		•		•								•	

SCHOLASTIC APTITUDE SCALE (1991)

	Taxonomy code	Overall rating	Norms: Scores	Norms: Size	Norms: Demographics	Norms: Recency	Norms: Total	Reliability: Internal consistency	Reliability: Stability	Reliability: Total	Val.: Total	Ages/Grades for Intended Use	Admin.: Group/Individual	Admin.: Testing time	Scores: Age equivalents	Scores: Grade equivalents	Scores: Percentile ranks	Scores: Standard scores	Scores: Other	Examiner qualifications	Input: Third Party	Input: Listen	Input: Read print	Input: Look at stimuli	Input: Other	Output: Speak, minor	Output: Speak, major	Output: Manipulate objects	Output: Mark answer sheet	Output: Point	Output: Draw	Output: Write print	Output: Other
General Aptitude Quotient	4000	B	A	A	A	A	A	A	A	A	B	6-0/17-11 yrs.	G	60+			•	•		EA		•	•	•		•				•		•[1]	
Verbal Reasoning	2210	B	A	A	A	A	A	B	B	B	A	6-0/17-11 yrs.	G	20			•	•		EA		•				•						•[1]	
Nonverbal Reasoning	2110	B	A	A	A	A	A	B	B	A	A	6-0/17-11 yrs.	G	20			•	•		EA		•		•						•		•[1]	
Quantitative Reasoning	1220	B	A	A	A	A	A	B	A	B	A	6-0/17-11 yrs.	G	20			•	•		EA		•	•			•						•[1]	

[1]For group administration only

SCHOOL BEHAVIOR CHECKLIST (1981)

	Taxonomy code	Overall rating	Norms: Scores	Norms: Size	Norms: Demographics	Norms: Recency	Norms: Total	Reliability: Internal consistency	Reliability: Stability	Reliability: Total	Val.: Total	Ages/Grades for Intended Use	Admin.: Group/Individual	Admin.: Testing time	Scores: Age equivalents	Scores: Grade equivalents	Scores: Percentile ranks	Scores: Standard scores	Scores: Other	Examiner qualifications	Input: Third Party	Input: Listen	Input: Read print	Input: Look at stimuli	Input: Other	Output: Speak, minor	Output: Speak, major	Output: Manipulate objects	Output: Mark answer sheet	Output: Point	Output: Draw	Output: Write print	Output: Other
Total Disability	4000	F	A	F/B[1]	F	B	F	F	F	F	F	4-0/13-11 yrs.	G	20			•	•		EA	•		•						•				
Low Need Achievement	3900	F	A	F/B[1]	F	B	F	F	F	F	F	4-0/13-11 yrs.	G	20			•	•		EA	•		•						•				
Aggression	3500	F	A	F/B[1]	F	B	F	F	F	F	F	4-0/13-11 yrs.	G	20			•	•		EA	•		•						•				
Anxiety	3100	F	A	F/B[1]	F	B	F	F	F	F	F	4-0/13-11 yrs.	G	20			•	•		EA	•		•						•				
Hostile Isolation	3500	F	A	F/B[1]	F	B	F	F	F	F	F	4-0/13-11 yrs.	G	20			•	•		EA	•		•						•				
Extraversion	3400	F	A	F/B[1]	F	B	F	F	F	F	F	4-0/13-11 yrs.	G	20			•	•		EA	•		•						•				
Normal Irritability	3900	F	A	F	F	B	F	F	F	F	F	40/6-11 yrs.	G	20			•	•		EA	•		•						•				
School Disturbance	4000	F	A	F	F	B	F	F	F	F	F	4-0/6-11 yrs.	G	20			•	•		EA	•		•						•				

[1]Rating for Form A1 appears first, for Form A2 second

| | | | Technical Characteristics | | | | | | | | | Nontechnical Characteristics | | | | | | | | | | | | | | | | | | | | | | |
| | | | Norms | | | | | Reliability | | | Val. | Ages/Grades for Intended Use | Admin. | | Scores | | | | | | | Test Formats — Input | | | | | Test Formats — Output | | | | | | | |
	Taxonomy code	Overall rating	Scores	Size	Demographics	Recency	Total	Internal consistency	Stability	Total	Total		Group/Individual	Testing time	Age equivalents	Grade equivalents	Percentile ranks	Standard scores	Other	Examiner qualifications	Third Party	Listen	Read print	Look at stimuli	Other	Speak, minor	Speak, major	Manipulate objects	Mark answer sheet	Point	Draw	Write print	Other
SCHOOL BEHAVIOR CHECKLIST (1981) (cont.)																																		
Academic Disability	1000	F	A	B	F	B	F	F	F	F	F	7-0/13-11 yrs.	G	20			•	•		EA	•		•							•			

¹Rating for Form A1 appears first, for Form A2 second

	Taxonomy code	Overall rating	Scores	Size	Demographics	Recency	Total	Internal consistency	Stability	Total	Total	Ages/Grades for Intended Use	Group/Individual	Testing time	Age equivalents	Grade equivalents	Percentile ranks	Standard scores	Other	Examiner qualifications	Third Party	Listen	Read print	Look at stimuli	Other	Speak, minor	Speak, major	Manipulate objects	Mark answer sheet	Point	Draw	Write print	Other
SCREENING ASSESSMENT FOR GIFTED ELEMENTARY STUDENTS — GIFTED NORMS (1987)																																	
Program Related-A	4000	F	A	A	F	A	F	F	F	F	F	7-0/12-11 yrs.	G	7			•	•		EA	•	•	•					•		•			
Program Related-B	4000	F	A	A	F	A	F	B	F	B	B	7-0/12-11 yrs.	G	7			•	•		EA	•	•	•							•			
Program Related-C	2200	F	A	A	F	A	F	F	F	F	F	7-0/12-11 yrs.	G	7			•	•		EA	•		•					•		•			
Program Related-D	4000	F	A	A	F	A	F	F	F	F	F	7-0/12-11 yrs.	G	7			•	•		EA	•	•	•					•		•			
Reasoning	2210	F	A	A	F	A	F	B	F	B	A	7-0/12-11 yrs.	G	7			•	•		EA	•		•							•			
School-Acquired Information	1000	F	A	A	F	A	F	A	F	B	B	7-0/12-11 yrs.	G	7			•	•		EA	•	•								•			
Divergent Production	2220	F	A	A	F	A	F	F	F	F	B	7-0/12-11 yrs.	G	7			•	•		EA	•		•					•		•			
SCREENING ASSESSMENT FOR GIFTED ELEMENTARY STUDENTS — NORMAL NORMS (1987)																																	
Program Related-A	4000	F	A	A	B	A	B	F	F	F	F	7-0/12-11 yrs.	G	7			•	•		EA	•	•	•					•		•			
Program Related-B	4000	B	A	A	B	A	B	B	F	B	B	7-0/12-11 yrs.	G	7			•	•		EA	•	•	•							•			
Program Related-C	2200	F	A	A	B	A	B	F	F	F	F	7-0/12-11 yrs.	G	7			•	•		EA	•		•					•		•			
Program Related-D	4000	F	A	A	B	A	B	F	F	F	F	7-0/12-11 yrs.	G	7			•	•		EA	•	•	•					•		•			
Reasoning	2210	B	A	A	B	A	B	B	F	B	A	7-0/12-11 yrs.	G	7			•	•		EA	•		•							•			
School-Acquired Information	1000	B	A	A	B	A	B	B	F	B	B	7-0/12-11 yrs.	G	7			•	•		EA	•	•								•			
Divergent Production	2220	F	A	A	B	A	B	F	F	F	F	7-0/12-11 yrs.	G	7			•	•		EA	•		•					•		•			
SCREENING CHILDREN FOR RELATED EARLY EDUCATIONAL NEEDS (1988)																																	
Early Achievement Quotient	4000	B	A	A	B	A	B	A	B	B	B	3-0/7-11 yrs.	I	22			•	•		EA	•	•	•			•	•	•	•	•		•	
Language	2200	B	A	A	B	A	B	B	B	B	A	3-0/7-11 yrs.	I	22			•	•		EA	•		•				•			•			
Reading	1300	B	A	A	B	A	B	B	B	B	A	3-0/7-11 yrs.	I	22			•	•		EA	•	•	•			•	•			•			
Writing	1600	B	A	A	B	A	B	B	B	B	A	3-0/7-11 yrs.	I	22			•	•		EA	•						•			•	•	•	
Math	1200	B	A	A	B	A	B	B	B	B	A	3-0/7-11 yrs.	I	22			•	•		EA	•		•			•	•	•	•			•	
SCREENING TEST OF ADOLESCENT LANGUAGE (1980)																																	
Total	2200	F	B	F	F	B	F	F	F	F	F	gr. 6–9	I	7			•			EA		•				•	•						
Vocabulary	2231	F	B	F	F	B	F	F	F	F	F	gr. 6–9	I	7			•			EA		•						•					
Auditory Memory Span	2232	F	B	F	F	B	F	F	F	F	F	gr. 6–9	I	7			•			EA		•						•					

	Taxonomy code	Overall rating	Scores	Size	Demographics	Recency	Total	Internal consistency	Stability	Total	Total (Val)	Ages/Grades for Intended Use	Group/Individual	Testing time	Age equivalents	Grade equivalents	Percentile ranks	Standard scores	Other	Examiner qualifications	Third Party	Listen	Read print	Look at stimuli	Other	Speak, minor	Speak, major	Manipulate objects	Mark answer sheet	Point	Draw	Write print	Other
SCREENING TEST OF ADOLESCENT LANGUAGE (1980) (cont.)																																	
Language Processing	2210	F	B	F	F	B	F	F	F	F	F	gr. 6–9	I	7			•			EA		•				•							
Proverb Explanation	2210	F	B	F	F	B	F	F	F	F	F	gr. 6–9	I	7			•			EA		•				•							
SCHUBERT GENERAL ABILITY BATTERY (1986)																																	
Total	1000	F	A	F	F	B	F	F	F	F	F	gr. 10–Adult	G	32			•	•		EA			•						•				
Word Meaning	1310	F	A	F	F	B	F	F	F	F	F	gr. 10–Adult	G	8			•	•		EA			•						•				
Verbal Analogies	1310	F	A	F	F	B	F	F	F	F	F	gr. 10–Adult	G	8			•	•		EA			•						•				
Arithmetic Problems	1210	F	A	F	F	B	F	F	F	F	F	gr. 10–Adult	G	8			•	•		EA			•						•				
Logical Answers	1310	F	A	F	F	B	F	F	F	F	F	gr. 10–Adult	G	8			•	•		EA			•						•				
SELF-DESCRIPTION QUESTIONNAIRE — II (1990)																																	
General Self	3700	F	A	A	F	A	F	F	F	F	F	gr. 7–12	G	20			•	•		EA			•						•				
General School	3710	F	A	A	F	A	F	F	F	F	F	gr. 7–12	G	20			•	•		EA			•						•				
Physical Abilities	3720	F	A	A	F	A	F	F	F	F	F	gr. 7–12	G	20			•	•		EA			•						•				
Physical Appearance	3720	F	A	A	F	A	F	F	F	F	F	gr. 7–12	G	20			•	•		EA			•						•				
Opposite-Sex Relations	3730	F	A	A	F	A	F	F	F	F	F	gr. 7–12	G	20			•	•		EA			•						•				
Same-Sex Relations	3730	F	A	A	F	A	F	F	F	F	F	gr. 7–12	G	20			•	•		EA			•						•				
Parent Relations	3730	F	A	A	F	A	F	F	F	F	F	gr. 7–12	G	20			•	•		EA			•						•				
Honesty-Trustworthiness	3740	F	A	A	F	A	F	F	F	F	F	gr. 7–12	G	20			•	•		EA			•						•				
Emotional Stability	3740	F	A	A	F	A	F	F	F	F	F	gr. 7–12	G	20			•	•		EA			•						•				
Math	3710	F	A	A	F	A	F	F	F	F	F	gr. 7–12	G	20			•	•		EA			•						•				
Verbal	3710	F	A	A	F	A	F	F	F	F	F	gr. 7–12	G	20			•	•		EA			•						•				
SELF-ESTEEM INDEX (1990)																																	
Self-Esteem Quotient	3700	B	A	A	A	A	A	A	F	B	A	8-0/18-11 yrs.	G	30			•	•		EA			•						•				
Familial Acceptance	3730	B	A	A	A	A	A	A	F	B	A	8-0/18-11 yrs.	G	30			•	•		EA			•						•				
Academic Competence	3710	B	A	A	A	A	A	B	F	B	A	8-0/18-11 yrs.	G	30			•	•		EA			•						•				
Peer Popularity	3730	B	A	A	A	A	A	B	F	B	A	8-0/18-11 yrs.	G	30			•	•		EA			•						•				
Personal Security	3740	B	A	A	A	A	A	B	F	B	A	8-0/18-11 yrs.	G	30			•	•		EA			•					·	•				

			Technical Characteristics									Nontechnical Characteristics																						
			Norms					Reliability			Val.		Admin.		Scores						Test Formats Input					Output							
	Taxonomy code	Overall rating	Scores	Size	Demographics	Recency	Total	Internal consistency	Stability	Total	Total	Ages/Grades for Intended Use	Group/Individual	Testing time	Age equivalents	Grade equivalents	Percentile ranks	Standard scores	Other	Examiner qualifications	Third Party	Listen	Read print	Look at stimuli	Other	Speak, minor	Speak, major	Manipulate objects	Mark answer sheet	Point	Draw	Write print	Other
SELF-ESTEEM INVENTORIES — SCHOOL FORM (1984)																																	
Total Self Score	3700	F	B	A	F	F	F	B	F	B	B	8-0/15-11 yrs.	G	7			•			EA		•	•						•				
Student Short Form Total Self Score	3700	F	F	A	F	F	F	F	F	F	F	8-0/15-11 yrs.	G	7					•¹	EA		•	•						•				
General Self Subscale Score	3700	F	F	A	F	F	F	F	F	F	F	8-0/15-11 yrs.	G	7					•²	EA		•	•						•				
Social Self-Peers Subscale Score	3730	F	F	A	F	F	F	F	F	F	F	8-0/15-11 yrs.	G	7					•²	EA		•	•						•				
Home-Parents Subscale Score	3700	F	F	A	F	F	F	F	F	F	F	8-0/15-11 yrs.	G	7					•²	EA		•	•						•				
School-Academic Subscale Score	3710	F	F	A	F	F	F	F	F	F	F	8-0/15-11 yrs.	G	7					•²	EA		•	•						•				

¹No norms provided; ²means and standard deviations provided for Grades 3, 6, and 9

Test	Taxonomy code	Overall rating	Scores	Size	Demographics	Recency	Total	Internal consistency	Stability	Total	Total	Ages/Grades	G/I	Testing time	Age eq	Grade eq	Percentile	Standard	Other	Examiner	Third Party	Listen	Read print	Look at stimuli	Other	Speak minor	Speak major	Manipulate	Mark answer	Point	Draw	Write print	Other
SENSORY INTEGRATION AND PRAXIS TESTS (1989)																																	
Space Visualization	2132	F	B	B	B	A	B	F	F	F	B	4-0/8-11 yrs.	I	10					•¹	ST		•		•				•					
Figure-Ground Perception	2131	F	B	B	B	A	B	F	F	F	B	4-0/8-11 yrs.	I	10					•¹	ST		•		•						•			
Manual Form Perception	2154	F	B	B	B	A	B	F	F	F	B	4-0/8-11 yrs.	I	10					•¹	ST		•			•²					•			
Kinesthesia	2140	F	B	B	B	A	B	F	F	F	B	4-0/8-11 yrs.	I	10					•¹	ST		•			•²					•			
Finger Identification	2140	F	B	B	B	A	B	F	F	F	B	4-0/8-11 yrs.	I	10					•¹	ST		•			•²						•		
Graphesthesia	2140	F	B	B	B	A	B	F	F	F	B	4-0/8-11 yrs.	I	10					•¹	ST		•			•²								•²
Localization of Tactile Stimulation	2140	F	B	B	B	A	B	F	F	F	B	4-0/8-11 yrs.	I	10					•¹	ST		•			•²					•			
Praxis on Verbal Command	2154	F	B	B	B	A	B	F	F	F	B	4-0/8-11 yrs.	I	10					•¹	ST		•											•²
Design Copying	2132	F	B	B	B	A	B	F	F	F	B	4-0/8-11 yrs.	I	10					•¹	ST		•		•							•		
Constructional Praxis	2132	F	B	B	B	A	B	F	F	F	B	4-0/8-11 yrs.	I	10					•¹	ST		•		•				•					
Postural Praxis	2151	F	B	B	B	A	B	F	F	F	B	4-0/8-11 yrs.	I	10					•¹	ST		•		•									•²
Oral Praxis	2154	F	B	B	B	A	B	F	F	F	B	4-0/8-11 yrs.	I	10					•¹	ST		•											•²
Sequencing Praxis	2154	F	B	B	B	A	B	F	F	F	B	4-0/8-11 yrs.	I	10					•¹	ST		•		•									•²
Bilateral Motor Coordination	2154	F	B	B	B	A	B	F	F	F	B	4-0/8-11 yrs.	I	10					•¹	ST		•											•²
Standing & Walking Balance	2151	F	B	B	B	A	B	F	F	F	B	4-0/8-11 yrs.	I	10					•¹	ST		•		•									
Motor Accuracy	2131	F	B	B	B	A	B	F	F	F	B	4-0/8-11 yrs.	I	10					•¹	ST		•		•								•	
Postrotary Nystagmus	2154	F	B	B	B	A	B	F	F	F	B	4-0/8-11 yrs.	I	10					•¹	ST		•			•²								•²

¹Means and standard deviations provided; ²various motor responses

Test	Taxonomy code	Overall rating	Scores	Size	Demographics	Recency	Total	Internal consistency	Stability	Total	Total	Ages/Grades	G/I	Testing time	Age eq	Grade eq	Percentile	Standard	Other	Examiner	Third Party	Listen	Read print	Look at stimuli	Other	Speak minor	Speak major	Manipulate	Mark answer	Point	Draw	Write print	Other
SEQUENTIAL ASSESSMENT OF MATHEMATICS INVENTORIES (1985)																																	
Total	1200	F	A	A	F	B	F	A	B	B	F	gr. K–8	I	60	•	•	•			EA		•	•	•				•		•		•	
Mathematical Language	1230	F	A	A	F	B	F	F	B	B	F	gr. K–8	I	60	•	•	•			EA		•		•						•			

Legend for columns: **Technical Characteristics** — Norms (Scores, Size, Demographics, Recency, Total), Reliability (Internal consistency, Stability, Total), Val. (Total). **Nontechnical Characteristics** — Ages/Grades for Intended Use; Admin. (Group/Individual, Testing time); Scores (Age equivalents, Grade equivalents, Percentile ranks, Standard scores, Other); Examiner qualifications; Test Formats — Input (Third Party, Listen, Read print, Look at stimuli, Other), Output (Speak minor, Speak major, Manipulate objects, Mark answer sheet, Point, Draw, Write print, Other).

SEQUENTIAL ASSESSMENT OF MATHEMATICS INVENTORIES (1985) (cont.)

	Taxonomy code	Overall rating	Scores	Size	Demographics	Recency	Norms Total	Internal consistency	Stability	Reliability Total	Val. Total	Ages/Grades for Intended Use	Group/Individual	Testing time	Age equivalents	Grade equivalents	Percentile ranks	Standard scores	Other	Examiner qualifications	Third Party	Listen	Read print	Look at stimuli	Other	Speak, minor	Speak, major	Manipulate objects	Mark answer sheet	Point	Draw	Write print	Other
Ordinality	1220	**F**	A	A	F	B	F	F	F	F	F	gr. K–8	I	60	•	•		•		EA		•	•	•		•				•		•	
Number & Notation	1200	**F**	A	A	F	B	F	B	F	B	F	gr. K–8	I	60	•	•		•		EA		•	•	•		•				•		•	
Computation	1220	**F**	A	A	F	B	F	B	F	B	F	gr. K–8	I	60	•	•		•		EA		•	•									•	
Measurement	1200	**F**	A	A	F	B	F	B	F	B	F	gr. K–8	I	60	•	•		•		EA		•	•	•		•				•		•	
Geometric Concepts	1200	**F**	A	A	F	B	F	B	F	B	F	gr. K–8	I	60	•	•		•		EA		•	•	•		•				•		•	
Mathematical Applications	1200	**F**	A	A	F	B	F	F	F	F	F	gr. K–8	I	60	•	•		•		EA		•	•			•						•	
Word Problems	1210	**F**	A	A	F	B	F	F	F	F	F	gr. K–8	I	60	•	•		•		EA		•	•			•							

SLOSSON INTELLIGENCE TEST FOR CHILDREN AND ADULTS — REVISED (1985)

	Taxonomy code	Overall rating	Scores	Size	Demographics	Recency	Norms Total	Internal consistency	Stability	Reliability Total	Val. Total	Ages/Grades for Intended Use	Group/Individual	Testing time	Age equivalents	Grade equivalents	Percentile ranks	Standard scores	Other	Examiner qualifications	Third Party	Listen	Read print	Look at stimuli	Other	Speak, minor	Speak, major	Manipulate objects	Mark answer sheet	Point	Draw	Write print	Other
Total	4000	**F**	A	B	F	B	F	F	B	B	F	2-0/18-0 yrs.	I	22	•		•	•		EA	•		•	•[1]		•	•	•		•	•		•[2]

[1] Observe motor tasks; [2] perform various movements

SLOSSON INTELLIGENCE TEST FOR CHILDREN AND ADULTS — REVISED (1991)

	Taxonomy code	Overall rating	Scores	Size	Demographics	Recency	Norms Total	Internal consistency	Stability	Reliability Total	Val. Total	Ages/Grades for Intended Use	Group/Individual	Testing time	Age equivalents	Grade equivalents	Percentile ranks	Standard scores	Other	Examiner qualifications	Third Party	Listen	Read print	Look at stimuli	Other	Speak, minor	Speak, major	Manipulate objects	Mark answer sheet	Point	Draw	Write print	Other
Total	4000	**F**	A	B	F	A	F	A	F	B	B	4-0/18+ yrs.	I	15	•		•	•		EA	•		•			•	•			•	•		•[1]

[1] Various motor responses

SLOSSON ORAL READING TEST, REVISED (1990)

	Taxonomy code	Overall rating	Scores	Size	Demographics	Recency	Norms Total	Internal consistency	Stability	Reliability Total	Val. Total	Ages/Grades for Intended Use	Group/Individual	Testing time	Age equivalents	Grade equivalents	Percentile ranks	Standard scores	Other	Examiner qualifications	Third Party	Listen	Read print	Look at stimuli	Other	Speak, minor	Speak, major	Manipulate objects	Mark answer sheet	Point	Draw	Write print	Other
Total	1320	**F**	A	F	F	A	F	A	F	B	F	gr. K–12	I	20	•	•	•	•		EA	•		•			•							

SOCIAL-EMOTIONAL DIMENSION SCALE (1986)

	Taxonomy code	Overall rating	Scores	Size	Demographics	Recency	Norms Total	Internal consistency	Stability	Reliability Total	Val. Total	Ages/Grades for Intended Use	Group/Individual	Testing time	Age equivalents	Grade equivalents	Percentile ranks	Standard scores	Other	Examiner qualifications	Third Party	Listen	Read print	Look at stimuli	Other	Speak, minor	Speak, major	Manipulate objects	Mark answer sheet	Point	Draw	Write print	Other
Behavior Quotient	3000	**B**	A	B	B	A	B	B	F	B	B	5-6/18-5 yrs.	I	7			•	•		EA	•		•						•				
Avoidance of Peer Interaction	3400	**F**	A	B	B	A	B	F	F	F	F	5-6/18-5 yrs.	I	7				•		EA	•		•						•				
Aggressive Interaction	3500	**F**	A	B	B	A	B	F	F	F	F	5-6/18-5 yrs.	I	7				•		EA	•		•						•				
Avoidance of Teacher Interaction	3400	**F**	A	B	B	A	B	F	F	F	F	5-6/18-5 yrs.	I	7				•		EA	•		•						•				
Inappropriate Behavior	3000	**F**	A	B	B	A	B	F	F	F	F	5-6/18-5 yrs.	I	7				•		EA	•		•						•				
Depressive Reaction	3300	**F**	A	B	B	A	B	F	F	F	F	5-6/18-5 yrs.	I	7				•		EA	•		•						•				
Physical/Fear Reaction	3100	**F**	A	B	B	A	B	F	F	F	F	5-6/18-5 yrs.	I	7				•		EA	•		•						•				

SOCIAL SKILLS RATING SYSTEM (1990)

Teacher Form:

	Taxonomy code	Overall rating	Scores	Size	Demographics	Recency	Norms Total	Internal consistency	Stability	Reliability Total	Val. Total	Ages/Grades for Intended Use	Group/Individual	Testing time	Age equivalents	Grade equivalents	Percentile ranks	Standard scores	Other	Examiner qualifications	Third Party	Listen	Read print	Look at stimuli	Other	Speak, minor	Speak, major	Manipulate objects	Mark answer sheet	Point	Draw	Write print	Other
Total Social Skills	3400	**F**	A	B	F	A	F	A	F	B	F	Preschool–gr. 12	I	20			•	•	•[1]	EA	•		•						•				
Total Problem Behavior	3000	**F**	A	B	F	A	F	B	F	B	F	Preschool–gr. 12	I	20			•	•	•[1]	EA	•		•						•				
Total Academic Competence	1000	**F**	A	B	F	A	F	A	F	B	F	Preschool–gr. 12	I	20			•	•	•[1]	EA	•		•						•				

[1] Trichotomous behavior levels provided

SOCIAL SKILLS RATING SYSTEM (1990) (cont.)

| | | Technical Characteristics | | | | | | | | | Nontechnical Characteristics | | | | | | | | | | | | | | | | | | | | | | |
| | | Norms | | | | | Reliability | | | Val. | Ages/Grades for Intended Use | Admin. | | Scores | | | | | | Input | | | | | Output | | | | | | | |
	Taxonomy code	Overall rating	Scores	Size	Demographics	Recency	Total	Internal consistency	Stability	Total	Total		Group/Individual	Testing time	Age equivalents	Grade equivalents	Percentile ranks	Standard scores	Other	Examiner qualifications	Third Party	Listen	Read print	Look at stimuli	Other	Speak, minor	Speak, major	Manipulate objects	Mark answer sheet	Point	Draw	Write print	Other
Teacher Form (cont.):																																	
Cooperation	3400	F	B	B	F	A	F	A	F	B	F	Preschool–gr. 12	I	20					•¹	EA	•		•						•				
Assertion	3400	F	B	B	F	A	F	B	F	B	F	Preschool–gr. 12	I	20					•¹	EA	•		•						•				
Self-Control	3830	F	B	B	F	A	F	B	F	B	F	Preschool–gr. 12	I	20					•¹	EA	•		•						•				
Externalizing	3500	F	B	B	F	A	F	B	F	B	F	Preschool–gr. 12	I	20					•¹	EA	•		•						•				
Internalizing	3000	F	B	B	F	A	F	F	F	F	F	Preschool–gr. 12	I	20					•¹	EA	•		•						•				
Hyperactivity	3810	F	B	B	F	A	F	B	F	B	F	Preschool–gr. 12	I	20					•¹	EA	•		•						•				
Parent Form:																																	
Total Social Skills	3400	F	A	B	F	A	F	B	F	B	F	Preschool–gr. 12	I	20			•	•	•¹	EA	•		•						•				
Total Problem Behavior	3000	F	A	B	F	A	F	B	F	B	F	Preschool–gr. 12	I	20			•	•	•¹	EA	•		•						•				
Cooperation	3400	F	B	B	F	A	F	F	F	F	F	Preschool–gr. 12	I	20					•¹	EA	•		•						•				
Assertion	3400	F	B	B	F	A	F	F	F	F	F	Preschool–gr. 12	I	20					•¹	EA	•		•						•				
Responsibility	3830	F	B	B	F	A	F	F	F	F	F	Preschool–gr. 12	I	20					•¹	EA	•		•						•				
Self-Control	3830	F	B	B	F	A	F	B	F	B	F	Preschool–gr. 12	I	20					•¹	EA	•		•						•				
Externalizing	3500	F	B	B	F	A	F	F	F	F	F	Preschool–gr. 12	I	20					•¹	EA	•		•						•				
Internalizing	3000	F	B	B	F	A	F	F	F	F	F	Preschool–gr. 12	I	20					•¹	EA	•		•						•				
Hyperactivity	3810	F	B	B	F	A	F	F	F	F	F	Preschool–gr. 12	I	20					•¹	EA	•		•						•				
Student Form:																																	
Total Social Skills	3400	F	A	B	F	A	F	B	F	B	F	gr. 3–12	I	20			•	•	•¹	EA			•						•				
Cooperation	3400	F	B	B	F	A	F	F	F	F	F	gr. 3–12	I	20					•¹	EA			•						•				
Assertion	3400	F	B	B	F	A	F	F	F	F	F	gr. 3–12	I	20					•¹	EA			•						•				
Empathy	3900	F	B	B	F	A	F	F	F	F	F	gr. 3–12	I	20					•¹	EA			•						•				
Self-Control	3830	F	B	B	F	A	F	F	F	F	F	gr. 3–12	I	20					•¹	EA			•						•				

¹Trichotomous behavior levels provided

SOUTHERN CALIFORNIA SENSORY INTEGRATION TESTS — REVISED (1980)

	Taxonomy code	Overall rating	Scores	Size	Demographics	Recency	Total	Internal consistency	Stability	Total	Total	Ages/Grades	Group/Individual	Testing time	Age equivalents	Grade equivalents	Percentile ranks	Standard scores	Other	Examiner qualifications	Third Party	Listen	Read print	Look at stimuli	Other	Speak, minor	Speak, major	Manipulate objects	Mark answer sheet	Point	Draw	Write print	Other
Space Visualization	2132	F	A	F	F	B	F	F	F	F	F	4-0/10-11 yrs.	I	7				•		ST	•		•					•		•			
Figure-Ground Perception	2131	F	A	F	F	B	F	F	F	F	F	4-0/10-11 yrs.	I	7				•		ST	•		•							•			
Position in Space	2131	F	A	F	F	B	F	F	F	F	F	4-0/10-11 yrs.	I	7				•		ST	•		•					•		•			
Design Copying	2132	F	A	F	F	B	F	F	B	B	F	4-0/10-11 yrs.	I	7				•		ST	•		•									•	

Technical Characteristics: **Norms** (Scores, Size, Demographics, Recency, Total); **Reliability** (Internal consistency, Stability, Total); **Val.** (Total).
Nontechnical Characteristics: **Admin.** (Group/Individual, Testing time); **Scores** (Age equivalents, Grade equivalents, Percentile ranks, Standard scores, Other); Examiner qualifications; **Test Formats** — Input (Third Party, Listen, Read print, Look at stimuli, Other), Output (Speak minor, Speak major, Manipulate objects, Mark answer sheet, Point, Draw, Write print, Other).

SOUTHERN CALIFORNIA SENSORY INTEGRATION TESTS — REVISED (1980) (cont.)

Test	Tax. code	Overall	Scores	Size	Demog.	Recency	Total	Int. cons.	Stability	Total	Val. Total	Ages/Grades	Grp/Ind	Time	Age eq	Grade eq	%ile	Std sc	Other	Exam. qual.	3rd Party	Listen	Read	Look	Other	Spk min	Spk maj	Manip	Mark	Point	Draw	Write	Other
Motor Accuracy-Revised	2132	F	A	F	F	B	F	F	F	F	F	4-0/10-11 yrs.	I	7				•		ST	•			•							•		
Kinesthesia	2140	F	A	F	F	B	F	F	F	F	F	4-0/10-11 yrs.	I	7				•		ST	•				•1								•2
Manual Form Perception	2140	F	A	F	F	B	F	F	F	F	F	4-0/10-11 yrs.	I	7				•		ST	•				•3					•			
Finger Identification	2140	F	A	F	F	B	F	F	F	F	F	4-0/10-11 yrs.	I	7				•		ST	•				•4					•			
Graphesthesia	2140	F	A	F	F	B	F	F	F	F	F	4-0/10-11 yrs.	I	7				•		ST	•				•5								•6
Localization of Tactile Stimuli	2140	F	A	F	F	B	F	F	F	F	F	4-0/10-11 yrs.	I	7				•		ST	•				•7								
Double Tactile Stimuli Perception	2140	F	A	F	F	B	F	F	F	F	F	4-0/10-11 yrs.	I	7				•		ST	•				•8					•			
Imitation of Postures	2151	F	A	F	F	B	F	F	F	F	F	4-0/10-11 yrs.	I	7				•		ST	•				•9								•10
Crossing Mid-Line of Body	2154	F	A	F	F	B	F	F	F	F	F	4-0/10-11 yrs.	I	7				•		ST	•				•1								•2
Bilateral Motor Coordination	2153	F	A	F	F	B	F	F	F	F	F	4-0/10-11 yrs.	I	7				•		ST	•				•1								•2
Right-Left Discrimination	2154	F	A	F	F	B	F	F	F	F	F	4-0/10-11 yrs.	I	7				•		ST	•												•11
Standing Balance: Eyes Open	2151	F	A	F	F	B	F	F	F	F	F	4-0/10-11 yrs.	I	7				•		ST	•												•12
Standing Balance: Eyes Closed	2151	F	A	F	F	B	F	F	F	F	F	4-0/10-11 yrs.	I	7				•		ST	•												•13

[1]Observe arm movements; [2]reproduce arm movements; [3]feel forms; [4]feel fingers touched; [5]feel shape of blocks "drawn" on hand; [6]draws on own hand with finger; [7]feels penmark on arm; [8]feel touch on body; [9]looks at positions/postures demonstrated by examiner; [10]reproduces examiner positions; [11]executes commands motorically; [12]balance on one foot with eyes open; [13]balance on one foot with eyes closed

STANFORD-BINET INTELLIGENCE SCALE, FOURTH EDITION (1986)

Test	Tax. code	Overall	Scores	Size	Demog.	Recency	Total	Int. cons.	Stability	Total	Val. Total	Ages/Grades	Grp/Ind	Time	Age eq	Grade eq	%ile	Std sc	Other	Exam. qual.	3rd Party	Listen	Read	Look	Other	Spk min	Spk maj	Manip	Mark	Point	Draw	Write	Other
Test Composite	4000	B	A	A	A	A	A	A	A	A	B	2-0/23-11 yrs.	I	60+				•1		R		•	•	•		•	•	•		•	•	•	•
Verbal Reasoning	2200	B	A	A	A	A	A	A	B	B	B	2-0/23-11 yrs.	I	22				•1		R		•		•		•	•						
Abstract/Visual Reasoning	2100	B	A	A	A	A	A	A	B	B	B	2-0/23-11 yrs.	I	22				•1		R		•		•				•		•	•		
Quantitative Reasoning	1200	B	A	A	A	A	A	A	F	B	B	2-0/23-11 yrs.	I	45				•1		R		•	•	•		•						•	
Short-Term Memory	2000	B	A	A	A	A	A	A	F	B	B	2-0/23-11 yrs.	I	22				•1		R		•		•			•	•		•			
Vocabulary	2231	B	A	A	A	A	A	B	F	B	B	2-0/23-11 yrs.	I	7				•2		R		•		•		•	•						
Bead Memory	2133	B	A	A	A	A	A	B	F	B	B	2-0/23-11 yrs.	I	7				•2		R		•		•				•		•			
Quantitative	1200	B	A	A	A	A	A	B	F	B	B	2-0/23-11 yrs.	I	22				•2		R		•		•				•		•			
Memory for Sentences	2232	B	A	A	A	A	A	B	F	B	B	2-0/23-11 yrs.	I	7				•2		R		•					•						
Pattern Analysis	2132	B	A	A	A	A	A	A	F	B	B	2-0/23-11 yrs.	I	22				•2		R		•		•				•					
Comprehension	2210	B	A	A	A	A	A	B	F	B	B	2-0/23-11 yrs.	I	7				•2		R		•					•						
Absurdities	2210	B	A	A	A	A	A	B	F	B	B	2-0/17-11 yrs.	I	7				•2		R		•		•			•						

[1]Standard Age Scores (SAS) are normalized standard scores with $\bar{x} = 100$, SD = 16; [2]SAS $\bar{x} = 50$, SD = 8

STANFORD-BINET INTELLIGENCE SCALE, FOURTH EDITION (1986) (cont.)

	Taxonomy code	Overall rating	Scores	Size	Demographics	Recency	Total	Internal consistency	Stability	Total	Total (Val)	Ages/Grades for Intended Use	Group/Individual	Testing time	Age equivalents	Grade equivalents	Percentile ranks	Standard scores	Other	Examiner qualifications	Third Party	Listen	Read print	Look at stimuli	Other	Speak, minor	Speak, major	Manipulate objects	Mark answer sheet	Point	Draw	Write print	Other
Memory for Digits	2242	B	A	A	A	A	A	B	F	B	B	4-11/23-11 yrs.	I	7				•2		R		•						•					
Copying	2132	B	A	A	A	A	A	B	F	B	B	2-0/17-11 yrs.	I	7				•2		R		•		•				•			•		
Memory for Objects	2133	F	A	A	A	A	A	F	F	F	B	4-11/23-11 yrs.	I	7				•2		R		•		•						•			
Matrices	2110	B	A	A	A	A	A	A	F	B	B	4-11/23-11 yrs.	I	7				•2		R		•		•						•		•	
Number Series	1210	B	A	A	A	A	A	A	F	B	B	4-11/23-11 yrs.	I	7				•2		R		•		•		•							
Paper Folding and Cutting	2131	B	A	A	A	A	A	A	F	B	B	9-11/23-11 yrs.	I	7				•2		R		•		•		•				•			
Verbal Relations	2210	B	A	A	A	A	A	A	F	B	B	9-11/23-11 yrs.	I	7				•2		R		•					•						
Equation Building	1210	B	A	A	A	A	A	A	F	B	B	9-11/23-11 yrs.	I	22				•2		R			•									•	

¹Standard Age Scores (SAS) are normalized standard scores with $\bar{X} = 100$, $SD = 16$; ²SAS $\bar{X} = 50$, $SD = 8$

STANFORD-BINET INTELLIGENCE SCALE, 1972 NORMS EDITION (1973)

	Taxonomy code	Overall rating	Scores	Size	Demographics	Recency	Total	Internal consistency	Stability	Total	Total (Val)	Ages/Grades for Intended Use	Group/Individual	Testing time	Age equivalents	Grade equivalents	Percentile ranks	Standard scores	Other	Examiner qualifications	Third Party	Listen	Read print	Look at stimuli	Other	Speak, minor	Speak, major	Manipulate objects	Mark answer sheet	Point	Draw	Write print	Other
Total	4000	F	A	B	F	F	F	F	F	F	F	2-0/18-11 yrs.	I	45	•		•			R		•		•		•	•	•		•	•	•	•

STREET SURVIVAL SKILLS QUESTIONNAIRE (1980)

	Taxonomy code	Overall rating	Scores	Size	Demographics	Recency	Total	Internal consistency	Stability	Total	Total (Val)	Ages/Grades for Intended Use	Group/Individual	Testing time	Age equivalents	Grade equivalents	Percentile ranks	Standard scores	Other	Examiner qualifications	Third Party	Listen	Read print	Look at stimuli	Other	Speak, minor	Speak, major	Manipulate objects	Mark answer sheet	Point	Draw	Write print	Other
Total Quotient	1000	F	A	F	F	B	F	F	F	F	B	9-0/15-11 yrs.	I	60+			•			EA		•	•	•						•			
Basic Concepts	1910	F	A	F	F	B	F	F	F	F	B	9-0/15-11 yrs.	I	7			•			EA		•	•	•						•			
Functional Signs	1910	F	A	F	F	B	F	F	F	F	B	9-0/15-11 yrs.	I	7			•			EA		•	•	•						•			
Tools	1930	F	A	F	F	B	F	F	F	F	B	9-0/15-11 yrs.	I	7			•			EA		•	•	•						•			
Domestics	1920	F	A	F	F	B	F	F	F	F	B	9-0/15-11 yrs.	I	7			•			EA		•	•	•						•			
Health and Safety	1910	F	A	F	F	B	F	F	F	F	B	9-0/15-11 yrs.	I	7			•			EA		•	•	•						•			
Public Services	1910	F	A	F	F	B	F	F	F	F	B	9-0/15-11 yrs.	I	7			•			EA		•	•	•						•			
Time	1230	F	A	F	F	B	F	F	F	F	B	9-0/15-11 yrs.	I	7			•			EA		•	•	•						•			
Monetary	1230	F	A	F	F	B	F	F	F	F	B	9-0/15-11 yrs.	I	7			•			EA		•	•	•						•			
Measurements	1230	F	A	F	F	B	F	F	F	F	B	9-0/15-11 yrs.	I	7			•			EA		•	•	•						•			

SUICIDAL IDEATION QUESTIONNAIRE (1988)

	Taxonomy code	Overall rating	Scores	Size	Demographics	Recency	Total	Internal consistency	Stability	Total	Total (Val)	Ages/Grades for Intended Use	Group/Individual	Testing time	Age equivalents	Grade equivalents	Percentile ranks	Standard scores	Other	Examiner qualifications	Third Party	Listen	Read print	Look at stimuli	Other	Speak, minor	Speak, major	Manipulate objects	Mark answer sheet	Point	Draw	Write print	Other
Form HS Total	3640	F	B	B/F/F¹	F	A	F	A	F	B	A/F/F¹	gr. 10–12	G	10			•			EA			•						•				
Form JR Total	3640	F	B	B/F/F¹	F	A	F	A	F	B	A/F/F¹	gr. 7–9	G	10			•			EA			•						•				

¹Rating for Total Population Norms appears first, Male Norms second, and Female Norms third

THE TEMPERAMENT ASSESSMENT BATTERY FOR CHILDREN (1988)

	Taxonomy code	Overall rating	Scores	Size	Demographics	Recency	Total	Internal consistency	Stability	Total	Total (Val)	Ages/Grades for Intended Use	Group/Individual	Testing time	Age equivalents	Grade equivalents	Percentile ranks	Standard scores	Other	Examiner qualifications	Third Party	Listen	Read print	Look at stimuli	Other	Speak, minor	Speak, major	Manipulate objects	Mark answer sheet	Point	Draw	Write print	Other
Parent Form:																																	
Activity	3810	F	A	B	F	B	F	F	F	F	F	3-0/7-11 yrs.	I	15			•			EA		•		•						•			

	Taxonomy code	Overall rating	Norms: Scores	Norms: Size	Norms: Demographics	Norms: Recency	Norms: Total	Reliability: Internal consistency	Reliability: Stability	Reliability: Total	Val.: Total	Ages/Grades for Intended Use	Admin.: Group/Individual	Admin.: Testing time	Scores: Age equivalents	Scores: Grade equivalents	Scores: Percentile ranks	Scores: Standard scores	Scores: Other	Examiner qualifications	Input: Third Party	Input: Listen	Input: Read print	Input: Look at stimuli	Input: Other	Output: Speak, minor	Output: Speak, major	Output: Manipulate objects	Output: Mark answer sheet	Output: Point	Output: Draw	Output: Write print	Output: Other
THE TEMPERAMENT ASSESSMENT BATTERY FOR CHILDREN (1988) (cont.)																																	
Parent Form (cont.):																																	
Adaptability	3900	F	A	B	F	B	F	F	F	F	F	3-0/7-11 yrs.	I	15				•		EA	•		•						•				
Approach/Withdrawal	3400	F	A	B	F	B	F	B	F	B	F	3-0/7-11 yrs.	I	15				•		EA	•		•						•				
Emotional Intensity	3900	F	A	B	F	B	F	F	F	F	F	3-0/7-11 yrs.	I	15				•		EA	•		•						•				
Ease-of-Management-Through-Distraction	3900	F	A	B	F	B	F	F	F	F	F	3-0/7-11 yrs.	I	15				•		EA	•		•						•				
Persistence	3820	F	A	B	F	B	F	F	F	F	F	3-0/7-11 yrs.	I	15				•		EA	•		•						•				
Teacher Form:																																	
Activity	3810	F	A	F	F	B	F	B	F	B	B	3-0/7-11 yrs.	I	15				•		EA	•		•						•				
Adaptability	3900	F	A	F	F	B	F	B	F	B	B	3-0/7-11 yrs.	I	15				•		EA	•		•						•				
Approach/Withdrawal	3400	F	A	F	F	B	F	B	F	B	B	3-0/7-11 yrs.	I	15				•		EA	•		•						•				
Emotional Intensity	3900	F	A	F	F	B	F	F	F	F	F	3-0/7-11 yrs.	I	15				•		EA	•		•						•				
Distractibility	3820	F	A	F	F	B	F	B	F	B	B	3-0/7-11 yrs.	I	15				•		EA	•		•						•				
Persistence	3820	F	A	F	F	B	F	B	F	B	B	3-0/7-11 yrs.	I	15				•		EA	•		•						•				
Clinician Form:																																	
Activity	3810	F	A	F	F	B	F	B	F	B	F	3-0/7-11 yrs.	I	15				•		EA	•		•						•				
Adaptability	3900	F	A	F	F	B	F	F	F	F	F	3-0/7-11 yrs.	I	15				•		EA	•		•						•				
Approach/Withdrawal	3400	F	A	F	F	B	F	F	F	F	F	3-0/7-11 yrs.	I	15				•		EA	•		•						•				
Distractibility	3820	F	A	F	F	B	F	F	F	F	F	3-0/7-11 yrs.	I	15				•		EA	•		•						•				
Persistence	3820	F	A	F	F	B	F	F	F	F	F	3-0/7-11 yrs.	I	15				•		EA	•		•						•				
TEMPLIN-DARLEY TESTS OF ARTICULATION — DIAGNOSTIC (1969)																																	
Total	2243	F	F	F	F	F	F	F	F	F	F	3-0/8-11 yrs.	I	22	•					ST	•		•	•		•							
TEMPLIN-DARLEY TESTS OF ARTICULATION — SCREEN (1969)																																	
Total	2243	F	F	F	F	F	F	F	F	F	F	3-0/8-11 yrs.	I	7	•					ST	•		•	•		•							
TEST FOR AUDITORY COMPREHENSION OF LANGUAGE — REVISED (1985)																																	
Total	2230	B	A	B	A	B	B	A	F	B	B	3-0/9-11 yrs.	I	45	•	•	•	•		EA	•		•							•			
Word Classes and Relations	2231	B	A	B	A	B	B	B	F	B	B	3-0/9-11 yrs.	I	7	•	•	•	•		EA	•		•							•			
Grammatic Morphemes	2232	B	A	B	A	B	B	B	F	B	B	3-0/9-11 yrs.	I	7	•	•	•	•		EA	•		•							•			
Elaborated Sentences	2232	B	A	B	A	B	B	A	F	B	B	3-0/9-11 yrs.	I	7	•	•	•	•		EA	•		•							•			

		Technical Characteristics									Nontechnical Characteristics																						
		Overall rating	Norms					Reliability			Val.	Ages/Grades for Intended Use	Admin.		Scores					Examiner qualifications	Input					Output							
	Taxonomy code	Overall rating	Scores	Size	Demographics	Recency	Total	Internal consistency	Stability	Total	Total	Ages/Grades for Intended Use	Group/Individual	Testing time	Age equivalents	Grade equivalents	Percentile ranks	Standard scores	Other	Examiner qualifications	Third Party	Listen	Read print	Look at stimuli	Other	Speak, minor	Speak, major	Manipulate objects	Mark answer sheet	Point	Draw	Write print	Other
TEST OF ACADEMIC PERFORMANCE (1989)																																	
Mathematics	1220	F	A	A	B	A	B	F	F	F	F	5-6/18-11 yrs.	G	15		•	•	•		EA		•	•						•			•	
Spelling	1630	F	A	A	B	A	B	B	B	B	F	5-6/18-11 yrs.	G	15		•	•	•		EA		•										•	
Reading Recognition	1320	F	A	A	B	A	B	A	A	A	F	5-6/18-11 yrs.	I	5		•	•	•		EA		•	•			•							
Reading Comprehension	1310	F	A	A	B	A	B	F	F	F	F	5-6/18-11 yrs.	I	10		•	•	•		EA		•	•					•					
Copying Rate	2250	F	A	A	B	A	B	F	F	F	F	5-6/13-11 yrs.	G	1		•	•	•		EA		•	•									•	
Written Composition	1600	F	A	A	B	A	B	F	F	F	F	8-0/18-11 yrs.	G	10		•	•	•		EA		•										•	
TEST OF ADOLESCENT/ADULT WORD FINDING (1990)																																	
Total	2230	B	A	A	B	A	B	B	B	B	B	12-0/80-11 yrs.	I	25			•	•		EA		•		•		•	•			•			
TEST OF ADOLESCENT LANGUAGE (1980)																																	
Adolescent Language	4000	F	A	A	F	B	F	A	A	A	B	11-0/18-5 yrs.	I	60				•		EA		•	•	•				•	•			•	
Receptive Language	4000	F	A	A	F	B	F	A	A	A	B	11-0/18-5 yrs.	G	60				•		EA		•	•	•					•				
Expressive Language	4000	F	A	A	F	B	F	A	A	A	B	11-0/18-5 yrs.	G	45				•		EA		•	•					•				•	
Spoken Language	2230	F	A	A	F	B	F	A	A	A	B	11-0/18-5 yrs.	I	45				•		EA		•	•				•	•					
Written Language	1000	F	A	A	F	B	F	A	A	A	B	11-0/18-5 yrs.	G	60				•		EA		•	•						•			•	
Vocabulary	4000	F	A	A	F	B	F	A	A	A	B	11-0/18-5 yrs.	I	60				•		EA		•	•	•				•	•			•	
Grammar	4000	F	A	A	F	B	F	A	A	A	B	11-0/18-5 yrs.	I	60				•		EA		•	•					•	•			•	
Listening	2230	F	A	A	F	B	F	B	B	B	B	11-0/18-5 yrs.	G	45				•		EA		•							•				
Speaking	2230	F	A	A	F	B	F	B	B	B	B	11-0/18-5 yrs.	I	22				•		EA		•					•						
Reading	1310	F	A	A	F	B	F	A	A	A	B	11-0/18-5 yrs.	G	45				•		EA		•	•						•				
Writing	1600	F	A	A	F	B	F	A	A	A	B	11-0/18-5 yrs.	G	45				•		EA		•	•									•	
Listening/Vocabulary	2231	F	A	A	F	B	F	F	F	F	B	11-0/18-5 yrs.	G	22			•	•		EA		•		•					•				
Listening/Grammar	2232	F	A	A	F	B	F	F	F	F	B	11-0/18-5 yrs.	G	22			•	•		EA		•							•				
Speaking/Vocabulary	2231	F	A	A	F	B	F	B	B	B	B	11-0/18-5 yrs.	I	7			•	•		EA		•						•					
Speaking/Grammar	2232	F	A	A	F	B	F	B	F	B	B	11-0/18-5 yrs.	I	7			•	•		EA		•						•					
Reading/Vocabulary	1310	F	A	A	F	B	F	B	B	B	B	11-0/18-5 yrs.	G	22			•	•		EA		•	•						•				
Reading/Grammar	1310	F	A	A	F	B	F	B	B	B	B	11-0/18-5 yrs.	G	22			•	•		EA		•	•						•				
Writing/Vocabulary	1600	F	A	A	F	B	F	B	A	B	B	11-0/18-5 yrs.	G	22			•	•		EA		•										•	
Writing/Grammar	1600	F	A	A	F	B	F	A	B	B	B	11-0/18-5 yrs.	G	22			•	•		EA		•	•									•	

	Taxonomy code	Overall rating	Norms: Scores	Size	Demographics	Recency	Total	Reliability: Internal consistency	Stability	Total	Val.: Total	Ages/Grades for Intended Use	Group/Individual	Testing time	Age equivalents	Grade equivalents	Percentile ranks	Standard scores	Other	Examiner qualifications	Third Party	Listen	Read print	Look at stimuli	Other	Speak, minor	Speak, major	Manipulate objects	Mark answer sheet	Point	Draw	Write print	Other
TEST OF ADOLESCENT LANGUAGE, SECOND EDITION (1987)																																	
Adolescent Language	4000	B	A	A	A	A	A	A	B	B	B	12-0/18-5 yrs.	I	60				•		EA		•		•		•		•		•		•	
Receptive Language	4000	B	A	A	A	A	A	A	B	B	B	12-0/18-5 yrs.	G	60				•		EA		•	•	•						•			
Expressive Language	4000	B	A	A	A	A	A	A	B	B	B	12-0/18-5 yrs.	G	45				•		EA		•	•					•				•	
Spoken Language	2230	B	A	A	A	A	A	A	B	B	B	12-0/18-5 yrs.	I	45				•		EA		•		•		•		•					
Written Language	1000	B	A	A	A	A	A	A	B	B	B	12-0/18-5 yrs.	G	60				•		EA		•	•							•		•	
Vocabulary	4000	B	A	A	A	A	A	A	B	B	B	12-0/18-5 yrs.	I	60				•		EA		•	•	•						•			
Grammar	4000	B	A	A	A	A	A	A	B	B	B	12-0/18-5 yrs.	I	60				•		EA		•	•					•				•	
Listening	2230	B	A	A	A	A	A	A	B	B	B	12-0/18-5 yrs.	G	45				•		EA		•		•						•			
Speaking	2230	B	A	A	A	A	A	A	B	B	B	12-0/18-5 yrs.	I	22				•		EA		•						•					
Reading	1310	B	A	A	A	A	A	A	B	B	B	12-0/18-5 yrs.	G	45				•		EA		•	•							•			
Writing	1600	B	A	A	A	A	A	A	B	B	B	12-0/18-5 yrs.	G	45				•		EA		•	•									•	
Listening/Vocabulary	2231	B	A	A	A	A	A	F	B	A		12-0/18-5 yrs.	G	22			•	•		EA		•		•						•			
Listening/Grammar	2232	B	A	A	A	A	A	F	B	A		12-0/18-5 yrs.	G	22			•	•		EA		•								•			
Speaking/Vocabulary	2231	B	A	A	A	A	B	B	B	A		12-0/18-5 yrs.	I	7			•	•		EA		•						•					
Speaking/Grammar	2232	B	A	A	A	A	B	F	B	A		12-0/18-5 yrs.	I	7			•	•		EA		•						•					
Reading/Vocabulary	1310	B	A	A	A	A	A	B	B	A		12-0/18-5 yrs.	G	22			•	•		EA		•	•							•			
Reading/Grammar	1310	B	A	A	A	A	B	B	B	A		12-0/18-5 yrs.	G	22			•	•		EA		•	•							•			
Writing/Vocabulary	1600	B	A	A	A	A	B	B	B	A		12-0/18-5 yrs.	G	22			•	•		EA		•	•									•	
Writing/Grammar	1600	B	A	A	A	A	A	B	B	A		12-0/18-5 yrs.	G	22			•	•		EA		•	•									•	
TEST OF ARTICULATION PERFORMANCE — SCREEN — IMITATION NORMS (1983)																																	
Articulation Quotient	2243	F	A	B	F	B	F	A	F	B	F	3-0/8-11 yrs.	I	7	•		•	•		EA		•		•		•							
TEST OF ARTICULATION PERFORMANCE — SCREEN — PICTURE/PROMPT NORMS (1983)																																	
Articulation Quotient	2243	F	A	B	F	B	F	A	F	B	F	3-0/8-11 yrs.	I	7	•		•	•		EA		•		•		•							
TEST OF AUDITORY-PERCEPTUAL SKILLS (1985)																																	
Auditory Quotient	2210	F	A	B	F	B	F	F	F	B	F	4-0/11-11 yrs.	I	22			•	•		EA		•				•	•						
Auditory Processing	2200	F	A	B	F	B	F	F	F	F	F	4-0/11-11 yrs.	I	7	•		•	•		EA		•						•					
Auditory Number Memory-Forward	2242	F	A	B	F	B	F	B	F	B	F	4-0/11-11 yrs.	I	7	•					EA		•						•					
Auditory Number Memory-Reversed	2242	F	A	B	F	B	F	F	F	F	F	4-0/11-11 yrs.	I	7	•					EA		•						•					
Auditory Sentence Memory	2232	F	A	B	F	B	F	F	F	F	F	4-0/11-11 yrs.	I	7	•					EA		•						•					

	Taxonomy code	Overall rating	Norms: Scores	Norms: Size	Norms: Demographics	Norms: Recency	Norms: Total	Reliability: Internal consistency	Reliability: Stability	Reliability: Total	Val.: Total	Ages/Grades for Intended Use	Group/Individual	Testing time	Age equivalents	Grade equivalents	Percentile ranks	Standard scores	Other	Examiner qualifications	Third Party	Listen	Read print	Look at stimuli	Other	Speak, minor	Speak, major	Manipulate objects	Mark answer sheet	Point	Draw	Write print	Other

TEST OF AUDITORY-PERCEPTUAL SKILLS (1985) (cont.)

Auditory Word Memory	2242	F	A	B	F	B	F	B	F	B	F	4-0/11-11 yrs.	I	7	•					EA		•					•						
Auditory Interpretation of Directions	2230	F	A	B	F	B	F	F	F	F	F	4-0/11-11 yrs.	I	7	•					EA		•					•						
Auditory Word Discrimination	2241	F	A	B	F	B	F	F	F	F	F	4-0/11-11 yrs.	I	7	•					EA		•				•							

TEST OF EARLY LANGUAGE DEVELOPMENT (1981)

| Language Quotient | 2200 | B | A | A | B | B | B | B | B | B | A | 3-0/7-11 yrs. | I | 22 | • | | • | • | | EA | | • | | • | | • | • | | | • | | | •[1] |

[1]Gestures

TEST OF EARLY LANGUAGE DEVELOPMENT, SECOND EDITION (1991)

| Total, Forms A & B | 2200 | A | A | A | A | A | A | A | A | A | A | 2-0/7-11 yrs. | I | 30 | • | | • | • | | EA | | • | | • | | • | • | | | • | | | •[1] |

[1]Various gestures and motor responses required

TEST OF EARLY MATHEMATICS ABILITY (1983)

| Math Quotient | 1200 | F | B | F | F | B | F | A | A | A | B | 4-0/8-11 yrs. | I | 22 | • | | • | • | | EA | | • | | • | | • | • | | | | | • | |

TEST OF EARLY MATHEMATICS ABILITY, SECOND EDITION (1990)

| Math Quotient | 1200 | B | A | B | A | B | B | A | B | B | A | 3-0/8-11 yrs. | I | 20 | | | • | • | | EA | | • | • | • | | • | • | • | | • | • | • | |

TEST OF EARLY READING ABILITY (1981)

| Reading Quotient | 1300 | B | A | A | B | B | B | A | A | A | A | 3-0/7-11 yrs. | I | 22 | • | | • | • | | EA | | • | • | • | | • | • | | | • | | | |

TEST OF EARLY READING ABILITY, SECOND EDITION (1989)

| Total Score, Forms A & B | 1300 | B | A | A | B | A | B | A | B | B | B | 3-0/9-11 yrs. | I | 15 | | | • | • | | EA | | • | • | • | | • | • | | | • | | | |

TEST OF EARLY READING ABILITY — DEAF OR HARD OF HEARING (1991)

| Form A | 1300 | B | A | B | A | A | B | A | B | B | A | 3-0/13-11 yrs. | I | 30 | | | • | • | | EA | | • | • | • | | • | • | | | • | | | |
| Form B | 1300 | B | A | B | A | A | B | A | B | B | A | 3-0/13-11 yrs. | I | 30 | | | • | • | | EA | | • | • | • | | • | • | | | • | | | |

TEST OF EARLY SOCIOEMOTIONAL DEVELOPMENT (1984)

Student Rating Scale	3000	F	A	A	B	B	B	F	B	B	F	3-0/7-11 yrs.	I	7			•	•		EA		•					•						
Teacher Rating Scale	3000	F	A	A	F	B	F	A	A	A	B	3-0/7-11 yrs.	I	7			•	•		EA			•						•				
Parent Rating Scale	3000	F	A	A	F	B	F	A	A	A	B	3-0/7-11 yrs.	I	7			•	•		EA			•						•				

TEST OF EARLY WRITTEN LANGUAGE (1988)

| Written Language Quotient | 1600 | B | A | A | B | A | B | B | B | B | B | 3-0/7-11 yrs. | I | 22 | | | • | • | | EA | | • | • | • | | • | • | | | • | | • | |

TEST OF GROSS MOTOR DEVELOPMENT (1985)

| Gross Motor Development Quotient | 2153 | F | A | B | F | B | F | F | F | F | B | 3-0/10-11 yrs. | I | 22 | | | | • | | EA | | • | • | | | | | | | | | | •[1] |

[1]Physical activities (e.g., run, jump)

Column groups: Technical Characteristics — Norms (Scores, Size, Demographics, Recency, Total); Reliability (Internal consistency, Stability, Total); Val. (Total). Nontechnical Characteristics — Admin. (Group/Individual, Testing time); Scores (Age equivalents, Grade equivalents, Percentile ranks, Standard scores, Other); Examiner qualifications; Test Formats — Input (Third Party, Listen, Read print, Look at stimuli, Other); Output (Speak minor, Speak major, Manipulate objects, Mark answer sheet, Point, Draw, Write print, Other).

TEST OF GROSS MOTOR DEVELOPMENT (1985) (cont.)

	Taxonomy code	Overall rating	Scores	Size	Demographics	Recency	Total	Internal consistency	Stability	Total	Val.	Ages/Grades for Intended Use	Group/Individual	Testing time	Age equivalents	Grade equivalents	Percentile ranks	Standard scores	Other	Examiner qualifications	Third Party	Listen	Read print	Look at stimuli	Other	Speak, minor	Speak, major	Manipulate objects	Mark answer sheet	Point	Draw	Write print	Other
Locomotor	2153	F	A	B	F	B	F	B	F	B	B	3-0/10-11 yrs.	I	7				•		EA		•		•									•[1]
Object Control	2153	F	A	B	F	B	F	F	F	F	B	3-0/10-11 yrs.	I	7				•		EA		•		•									•[1]

[1]Physical activities (e.g., run, jump)

TEST OF LANGUAGE COMPETENCE (1985)

	Taxonomy code	Overall rating	Scores	Size	Demographics	Recency	Total	Internal consistency	Stability	Total	Val.	Ages/Grades for Intended Use	Group/Individual	Testing time	Age equivalents	Grade equivalents	Percentile ranks	Standard scores	Other	Examiner qualifications	Third Party	Listen	Read print	Look at stimuli	Other	Speak, minor	Speak, major	Manipulate objects	Mark answer sheet	Point	Draw	Write print	Other
Composite	2210	F	A	A	F	B	F	F	F	F	B	9-0/18-11 yrs.	I	45	•			•		EA		•	•	•			•					•	
Partial	2210	F	A	A	F	B	F	F	F	F	F	9-0/18-11 yrs.	I	22	•			•		EA		•	•	•			•						
Understanding Ambiguous Sentences	2210	F	A	A	F	B	F	F	F	F	B	9-0/18-11 yrs.	I	7	•			•		EA		•	•				•						
Making Inferences	2210	F	A	A	F	B	F	F	F	F	B	9-0/18-11 yrs.	I	7	•			•		EA		•	•				•			•			
Recreating Sentences	2210	F	A	A	F	B	F	F	F	F	B	9-0/18-11 yrs.	I	7	•			•		EA		•					•						
Understanding Metaphoric Expressions	2210	F	A	A	F	B	F	F	F	F	B	9-0/18-11 yrs.	I	7	•			•		EA		•	•				•						

TEST OF LANGUAGE DEVELOPMENT — INTERMEDIATE (1982)

	Taxonomy code	Overall rating	Scores	Size	Demographics	Recency	Total	Internal consistency	Stability	Total	Val.	Ages/Grades for Intended Use	Group/Individual	Testing time	Age equivalents	Grade equivalents	Percentile ranks	Standard scores	Other	Examiner qualifications	Third Party	Listen	Read print	Look at stimuli	Other	Speak, minor	Speak, major	Manipulate objects	Mark answer sheet	Point	Draw	Write print	Other
Overall Spoken Language	2230	B	A	B	B	B	B	A	A	A	B	8-6/12-11 yrs.	I	45				•		EA		•					•	•						
Listening	2230	B	A	B	B	B	B	A	B	B	B	8-6/12-11 yrs.	I	22				•		EA		•						•						
Speaking	2230	B	A	B	B	B	B	A	B	B	B	8-6/12-11 yrs.	I	22				•		EA		•					•	•						
Semantics	2231	B	A	B	B	B	B	A	B	B	B	8-6/12-11 yrs.	I	22				•		EA		•						•						
Syntax	2232	B	A	B	B	B	B	A	B	B	B	8-6/12-11 yrs.	I	22				•		EA		•					•	•						
Sentence Combining	2232	B	A	B	B	B	B	A	B	B	A	8-6/12-11 yrs.	I	7			•	•		EA		•						•						
Characteristics	2231	B	A	B	B	B	B	A	B	B	A	8-6/12-11 yrs.	I	7			•	•		EA		•						•						
Word Ordering	2232	B	A	B	B	B	B	B	B	B	B	8-6/12-11 yrs.	I	7			•	•		EA		•							•					
Generals	2231	B	A	B	B	B	B	B	B	B	A	8-6/12-11 yrs.	I	7			•	•		EA		•						•						
Grammatic Comprehension	2232	B	A	B	B	B	B	A	B	B	A	8-6/12-11 yrs.	I	7			•	•		EA		•						•						

TEST OF LANGUAGE DEVELOPMENT — INTERMEDIATE, SECOND EDITION (1988)

	Taxonomy code	Overall rating	Scores	Size	Demographics	Recency	Total	Internal consistency	Stability	Total	Val.	Ages/Grades for Intended Use	Group/Individual	Testing time	Age equivalents	Grade equivalents	Percentile ranks	Standard scores	Other	Examiner qualifications	Third Party	Listen	Read print	Look at stimuli	Other	Speak, minor	Speak, major	Manipulate objects	Mark answer sheet	Point	Draw	Write print	Other
Spoken Language	2230	B	A	B	B	B	B	A	B	B	B	8-6/12-11 yrs.	I	45				•		EA		•					•	•						
Short Form	2230	B	A	B	B	B	B	A	F	B	B	8-6/12-11 yrs.	I	22				•		EA		•						•						
Listening	2230	B	A	B	B	B	B	A	B	B	B	8-6/12-11 yrs.	I	22				•		EA		•					•	•						
Speaking	2230	B	A	B	B	B	B	A	A	A	B	8-6/12-11 yrs.	I	22				•		EA		•						•						
Semantics	2231	B	A	B	B	B	B	A	B	B	B	8-6/12-11 yrs.	I	22				•		EA		•					•	•						
Syntax	2232	B	A	B	B	B	B	A	B	B	B	8-6/12-11 yrs.	I	22				•		EA		•					•	•						
Sentence Combining	2232	B	A	B	B	B	B	B	B	B	A	8-6/12-11 yrs.	I	7			•	•		EA		•						•						

	Taxonomy code	Overall rating	Norms: Scores	Size	Demographics	Recency	Total	Rel: Internal consistency	Stability	Total	Val: Total	Ages/Grades for Intended Use	Group/Individual	Testing time	Age equivalents	Grade equivalents	Percentile ranks	Standard scores	Other	Examiner qualifications	Third Party	Listen	Read print	Look at stimuli	Other	Speak, minor	Speak, major	Manipulate objects	Mark answer sheet	Point	Draw	Write print	Other
TEST OF LANGUAGE DEVELOPMENT — INTERMEDIATE, SECOND EDITION (1988) (cont.)																																	
Vocabulary	2231	B	A	B	B	B	B	B	F	B	A	8-6/12-11 yrs.	I	7			•	•		EA		•				•							
Word Ordering	2232	B	A	B	B	B	B	B	B	B	A	8-6/12-11 yrs.	I	7			•	•		EA		•					•						
Generals	2231	B	A	B	B	B	B	B	B	B	A	8-6/12-11 yrs.	I	7			•	•		EA		•					•						
Grammatic Comprehension	2232	B	A	B	B	B	B	A	B	B	A	8-6/12-11 yrs.	I	7			•	•		EA		•				•							
Malapropisms	2231	B	A	B	B	B	B	A	B	B	A	8-6/12-11 yrs.	I	7			•	•		EA		•				•							
TEST OF LANGUAGE DEVELOPMENT — PRIMARY (1982)																																	
Spoken Language	2230	F	A	B	F	B	F	A	B	B	A	4-0/8-11 yrs.	I	45				•		EA		•		•		•	•			•			
Listening	2230	F	A	B	F	B	F	F	F	F	F	4-0/8-11 yrs.	I	22				•		EA		•		•						•			
Speaking	2230	F	A	B	F	B	F	A	F	B	F	4-0/8-11 yrs.	I	22				•		EA		•				•	•						
Semantics	2231	F	A	B	F	B	F	B	F	B	F	4-0/8-11 yrs.	I	22				•		EA		•		•						•			
Syntax	2232	F	A	B	F	B	F	A	F	B	F	4-0/8-11 yrs.	I	22				•		EA		•		•		•	•			•			
Picture Vocabulary	2231	F	A	B	F	B	F	F	B	B	A	4-0/8-11 yrs.	I	7	•		•	•		EA		•		•						•			
Oral Vocabulary	2231	F	A	B	F	B	F	B	B	B	A	4-0/8-11 yrs.	I	7	•		•	•		EA		•					•						
Grammatic Understanding	2232	F	A	B	F	B	F	F	B	B	A	4-0/8-11 yrs.	I	7	•		•	•		EA		•		•						•			
Sentence Imitation	2232	F	A	B	F	B	F	A	B	B	A	4-0/8-11 yrs.	I	7	•		•	•		EA		•					•						
Grammatic Completion	2232	F	A	B	F	B	F	B	B	B	A	4-0/8-11 yrs.	I	7	•		•	•		EA		•				•							
Word Discrimination	2241	F	A	B	F	B	F	B	B	B	B	4-0/8-11 yrs.	I	7	•		•	•		EA		•				•							
Word Articulation	2243	F	A	B	F	B	F	B	B	B	B	4-0/8-11 yrs.	I	7	•		•	•		EA		•				•							
TEST OF LANGUAGE DEVELOPMENT — PRIMARY, SECOND EDITION (1988)																																	
Spoken Language	2230	B	A	A	B	B	B	A	B	B	B	4-0/8-11 yrs.	I	45				•		EA		•		•		•	•			•			
Short Form	2230	B	A	A	B	B	B	A	F	B	B	4-0/8-11 yrs.	I	22				•		EA		•		•		•				•			
Listening	2230	B	A	A	B	B	B	A	B	B	B	4-0/8-11 yrs.	I	22				•		EA		•		•						•			
Speaking	2230	B	A	A	B	B	B	A	B	B	B	4-0/8-11 yrs.	I	22				•		EA		•				•	•						
Semantics	2231	B	A	A	B	B	B	A	B	B	B	4-0/8-11 yrs.	I	22				•		EA		•		•			•			•			
Syntax	2232	B	A	A	B	B	B	A	B	B	B	4-0/8-11 yrs.	I	22				•		EA		•		•		•		•					
Phonology	2240	B	A	A	B	B	B	A	B	B	B	4-0/8-11 yrs.	I	22				•		EA		•		•		•	•			•			
Picture Vocabulary	2231	B	A	A	B	B	B	B	B	B	A	4-0/8-11 yrs.	I	7	•		•	•		EA		•		•						•			
Oral Vocabulary	2231	B	A	A	B	B	B	B	B	B	A	4-0/8-11 yrs.	I	7	•		•	•		EA		•					•						
Grammatic Understanding	2232	B	A	A	B	B	B	B	F	B	A	4-0/8-11 yrs.	I	7	•		•	•		EA		•		•						•			

	Technical Characteristics										Nontechnical Characteristics																					
			Norms					Reliability			Val.	Ages/Grades for Intended Use	Admin.		Scores						Test Formats — Input					Test Formats — Output						
	Taxonomy code	Overall rating	Scores	Size	Demographics	Recency	Total	Internal consistency	Stability	Total	Total		Group/Individual	Testing time	Age equivalents	Grade equivalents	Percentile ranks	Standard scores	Other	Examiner qualifications	Third Party	Listen	Read print	Look at stimuli	Other	Speak, minor	Speak, major	Manipulate objects	Mark answer sheet	Point	Draw	Write print	Other
TEST OF LANGUAGE DEVELOPMENT — PRIMARY, SECOND EDITION (1988) (cont.)																																	
Sentence Imitation	2232	B	A	A	B	B	B	A	B	B	A	4-0/8-11 yrs.	I	7	•		•	•		EA		•					•						
Grammatic Completion	2232	B	A	A	B	B	B	A	B	B	A	4-0/8-11 yrs.	I	7	•		•	•		EA		•				•							
Word Discrimination	2241	B	A	A	B	B	B	B	B	B	A	4-0/8-11 yrs.	I	7	•		•	•		EA		•				•							
Word Articulation	2243	B	A	A	B	B	B	A	B	B	A	4-0/8-11 yrs.	I	7	•		•	•		EA		•				•							
TEST OF LEGIBLE HANDWRITING (1989)																																	
Legibility Quotient	1640	F	A	B	B	A	B	F	F	F	F	7-0/18-6 yrs.	G	10			•	•		EA		•	•									•	
Single Sample	1640	B	B	B	B	A	B	B	B	B	B	7-0/18-6 yrs.	G	10			•			EA		•	•									•	
TEST OF MATHEMATICAL ABILITIES (1984)																																	
Total Math Quotient	4000	B	A	B	B	B	B	F	B	B	A	8-6/18-11 yrs.	I	60				•		EA		•	•			•	•		•			•	
Attitude Towards Math	3210	F	A	B	B	B	B	F	F	F	F	8-6/18-11 yrs.	G	7			•	•		EA		•	•			•	•						
Vocabulary	1230	B	A	B	B	B	B	B	B	B	B	8-6/18-11 yrs.	G	22			•	•		EA		•	•									•	
Computation	1220	B	A	B	B	B	B	F	B	B	B	8-6/18-11 yrs.	G	22			•	•		EA		•	•									•	
General Information	1230	B	A	B	B	B	B	A	B	B	A	8-6/18-11 yrs.	I	22			•	•		EA		•				•	•						
Story Problems	1210	F	A	B	B	B	B	F	F	F	A	8-6/18-11 yrs.	G	22			•	•		EA		•	•									•	
TEST OF NONVERBAL INTELLIGENCE (1982)																																	
TONI Quotient, Forms A & B	2110	B	A	B	B	B	B	B	F	B	A	5-0/85-11 yrs.	I	7			•	•		EA				•						•			
TEST OF NONVERBAL INTELLIGENCE, SECOND EDITION (1990)																																	
TONI Quotient, Forms A & B	2110	B	A	B	A	B	B	A	B	B	A	5-0/85-11 yrs.	I	15			•	•		EA				•						•			
TEST OF PICTURES/FORMS/LETTERS/NUMBERS/SPATIAL ORIENTATION AND SEQUENCING SKILLS (1991)																																	
Spatial Relationships (Pictures)	2131	F	A	F	F	A	F	F	F	F	B	5-0/6-11 yrs.	I	2			•	•		EA		•	•							•			
Spatial Relationships (Forms)	2131	F	A	F	F	A	F	F	F	F	F	5-0/8-11 yrs.	I	2			•	•		EA		•	•							•			
Reversed Letters & Numbers	2250	F	A	F	F	A	F	F	F	F	B	5-0/7-11 yrs.	I	2			•	•		EA		•	•							•			
Reversed Letters in Words	2250	F	A	F	F	A	F	B	F	B	B	5-0/8-11 yrs.	I	2			•	•		EA		•	•							•			
Reversed Letters from Non-Reversed Letters	2250	F	A	F	F	A	F	B	F	B	B	5-0/8-11 yrs.	I	2			•	•		EA		•	•							•			
Reversed Numbers from Non-Reversed Numbers	2250	F	A	F	F	A	F	B	F	B	B	5-0/6-11 yrs.	I	2			•	•		EA		•	•							•			
Letter Sequencing	2250	F	A	F	F	A	F	F	F	F	F	5-0/8-11 yrs.	I	2			•	•		EA		•	•							•			
TEST OF PRACTICAL KNOWLEDGE (1983)																																	
Total	1000	F	A	A	F	B	F	A	F	B	A	gr. 8–12	G	45			•	•		EA		•	•						•				
Social	1910	F	A	A	F	B	F	B	B	B	A	gr. 8–12	G	22			•	•		EA		•	•						•				

	Taxonomy code	Overall rating	Norms: Scores	Norms: Size	Norms: Demographics	Norms: Recency	Norms: Total	Rel: Internal consistency	Rel: Stability	Rel: Total	Val: Total	Ages/Grades for Intended Use	Group/Individual	Testing time	Age equivalents	Grade equivalents	Percentile ranks	Standard scores	Other (Scores)	Examiner qualifications	Third Party	Listen	Read print	Look at stimuli	Other (Input)	Speak, minor	Speak, major	Manipulate objects	Mark answer sheet	Point	Draw	Write print	Other (Output)
TEST OF PRACTICAL KNOWLEDGE (1983) (cont.)																																	
Personal	1910	F	A	A	F	B	F	B	B	B	A	gr. 8–12	G	22			•	•		EA	•	•							•				
Occupational	1830	F	A	A	F	B	F	B	F	B	A	gr. 8–12	G	22			•	•		EA	•	•							•				
TEST OF PROBLEM SOLVING (1984)																																	
Total	2210	F	A	B	F	A	F	B	F	B	B	6-0/11-11 yrs.	I	25	•		•	•		EA	•			•			•						
Explaining Inferences	2210	F	A	B	F	A	F	F	F	F	B	6-0/11-11 yrs.	I	5	•		•	•		EA	•			•			•						
Determining Causes	2210	F	A	B	F	A	F	F	F	F	B	6-0/11-11 yrs.	I	5	•		•	•		EA	•						•						
Negative Why Questions	2210	F	A	B	F	A	F	F	F	F	B	6-0/11-11 yrs.	I	5	•		•	•		EA	•			•			•						
Determining Solutions	2210	F	A	B	F	A	F	F	F	F	B	6-0/11-11 yrs.	I	5	•		•	•		EA	•			•			•						
Avoiding Problems	2210	F	A	B	F	A	F	F	F	F	B	6-0/11-11 yrs.	I	5	•		•	•		EA	•			•			•						
TEST OF READING COMPREHENSION (1978)																																	
Reading Comprehension Quotient	1310	F	A	B	F	B	F	B	F	B	A	7-0/17-11 yrs.	G	60				•		EA	•	•							•				
General Vocabulary	1310	F	A	B	F	B	F	B	F	B	A	7-0/17-11 yrs.	G	22			•	•		EA	•	•							•				
Syntactic Similarities	1310	F	A	B	F	B	F	B	F	B	A	7-0/17-11 yrs.	G	22			•	•		EA	•	•							•				
Paragraph Reading	1310	F	A	B	F	B	F	B	F	B	A	7-0/17-11 yrs.	G	22			•	•		EA	•	•							•				
Sentence Sequencing	1310	F	A	B	F	B	F	B	F	B	A	7-0/17-11 yrs.	G	22			•	•		EA	•	•							•				
Mathematics Vocabulary	1230	F	A	B	F	B	F	A	F	B	A	7-0/17-11 yrs.	G	22			•	•		EA	•	•							•				
Social Studies Vocabulary	1500	F	A	B	F	B	F	A	F	B	A	7-0/17-11 yrs.	G	22			•	•		EA	•	•							•				
Science Vocabulary	1400	F	A	B	F	B	F	B	F	B	A	7-0/17-11 yrs.	G	22			•	•		EA	•	•							•				
Reading the Directions of Schoolwork	1000	F	A	B	F	B	F	B	F	B	VA.	7-0/17-11 yrs.	G	22			•	•		EA	•	•							•			•	•
TEST OF READING COMPREHENSION — REVISED (1986)																																	
Reading Comprehension Quotient	1310	B	A	B	B	B	B	A	F	B	B	7-0/17-11 yrs.	G	60				•		EA	•	•							•				
General Vocabulary	1310	B	A	B	B	B	B	A	F	B	A	7-0/17-11 yrs.	G	22			•	•		EA	•	•							•				
Syntactic Similarities	1310	B	A	B	B	B	B	A	F	B	A	7-0/17-11 yrs.	G	22			•	•		EA	•	•							•				
Paragraph Reading	1310	B	A	B	B	B	B	A	F	B	A	7-0/17-11 yrs.	G	22			•	•		EA	•	•							•				
Sentence Sequencing	1310	B	A	B	B	B	B	B	F	B	A	7-0/17-11 yrs.	G	22			•	•		EA	•	•							•				
Mathematics Vocabulary	1230	B	A	B	B	B	B	A	F	B	A	7-0/17-11 yrs.	G	22			•	•		EA	•	•							•				
Social Studies Vocabulary	1500	B	A	B	B	B	B	A	F	B	A	7-0/17-11 yrs.	G	22			•	•		EA	•	•							•				
Science Vocabulary	1400	B	A	B	B	B	B	A	F	B	A	7-0/17-11 yrs.	G	22			•	•		EA	•	•							•				
Reading the Directions of Schoolwork	1000	B	A	B	B	B	B	A	F	B	A	7-0/17-11 yrs.	G	22			•	•		EA	•	•							•			•	•

	Taxonomy code	Overall rating	Norms: Scores	Size	Demographics	Recency	Total	Reliability: Internal consistency	Stability	Total	Val. Total	Ages/Grades for Intended Use	Group/Individual	Testing time	Age equivalents	Grade equivalents	Percentile ranks	Standard scores	Other	Examiner qualifications	Third Party	Listen	Read print	Look at stimuli	Other	Speak, minor	Speak, major	Manipulate objects	Mark answer sheet	Point	Draw	Write print	Other
TEST OF RELATIONAL CONCEPTS (1988)																																	
Concept Score	2230	F	A	A	A	A	A	A	B	B	F	3-0/7-11 yrs.	I	7			•	•		EA		•		•						•			
TEST OF VISUAL-MOTOR SKILLS (1986)																																	
Total	2132	F	A	B	F	A	F	B	F	B	B	2-0/12-11 yrs.	I	7	•		•	•		EA		•		•							•		
TEST OF VISUAL-PERCEPTUAL SKILLS (1982)																																	
Perceptual Quotient	2130	F	A	B	F	B	F	A	F	B	B	4-0/12-11 yrs.	I	22	•		•	•		EA		•		•						•			
Visual Discrimination	2131	F	A	B	F	B	F	F	F	F	B	4-0/12-11 yrs.	I	7	•					EA		•		•						•			
Visual Memory	2133	F	A	B	F	B	F	F	F	F	B	4-0/12-11 yrs.	I	7	•					EA		•		•						•			
Visual-Spatial Relations	2131	F	A	B	F	B	F	F	F	F	B	4-0/12-11 yrs.	I	7	•					EA		•		•						•			
Visual Form Constancy	2131	F	A	B	F	B	F	F	F	F	B	4-0/12-11 yrs.	I	7	•					EA		•		•						•			
Visual-Sequential Memory	2133	F	A	B	F	B	F	B	F	B	B	4-0/12-11 yrs.	I	7	•					EA		•		•						•			
Visual Figure-Ground	2131	F	A	B	F	B	F	F	F	F	B	4-0/12-11 yrs.	I	7	•					EA		•		•						•			
Visual Closure	2131	F	A	B	F	B	F	F	F	F	B	4-0/12-11 yrs.	I	7	•					EA		•		•						•			
TEST OF WORD FINDING (1986)																																	
Total	2231	B	A	A	B	A	B	F	B	B	A	6-6/12-11 yrs.	I	22			•	•		EA		•		•		•				•			
TEST OF WRITTEN LANGUAGE (1983)																																	
Written Language Quotient	1600	F	A	A	A	B	B	F	A	B	F	7-0/18-11 yrs.	G	45				•		EA		•	•	•								•	
Vocabulary	1610	F	A	A	A	B	B	F	F	F	B	7-0/18-11 yrs.	G	22			•	•		EA		•		•								•	
Thematic Maturity	1610	F	A	A	A	B	B	F	F	F	F	8-0/18-11 yrs.	G	22			•	•		EA		•		•								•	
Handwriting	1640	F	A	A	A	B	B	F	B	B	F	8-0/18-11 yrs.	G	22			•	•		EA		•		•								•	
Spelling	1630	B	A	A	A	B	B	A	B	B	B	7-0/14-11 yrs.	G	7			•	•		EA		•										•	
Word Usage	1610	B	A	A	A	B	B	B	F	B	B	7-0/14-11 yrs.	G	7			•	•		EA		•	•									•	
Style	1620	B	A	A	A	B	B	B	B	B	B	7-0/18-11 yrs.	G	7			•	•		EA		•	•									•	
TEST OF WRITTEN LANGUAGE, SECOND EDITION (1988)																																	
Overall Written Language	1600	B	A	B	B	A	B	A	B	B	B	7-6/17-11 yrs.	G	60+				•		EA		•	•	•								•	
Contrived Writing	1600	B	A	B	B	A	B	A	B	B	B	7-6/17-11 yrs.	G	45				•		EA		•	•									•	
Spontaneous Writing	1600	B	A	B	B	A	B	A	B	B	B	7-6/17-11 yrs.	G	45				•		EA		•	•									•	
Vocabulary	1610	B	A	B	B	A	B	B	B	B	B	7-6/17-11 yrs.	G	7			•	•		EA		•	•									•	
Spelling	1630	B	A	B	B	A	B	B/A¹	B	B	B	7-6/17-11 yrs.	G	22			•	•		EA		•										•	

¹Form A rating appears first, Form B second

	Taxonomy code	Overall rating	Norms: Scores	Size	Demographics	Recency	Total	Rel: Internal consistency	Stability	Total	Val. Total	Ages/Grades for Intended Use	Group/Individual	Testing time	Age equivalents	Grade equivalents	Percentile ranks	Standard scores	Other	Examiner qualifications	Third Party	Listen	Read print	Look at stimuli	Other	Speak, minor	Speak, major	Manipulate objects	Mark answer sheet	Point	Draw	Write print	Other
TEST OF WRITTEN LANGUAGE, SECOND EDITION (1988) (cont.)																																	
Style	1620	**B**	A	B	B	A	B	B/A¹	B	B	B	7-6/17-11 yrs.	G	22			•	•		EA		•										•	
Logical Sentences	1610	**B**	A	B	B	A	B	F/B¹	B	B	B	7-6/17-11 yrs.	G	7			•	•		EA		•	•									•	
Sentence Combining	1610	**F/B¹**	A	B	B	A	B	F/A¹	F	F/B¹	B	7-6/17-11 yrs.	G	7			•	•		EA		•	•									•	
Thematic Maturity	1610	**B**	A	B	B	A	B	F/B¹	B	B	B	7-6/17-11 yrs.	G	22			•	•		EA		•		•								•	
Contextual Vocabulary	1610	**B**	A	B	B	A	B	F/B¹	B	B	B	7-6/17-11 yrs.	G	22			•	•		EA		•		•								•	
Syntactic Maturity	1610	**B**	A	B	B	A	B	A	F	B	B	7-6/17-11 yrs.	G	22			•	•		EA		•		•								•	
Contextual Spelling	1630	**B**	A	B	B	A	B	A	F	B	B	7-6/17-11 yrs.	G	22			•	•		EA		•		•								•	
Contextual Style	1620	**B**	A	B	B	A	B	F	B	B	B	7-6/17-11 yrs.	G	22			•	•		EA		•		•								•	

¹Form A rating appears first, Form B second

	Taxonomy code	Overall rating	Norms: Scores	Size	Demographics	Recency	Total	Rel: Internal consistency	Stability	Total	Val. Total	Ages/Grades for Intended Use	Group/Individual	Testing time	Age equivalents	Grade equivalents	Percentile ranks	Standard scores	Other	Examiner qualifications	Third Party	Listen	Read print	Look at stimuli	Other	Speak, minor	Speak, major	Manipulate objects	Mark answer sheet	Point	Draw	Write print	Other
TEST OF WRITTEN SPELLING (1976)																																	
Total	1630	**B**	A	B	B	B	B	B	F	B	B	5-0/13-5 yrs.	G	22	•	•		•		EA		•										•	
Predictable Words	1630	**B**	A	B	B	B	B	B	F	B	B	5-0/13-5 yrs.	G	7	•	•		•		EA		•										•	
Unpredictable Words	1630	**B**	A	B	B	B	B	B	F	B	B	5-0/13-5 yrs.	G	7	•	•		•		EA		•										•	
TEST OF WRITTEN SPELLING, SECOND EDITION (1986)																																	
Total	1630	**B**	A	B	A	B	A	A	A	A	B	6-6/18-5 yrs.	G	22			•	•		EA		•										•	
Predictable Words	1630	**B**	A	B	A	B	A	A	A	A	B	6-6/18-5 yrs.	G	7			•	•		EA		•										•	
Unpredictable Words	1630	**B**	A	B	A	B	A	A	A	A	B	6-6/18-5 yrs.	G	7			•	•		EA		•										•	
TESTS FOR EVERYDAY LIVING (1979)																																	
Total Battery	1000	**F**	F	B	F	B	F	A	F	B	F	gr. 7–12	G	60					•¹	EA		•	•	•				•				•	
Purchasing Habits	1910	**F**	F	B	F	B	F	F	F	F	B	gr. 7–12	G	22					•¹	EA		•	•	•				•					
Banking	1910	**F**	F	B	F	B	F	F	F	F	B	gr. 7–12	G	22					•¹	EA		•	•	•				•				•	
Budgeting	1910	**F**	F	B	F	B	F	F	F	F	B	gr. 7–12	G	22					•¹	EA		•	•	•				•				•	
Health Care	1910	**F**	F	B	F	B	F	F	F	F	B	gr. 7–12	G	22					•¹	EA		•	•					•					
Home Management	1910	**F**	F	B	F	B	F	F	F	F	B	gr. 7–12	G	22					•¹	EA		•	•	•				•					
Job Search Skills	1830	**F**	F	B	F	B	F	B	F	B	B	gr. 7–12	G	22					•¹	EA		•	•	•				•					
Job Related Behavior	1830	**F**	F	B	F	B	F	B	F	B	B	gr. 7–12	G	22					•¹	EA		•	•	•				•					
TEL Reading Scale	1310	**F**	F	B	F	B	F	B	F	B	B	gr. 7–12	G	22					•¹	EA		•	•	•				•				•	

¹Compare mean and standard deviation with reference groups

	Taxonomy code	Overall rating	Norms: Scores	Size	Demographics	Recency	Total	Reliability: Internal consistency	Stability	Total	Val. Total	Ages/Grades for Intended Use	Group/Individual	Testing time	Age equivalents	Grade equivalents	Percentile ranks	Standard scores	Other	Examiner qualifications	Third Party	Listen	Read print	Look at stimuli	Other	Speak, minor	Speak, major	Manipulate objects	Mark answer sheet	Point	Draw	Write print	Other
TORRANCE TESTS OF CREATIVE THINKING (1974)																																	
Verbal Fluency	2220	F	A	A	F	F	F	F	B	B	F	gr. K–Adult	G¹	22				•		ST	•												•²
Verbal Flexibility	2220	F	A	A	F	F	F	F	B	B	F	gr. K–Adult	G¹	22				•		ST	•												•²
Verbal Originality	2220	F	A	A	F	F	F	F	F	F	F	gr. K–Adult	G¹	22				•		ST	•												•²
Figural Fluency	2110	F	A	A	F	F	F	F	F	F	F	gr. K–Adult	I	22				•		ST	•			•							•		•²
Figural Flexibility	2110	F	A	A	F	F	F	F	F	F	F	gr. K–Adult	I	22				•		ST	•			•							•		•²
Figural Originality	2110	F	A	A	F	F	F	F	F	F	F	gr. K–Adult	I	22				•		ST	•			•							•		•²
Figural Elaboration	2110	F	A	A	F	F	F	F	B	B	F	gr. K–Adult	I	22				•		ST	•			•							•		•²

¹Given individually in Grades K–3, can be group or individual in Grades 4+; ²verbal responses acceptable in Grades K–3

	Taxonomy code	Overall rating	Norms: Scores	Size	Demographics	Recency	Total	Reliability: Internal consistency	Stability	Total	Val. Total	Ages/Grades for Intended Use	Group/Individual	Testing time	Age equivalents	Grade equivalents	Percentile ranks	Standard scores	Other	Examiner qualifications	Third Party	Listen	Read print	Look at stimuli	Other	Speak, minor	Speak, major	Manipulate objects	Mark answer sheet	Point	Draw	Write print	Other
THE TRANSITION BEHAVIOR SCALE (1989)																																	
Total	4000	F	B	B	F	A	F	F	F	F	B/F/F¹	gr. 11–12	I	15			•			EA	•		•							•			
Work Related	4000	F	A	B	F	A	F	F	F	F	B/F/F¹	gr. 11–12	I	15			•	•		EA	•		•							•			
Interpersonal Relations	3400	F	A	B	F	A	F	F	F	F	B/F/F¹	gr. 11–12	I	15			•	•		EA	•		•							•			
Social/Community Expectations	4000	F	A	B	F	A	F	F	F	F	B/F/F¹	gr. 11–12	I	15			•	•		EA	•		•							•			

¹Rating for Total Population Norms appears first, Male Norms second, and Female Norms third

	Taxonomy code	Overall rating	Norms: Scores	Size	Demographics	Recency	Total	Reliability: Internal consistency	Stability	Total	Val. Total	Ages/Grades for Intended Use	Group/Individual	Testing time	Age equivalents	Grade equivalents	Percentile ranks	Standard scores	Other	Examiner qualifications	Third Party	Listen	Read print	Look at stimuli	Other	Speak, minor	Speak, major	Manipulate objects	Mark answer sheet	Point	Draw	Write print	Other
UTAH TEST OF LANGUAGE DEVELOPMENT — REVISED EDITION (1978)																																	
Total	4000	F	A	F	F	F	F	F	F	F	B	2-0/14-11 yrs.	I	22	•		•	•		EA	•	•	•			•	•	•		•	•	•	•¹

¹Behavioral responses

	Taxonomy code	Overall rating	Norms: Scores	Size	Demographics	Recency	Total	Reliability: Internal consistency	Stability	Total	Val. Total	Ages/Grades for Intended Use	Group/Individual	Testing time	Age equivalents	Grade equivalents	Percentile ranks	Standard scores	Other	Examiner qualifications	Third Party	Listen	Read print	Look at stimuli	Other	Speak, minor	Speak, major	Manipulate objects	Mark answer sheet	Point	Draw	Write print	Other
UTAH TEST OF LANGUAGE DEVELOPMENT, THIRD EDITION (1989)																																	
Language Quotient	2230	B	A	A	B	A	B	B	F	B	B	3-0/9-11 yrs.	I	30			•	•		EA	•		•			•	•			•			
Language Comprehension	2230	B	A	A	B	A	B	B	F	B	A	3-0/9-11 yrs.	I	30			•	•		EA	•		•			•				•			
Language Expression	2230	B	A	A	B	A	B	B	F	B	A	3-0/9-11 yrs.	I	30			•	•		EA	•		•			•	•						
THE VANE KINDERGARTEN TEST (1984)																																	
Total	2000	B	A	B	B	B	B	F	B	B	B	4-0/6-5 yrs.	I	30				•		EA	•		•					•			•		
Perceptual-Motor	2132	B	A	B	B	B	B	F	B	B	B	4-0/6-5 yrs.	G	30	•			•		EA	•		•								•		
Man	2110	B	A	B	B	B	B	F	B	B	B	4-0/6-5 yrs.	G	30	•			•		EA	•										•		
Vocabulary	2231	F	A	B	B	B	B	F	F	F	B	4-0/6-5 yrs.	I	30	•			•		EA	•							•					

| | | | Technical Characteristics | | | | | | | | | Nontechnical Characteristics | | | | | | | | | | | | | | | | | | | | | | |
| | | | Norms | | | | | Reliability | | | Val. | Ages/Grades for Intended Use | Admin. | | Scores | | | | | | Input | | | | | Output | | | | | | | |
	Taxonomy code	Overall rating	Scores	Size	Demographics	Recency	Total	Internal consistency	Stability	Total	Total		Group/Individual	Testing time	Age equivalents	Grade equivalents	Percentile ranks	Standard scores	Other	Examiner qualifications	Third Party	Listen	Read print	Look at stimuli	Other	Speak, minor	Speak, major	Manipulate objects	Mark answer sheet	Point	Draw	Write print	Other
VINELAND ADAPTIVE BEHAVIOR SCALES — CLASSROOM EDITION (1985)																																	
Adaptive Behavior Composite	4000	F	A	A	F	B	F	A	F	B	B	3-0/12-11 yrs.	I	22	•		•	•	•¹	EA	•		•						•				
Communication Domain	4000	F	A	A	F	B	F	A	F	B	A	3-0/12-11 yrs.	I	22	•		•	•	•¹	EA	•		•						•				
Daily Living Skills Domain	1900	F	A	A	F	B	F	A	F	B	A	3-0/12-11 yrs.	I	22	•		•	•	•¹	EA	•		•						•				
Socialization Domain	3400	F	A	A	F	B	F	A	F	B	B	3-0/12-11 yrs.	I	22	•		•	•	•¹	EA	•		•						•				
Motor Skills Domain	2150	F	A²	A	F	B	F	F	F	F	A	3-0/12-11 yrs.	I	22	•		•	•²	•¹	EA	•		•						•				
Receptive Communication	2230	F	F	A	F	B	F	F	F	F	F	3-0/12-11 yrs.	I	22	•		•	•²	•¹	EA	•		•						•				
Expressive Communication	2230	F	F	A	F	B	F	B	F	B	F	3-0/12-11 yrs.	I	22	•		•	•²	•¹	EA	•		•						•				
Written Communication	1600	F	F	A	F	B	F	B	F	B	F	3-0/12-11 yrs.	I	22	•		•	•²	•¹	EA	•		•						•				
Personal Living Skills	1920	F	F	A	F	B	F	B	F	B	F	3-0/12-11 yrs.	I	22	•		•	•²	•¹	EA	•		•						•				
Domestic Living Skills	1920	F	F	A	F	B	F	A	F	B	F	3-0/12-11 yrs.	I	22	•		•	•²	•¹	EA	•		•						•				
Community Living Skills	1900	F	F	A	F	B	F	A	F	B	F	3-0/12-11 yrs.	I	22	•		•	•²	•¹	EA	•		•						•				
Interpersonal Relationships	3400	F	F	A	F	B	F	B	F	B	F	3-0/12-11 yrs.	I	22	•		•	•²	•¹	EA	•		•						•				
Play and Leisure Time	3900	F	F	A	F	B	F	F	F	F	F	3-0/12-11 yrs.	I	22	•		•	•²	•¹	EA	•		•						•				
Coping Skills	3840	F	F	A	F	B	F	A	F	B	F	3-0/12-11 yrs.	I	22	•		•	•²	•¹	EA	•		•						•				
Gross Motor Skills	2150	F	F	A	F	B	F	F	F	F	F	3-0/12-11 yrs.	I	22	•		•	•²	•¹	EA	•		•						•				
Fine Motor Skills	2150	F	F	A	F	B	F	F	F	F	F	3-0/12-11 yrs.	I	22	•		•	•²	•¹	EA	•		•						•				

¹Adaptive levels; ²estimated standard scores from 6-0/12-11 yrs.

	Taxonomy code	Overall rating	Scores	Size	Demographics	Recency	Total	Internal consistency	Stability	Total	Total	Ages/Grades	Group/Individual	Testing time	Age equivalents	Grade equivalents	Percentile ranks	Standard scores	Other	Examiner qualifications	Third Party	Listen	Read print	Look at stimuli	Other	Speak, minor	Speak, major	Manipulate objects	Mark answer sheet	Point	Draw	Write print	Other
VINELAND ADAPTIVE BEHAVIOR SCALES — INTERVIEW EDITION, EXPANDED FORM (1984)																																	
Adaptive Behavior Composite	4000	B	A	A	A	B	B	B¹	F	B	B¹	0-0/18-7 yrs.	G	45	•		•	•		EA	•	•						•					
Communication Domain	4000	B	A	A	A	B	B	B¹	F	B	B¹	0-0/18-7 yrs.	G	22	•		•	•		EA	•	•						•					
Daily Living Skills Domain	1900	B	A	A	A	B	B	B¹	F	B	B¹	0-0/18-7 yrs.	G	22	•		•	•		EA	•	•						•					
Socialization Domain	3400	B	A	A	A	B	B	B¹	F	B	B¹	0-0/18-7 yrs.	G	22	•		•	•		EA	•	•						•					
Motor Skills Domain	2150	B	A	A	A	B	B	B¹	F	B	B¹	0-0/5-11 yrs.	G	22	•		•	•		EA	•	•						•					
Receptive Communication	2230	F	A	A	A	B	B	B	F	B	F	0-0/4-11 yrs.	G	22			•	•		EA	•	•						•					
Expressive Communication	2230	F	A	A	A	B	B	B	F	B	F	0-0/18-7 yrs.	G	22	•		•	•		EA	•	•						•					
Written Communication	1600	F	A	A	A	B	B	B	F	B	F	2-0/18-7 yrs.	G	22	•		•	•		EA	•	•						•					
Personal Living Skills	1920	F	A	A	A	B	B	B	F	B	F	0-0/18-7 yrs.	G	22	•		•	•		EA	•	•						•					
Domestic Living Skills	1920	F	A	A	A	B	B	B	F	B	F	1-0/18-7 yrs.	G	22	•		•	•		EA	•	•						•					

¹Estimates based on Survey Form Data

			Technical Characteristics									Nontechnical Characteristics																					
			Norms					Reliability			Val.	Ages/Grades for Intended Use	Admin.		Scores					Examiner qualifications	Test Formats												
																					Input					Output							
	Taxonomy code	Overall rating	Scores	Size	Demographics	Recency	Total	Internal consistency	Stability	Total	Total		Group/Individual	Testing time	Age equivalents	Grade equivalents	Percentile ranks	Standard scores	Other		Third Party	Listen	Read print	Look at stimuli	Other	Speak, minor	Speak, major	Manipulate objects	Mark answer sheet	Point	Draw	Write print	Other
VINELAND ADAPTIVE BEHAVIOR SCALES — INTERVIEW EDITION, EXPANDED FORM (1984) (cont.)																																	
Community Living Skills	1900	F	A	A	A	B	B	B	F	B	F	1-0/18-7 yrs.	G	22	•		•	•		EA	•	•					•						
Interpersonal Relationships	3400	F	A	A	A	B	B	B	F	B	F	0-0/18-7 yrs.	G	22	•		•	•		EA	•	•					•						
Play and Leisure Time	3900	F	A	A	A	B	B	B	F	B	F	0-0/18-7 yrs.	G	22	•		•	•		EA	•	•					•						
Coping Skills	3840	F	A	A	A	B	B	B	F	B	F	1-0/18-7 yrs.	G	22	•		•	•		EA	•	•					•						
Gross Motor Skills	2150	F	A	A	A	B	B	B	F	B	F	0-0/5-11 yrs.	G	22	•		•	•		EA	•	•					•						
Fine Motor Skills	2150	F	A	A	A	B	B	B	F	B	F	0-0/5-11 yrs.	G	22	•		•	•		EA	•	•					•						

[1]Estimates based on Survey Form Data

	Taxonomy code	Overall rating	Scores	Size	Demographics	Recency	Total	Internal consistency	Stability	Total	Total	Ages/Grades	Group/Individual	Testing time	Age equivalents	Grade equivalents	Percentile ranks	Standard scores	Other	Examiner qual.	Third Party	Listen	Read print	Look at stimuli	Other	Speak, minor	Speak, major	Manipulate objects	Mark answer sheet	Point	Draw	Write print	Other
VINELAND ADAPTIVE BEHAVIOR SCALES — INTERVIEW EDITION, SURVEY FORM (1984)																																	
Adaptive Behavior Composite	4000	B	A	A	A	B	B	A	B	B	A	0-0/18-7 yrs.	G	45	•		•	•		EA	•	•					•						
Communication Domain	4000	B	A	A	A	B	B	B	B	B	A	0-0/18-7 yrs.	G	22	•		•	•		EA	•	•					•						
Daily Living Skills Domain	1900	B	A	A	A	B	B	B	B	B	B	0-0/18-7 yrs.	G	22	•		•	•		EA	•	•					•						
Socialization Domain	3400	B	A	A	A	B	B	B	F	B	B	0-0/18-7 yrs.	G	22	•		•	•		EA	•	•					•						
Motor Skills Domain	2150	B	A	A	A	B	B	B	B	B	B	0-0/5-11 yrs.	G	22	•		•	•		EA	•	•					•						
Receptive Communication	2230	F	A	A	A	B	B	F	F	F	F	0-0/4-11 yrs.	G	22	•		•	•		EA	•	•					•						
Expressive Communication	2230	F	A	A	A	B	B	F	F	F	F	0-0/18-7 yrs.	G	22	•		•	•		EA	•	•					•						
Written Communication	1600	F	A	A	A	B	B	B	F	B	F	2-0/18-7 yrs.	G	22	•		•	•		EA	•	•					•						
Personal Living Skills	1920	F	A	A	A	B	B	F	F	F	F	0-0/18-7 yrs.	G	22	•		•	•		EA	•	•					•						
Domestic Living Skills	1920	F	A	A	A	B	B	F	F	F	F	1-0/18-7 yrs.	G	22	•		•	•		EA	•	•					•						
Community Living Skills	1900	F	A	A	A	B	B	F	F	F	F	1-0/18-7 yrs.	G	22	•		•	•		EA	•	•					•						
Interpersonal Relationships	3400	F	A	A	A	B	B	F	F	F	F	0-0/18-7 yrs.	G	22	•		•	•		EA	•	•					•						
Play and Leisure Time	3900	F	A	A	A	B	B	F	F	F	F	0-0/18-7 yrs.	G	22	•		•	•		EA	•	•					•						
Coping Skills	3840	F	A	A	A	B	B	F	F	F	F	1-0/18-7 yrs.	G	22	•		•	•		EA	•	•					•						
Gross Motor Skills	2150	F	A	A	A	B	B	F	F	F	F	0-0/5-11 yrs.	G	22	•		•	•		EA	•	•					•						
Fine Motor Skills	2150	F	A	A	A	B	B	F	F	F	F	0-0/5-11 yrs.	G	22	•		•	•		EA	•	•					•						
THE VISUAL AURAL DIGIT SPAN TEST (1977)																																	
Total	2200	F	B	B	F	B	F	F	F	F	B	5-6/12-11 yrs.	I	22	•		•			EA		•	•				•						•
Intrasensory Integration	2250	F	B	B	F	B	F	F	B	B	B	5-6/12-11 yrs.	I	22	•		•			EA		•	•				•						•
Intersensory Integration	2250	F	B	B	F	B	F	F	B	B	B	5-6/12-11 yrs.	I	22	•		•			EA		•	•				•						•
Aural Input	2200	F	B	B	F	B	F	F	B	B	B	5-6/12-11 yrs.	I	22	•		•			EA		•					•						•

		Technical Characteristics									Nontechnical Characteristics																						
		Norms					Reliability			Val.	Ages/Grades for Intended Use	Admin.		Scores						Input					Output							
	Taxonomy code	Overall rating	Scores	Size	Demographics	Recency	Total	Internal consistency	Stability	Total	Total		Group/Individual	Testing time	Age equivalents	Grade equivalents	Percentile ranks	Standard scores	Other	Examiner qualifications	Third Party	Listen	Read print	Look at stimuli	Other	Speak, minor	Speak, major	Manipulate objects	Mark answer sheet	Point	Draw	Write print	Other
THE VISUAL AURAL DIGIT SPAN TEST (1977) (cont.)																																	
Visual Input	2250	F	B	B	F	B	F	F	B	B	B	5-6/12-11 yrs.	I	22	•		•			EA		•	•				•					•	
Oral Expression	2200	F	B	B	F	B	F	F	B	B	B	5-6/12-11 yrs.	I	22	•		•			EA		•	•				•						
Written Expression	2250	F	B	B	F	B	F	F	B	B	F	5-6/12-11 yrs.	I	22	•		•			EA		•	•									•	
Aural-Oral	2242	F	B	B	F	B	F	F	B	B	F	5-6/12-11 yrs.	I	7	•		•			EA		•					•						
Visual-Oral	2250	F	B	B	F	B	F	F	F	F	B	5-6/12-11 yrs.	I	7	•		•			EA		•	•				•						
Aural-Written	2250	F	B	B	F	B	F	F	F	F	B	5-6/12-11 yrs.	I	7	•		•			EA		•										•	
Visual-Written	2250	F	B	B	F	B	F	F	F	F	F	5-6/12-11 yrs.	I	7	•		•			EA		•	•									•	
WALKER-McCONNELL SCALE OF SOCIAL COMPETENCE AND SCHOOL ADJUSTMENT (1988)																																	
Total Score	3000	B	A	A	B	B	B	A	B	B	A	gr. K–6	I	15			•	•		EA	•		•							•			
Subscale 1: Teacher-Preferred Social Behavior	3400	B	A	A	B	B	B	A	A	A	A	gr. K–6	I	15			•	•		EA	•		•							•			
Subscale 2: Peer-Preferred Social Behavior	3400	B	A	A	B	B	B	A	B	B	A	gr. K–6	I	15			•	•		EA	•		•							•			
School Adjustment Behavior	3000	B	A	A	B	B	B	A	A	A	A	gr. K–6	I	15			•	•		EA	•		•							•			
WALKER PROBLEM BEHAVIOR IDENTIFICATION CHECKLIST — REVISED 1983 (1983)																																	
Total	3000	F	A	B	F	B	F	F	F	F	B	gr. Pre K–6	I	7				•		EA	•		•							•			
Acting Out	3500	F	A	B	F	B	F	F	F	F	B	gr. Pre K–6	I	7				•		EA	•		•							•			
Withdrawal	3400	F	A	B	F	B	F	F	F	F	F	gr. Pre K–6	I	7				•		EA	•		•							•			
Distractibility	3820	F	A	B	F	B	F	F	F	F	B	gr. Pre K–6	I	7				•		EA	•		•							•			
Disturbed Peer Relations	3400	F	A	B	F	B	F	F	F	F	F	gr. Pre K–6	I	7				•		EA	•		•							•			
Immaturity	3840	F	A	B	F	B	F	F	F	F	B	gr. Pre K–6	I	7				•		EA	•		•							•			
THE WATKINS BENDER-GESTALT SCORING SYSTEM (1976)																																	
Total Score	2132	B	B	A	B	B	B	F	B	B	B	5-0/14-11 yrs.	G	30					•¹	ST		•		•							•		
WECHSLER ADULT INTELLIGENCE SCALE — REVISED (1981)																																	
Full Scale	4000	B	A	A	A	B	B	A	A	A	B	16-0/Adult yrs.	I	60+	•			•		R		•	•	•		•	•	•	•	•	•		
Verbal Scale	4000	B	A	A	A	B	B	A	A	A	B	16-0/Adult yrs.	I	45	•			•		R		•	•	•		•	•						
Performance Scale	2100	B	A	A	A	B	B	A	B	B	B	16-0/Adult yrs.	I	45	•			•		R		•		•			•	•		•	•		
Information	1100	B	A	A	A	B	B	B	A	B	B	16-0/Adult yrs.	I	7	•			•		R		•					•						
Digit Span	2242	B	A	A	A	B	B	B	B	B	B	16-0/Adult yrs.	I	7	•			•		R		•					•						
Vocabulary	2231	B	A	A	A	B	B	A	B	B	B	16-0/Adult yrs.	I	7	•			•		R		•	•				•						

¹Cutoff scores based on means and standard deviations

	Taxonomy code	Overall rating	Scores	Size	Demographics	Recency	Norms Total	Internal consistency	Stability	Reliability Total	Val. Total	Ages/Grades for Intended Use	Group/Individual	Testing time	Age equivalents	Grade equivalents	Percentile ranks	Standard scores	Other	Examiner qualifications	Third Party	Listen	Read print	Look at stimuli	Input Other	Speak, minor	Speak, major	Manipulate objects	Mark answer sheet	Point	Draw	Write print	Output Other
WECHSLER ADULT INTELLIGENCE SCALE — REVISED (1981) (cont.)																																	
Arithmetic	1210	B	A	A	A	B	B	B	B	B	B	16-0/Adult yrs.	I	7	•			•		R	•			•		•	•	•					
Comprehension	2210	B	A	A	A	B	B	B	B	B	B	16-0/Adult yrs.	I	7	•			•		R	•						•						
Similarities	2231	B	A	A	A	B	B	B	B	B	B	16-0/Adult yrs.	I	7	•			•		R	•						•						
Picture Completion	2131	B	A	A	A	B	B	B	B	B	B	16-0/Adult yrs.	I	7	•			•		R	•			•		•				•			
Picture Arrangement	2110	F	A	A	A	B	B	F	F	F	B	16-0/Adult yrs.	I	7	•			•		R	•			•				•					
Block Design	2132	B	A	A	A	B	B	B	B	B	B	16-0/Adult yrs.	I	7	•			•		R	•			•				•					
Object Assembly	2132	F	A	A	A	B	B	F	F	F	B	16-0/Adult yrs.	I	7	•			•		R	•			•				•					
Digit Symbol	2132	B	A	A	A	B	B	B	B	B	B	16-0/Adult yrs.	I	7	•			•		R	•			•								•	
WECHSLER INTELLIGENCE SCALE FOR CHILDREN — REVISED (1974)																																	
Full Scale	4000	F	A	A	A	F	F	A	B	B	B	6-6/16-6 yrs.	I	60+	•			•		R	•	•		•		•	•	•		•	•		
Verbal Scale	4000	F	A	A	A	F	F	A	B	B	B	6-6/16-6 yrs.	I	45	•			•		R	•	•		•		•	•						
Performance Scale	2100	F	A	A	A	F	F	A	B	B	B	6-6/16-6 yrs.	I	45	•			•		R	•			•		•		•		•	•		
Information	1100	F	A	A	A	F	F	B	B	B	B	6-6/16-6 yrs.	I	7	•			•		R	•					•	•						
Comprehension	2210	F	A	A	A	F	F	F	B	B	B	6-6/16-6 yrs.	I	7	•			•		R	•						•						
Similarities	2231	F	A	A	A	F	F	B	B	B	B	6-6/16-6 yrs.	I	7	•			•		R	•						•						
Arithmetic	1210	F	A	A	A	F	F	F	B	B	B	6-6/16-6 yrs.	I	7	•			•		R	•	•		•		•							
Vocabulary	2231	F	A	A	A	F	F	B	B	B	B	6-6/16-6 yrs.	I	7	•			•		R	•						•						
Digit Span	2242	F	A	A	A	F	F	F	F	F	F	6-6/16-6 yrs.	I	7	•			•		R	•						•						
Picture Completion	2131	F	A	A	A	F	F	F	F	F	F	6-6/16-6 yrs.	I	7	•			•		R	•			•		•				•			
Picture Arrangement	2110	F	A	A	A	F	F	F	F	F	B	6-6/16-6 yrs.	I	7	•			•		R	•			•				•					
Block Design	2132	F	A	A	A	F	F	B	F	B	B	6-6/16-6 yrs.	I	7	•			•		R	•			•				•					
Object Assembly	2132	F	A	A	A	F	F	F	F	F	B	6-6/16-6 yrs.	I	7	•			•		R	•			•				•					
Coding	2132	F	A	A	A	F	F	F	F	F	F	6-6/16-6 yrs.	I	7	•			•		R	•			•								•	
Mazes	2132	F	A	A	A	F	F	F	F	F	F	6-6/16-6 yrs.	I	7	•			•		R	•			•								•	
WECHSLER INTELLIGENCE SCALE FOR CHILDREN — THIRD EDITION (1991)																																	
Full Scale IQ	4000	A	A	A	A	A	A	A	A	A	A	6-0/16-11 yrs.	I	60+			•	•		R	•	•		•		•	•	•		•	•		
Verbal IQ	4000	A	A	A	A	A	A	A	A	A	A	6-0/16-11 yrs.	I	45			•	•		R	•	•		•		•	•						
Performance IQ	2100	B	A	A	A	A	A	A	B	B	A	6-0/16-11 yrs.	I	45			•	•		R	•			•		•		•		•	•		
Verbal Comprehension Index	4000	B	A	A	A	A	A	F	A	B	A	6-0/16-11 yrs.	I	10			•	•		R	•					•	•						

		Technical Characteristics										Nontechnical Characteristics																						
			Norms					Reliability			Val.	Ages/Grades for Intended Use	Admin.		Scores					Examiner qualifications	Third Party	Input				Output							
	Taxonomy code	Overall rating	Scores	Size	Demographics	Recency	Total	Internal consistency	Stability	Total	Total		Group/Individual	Testing time	Age equivalents	Grade equivalents	Percentile ranks	Standard scores	Other			Listen	Read print	Look at stimuli	Other	Speak, minor	Speak, major	Manipulate objects	Mark answer sheet	Point	Draw	Write print	Other
WECHSLER INTELLIGENCE SCALE FOR CHILDREN — THIRD EDITION (1991) (cont.)																																	
Perceptual Organization Index	2100	B	A	A	A	A	A	F	B	B	B	6-0/16-11 yrs.	I	10			•	•		R		•		•		•	•	•		•			
Freedom from Distractibility Index	4000	B	A	A	A	A	A	F	B	B	A	6-0/16-11 yrs.	I	10			•	•		R		•	•	•		•	•						
Processing Speed Index	2132	B	A	A	A	A	A	F	B	B	A	6-0/16-11 yrs.	I	10			•	•		R		•		•						•	•		
Information	1100	B	A	A	A	A	A	B	B	B	B	6-0/16-11 yrs.	I	10				•		R		•				•	•						
Similarities	2231	B	A	A	A	A	A	B	B	B	B	6-0/16-11 yrs.	I	10				•		R		•					•						
Arithmetic	1210	F	A	A	A	A	A	F	F	F	B	6-0/16-11 yrs.	I	10				•		R		•	•	•		•							
Vocabulary	2231	B	A	A	A	A	A	B	B	B	B	6-0/16-11 yrs.	I	10				•		R		•					•						
Comprehension	2210	F	A	A	A	A	A	F	F	F	B	6-0/16-11 yrs.	I	10				•		R		•					•						
Picture Completion	2131	B	A	A	A	A	A	F	B	B	B	6-0/16-11 yrs.	I	10				•		R		•		•		•	•			•			
Coding	2132	F	A	A	A	A	A	F	F	F	B	6-0/16-11 yrs.	I	10				•		R		•		•								•	
Picture Arrangement	2110	F	A	A	A	A	A	F	F	F	B	6-0/16-11 yrs.	I	10				•		R		•		•				•					
Block Design	2132	B	A	A	A	A	A	B	F	B	B	6-0/16-11 yrs.	I	10				•		R		•		•				•					
Object Assembly	2132	F	A	A	A	A	A	F	F	F	B	6-0/16-11 yrs.	I	10				•		R		•		•				•					
Digit Span	2242	B	A	A	A	A	A	B	F	B	B	6-0/16-11 yrs.	I	10				•		R		•					•						
Symbol Search	2132	F	A	A	A	A	A	F	F	F	B	6-0/16-11 yrs.	I	10				•		R		•		•						•			
Mazes	2132	F	A	A	A	A	A	F	F	F	B	6-0/16-11 yrs.	I	10				•		R		•		•							•		
WECHSLER MEMORY SCALE — REVISED (1987)																																	
General Memory	4000	F	A	F	A	A	F	B	F	B	B	16-0/Adult yrs.	I	45			•	•		EA		•		•		•	•			•	•		
Attention/Concentration	2000	F	A	F	A	A	F	A	B	B	B	16-0/Adult yrs.	I	22			•	•		EA		•		•						•			
Verbal Memory	2000	F	A	F	A	A	F	F	F	F	B	16-0/Adult yrs.	I	22			•	•		EA		•				•	•						
Visual Memory	2100	F	A	F	A	A	F	F	F	F	B	16-0/Adult yrs.	I	22			•	•		EA		•		•						•	•		
Delayed Recall	2000	F	A	F	A	A	F	F	B	B	B	16-0/Adult yrs.	I	22			•	•		EA		•		•		•	•			•	•		
Information and Orientation Questions	1100	F	B	F	A	A	F	F	F	F	F	16-0/Adult yrs.	I	7				•		EA		•				•	•						
Mental Control	2244	F	B	F	A	A	F	F	F	F	F	16-0/Adult yrs.	I	7				•		EA		•					•						
Figural Memory	2133	F	B	F	A	A	F	F	F	F	F	16-0/Adult yrs.	I	7				•		EA		•		•						•			
Logical Memory I	2230	F	B	F	A	A	F	F	F	F	F	16-0/Adult yrs.	I	7				•		EA		•					•						
Visual Paired Associates I	2133	F	B	F	A	A	F	F	F	F	F	16-0/Adult yrs.	I	7				•		EA		•		•						•			
Verbal Paired Associates I	2242	F	B	F	A	A	F	F	F	F	F	16-0/Adult yrs.	I	7				•		EA		•				•							
Visual Reproduction I	2132	F	B	F	A	A	F	F	F	F	F	16-0/Adult yrs.	I	7				•		EA		•		•							•		

			Technical Characteristics									Nontechnical Characteristics																						
			Norms					Reliability			Val.		Admin.		Scores						Input					Output								
	Taxonomy code	Overall rating	Scores	Size	Demographics	Recency	Total	Internal consistency	Stability	Total	Total	Ages/Grades for Intended Use	Group/Individual	Testing time	Age equivalents	Grade equivalents	Percentile ranks	Standard scores	Other	Examiner qualifications	Third Party	Listen	Read print	Look at stimuli	Other	Speak, minor	Speak, major	Manipulate objects	Mark answer sheet	Point	Draw	Write print	Other
WECHSLER MEMORY SCALE — REVISED (1987) (cont.)																																	
Digit Span	2242	F	B	F	A	A	F	F	F	F	F	16-0/Adult yrs.	I	7				•		EA		•				•							
Visual Memory Span	2133	F	B	F	A	A	F	F	F	F	F	16-0/Adult yrs.	I	7				•		EA		•		•						•			
Logical Memory II	2230	F	B	F	A	A	F	F	F	F	F	16-0/Adult yrs.	I	7				•		EA		•				•							
Visual Paired Associates II	2133	F	B	F	A	A	F	F	F	F	F	16-0/Adult yrs.	I	7				•		EA		•		•						•			
Verbal Paired Associates II	2242	F	B	F	A	A	F	F	F	F	F	16-0/Adult yrs.	I	7				•		EA		•						•					
Visual Reproduction II	2132	F	B	F	A	A	F	F	F	F	F	16-0/Adult yrs.	I	7				•		EA		•		•							•		
WECHSLER PRESCHOOL AND PRIMARY SCALE OF INTELLIGENCE (1967)																																	
Full Scale	4000	F	A	A	A	F	F	A	A	A	F	4-0/6-5 yrs.	I	60	•			•		R		•		•		•	•	•		•	•		
Verbal Scale	4000	F	A	A	A	F	F	A	B	B	F	4-0/6-5 yrs.	I	45	•			•		R		•		•		•	•			•			
Performance Scale	2100	F	A	A	A	F	F	A	B	B	F	4-0/6-5 yrs.	I	45	•			•		R		•		•		•		•		•	•		
Information	1100	F	A	A	A	F	F	B	F	B	F	4-0/6-5 yrs.	I	7	•			•		R		•				•				•			
Comprehension	2210	F	A	A	A	F	F	B	F	B	F	4-0/6-5 yrs.	I	7	•			•		R		•					•						
Similarities	2231	F	A	A	A	F	F	B	F	B	F	4-0/6-5 yrs.	I	7	•			•		R		•				•							
Arithmetic	1210	F	A	A	A	F	F	B	F	B	F	4-0/6-5 yrs.	I	7	•			•		R		•		•		•				•			
Vocabulary	2231	F	A	A	A	F	F	B	F	B	F	4-0/6-5 yrs.	I	7	•			•		R		•					•						
Sentences	2232	F	A	A	A	F	F	B	F	B	F	4-0/6-5 yrs.	I	7	•			•		R		•					•						
Picture Completion	2131	F	A	A	A	F	F	B	F	B	F	4-0/6-5 yrs.	I	7	•			•		R		•		•		•				•			
Block Design	2132	F	A	A	A	F	F	B	F	B	F	4-0/6-5 yrs.	I	7	•			•		R		•		•				•					
Animal House	2132	F	A	A	A	F	F	F	F	F	F	4-0/6-5 yrs.	I	7	•			•		R		•		•				•					
Mazes	2132	F	A	A	A	F	F	B	F	B	F	4-0/6-5 yrs.	I	7	•			•		R		•		•							•		
Geometric Designs	2132	F	A	A	A	F	F	B	F	B	F	4-0/6-5 yrs.	I	7	•			•		R		•		•							•		
WEISS COMPREHENSIVE ARTICULATION TEST (1980)																																	
Picture Test	2243	F	F	F	F	B	F	F	F	F	F	2-6/Adult yrs.	I	7	•					ST		•		•		•							
Sentence Test	2243	F	F	F	F	B	F	F	F	F	F	2-6/Adult yrs.	I	7	•					ST		•	•				•						
WEPMAN'S AUDITORY DISCRIMINATION TEST — SECOND EDITION (1987)																																	
Total	2241	F	A	B	B	A	B	F	F	F	F	4-0/8-11 yrs.	I	7			•	•		EA		•				•							
WIDE RANGE ACHIEVEMENT TEST (1978)																																	
Reading	1320	F	A	A	F	B	F	F	F	F	F	gr. K–Adult	I	7		•	•	•		EA			•			•							
Spelling	1630	F	A	A	F	B	F	F	F	F	F	gr. K–Adult	I	7		•	•	•		EA		•										•	

	Taxonomy code	Overall rating	Scores	Size	Demographics	Recency	Total	Internal consistency	Stability	Total	Total (Val.)	Ages/Grades for Intended Use	Group/Individual	Testing time	Age equivalents	Grade equivalents	Percentile ranks	Standard scores	Other	Examiner qualifications	Third Party	Listen	Read print	Look at stimuli	Other	Speak, minor	Speak, major	Manipulate objects	Mark answer sheet	Point	Draw	Write print	Other
WIDE RANGE ACHIEVEMENT TEST (1978) (cont.)																																	
Arithmetic	1220	F	A	A	F	B	F	F	F	F	F	gr. K–Adult	I	7	•	•	•			EA		•	•	•			•			•			•	•[1]
WIDE RANGE ACHIEVEMENT TEST — REVISED (1984)																																	
Reading	1320	B	A	A	B	B	B	A	F	B	B	5-0/Adult yrs.	I	7	•	•	•			EA		•	•				•							
Spelling	1630	B	A	A	B	B	B	A	F	B	B	5-0/Adult yrs.	I	7	•	•	•			EA		•											•	
Arithmetic	1220	B	A	A	B	B	B	B	F	B	B	5-0/Adult yrs.	I	7	•	•	•			EA		•	•	•			•						•	
WIDE RANGE ASSESSMENT OF MEMORY AND LEARNING (1990)																																	
General Memory	2000	B	A	A	A	A	A	A	F	B	A	5-0/15-11 yrs.	I	60 +				•		EA		•		•			•	•		•	•	•		
Memory Screening Index	2000	F	A	A	A	A	A	F	F	F	A	5-0/15-11 yrs.	I	40				•		EA		•		•			•			•	•			
Verbal Memory	2200	B	A	A	A	A	A	A	F	B	A	5-0/15-11 yrs.	I	30				•		EA		•		•			•							
Visual Memory	2133	B	A	A	A	A	A	A	F	B	A	5-0/15-11 yrs.	I	30				•		EA		•		•						•	•	•		
Learning	2000	B	A	A	A	A	A	A	F	B	A	5-0/15-11 yrs.	I	30				•		EA		•					•	•		•	•			
Picture Memory	2133	B	A	A	A	A	A	B	F	B	A	5-0/15-11 yrs.	I	10	•			•		EA		•		•										
Design Memory	2133	B	A	A	A	A	A	B	F	B	A	5-0/15-11 yrs.	I	10	•			•		EA		•		•								•		
Verbal Learning	2242	F	A	A	A	A	A	F	F	F	A	5-0/15-11 yrs.	I	10	•			•		EA		•						•						
Story Memory	2233	B	A	A	A	A	A	B	F	B	A	5-0/15-11 yrs.	I	10	•			•		EA		•						•						
Finger Windows	2133	B	A	A	A	A	A	B	F	B	A	5-0/15-11 yrs.	I	10	•			•		EA		•		•						•				
Sound Symbol	2244	B	A	A	A	A	A	A	F	B	A	5-0/15-11 yrs.	I	10	•			•		EA		•		•		•								
Sentence Memory	2232	B	A	A	A	A	A	B	F	B	A	5-0/15-11 yrs.	I	10	•			•		EA		•						•						
Visual Learning	2133	B	A	A	A	A	A	B	F	B	A	5-0/15-11 yrs.	I	10	•			•		EA		•		•						•				
Number/Letter Memory	2242	B	A	A	A	A	A	B	F	B	A	5-0/15-11 yrs.	I	10	•			•		EA		•						•						
WIDE RANGE INTELLIGENCE–PERSONALITY TEST (1978)																																	
Intelligence Score	4000	F	A	B	F	F	F	B	F	B	F	9-6/Adult yrs.	G	60		•	•			EA		•	•	•						•		•	•	
Vocabulary	1310	F	A	B	F	F	F	B	F	B	F	9-6/Adult yrs.	G	7		•	•			EA		•	•										•	
Number Series	2110	F	A	B	F	F	F	B	F	B	F	9-6/Adult yrs.	G	7		•	•			EA		•	•										•	
Coding	2132	F	A	B	F	F	F	B	F	B	F	9-6/Adult yrs.	G	7		•	•			EA		•		•								•		
Picture Reasoning	2110	F	A	B	F	F	F	B	F	B	F	9-6/Adult yrs.	G	7		•	•			EA		•		•									•	
Space Series	2110	F	A	B	F	F	F	B	F	B	F	9-6/Adult yrs.	G	7		•	•			EA		•		•									•	
Verbal Reasoning	1310	F	A	B	F	F	F	B	F	B	F	9-6/Adult yrs.	G	7		•	•			EA		•	•										•	

[1] Show fingers

	Taxonomy code	Overall rating	Scores	Size	Demographics	Recency	Total	Internal consistency	Stability	Total	Total (Val.)	Ages/Grades for Intended Use	Group/Individual	Testing time	Age equivalents	Grade equivalents	Percentile ranks	Standard scores	Other	Examiner qualifications	Third Party	Listen	Read print	Look at stimuli	Other	Speak, minor	Speak, major	Manipulate objects	Mark answer sheet	Point	Draw	Write print	Other
WIDE RANGE INTELLIGENCE–PERSONALITY TEST (1978) (cont.)																																	
Social Concept	3400	F	A	B	F	F	F	B	F	B	F	9-6/Adult yrs.	G	7			•	•		EA		•		•					•		•		
Arithmetic	1220	F	A	B	F	F	F	B	F	B	F	9-6/Adult yrs.	G	7			•	•		EA		•	•									•	
Space Completion	2131	F	A	B	F	F	F	B	F	B	F	9-6/Adult yrs.	G	7			•	•		EA		•		•					•				
Spelling	1630	F	A	B	F	F	F	B	F	B	F	9-6/Adult yrs.	G	7			•	•		EA		•										•	
WIDE RANGE INTEREST – OPINION TEST (1979)																																	
Art	3220	F	A	B	F	B	F	F	F	F	F	5-0/Adult yrs.	G	45				•		EA		•		•					•				
Literature	3220	F	A	B	F	B	F	F	F	F	F	5-0/Adult yrs.	G	45				•		EA		•		•					•				
Music	3220	F	A	B	F	B	F	F	F	F	F	5-0/Adult yrs.	G	45				•		EA		•		•					•				
Drama	3220	F	A	B	F	B	F	F	F	F	F	5-0/Adult yrs.	G	45				•		EA		•		•					•				
Sales	3220	F	A	B	F	B	F	F	F	F	F	5-0/Adult yrs.	G	45				•		EA		•		•					•				
Management	3220	F	A	B	F	B	F	F	F	F	F	5-0/Adult yrs.	G	45				•		EA		•		•					•				
Office Work	3220	F	A	B	F	B	F	F	F	F	F	5-0/Adult yrs.	G	45				•		EA		•		•					•				
Personal Service	3220	F	A	B	F	B	F	F	F	F	F	5-0/Adult yrs.	G	45				•		EA		•		•					•				
Protective Service	3220	F	A	B	F	B	F	F	F	F	F	5-0/Adult yrs.	G	45				•		EA		•		•					•				
Social Service	3220	F	A	B	F	B	F	F	F	F	F	5-0/Adult yrs.	G	45				•		EA		•		•					•				
Social Science	3220	F	A	B	F	B	F	F	F	F	F	5-0/Adult yrs.	G	45				•		EA		•		•					•				
Biological Science	3220	F	A	B	F	B	F	F	F	F	F	5-0/Adult yrs.	G	45				•		EA		•		•					•				
Physical Science	3220	F	A	B	F	B	F	F	F	F	F	5-0/Adult yrs.	G	45				•		EA		•		•					•				
Number	3220	F	A	B	F	B	F	F	F	F	F	5-0/Adult yrs.	G	45				•		EA		•		•					•				
Mechanics	3220	F	A	B	F	B	F	F	F	F	F	5-0/Adult yrs.	G	45				•		EA		•		•					•				
Machine Operation	3220	F	A	B	F	B	F	F	F	F	F	5-0/Adult yrs.	G	45				•		EA		•		•					•				
Outdoor	3220	F	A	B	F	B	F	F	F	F	F	5-0/Adult yrs.	G	45				•		EA		•		•					•				
Athletics	3220	F	A	B	F	B	F	F	F	F	F	5-0/Adult yrs.	G	45				•		EA		•		•					•				
Sedentariness	3220	F	A	B	F	B	F	F	F	F	F	5-0/Adult yrs.	G	45				•		EA		•		•					•				
Risk	3220	F	A	B	F	B	F	F	F	F	F	5-0/Adult yrs.	G	45				•		EA		•		•					•				
Ambition	3220	F	A	B	F	B	F	F	F	F	F	5-0/Adult yrs.	G	45				•		EA		•		•					•				
Skill Level	3220	F	A	B	F	B	F	F	F	F	F	5-0/Adult yrs.	G	45				•		EA		•		•					•				
Sex Stereotype	3220	F	A	B	F	B	F	F	F	F	F	5-0/Adult yrs.	G	45				•		EA		•		•					•				
Agreement	3220	F	A	B	F	B	F	F	F	F	F	5-0/Adult yrs.	G	45				•		EA		•		•					•				

	Taxonomy code	Overall rating	Norms: Scores	Norms: Size	Norms: Demographics	Norms: Recency	Norms: Total	Rel: Internal consistency	Rel: Stability	Rel: Total	Val: Total	Ages/Grades for Intended Use	Group/Individual	Testing time	Age equivalents	Grade equivalents	Percentile ranks	Standard scores	Other	Examiner qualifications	Third Party	Listen	Read print	Look at stimuli	Other	Speak, minor	Speak, major	Manipulate objects	Mark answer sheet	Point	Draw	Write print	Other
WIDE RANGE INTEREST – OPINION TEST (1979) (cont.)																																	
Negative	3220	F	A	B	F	B	F	F	F	F	F	5-0/Adult yrs.	G	45			•			EA		•		•					•				
Positive	3220	F	A	B	F	B	F	F	F	F	F	5-0/Adult yrs.	G	45			•			EA		•		•					•				
WOODCOCK–JOHNSON PSYCHO-EDUCATIONAL BATTERY — PART ONE (1978)																																	
Full Scale Cluster	4000	B	B	B	A	B	B	A	F	B	A	gr. K–Adult	I	60+	•	•	•	•		EA		•	•	•		•	•			•	•		
Brief Scale Cluster	4000	B	B	B	A	B	B	A	F	B	A	gr. K–Adult	I	7	•	•	•	•		EA		•	•	•		•							
Verbal Cluster	2000	B	B	B	A	B	B	B	F	B	B	gr. K–Adult	I	22	•	•	•	•		EA		•		•		•				•			
Reasoning Cluster	2000	B	B	B	A	B	B	B	F	B	B	gr. K–Adult	I	22	•	•	•	•		EA		•		•		•				•			
Perceptual Speed Cluster	2131	F	B	B	A	B	B	F	F	F	B	gr. K–Adult	I	7	•	•	•	•		EA		•		•		•				•	•		
Memory Cluster	2200	B	B	B	A	B	B	B	F	B	B	gr. K–Adult	I	7	•	•	•	•	•¹	EA		•				•	•						
Reading Aptitude Cluster	2000	B	B	B	A	B	B	A	F	B	B	gr. K–Adult	I	22	•	•	•	•	•¹	EA		•		•		•	•						
Mathematics Aptitude Cluster	2000	B	B	B	A	B	B	B	F	B	B	gr. K–Adult	I	22	•	•	•	•	•¹	EA		•		•		•				•	•		
Written Language Aptitude Cluster	4000	B	B	B	A	B	B	A	F	B	B	gr. K–Adult	I	22	•	•	•	•	•¹	EA		•	•	•		•					•		
Knowledge Aptitude Cluster	4000	B	B	B	A	B	B	A	F	B	B	gr. K–Adult	I	22	•	•	•	•	•¹	EA		•	•	•		•	•						
Picture Vocabulary	2231	B	B	B	A	B	B	B	F	B	B	gr. K–Adult	I	7	•	•	•	•	•¹	EA		•		•		•							
Spatial Relations	2131	F	B	B	A	B	B	B	F	B	F	gr. K–Adult	I	7	•	•	•	•	•¹	EA		•		•		•				•			
Memory for Sentences	2232	F	B	B	A	B	B	F	F	F	B	gr. K–Adult	I	7	•	•	•	•	•¹	EA		•					•						
Visual-Auditory Learning	2000	B	B	B	A	B	B	B	F	B	B	gr. K–Adult	I	7	•	•	•	•	•¹	EA		•		•			•						
Blending	2244	B	B	B	A	B	B	B	F	B	B	gr. K–Adult	I	7	•	•	•	•	•¹	EA		•				•							
Quantitative Concepts	1230	B	B	B	A	B	B	B	F	B	B	gr. K–Adult	I	7	•	•	•	•	•¹	EA		•	•	•				•					
Visual Matching	2131	F	B	B	A	B	B	F	F	F	F	gr. K–Adult	I	7	•	•	•	•	•¹	EA		•		•								•	
Antonyms-Synonyms	2231	B	B	B	A	B	B	B	F	B	B	gr. K–Adult	I	7	•	•	•	•	•¹	EA		•				•							
Analysis-Synthesis	2110	B	B	B	A	B	B	B	F	B	B	gr. K–Adult	I	7	•	•	•	•	•¹	EA		•		•						•			
Numbers Reversed	2242	F	B	B	A	B	B	F	F	F	B	gr. K–Adult	I	7	•	•	•	•	•¹	EA		•					•						
Concept Formation	2000	B	B	B	A	B	B	B	F	B	B	gr. K–Adult	I	7	•	•	•	•	•¹	EA		•		•		•							
Analogies	2210	B	B	B	A	B	B	B	F	B	B	gr. K–Adult	I	7	•	•	•	•	•¹	EA		•				•							
¹Means and standard deviations																																	
WOODCOCK–JOHNSON PSYCHO-EDUCATIONAL BATTERY — PART TWO (1978)																																	
Reading Achievement Cluster	1300	B	B	B	A	B	B	A	F	B	A	gr. K–Adult	I	22	•	•	•	•		EA		•	•			•							
Mathematics Achievement Cluster	1200	B	B	B	A	B	B	A	F	B	A	gr. K–Adult	I	7	•	•	•	•		EA		•	•	•		•						•	

	Taxonomy code	Overall rating	Norms: Scores	Size	Demographics	Recency	Norms Total	Internal consistency	Stability	Reliab. Total	Val. Total	Ages/Grades for Intended Use	Group/Individual	Testing time	Age equivalents	Grade equivalents	Percentile ranks	Standard scores	Scores Other	Examiner qualifications	Third Party	Listen	Read print	Look at stimuli	Input Other	Speak, minor	Speak, major	Manipulate objects	Mark answer sheet	Point	Draw	Write print	Output Other
WOODCOCK–JOHNSON PSYCHO-EDUCATIONAL BATTERY — PART TWO (1978) (cont.)																																	
Written Language Achievement Cluster	1600	B	B	B	A	B	B	A	F	B	A	gr. K–Adult	I	7	•	•	•	•		EA		•	•			•						•	
Knowledge Cluster	1000	B	B	B	A	B	B	A	F	B	A	gr. K–Adult	I	22	•	•	•	•		EA		•		•		•							
Skills Cluster	1000	B	B	B	A	B	B	A	F	B	B	gr. K–Adult	I	22	•	•	•	•		EA		•	•	•		•						•	
Letter-Word Identification	1320	B	B	B	A	B	B	A	F	B	B	gr. K–Adult	I	7	•	•	•	•		EA		•	•			•							
Word Attack	1330	B	B	B	A	B	B	A	F	B	B	gr. K–Adult	I	7	•	•	•	•		EA		•	•			•							
Passage Comprehension	1310	B	B	B	A	B	B	B	F	B	B	gr. K–Adult	I	7	•	•	•	•		EA		•	•			•							
Calculation	1220	B	B	B	A	B	B	B	F	B	B	gr. K–Adult	I	7	•	•	•	•		EA		•	•			•						•	
Applied Problems	1210	B	B	B	A	B	B	B	F	B	B	gr. K–Adult	I	7	•	•	•	•		EA		•	•			•						•	
Dictation	1600	B	B	B	A	B	B	B	F	B	B	gr. K–Adult	I	7	•	•	•	•		EA		•										•	
Proofing	1600	B	B	B	A	B	B	B	F	B	B	gr. K–Adult	I	7	•	•	•	•		EA		•	•			•							
Science	1400	B	B	B	A	B	B	B	F	B	B	gr. K–Adult	I	7	•	•	•	•		EA		•		•		•							
Social Studies	1500	B	B	B	A	B	B	B	F	B	B	gr. K–Adult	I	7	•	•	•	•		EA		•		•		•							
Humanities	1500	B	B	B	A	B	B	B	F	B	B	gr. K–Adult	I	7	•	•	•	•		EA		•		•		•							
WOODCOCK–JOHNSON PSYCHO-EDUCATIONAL BATTERY — PART THREE (1978)																																	
Scholastic Interest Cluster	3210	B	B	B	A	B	B	B	F	B	B	gr. K–Adult	I	7	•	•	•	•		EA		•	•			•							
Non-Scholastic Interest Cluster	3230	B	B	B	A	B	B	B	F	B	B	gr. K–Adult	I	7	•	•	•	•		EA		•	•			•							
Reading Interest	3210	B	B	B	A	B	B	B	F	B	B	gr. K–Adult	I	7	•	•	•	•		EA		•	•			•							
Mathematics Interest	3210	B	B	B	A	B	B	B	F	B	B	gr. K–Adult	I	7	•	•	•	•		EA		•	•			•							
Language Interest	3210	B	B	B	A	B	B	B	F	B	B	gr. K–Adult	I	7	•	•	•	•		EA		•	•			•							
Physical Interest	3230	F	B	B	A	B	B	F	F	F	B	gr. K–Adult	I	7	•	•	•	•		EA		•	•			•							
Social Interest	3230	F	B	B	A	B	B	F	F	F	B	gr. K–Adult	I	7	•	•	•	•		EA		•	•			•							
WOODCOCK–JOHNSON PSYCHO-EDUCATIONAL BATTERY — REVISED — TESTS OF ACHIEVEMENT (1989)																																	
Early Development Scale	1000	B	A	A	A	A	A	A	F	B	B	2-0/80+ yrs.	I	60+	•	•	•	•		EA		•	•	•		•	•			•		•	
Broad Reading	1300	B	A	A	A	A	A	B	B	B	A	5-0/80+ yrs.	I	20	•	•	•	•		EA		•	•	•		•				•			
Basic Reading Skills	1320	B	A	A	A	A	A	A	F	B	B	5-0/80+ yrs.	I	20	•	•	•	•		EA		•	•	•		•				•			
Reading Comprehension	1310	B	A	A	A	A	A	A	F	B	B	5-0/80+ yrs.	I	20	•	•	•	•		EA		•	•			•				•			
Broad Mathematics	1200	B	A	A	A	A	A	B	B	B	A	5-0/80+ yrs.	I	20	•	•	•	•		EA		•	•			•						•	•
Basic Mathematics Skills	1200	B	A	A	A	A	A	A	F	B	B	5-0/80+ yrs.	I	20	•	•	•	•		EA		•	•			•						•	•
Mathematics Reasoning	1210	B	A	A	A	A	A	A	F	B	B	2-0/80+ yrs.	I	10	•	•	•	•		EA		•	•									•	

WOODCOCK–JOHNSON PSYCHO-EDUCATIONAL BATTERY — REVISED — TESTS OF ACHIEVEMENT (1989) (cont.)

			Norms					Reliability			Val.		Admin.		Scores						Input					Output							
	Taxonomy code	Overall rating	Scores	Size	Demographics	Recency	Total	Internal consistency	Stability	Total	Total	Ages/Grades for Intended Use	Group/Individual	Testing time	Age equivalents	Grade equivalents	Percentile ranks	Standard scores	Other	Examiner qualifications	Third Party	Listen	Read print	Look at stimuli	Other	Speak, minor	Speak, major	Manipulate objects	Mark answer sheet	Point	Draw	Write print	Other
Broad Written Language	1600	B	A	A	A	A	A	A	F	B	A	5-0/80+ yrs.	I	20	•	•	•	•		EA		•	•									•	
Basic Writing Skills	1600	B	A	A	A	A	A	A	B	B	B	5-0/80+ yrs.	I	20	•	•	•	•		EA		•	•									•	
Written Expression	1600	B	A	A	A	A	A	A	F	B	B	5-0/80+ yrs.	I	20	•	•	•	•		EA		•	•	•								•	
Broad Knowledge	1000	B	A	A	A	A	A	A	B	B	A	2-0/80+ yrs.	I	30	•	•	•	•		EA		•	•	•			•					•	
Skills	1000	B	A	A	A	A	A	A	F	B	B	2-0/80+ yrs.	I	30	•	•	•	•		EA		•	•	•		•						•	
Test 22: Letter-Word Identification	1320	B	A	A	A	A	A	A	B	B	B	2-0/80+ yrs.	I	10	•	•	•	•		EA		•	•	•		•				•			
Test 23: Passage Comprehension	1310	B	A	A	A	A	A	B	B	B	B	5-0/80+ yrs.	I	10	•	•	•	•		EA		•	•	•		•							
Test 24: Calculation	1220	B	A	A	A	A	A	A	B	B	B	5-0/80+ yrs.	I	10	•	•	•	•		EA		•									•	•	
Test 25: Applied Problems	1210	B	A	A	A	A	A	A	B	B	B	2-0/80+ yrs.	I	10	•	•	•	•		EA		•	•									•	
Test 26: Dictation	1600	B	A	A	A	A	A	A	B	B	B	2-0/80+ yrs.	I	10	•	•	•	•		EA		•	•									•	
Test 27: Writing Samples	1610	B	A	A	A	A	A	B	F	B	B	5-0/80+ yrs.	I	10	•	•	•	•		EA		•	•									•	
Test 28: Science	1400	B	A	A	A	A	A	B	B	B	B	2-0/80+ yrs.	I	10	•	•	•	•		EA		•		•			•			•			
Test 29: Social Studies	1500	B	A	A	A	A	A	B	B	B	B	2-0/80+ yrs.	I	10	•	•	•	•		EA		•		•			•			•			
Test 30: Humanities	5000	B	A	A	A	A	A	B	B	B	B	2-0/80+ yrs.	I	10	•	•	•	•		EA		•		•			•			•			
Test 31: Word Attack	1330	B	A	A	A	A	A	A	F	B	B	5-0/80+ yrs.	I	10	•	•	•	•		EA		•	•			•							
Test 32: Reading Vocabulary	1310	B	A	A	A	A	A	A	F	B	B	5-0/80+ yrs.	I	10	•	•	•	•		EA		•	•			•							
Test 33: Quantitative Concepts	1230	B	A	A	A	A	A	B	F	B	B	5-0/80+ yrs.	I	10	•	•	•	•		EA		•	•	•		•							
Test 34: Proofing	1600	B	A	A	A	A	A	B	B	B	B	5-0/80+ yrs.	I	10	•	•	•	•		EA		•	•									•	
Test 35: Writing Fluency	1600	F	A	A	A	A	A	F	F	F	B	5-0/80+ yrs.	I	10	•	•	•	•		EA		•	•	•								•	
Punctuation & Capitalization	1620	B	A	A	A	A	A	B	B	B	B	5-0/80+ yrs.	I	10	•	•	•	•		EA		•	•									•	
Spelling	1630	B	A	A	A	A	A	B	B	B	B	5-0/80+ yrs.	I	10	•	•	•	•		EA		•	•									•	
Usage	1610	B	A	A	A	A	A	B	B	B	B	5-0/80+ yrs.	I	10	•	•	•	•		EA		•	•									•	
Handwriting	1640	F	A	A	A	A	A	F	F	F	F	5-0/80+ yrs.	I	10	•	•	•	•		EA		•	•									•	

WOODCOCK–JOHNSON PSYCHO-EDUCATIONAL BATTERY — REVISED — TESTS OF COGNITIVE ABILITY (1989)

			Norms					Reliability			Val.		Admin.		Scores						Input					Output							
	Taxonomy code	Overall rating	Scores	Size	Demographics	Recency	Total	Internal consistency	Stability	Total	Total	Ages/Grades for Intended Use	Group/Individual	Testing time	Age equivalents	Grade equivalents	Percentile ranks	Standard scores	Other	Examiner qualifications	Third Party	Listen	Read print	Look at stimuli	Other	Speak, minor	Speak, major	Manipulate objects	Mark answer sheet	Point	Draw	Write print	Other
Early Development Scale	2000	B	A	A	A	A	A	A	B	B	A	2-0/80+ yrs.	I	60+	•	•	•	•		EA		•		•	•	•				•			
Standard Scale	2000	B	A	A	A	A	A	A	F	B	A	5-0/80+ yrs.	I	60+	•	•	•	•		EA		•		•	•	•				•			
Extended Scale	2000	B	A	A	A	A	A	A	F	B	A	5-0/80+ yrs.	I	60+	•	•	•	•		EA		•		•	•	•				•	•		
Long-Term Retrieval	2200	B	A	A	A	A	A	A	B	B	A	5-0/80+ yrs.	I	40	•	•	•	•		EA		•		•						•			
Short-Term Retrieval	2200	B	A	A	A	A	A	B	F	B	A	5-0/80+ yrs.	I	30	•	•	•	•		EA		•						•					

WOODCOCK–JOHNSON PSYCHO-EDUCATIONAL BATTERY — REVISED — TESTS OF COGNITIVE ABILITY (1989) (cont.)

	Taxonomy code	Overall rating	Norms: Scores	Size	Demographics	Recency	Total	Rel: Internal consistency	Stability	Total	Val. Total	Ages/Grades for Intended Use	Group/Individual	Testing time	Age equivalents	Grade equivalents	Percentile ranks	Standard scores	Other	Examiner qualifications	Third Party	Listen	Read print	Look at stimuli	Other	Speak, minor	Speak, major	Manipulate objects	Mark answer sheet	Point	Draw	Write print	Other
Processing Speed	2000	B	A	A	A	A	A	B	B	B	A	5-0/80+ yrs.	I	20	•	•	•	•		EA		•		•						•	•		
Auditory Processing	2244	B	A	A	A	A	A	B	F	B	A	5-0/80+ yrs.	I	30	•	•	•	•		EA		•		•		•							
Visual Processing	2131	B	A	A	A	A	A	B	F	B	A	5-0/80+ yrs.	I	30	•	•	•	•		EA		•		•		•							
Comprehension-Knowledge	2231	B	A	A	A	A	A	A	B	B	A	5-0/80+ yrs.	I	40	•	•	•	•		EA		•		•		•							
Fluid Reasoning	2000	B	A	A	A	A	A	A	B	B	A	5-0/80+ yrs.	I	40	•	•	•	•		EA		•		•		•	•						
Oral Language	2200	B	A	A	A	A	A	A	B	B	B	5-0/80+ yrs.	I	40	•	•	•	•		EA		•		•		•							
Reading Aptitude	2000	B	A	A	A	A	A	A	F	B	B	5-0/80+ yrs.	I	40	•	•	•	•		EA		•		•		•	•			•			
Mathematics Aptitude	2000	B	A	A	A	A	A	A	F	B	B	5-0/80+ yrs.	I	40	•	•	•	•		EA		•		•		•	•			•			
Written Language Aptitude	2000	B	A	A	A	A	A	A	F	B	B	5-0/80+ yrs.	I	40	•	•	•	•		EA		•		•		•	•			•			
Knowledge Aptitude	2000	B	A	A	A	A	A	A	F	B	B	5-0/80+ yrs.	I	40	•	•	•	•		EA		•		•		•	•						
Oral Language Aptitude	2000	B	A	A	A	A	A	A	F	B	B	5-0/80+ yrs.	I	40	•	•	•	•		EA		•		•		•	•					•	
Test 1: Memory for Names	2242	F	A	A	A	A	A	A	F	B	F	2-0/80+ yrs.	I	10	•	•	•	•		EA		•		•						•			
Test 2: Memory for Sentences	2232	F	A	A	A	A	A	B	F	B	F	2-0/80+ yrs.	I	10	•	•	•	•		EA		•				•							
Test 3: Visual Matching	2250	B	A	A	A	A	A	F	B	B	B	2-0/80+ yrs.	I	10	•	•	•	•		EA		•		•					•				
Test 4: Incomplete Words	2244	F	A	A	A	A	A	F	F	F	F	2-0/80+ yrs.	I	10	•	•	•	•		EA		•			•								
Test 5: Visual Closure	2131	F	A	A	A	A	A	F	F	F	F	2-0/80+ yrs.	I	10	•	•	•	•		EA		•		•		•							
Test 6: Picture Vocabulary	2231	F	A	A	A	A	A	B	F	B	F	2-0/80+ yrs.	I	10	•	•	•	•		EA		•		•		•				•			
Test 7: Analysis-Synthesis	2210	B	A	A	A	A	A	A	F	B	B	5-0/80+ yrs.	I	10	•	•	•	•		EA		•		•		•							
Test 8: Visual-Auditory Learning	2200	B	A	A	A	A	A	A	F	B	B	5-0/80+ yrs.	I	10	•	•	•	•		EA		•		•				•					
Test 9: Memory for Words	2242	F	A	A	A	A	A	B	F	B	F	5-0/80+ yrs.	I	10	•	•	•	•		EA		•						•					
Test 10: Cross Out	2132	F	A	A	A	A	A	F	F	F	F	5-0/80+ yrs.	I	10	•	•	•	•		EA		•		•	•				•				
Test 11: Sound Blending	2244	B	A	A	A	A	A	B	F	B	B	5-0/80+ yrs.	I	10	•	•	•	•		EA		•				•							
Test 12: Picture Recognition	2131	F	A	A	A	A	A	B	F	B	F	5-0/80+ yrs.	I	10	•	•	•	•		EA		•		•		•					•		
Test 13: Oral Vocabulary	2231	B	A	A	A	A	A	B	B	B	B	5-0/80+ yrs.	I	10	•	•	•	•		EA		•				•							
Test 14: Concept Formation	2000	F	A	A	A	A	A	A	F	B	F	5-0/80+ yrs.	I	10	•	•	•	•		EA		•		•			•						
Test 15: Delayed Recall-Memory for Names	2242	F	A	A	A	A	A	A	F	B	F	5-0/80+ yrs.	I	10	•	•	•	•		EA		•		•						•			
Test 16: Delayed Recall-Visual-Auditory Learning	2200	F	A	A	A	A	A	A	F	B	F	5-0/80+ yrs.	I	10	•	•	•	•		EA		•		•		•							
Test 17: Numbers Reversed	2242	F	A	A	A	A	A	B	F	B	F	5-0/80+ yrs.	I	10	•	•	•	•		EA		•						•					
Test 18: Sound Patterns	2241	F	A	A	A	A	A	B	F	B	F	5-0/80+ yrs.	I	10	•	•	•	•		EA		•				•							

			Technical Characteristics									Nontechnical Characteristics																						
			Norms					Reliability			Val.	Ages/Grades for Intended Use	Admin.		Scores						Test Formats — Input					Output							
	Taxonomy code	Overall rating	Scores	Size	Demographics	Recency	Total	Internal consistency	Stability	Total	Total		Group/Individual	Testing time	Age equivalents	Grade equivalents	Percentile ranks	Standard scores	Other	Examiner qualifications	Third Party	Listen	Read print	Look at stimuli	Other	Speak, minor	Speak, major	Manipulate objects	Mark answer sheet	Point	Draw	Write print	Other
WOODCOCK–JOHNSON PSYCHO-EDUCATIONAL BATTERY — REVISED — TESTS OF COGNITIVE ABILITY (1989) (cont.)																																	
Test 19: Spatial Relations	2110	F	A	A	A	A	A	B	F	B	F	5-0/80+ yrs.	I	10	•	•	•	•		EA		•		•						•			
Test 20: Listening Comprehension	2230	F	A	A	A	A	A	B	F	B	F	5-0/80+ yrs.	I	10	•	•	•	•		EA		•				•							
Test 21: Verbal Analogies	2210	B	A	A	A	A	A	B	F	B	B	5-0/80+ yrs.	I	10	•	•	•	•		EA		•				•							
WOODCOCK LANGUAGE PROFICIENCY BATTERY — REVISED (1991)																																	
Oral Language	2200	B	A	A	A	A	A	A	A	A	B	2-0/95-11 yrs.	I	25	•	•	•	•		EA		•	•	•		•	•						
Broad Reading	1300	B	A	A	A	A	A	A	A	A	B	2-0/95-11 yrs.	I	10	•	•	•	•		EA		•	•			•				•			
Basic Reading Skills	1330	B	A	A	A	A	A	F	B	B	B	2-0/95-11 yrs.	I	10	•	•	•	•		EA		•	•			•				•			
Reading Comprehension	1310	B	A	A	A	A	A	F	B	B	B	2-0/95-11 yrs.	I	10	•	•	•	•		EA		•	•			•				•			
Broad Written Language	1600	B	A	A	A	A	A	F	B	B	B	2-0/95-11 yrs.	I	10	•	•	•	•		EA		•		•								•	
Basic Writing Skills	1600	B	A	A	A	A	A	A	A	A	B	2-0/95-11 yrs.	I	10	•	•	•	•		EA		•							•				
Written Expression	1610	B	A	A	A	A	A	F	B	B	B	2-0/95-11 yrs.	I	10	•	•	•	•		EA		•		•								•	
Broad English Ability—ED	4000	B	A	A	A	A	A	F	B	B	B	2-0/95-11 yrs.	I	20	•	•	•	•		EA		•	•	•		•	•			•		•	
Broad English Ability—Standard	4000	B	A	A	A	A	A	F	B	B	B	2-0/95-11 yrs.	I	35	•	•	•	•		EA		•	•	•		•	•			•		•	
Memory for Sentences	2232	B	A	A	A	A	A	B	F	B	B	2-0/95-11 yrs.	I	5	•	•	•	•		EA		•				•							
Picture Vocabulary	2231	B	A	A	A	A	A	B	F	B	B	2-0/95-11 yrs.	I	5	•	•	•	•		EA		•		•		•							
Oral Vocabulary	2231	B	A	A	A	A	A	B	B	B	B	2-0/95-11 yrs.	I	5	•	•	•	•		EA		•	•			•							
Listening Comprehension	2230	B	A	A	A	A	A	B	F	B	B	2-0/95-11 yrs.	I	5	•	•	•	•		EA		•				•							
Verbal Analogies	2210	B	A	A	A	A	A	F	B	B	B	2-0/95-11 yrs.	I	5	•	•	•	•		EA		•	•			•							
Letter-Word Identification	1330	B	A	A	A	A	A	A	B	B	B	2-0/95-11 yrs.	I	5	•	•	•	•		EA		•	•	•						•			
Passage Comprehension	1310	B	A	A	A	A	A	B	B	B	B	2-0/95-11 yrs.	I	5	•	•	•	•		EA		•	•							•			
Word Attack	1330	B	A	A	A	A	A	F	B	B	B	2-0/95-11 yrs.	I	5	•	•	•	•		EA		•	•			•							
Reading Vocabulary	1310	F	A	A	A	A	A	F	B	B	F	2-0/95-11 yrs.	I	5	•	•	•	•		EA		•	•			•							
Dictation	1630	B	A	A	A	A	A	A	B	B	B	2-0/95-11 yrs.	I	5	•	•	•	•		EA		•										•	
Writing Samples	1610	B	A	A	A	A	A	F	B	B	B	2-0/95-11 yrs.	I	5	•	•	•	•		EA		•		•								•	
Proofing	1620	F	A	A	A	A	A	B	B	B	F	2-0/95-11 yrs.	I	5	•	•	•	•		EA		•							•				
Writing Fluency	1610	F	A	A	A	A	A	F	F	F	F	2-0/95-11 yrs.	I	5	•	•	•	•		EA		•		•								•	
Punctuation & Capitalization	1620	F	A	A	A	A	A	B	B	B	F	2-0/95-11 yrs.	I	5	•	•	•	•		EA		•	•						•			•	
Spelling	1630	F	A	A	A	A	A	B	B	B	F	2-0/95-11 yrs.	I	5	•	•	•	•		EA		•	•									•	
Usage	1610	F	A	A	A	A	A	B	B	B	F	2-0/95-11 yrs.	I	5	•	•	•	•		EA		•	•	•			•					•	•

	Taxonomy code	Overall rating	Norms: Scores	Norms: Size	Norms: Demographics	Norms: Recency	Norms: Total	Rel: Internal consistency	Rel: Stability	Rel: Total	Val: Total	Ages/Grades for Intended Use	Group/Individual	Testing time	Age equivalents	Grade equivalents	Percentile ranks	Standard scores	Other	Examiner qualifications	Third Party	Listen	Read print	Look at stimuli	Other	Speak, minor	Speak, major	Manipulate objects	Mark answer sheet	Point	Draw	Write print	Other
WOODCOCK LANGUAGE PROFICIENCY BATTERY — REVISED (1991) (cont.)																																	
Handwriting	1640	**F**	A	A	A	A	A	F	F	F	F	2-0/95-11 yrs.	I	5	•	•	•	•		EA		•		•								•	
WOODCOCK READING MASTERY TESTS (1973)																																	
Total Reading	1300	**F**	A	A	B	F	F	B	B	B	B	gr. K–12	I	45	•	•	•	•		EA		•	•	•		•							
Letter Identification	1320	**F**	A	A	B	F	F	F	F	F	B	gr. K–12	I	7	•	•	•	•		EA		•	•			•							
Word Identification	1320	**F**	A	A	B	F	F	B	A	B	B	gr. K–12	I	7	•	•	•	•		EA		•	•			•							
Word Attack	1330	**F**	A	A	B	F	F	B	B	B	B	gr. K–12	I	7	•	•	•	•		EA		•	•			•							
Word Comprehension	1310	**F**	A	A	B	F	F	B	F	B	B	gr. K–12	I	7	•	•	•	•		EA		•	•			•							
Passage Comprehension	1310	**F**	A	A	B	F	F	B	F	B	B	gr. K–12	I	7	•	•	•	•		EA		•	•	•		•							
WOODCOCK READING MASTERY TESTS — REVISED (1988)																																	
Total Reading–Full Scale	1300	**B**	A	B	A	A	B	A	F	B	B	5-0/Adult yrs.	I	45	•	•	•	•		EA		•	•	•		•							
Total Reading–Short Scale	1300	**B**	A	B	A	A	B	A	F	B	B	5-0/Adult yrs.	I	22	•	•	•	•		EA		•	•	•		•							
Readiness Cluster	4000	**F**	A	B	A	A	B	F	F	F	F	5-0/Adult yrs.	I	22	•	•	•	•		EA		•	•			•	•						
Basic Skills Cluster	1300	**F**	A	B	A	A	B	A	F	B	F	5-0/Adult yrs.	I	22	•	•	•	•		EA		•	•			•							
Reading Comprehension Cluster	1310	**F**	A	B	A	A	B	A	F	B	F	5-0/Adult yrs.	I	22	•	•	•	•		EA		•	•	•		•							
Visual-Auditory Learning	2000	**F**	A	B	A	A	B	B	F	B	F	5-0/Adult yrs.	I	7	•	•	•	•		EA		•		•				•					
Letter Identification	1320	**F**	A	B	A	A	B	F	F	F	F	5-0/Adult yrs.	I	7	•	•	•	•		EA		•	•			•							
Word Identification	1320	**B**	A	B	A	A	B	A	F	B	B	5-0/Adult yrs.	I	7	•	•	•	•		EA		•	•			•							
Word Attack	1330	**B**	A	B	A	A	B	A	F	B	B	5-0/Adult yrs.	I	7	•	•	•	•		EA		•	•			•							
Word Comprehension	1310	**B**	A	B	A	A	B	A	F	B	B	5-0/Adult yrs.	I	7	•	•	•	•		EA		•	•			•							
Passage Comprehension	1310	**B**	A	B	A	A	B	A	F	B	B	5-0/Adult yrs.	I	7	•	•	•	•		EA		•	•	•		•							
THE WORD TEST (1981)																																	
Total Test	2200	**F**	A	F	F	B	F	A	F	B	B	7-0/11-11 yrs.	I	45	•		•	•		EA		•				•	•						
Associations	2210	**F**	A	F	F	B	F	F	F	F	B	7-0/11-11 yrs.	I	7	•		•	•		EA		•				•							
Synonyms	2231	**F**	A	F	F	B	F	B	F	B	B	7-0/11-11 yrs.	I	7	•		•	•		EA		•				•							
Semantic Absurdities	2210	**F**	A	F	F	B	F	B	F	B	B	7-0/11-11 yrs.	I	7	•		•	•		EA		•					•						
Antonyms	2231	**F**	A	F	F	B	F	B	F	B	B	7-0/11-11 yrs.	I	7	•		•	•		EA		•				•							
Definitions	2231	**F**	A	F	F	B	F	B	F	B	B	7-0/11-11 yrs.	I	7	•		•	•		EA		•					•						
Multiple Definitions	2231	**F**	A	F	F	B	F	B	F	B	B	7-0/11-11 yrs.	I	7	•		•	•		EA		•					•						

			Norms					Reliability			Val.		Admin.		Scores						Input					Output							
	Taxonomy code	Overall rating	Scores	Size	Demographics	Recency	Total	Internal consistency	Stability	Total	Total	Ages/Grades for Intended Use	Group/Individual	Testing time	Age equivalents	Grade equivalents	Percentile ranks	Standard scores	Other	Examiner qualifications	Third Party	Listen	Read print	Look at stimuli	Other	Speak, minor	Speak, major	Manipulate objects	Mark answer sheet	Point	Draw	Write print	Other
THE WORD TEST: ADOLESCENT (1989)																																	
Total	2200	F	A	A	F	A	F	F	A	B	B	12-0/17-11 yrs.	I	25	•		•	•		EA		•	•	•		•	•						
Brand Names	2210	F	A	A	F	A	F	F	F	F	B	12-0/17-11 yrs.	I	8	•		•	•		EA		•	•				•						
Synonyms	2231	F	A	A	F	A	F	F	B	B	B	12-0/17-11 yrs.	I	8	•		•	•		EA		•	•			•							
Signs of the Times	2210	F	A	A	F	A	F	F	F	F	B	12-0/17-11 yrs.	I	8	•		•	•		EA		•	•	•			•						
Definitions	2231	F	A	A	F	A	F	F	B	B	B	12-0/17-11 yrs.	I	8	•		•	•		EA		•	•			•							
THE WORD TEST — R: ELEMENTARY (1990)																																	
Total	2200	F	A	A	F	A	F	F	A	B	A	7-0/11-11 yrs.	I	30	•		•	•		EA		•				•	•						
Associations	2210	F	A	A	F	A	F	F	B	B	A	7-0/11-11 yrs.	I	6	•		•	•		EA		•					•						
Synonyms	2231	F	A	A	F	A	F	F	B	B	A	7-0/11-11 yrs.	I	6	•		•	•		EA		•				•							
Semantic Absurdities	2231	F	A	A	F	A	F	F	B	B	A	7-0/11-11 yrs.	I	6	•		•	•		EA		•				•							
Antonyms	2231	F	A	A	F	A	F	F	B	B	A	7-0/11-11 yrs.	I	6	•		•	•		EA		•				•							
Definitions	2231	F	A	A	F	A	F	F	F	F	A	7-0/11-11 yrs.	I	6	•		•	•		EA		•					•						
Multiple Definitions	2231	F	A	A	F	A	F	F	F	F	A	7-0/11-11 yrs.	I	6	•		•	•		EA		•					•						
WRITTEN LANGUAGE ASSESSMENT (1989)																																	
Written Language Quotient	1600	F	A	B	F	A	F	A	F	B	F	8-0/19-11 yrs.	G	60			•	•		EA		•		•								•	
General Writing Ability	1600	F	A	B	F	A	F	B	F	B	F	8-0/19-11 yrs.	G	60			•	•		EA		•		•								•	
Productivity	1650	F	A	B	F	A	F	B	F	B	F	8-0/19-11 yrs.	G	60			•	•		EA		•		•								•	
Word Complexity	1650	F	A	B	F	A	F	B	F	B	B	8-0/19-11 yrs.	G	60			•	•		EA		•		•								•	
Readability	1650	F	A	B	F	A	F	F	F	F	F	8-0/19-11 yrs.	G	60			•	•		EA		•		•								•	

APPENDIX B

ACHIEVEMENT

1000   Overall Achievement

B	Adaptive Behavior Inventory	Academic Skills/Normal & Retarded Norms
B	Diagnostic Achievement Battery, 2nd Edition	Written Language
B	Diagnostic Achievement Test for Adolescents	Achievement Screener
B	Diagnostic Achievement Test for Adolescents	Overall Achievement
B	Kaufman Test of Educational Achievement–Comprehensive Form	Battery Composite
B	Peabody Individual Achievement Test–Revised	Total Test
B	Quick-Score Achievement Test	General Achievement Quotient
B	Scholastic Abilities Test for Adults	Achievement Screener
B	Scholastic Abilities Test for Adults	Total Achievement
B	Screening Assessment for Gifted Elementary Students	School-Acquired Information/Normal Norms
B	Test of Adolescent Language, 2nd Edition	Written Language
B	Test of Reading Comprehension Revised	Reading the Directions of Schoolwork
B	Woodcock-Johnson Psycho-Educational Battery–Part 2	Knowledge Cluster
B	Woodcock-Johnson Psycho-Educational Battery–Part 2	Skills Cluster
B	Woodcock-Johnson Psycho-Educational Battery–Revised–Tests of Achievement	Broad Knowledge
B	Woodcock-Johnson Psycho-Educational Battery–Revised–Tests of Achievement	Early Development Scale
B	Woodcock-Johnson Psycho-Educational Battery–Revised–Tests of Achievement	Skills
F	AAMD Adaptive Behavior Skills–School Edition	Factor 2: Community Self-Sufficiency
F	Conners' Parent Rating Scales–48	Learning Problem
F	Conners' Parent Rating Scales–93	Learning Problem
F	Diagnostic Achievement Battery	Written Language
F	Diagnostic Screening Test: Achievement	Total
F	Emotional & Behavior Problem Scale	Learning/Comprehension Disorder
F	Kaufman Test of Educational Achievement–Brief Form	Battery Composite
F	Peabody Individual Achievement Test	Total Test
F	School Behavior Checklist	Academic Disability
F	Schubert General Ability Battery	Total
F	Screening Assessment for Gifted Elementary Students	School-Acquired Information/Gifted Norms
F	Social Skills Rating System	Total Academic Competence
F	Street Survival Skills Questionnaire	Total Quotient
F	Test of Adolescent Language	Written Language
F	Test of Practical Knowledge	Total
F	Test of Reading Comprehension	Reading the Directions of Schoolwork
F	Tests for Everyday Living	Total Battery

1100   Basic Information

B	Detroit Tests of Learning Aptitude, 3rd Edition	Basic Information
B	Detroit Tests of Learning Aptitude–Adult	Basic Information
B	Kaufman Assessment Battery for Children	Faces & Places
B	Peabody Individual Achievement Test–Revised	General Information
B	Quick-Score Achievement Test	Facts
B	Wechsler Adult Intelligence Scale–Revised	Information
B	Wechsler Intelligence Scale for Children–3rd Edition	Information
F	Career Maturity Inventory Competence Test	Part 2: Occupational Information

F	Computer Aptitude, Literacy, & Interest Profile	Literacy
F	Diagnostic Screening Test: Achievement	Practical Knowledge
F	Learning Disability Evaluation Scale, The	Thinking
F	Peabody Individual Achievement Test	General Information
F	Wechsler Intelligence Scale for Children–Revised	Information
F	Wechsler Memory Scale–Revised	Information & Orientation Questions
F	Wechsler Preschool & Primary Scale of Intelligence	Information

1200   Math, General

B	Basic Achievement Skills Individual Screener	Mathematics
B	Diagnostic Achievement Battery, 2nd Edition	Math
B	Diagnostic Achievement Test for Adolescents	Mathematics
B	Kaufman Assessment Battery for Children	Arithmetic
B	Kaufman Test of Educational Achievement–Comprehensive Form	Mathematics Composite
B	KeyMath–Revised	Total Test
B	Peabody Individual Achievement Test–Revised	Mathematics
B	Scholastic Abilities Test for Adults	Mathematics
B	Screening Children for Related Early Educational Needs	Math
B	Stanford-Binet Intelligence Scale, 4th Edition	Quantitative
B	Stanford-Binet Intelligence Scale, 4th Edition	Quantitative Reasoning
B	Test of Early Mathematics Ability, 2nd Edition	Math Quotient
B	Woodcock-Johnson Psycho-Educational Battery–Part 2	Mathematics Achievement Cluster
B	Woodcock-Johnson Psycho-Educational Battery–Revised–Tests of Achievement	Basic Mathematics Skills
B	Woodcock-Johnson Psycho-Educational Battery–Revised–Tests of Achievement	Broad Mathematics
F	Basic School Skills Inventory–Diagnostic	Mathematics
F	Cognitive Levels Test	Quantitative Reasoning
F	Diagnostic Achievement Battery	Applied Mathematics
F	Diagnostic Screening Test: Math, 3rd Edition	Metric
F	Diagnostic Screening Test: Math, 3rd Edition	Money
F	Diagnostic Screening Test: Math, 3rd Edition	Percent
F	Diagnostic Screening Test: Math, 3rd Edition	Time
F	Diagnostic Screening Test: Math, 3rd Edition	Total Specialized
F	Diagnostic Screening Test: Math, 3rd Edition	U.S. Measure
F	Kaufman Test of Educational Achievement–Brief Form	Mathematics
F	KeyMath Diagnostic Arithmetic Test	Total
F	Luria-Nebraska Neuropsychological Battery: Children's Revision	C9
F	Peabody Individual Achievement Test	Mathematics
F	Sequential Assessment of Mathematics Inventories	Geometric Concepts
F	Sequential Assessment of Mathematics Inventories	Mathematical Applications
F	Sequential Assessment of Mathematics Inventories	Measurement
F	Sequential Assessment of Mathematics Inventories	Number & Notation
F	Sequential Assessment of Mathematics Inventories	Total
F	Test of Early Mathematics Ability	Math Quotient

1210   Math Reasoning/Problem Solving

B	Detroit Tests of Learning Aptitude–Adult	Mathematical Problems
B	Diagnostic Achievement Battery, 2nd Edition	Math Reasoning
B	Diagnostic Achievement Test for Adolescents	Math Problem Solving
B	Kaufman Test of Educational Achievement–Comprehensive Form	Mathematics Applications

B	KeyMath–Revised	Applications Area
B	KeyMath–Revised	Basic Concepts Area
B	KeyMath–Revised	Geometry
B	KeyMath–Revised	Interpreting Data
B	KeyMath–Revised	Measurement
B	KeyMath–Revised	Numeration
B	KeyMath–Revised	Problem Solving
B	KeyMath–Revised	Rational Numbers
B	KeyMath–Revised	Time & Money
B	Scholastic Abilities Test for Adults	Math Application
B	Scholastic Abilities Test for Adults	Quantitative Reasoning
B	Stanford-Binet Intelligence Scale, 4th Edition	Equation Building
B	Stanford-Binet Intelligence Scale, 4th Edition	Number Series
B	Wechsler Adult Intelligence Scale–Revised	Arithmetic
B	Woodcock-Johnson Psycho-Educational Battery–Part 2	Applied Problems
B	Woodcock-Johnson Psycho-Educational Battery–Revised–Tests of Achievement	Mathematics Reasoning
B	Woodcock-Johnson Psycho-Educational Battery–Revised–Tests of Achievement	Test 25: Applied Problems
F	Diagnostic Achievement Battery	Math Reasoning
F	KeyMath Diagnostic Arithmetic Test	Estimation
F	KeyMath Diagnostic Arithmetic Test	Fractions
F	KeyMath Diagnostic Arithmetic Test	Geometry & Symbols
F	KeyMath Diagnostic Arithmetic Test	Measurement
F	KeyMath Diagnostic Arithmetic Test	Missing Problems
F	KeyMath Diagnostic Arithmetic Test	Money
F	KeyMath Diagnostic Arithmetic Test	Numeration
F	KeyMath Diagnostic Arithmetic Test	Time
F	KeyMath Diagnostic Arithmetic Test	Word Problems
F	Pictorial Test of Intelligence	Size & Number
F	Schubert General Ability Battery	Arithmetic Problems
F	Sequential Assessment of Mathematics Inventories	Word Problems
F	Test of Mathematical Abilities	Story Problems
F	Wechsler Intelligence Scale for Children–Revised	Arithmetic
F	Wechsler Intelligence Scale for Children–3rd Edition	Arithmetic
F	Wechsler Preschool & Primary Scale of Intelligence	Arithmetic

1220   Math Calculation

B	Detroit Tests of Learning Aptitude–Adult	Quantitative Relations
B	Diagnostic Achievement Battery, 2nd Edition	Calculation
B	Diagnostic Achievement Test for Adolescents	Math Calculation
B	Kaufman Test of Educational Achievement–Comprehensive Form	Mathematics Computation
B	KeyMath–Revised	Division
B	KeyMath–Revised	Mental Computation
B	KeyMath–Revised	Operations Area
B	KeyMath–Revised	Subtraction
B	Occupational Aptitude Survey & Interest Schedule, 2nd Edition	Aptitude Survey–Computation
B	Quick-Score Achievement Test	Arithmetic
B	Scholastic Abilities Test for Adults	Math Calculation
B	Scholastic Aptitude Scale	Quantitative Reasoning
B	Test of Mathematical Abilities	Computation
B	Wide Range Achievement Test–Revised	Arithmetic
B	Woodcock-Johnson Psycho-Educational Battery–Part 2	Calculation

B	Woodcock-Johnson Psycho-Educational Battery–Revised–Tests of Achievement	Test 24: Calculation
F	Computer Aptitude, Literacy, & Interest Profile	Estimation
F	Diagnostic Achievement Battery	Math Calculation
F	Diagnostic Screening Test: Math, 3rd Edition	Addition
F	Diagnostic Screening Test: Math, 3rd Edition	Complex Computation
F	Diagnostic Screening Test: Math, 3rd Edition	Decimals
F	Diagnostic Screening Test: Math, 3rd Edition	Division
F	Diagnostic Screening Test: Math, 3rd Edition	Manipulation in Fractions
F	Diagnostic Screening Test: Math, 3rd Edition	Multiplication
F	Diagnostic Screening Test: Math, 3rd Edition	Process
F	Diagnostic Screening Test: Math, 3rd Edition	Sequencing
F	Diagnostic Screening Test: Math, 3rd Edition	Simple Computation
F	Diagnostic Screening Test: Math, 3rd Edition	Simple Fractions
F	Diagnostic Screening Test: Math, 3rd Edition	Special Manipulations
F	Diagnostic Screening Test: Math, 3rd Edition	Subtraction
F	Diagnostic Screening Test: Math, 3rd Edition	Total Basic
F	Diagnostic Screening Test: Math, 3rd Edition	Use of Zero
F	KeyMath Diagnostic Arithmetic Test	Addition
F	KeyMath Diagnostic Arithmetic Test	Division
F	KeyMath Diagnostic Arithmetic Test	Mental Computation
F	KeyMath Diagnostic Arithmetic Test	Multiplication
F	KeyMath Diagnostic Arithmetic Test	Numerical Reasoning
F	KeyMath Diagnostic Arithmetic Test	Subtraction
F	KeyMath Revised	Addition
F	KeyMath Revised	Multiplication
F	Learning Disability Evaluation Scale, The	Mathematical Calculations
F	Occupational Aptitude Survey & Interest Schedule	Aptitude Survey–Computation/Male & Female Norms
F	Sequential Assessment of Mathematics Inventories	Computation
F	Sequential Assessment of Mathematics Inventories	Ordinality
F	Test of Academic Performance	Mathematics
F	Wide Range Achievement Test	Arithmetic
F	Wide Range Intelligence–Personality Test	Arithmetic

1230 Math Vocabulary/Concepts

B	Test of Mathematical Abilities	General Information
B	Test of Mathematical Abilities	Vocabulary
B	Test of Reading Comprehension–Revised	Mathematics Vocabulary
B	Woodcock-Johnson Psycho-Educational Battery–Part 1	Quantitative Concepts
B	Woodcock-Johnson Psycho-Educational Battery–Revised–Tests of Achievement	Test 33: Quantitative Concepts
F	AAMD Adaptive Behavior Scales	Number & Time Concept
F	AAMD Adaptive Behavior Scales–Public School Version	Numbers & Time/Normal & Special Norms
F	AAMD Adaptive Behavior Scales–School Edition	Numbers & Time/Normal & Special Norms
F	Sequential Assessment of Mathematics Inventories	Mathematical Language
F	Street Survival Skills Questionnaire	Mathematics Vocabulary
F	Street Survival Skills Questionnaire	Measurements
F	Street Survival Skills Questionnaire	Monetary
F	Street Survival Skills Questionnaire	Time
F	Test of Reading Comprehension	Mathematics Vocabulary

1300 Reading, General

B	Basic Achievement Skills Individual Screener	Reading
B	Diagnostic Achievement Battery, 2nd Edition	Reading
B	Diagnostic Achievement Test for Adolescents	Reading
B	Gray Oral Reading Tests–Revised	Oral Reading Quotient
B	Gray Oral Reading Tests–Revised	Passage Score
B	Kaufman Test of Educational Achievement-Comprehensive Form	Reading Composite
B	Peabody Individual Achievement Test–Revised	Total Reading
B	Screening Children for Related Early Educational Needs	Reading
B	Test of Early Reading Ability	Reading Quotient
B	Test of Early Reading Ability, 2nd Edition	Total Score
B	Test of Early Reading Ability–Deaf or Hard of Hearing	Form A
B	Test of Early Reading Ability–Deaf or Hard of Hearing	Form B
B	Woodcock Language Proficiency Battery–Revised	Broad Reading
B	Woodcock Reading Mastery Tests–Revised	Total Reading–Full Scale
B	Woodcock Reading Mastery Tests–Revised	Total Reading–Short Scale
B	Woodcock-Johnson Psycho-Educational Battery–Part 2	Reading Achievement Cluster
B	Woodcock-Johnson Psycho-Educational Battery–Revised–Tests of Achievement	Broad Reading
F	Basic School Skills Inventory–Diagnostic	Reading
F	Comprehensive Behavior Rating Scale for Children	Reading Problems/Total, Male & Female Norms
F	Diagnostic Achievement Battery	Reading
F	Diagnostic Reading Scales	Instructional Level
F	Gray Oral Reading Tests	Total Passage Score
F	Kaufman Test of Educational Achievement-Brief Form	Reading
F	Learning Disability Evaluation Scale, The	Reading
F	Luria-Nebraska Neuropsychological Battery: Children's Revision	C10
F	Woodcock Reading Mastery Tests	Total Reading
F	Woodcock Reading Mastery Tests–Revised	Basic Skills Cluster

1310 Reading Comprehension

A	Kaufman Assessment Battery for Children	Reading/Understanding
B	Diagnostic Achievement Battery, 2nd Edition	Reading Comprehension
B	Diagnostic Achievement Test for Adolescents	Reading Comprehension
B	Formal Reading Inventory	Silent Reading Quotient
B	Gray Oral Reading Tests–Revised	Comprehension Score
B	Kaufman Test of Educational Achievement-Comprehensive Form	Reading Comprehension
B	Occupational Aptitude Survey & Interest Schedule, 2nd Edition	Aptitude Survey–Vocabulary
B	Peabody Individual Achievement Test–Revised	Reading Comprehension
B	Scholastic Abilities Test for Adults	Reading
B	Scholastic Abilities Test for Adults	Reading Comprehension
B	Scholastic Abilities Test for Adults	Reading Vocabulary
B	Test of Adolescent Language, 2nd Edition	Reading
B	Test of Adolescent Language, 2nd Edition	Reading/Grammar
B	Test of Adolescent Language, 2nd Edition	Reading/Vocabulary
B	Test of Reading Comprehension–Revised	General Vocabulary
B	Test of Reading Comprehension–Revised	Paragraph Reading
B	Test of Reading Comprehension–Revised	Reading Comprehension Quotient
B	Test of Reading Comprehension–Revised	Sentence Sequencing
B	Test of Reading Comprehension–Revised	Syntactic Similarities
B	Woodcock Language Proficiency Battery–Revised	Passage Comprehension

B	Woodcock Language Proficiency Battery–Revised	Reading Comprehension
B	Woodcock Reading Mastery Tests–Revised	Passage Comprehension
B	Woodcock Reading Mastery Tests–Revised	Word Comprehension
B	Woodcock-Johnson Psycho-Educational Battery–Part 2	Passage Comprehension
B	Woodcock-Johnson Psycho-Educational Battery–Revised–Tests of Achievement	Reading Comprehension
B	Woodcock-Johnson Psycho-Educational Battery–Revised–Tests of Achievement	Test 23: Passage Comprehension
B	Woodcock-Johnson Psycho-Educational Battery–Revised–Tests of Achievement	Test 32: Reading Vocabulary
F	Diagnostic Achievement Battery	Reading Comprehension
F	Diagnostic Reading Scales	Independent Level
F	Diagnostic Screening Test: Reading, 3rd Edition	Passage Comprehension
F	Gilmore Oral Reading Test	Comprehension
F	Jordan Left-Right Reversal Test, 1990 Edition	Level II Total
F	Peabody Individual Achievement Test	Reading Comprehension
F	Schubert General Ability Battery	Logical Answers
F	Schubert General Ability Battery	Verbal Analogies
F	Schubert General Ability Battery	Word Meaning
F	Test of Academic Performance	Reading Comprehension
F	Test of Adolescent Language	Reading
F	Test of Adolescent Language	Reading/Grammar
F	Test of Adolescent Language	Reading/Vocabulary
F	Test of Reading Comprehension	General Vocabulary
F	Test of Reading Comprehension	Paragraph Reading
F	Test of Reading Comprehension	Reading Comprehension Quotient
F	Test of Reading Comprehension	Sentence Sequencing
F	Test of Reading Comprehension	Syntactic Similarities
F	Tests for Everyday Living	Reading Scale
F	Wide Range Intelligence–Personality Test	Verbal Reasoning
F	Wide Range Intelligence–Personality Test	Vocabulary
F	Woodcock Language Proficiency Battery–Revised	Reading Vocabulary
F	Woodcock Reading Mastery Tests	Passage Comprehension
F	Woodcock Reading Mastery Tests	Word Comprehension
F	Woodcock Reading Mastery Tests–Revised	Reading Comprehension Cluster

1320   Word and Letter Recognition

A	Kaufman Assessment Battery for Children	Reading/Decoding
B	Diagnostic Achievement Battery, 2nd Edition	Alphabet/Word Knowledge
B	Diagnostic Achievement Test for Adolescents	Word Identification
B	Kaufman Test of Educational Achievement–Comprehensive Form	Reading/Decoding
B	Peabody Individual Achievement Test–Revised	Reading Recognition
B	Quick-Score Achievement Test	Reading
B	Wide Range Achievement Test–Revised	Reading
B	Woodcock Reading Mastery Tests–Revised	Word Identification
B	Woodcock-Johnson Psycho-Educational Achievement Test–Part 2	Letter-Word Identification
B	Woodcock-Johnson Psycho-Educational Battery–Revised–Tests of Achievement	Basic Reading Skills
B	Woodcock-Johnson Psycho-Educational Battery–Revised–Tests of Achievement	Test 22: Letter-Word Identification
F	Boder Test of Reading & Spelling Patterns	Reading
F	Comprehensive Test of Visual Functioning	Reading Word Analysis

F   Comprehensive Test of Visual Functioning · Visual/Letter Recognition
F   Diagnostic Achievement Battery · Alphabet/Word Knowledge
F   Diagnostic Screening Test: Reading, 3rd Edition · Phonics Total
F   Diagnostic Screening Test: Reading, 3rd Edition · Sight Total
F   Diagnostic Screening Test: Reading, 3rd Edition · Word Reading
F   Diagnostic Spelling Potential Test · Sight Word Recognition
F   Gilmore Oral Reading Test · Accuracy
F   Luria-Nebraska Neuropsychological Battery: Children's Revision · C8
F   Occupational Aptitude Survey & Interest Schedule · Aptitude Survey–Vocabulary/Male & Female Norms

F   Peabody Individual Achievement Test · Reading Recognition
F   Prescriptive Reading Performance Test · Total
F   Slosson Oral Reading Test, Revised · Total
F   Test of Academic Performance · Reading Recognition
F   Wide Range Achievement Test · Reading
F   Woodcock Reading Mastery Tests · Letter Identification
F   Woodcock Reading Mastery Tests · Word Identification
F   Woodcock Reading Mastery Tests–Revised · Letter Identification

1330   Word and Phonic Analysis

B   Woodcock Language Proficiency Battery–Revised · Basic Reading Skills
B   Woodcock Language Proficiency Battery–Revised · Letter-Word Identification
B   Woodcock Language Proficiency Battery–Revised · Word Attack
B   Woodcock Reading Mastery Tests–Revised · Word Attack
B   Woodcock-Johnson Psycho-Educational Battery–Part 2 · Word Attack
B   Woodcock-Johnson Psycho-Educational Battery–Revised–Tests of Achievement · Test 31: Word Attack
F   Diagnostic Spelling Potential Test · Phonetic Word Recognition
F   Goldman-Fristoe-Woodcock Auditory Skills Test Battery · Reading of Symbols
F   Goldman-Fristoe-Woodcock Auditory Skills Test Battery · Sound-Symbol Association
F   Goldman-Fristoe-Woodcock Auditory Skills Test Battery · Spelling of Sounds
F   Woodcock Reading Mastery Tests · Word Attack

1340   Reading Rate

F   Gilmore Oral Reading Test · Rate

1400   Science

B   Diagnostic Achievement Test for Adolescents · Science
B   Test of Reading Comprehension–Revised · Science Vocabulary
B   Woodcock-Johnson Psycho-Educational Battery–Part 2 · Science
B   Woodcock-Johnson Psycho-Educational Battery–Revised–Tests of Achievement · Test 28: Science
F   Diagnostic Screening Test: Achievement · Science
F   Test of Reading Comprehension · Science Vocabulary

1500   Social Studies

B   Diagnostic Achievement Test for Adolescents · Social Studies
B   Test of Reading Comprehension–Revised · Social Studies Vocabulary

B	Woodcock-Johnson Psycho-Educational Battery–Part 2	Humanities
B	Woodcock-Johnson Psycho-Educational Battery–Part 2	Social Studies
B	Woodcock-Johnson Psycho-Educational Battery–Revised–Tests of Achievement	Test 29: Social Studies
F	Diagnostic Screening Test: Achievement	Social Studies
F	Test of Reading Comprehension	Social Studies Vocabulary

1600   Writing, General

B	Diagnostic Achievement Battery, 2nd Edition	Writing
B	Diagnostic Achievement Test for Adolescents	Writing
B	Quick-Score Achievement Test	Writing
B	Scholastic Abilities Test for Adults	Writing
B	Scholastic Abilities Test for Adults	Writing Composition
B	Scholastic Abilities Test for Adults	Writing Mechanics
B	Screening Children for Related Early Educational Needs	Writing
B	Test of Adolescent Language, 2nd Edition	Writing
B	Test of Adolescent Language, 2nd Edition	Writing/Grammar
B	Test of Adolescent Language, 2nd Edition	Writing/Vocabulary
B	Test of Early Written Language	Written Language Quotient
B	Test of Written Language, 2nd Edition	Contrived Writing
B	Test of Written Language, 2nd Edition	Overall Written Language
B	Test of Written Language, 2nd Edition	Spontaneous Writing
B	Woodcock Language Proficiency Battery–Revised	Basic Writing Skills
B	Woodcock Language Proficiency Battery–Revised	Broad Written Language
B	Woodcock-Johnson Psycho-Educational Battery–Part 2	Dictation
B	Woodcock-Johnson Psycho-Educational Battery–Part 2	Proofing
B	Woodcock-Johnson Psycho-Educational Battery–Part 2	Written Language Achievement Cluster
B	Woodcock-Johnson Psycho-Educational Battery–Revised–Tests of Achievement	Basic Writing Skills
B	Woodcock-Johnson Psycho-Educational Battery–Revised–Tests of Achievement	Broad Written Language
B	Woodcock-Johnson Psycho-Educational Battery–Revised–Tests of Achievement	Test 26: Dictation
B	Woodcock-Johnson Psycho-Educational Battery–Revised–Tests of Achievement	Test 34: Proofing
B	Woodcock-Johnson Psycho-Educational Battery–Revised–Tests of Achievement	Test 35: Writing Fluency
B	Woodcock-Johnson Psycho-Educational Battery–Revised–Tests of Achievement	Written Expression
F	Basic Achievement Skills Individual Screener	Writing
F	Basic School Skills Inventory–Diagnostic	Writing
F	Comprehensive Test of Visual Functioning	Visual/Writing Integration
F	Diagnostic Achievement Battery	Writing
F	Diagnostic Screening Test: Language, 2nd Edition	Applied Knowledge
F	Diagnostic Screening Test: Language, 2nd Edition	Formal Knowledge
F	Diagnostic Screening Test: Language, 2nd Edition	Total Test
F	Learning Disability Evaluation Scale, The	Writing
F	Luria-Nebraska Neuropsychological Battery: Children's Revision	C7
F	Peabody Individual Achievement Test-Revised	Written Expression I
F	Peabody Individual Achievement Test-Revised	Written Expression II
F	Peabody Individual Achievement Test-Revised	Written Language Composite
F	Test of Academic Performance	Written Composition
F	Test of Adolescent Language	Writing

F	Test of Adolescent Language	Writing/Grammar
F	Test of Adolescent Language	Writing/Vocabulary
F	Test of Written Language	Written Language Quotient
F	Vineland Adaptive Behavior Scales–Classroom Edition	Written Communication
F	Vineland Adaptive Behavior Scales–Interview Edition	Written Communication
F	Vineland Adaptive Behavior Scales–Interview Edition	Written Communication
F	Written Language Assessment	General Writing Ability
F	Written Language Assessment	Written Language Quotient

1610   Writing Composition

B	Test of Written Language	Word Usage
B	Test of Written Language, 2nd Edition	Contextual Vocabulary
B	Test of Written Language, 2nd Edition	Logical Sentences
B	Test of Written Language, 2nd Edition	Sentence Combining
B	Test of Written Language, 2nd Edition	Syntactic Maturity
B	Test of Written Language, 2nd Edition	Thematic Maturity
B	Test of Written Language, 2nd Edition	Vocabulary
B	Woodcock Language Proficiency Battery–Revised	Writing Samples
B	Woodcock Language Proficiency Battery–Revised	Written Expression
B	Woodcock-Johnson Psycho-Educational Battery–Revised–Tests of Achievement	Test 27: Writing Samples
B	Woodcock-Johnson Psycho-Educational Battery–Revised–Tests of Achievement	Usage
F	Diagnostic Achievement Battery	Written Vocabulary
F	Diagnostic Achievement Battery, 2nd Edition	Writing Composition
F	Diagnostic Achievement Test for Adolescents	Writing Composition
F	Diagnostic Screening Test: Language, 2nd Edition	Grammar
F	Diagnostic Screening Test: Language, 2nd Edition	Sentence Structure
F	Test of Written Language	Thematic Maturity
F	Test of Written Language	Vocabulary
F	Woodcock Language Proficiency Battery–Revised	Usage
F	Woodcock Language Proficiency Battery–Revised	Writing Fluency

1620   Writing Conventions

B	Diagnostic Achievement Battery, 2nd Edition	Capitalization
B	Diagnostic Achievement Battery, 2nd Edition	Punctuation
B	Test of Written Language	Style
B	Test of Written Language, 2nd Edition	Contextual Style
B	Test of Written Language, 2nd Edition	Style
B	Woodcock-Johnson Psycho-Educational Battery–Revised–Tests of Achievement	Punctuation & Capitalization
F	Diagnostic Achievement Battery	Capitalization
F	Diagnostic Achievement Battery	Punctuation
F	Diagnostic Screening Test: Language, 2nd Edition	Capitalization
F	Diagnostic Screening Test: Language, 2nd Edition	Punctuation
F	Woodcock Language Proficiency Battery–Revised	Proofing
F	Woodcock Language Proficiency Battery–Revised	Punctuation & Capitalization

1630   Spelling

B   Basic Achievement Skills Individual Screener   Spelling
B   Diagnostic Achievement Battery, 2nd Edition   Spelling
B   Diagnostic Achievement Test for Adolescents   Spelling
B   Kaufman Test of Educational Achievement–Comprehensive Form   Spelling
B   Peabody Individual Achievement Test–Revised   Spelling
B   Test of Written Language   Spelling
B   Test of Written Language, 2nd Edition   Contextual Spelling
B   Test of Written Language, 2nd Edition   Spelling
B   Test of Written Spelling   Predictable Words
B   Test of Written Spelling   Total
B   Test of Written Spelling   Unpredictable Words
B   Test of Written Spelling, 2nd Edition   Predictable Words
B   Test of Written Spelling, 2nd Edition   Total
B   Test of Written Spelling, 2nd Edition   Unpredictable Words
B   Wide Range Achievement Test–Revised   Spelling
B   Woodcock Language Proficiency Battery–Revised   Dictation
B   Woodcock-Johnson Psycho-Educational Battery–Revised–Tests of   Spelling
      Achievement
F   Diagnostic Achievement Battery   Spelling
F   Diagnostic Analysis of Reading Errors   Correct Score
F   Diagnostic Screening Test: Language, 2nd Edition   Spelling Rules
F   Diagnostic Screening Test: Spelling, 3rd Edition   Phonics Spelling
F   Diagnostic Screening Test: Spelling, 3rd Edition   Sight Spelling
F   Diagnostic Screening Test: Spelling, 3rd Edition   Total Spelling
F   Diagnostic Spelling Potential Test   Auditory-Visual Recognition
F   Diagnostic Spelling Potential Test   Spelling
F   Diagnostic Spelling Potential Test   Visual Recognition
F   Kaufman Test of Educational Achievement–Brief Form   Spelling
F   Learning Disability Evaluation Scale, The   Spelling
F   Luria-Nebraska Neuropsychological Battery: Children's Revision   01
F   Peabody Individual Achievement Test   Spelling
F   Test of Academic Performance   Spelling
F   Wide Range Achievement Test   Spelling
F   Wide Range Intelligence–Personality Test   Spelling
F   Woodcock Language Proficiency Battery–Revised   Spelling

1640   Penmanship

B   Test of Legible Handwriting   Legibility Quotient
F   Luria-Nebraska Neuropsychological Battery: Children's Revision   02
F   Test of Legible Handwriting   Single Sample
F   Test of Written Language   Handwriting
F   Woodcock Language Proficiency Battery–Revised   Handwriting
F   Woodcock-Johnson Psycho-Educational Battery–Revised–Tests of   Handwriting
      Achievement

1650   Writing Productivity

F   Written Language Assessment   Productivity
F   Written Language Assessment   Readability
F   Written Language Assessment   Word Complexity

1700   Reference Skills

B   Diagnostic Achievement Test for Adolescents   Reference Skills

1800   Occupational Skills, General

B   Adaptive Behavior Inventory   Occupational Skills/Normal & Retarded Norms
F   Career Maturity Inventory Competence Test   Part 4: Planning

1810   Clerical Skills

No scores reviewed

1820   Mechanical Skills

No scores reviewed

1830   Other Occupational Skills

F   AAMD Adaptive Behavior Scales   Occupation–Domestic
F   AAMD Adaptive Behavior Scales   Occupation–General
F   AAMD Adaptive Behavior Scales–Public School Version   Domestic Activity/Normal & Special Norms
F   AAMD Adaptive Behavior Scales–Public School Version   Vocational Activity/Normal & Special Norms
F   AAMD Adaptive Behavior Scales–School Edition   Prevocational Activity/Normal &
                                                                                 Special Norms
F   Tests for Everyday Living   Job Related Behavior
F   Tests for Everyday Living   Job Search Skills
F   Test of Practical Knowledge   Occupational

1900   Adaptive Behavior, General

B   Inventory for Client & Agency Planning   Personal Living Skills
B   Scales of Independent Behavior   Community Living Skills
B   Scales of Independent Behavior   Personal Living Skills
B   Vineland Adaptive Behavior Scales–Interview Edition, Expanded Form   Daily Living Skills Domain
B   Vineland Adaptive Behavior Scales–Interview Edition, Survey Form   Daily Living Skills Domain
F   Basic School Skills Inventory–Diagnostic   Daily Living Skills
F   Parent Rating of Student Behavior   Self-Care
F   Responsibility & Independence Scale for Adolescents   Adaptive Behavior Total
F   Responsibility & Independence Scale for Adolescents   Independence
F   Responsibility & Independence Scale for Adolescents   Responsibility
F   Vineland Adaptive Behavior Scales–Classroom Edition   Community Living Skills
F   Vineland Adaptive Behavior Scales–Classroom Edition   Daily Living Skills Domain
F   Vineland Adaptive Behavior Scales–Interview Edition, Expanded Form   Community Living Skills
F   Vineland Adaptive Behavior Scales–Interview Edition, Survey Form   Community Living Skills

1910   Knowledge of Everyday Situations

F   Normative Adaptive Behavior Checklist   Home Living
F   Normative Adaptive Behavior Checklist   Independent Living

F	Street Survival Skills Questionnaire	Basic Concepts
F	Street Survival Skills Questionnaire	Health & Safety
F	Street Survival Skills Questionnaire	Functional Signs
F	Street Survival Skills Questionnaire	Public Services
F	Tests for Everyday Living	Banking
F	Tests for Everyday Living	Budgeting
F	Tests for Everyday Living	Health Care
F	Tests for Everyday Living	Home Management
F	Tests for Everyday Living	Purchasing Habits
F	Test of Practical Knowledge	Personal
F	Test of Practical Knowledge	Social

1920 Self-Help Skills

B	Adaptive Behavior Inventory	Self-Care Skills/Normal & Retarded Norms
B	Scales of Independent Behavior	Domestic Skills
B	Scales of Independent Behavior	Dressing
B	Scales of Independent Behavior	Eating & Meal Preparation
B	Scales of Independent Behavior	Home/Community Orientation
B	Scales of Independent Behavior	Toileting
F	AAMD Adaptive Behavior Scales	Independent Living
F	AAMD Adaptive Behavior Scales–Public School Version	Independent Living/Normal & Special Norms
F	AAMD Adaptive Behavior Scales–School Edition	Factor 1: Personal Self-Sufficiency/Normal & Special Norms
F	AAMD Adaptive Behavior Scales–School Edition	Factor 3: Personal-Social Responsibility/ Normal & Special Norms
F	AAMD Adaptive Behavior Scales–School Edition	Independent Functioning/Normal & Special Norms
F	Developmental Profile II	Self-Help
F	Devereux Child Behavior Rating Scale	Messiness, Sloppiness
F	Devereux Child Behavior Rating Scale	Poor Self-Care
F	Normative Adaptive Behavior Checklist	Self-Help
F	Scales of Independent Behavior	Early Developmental Scale
F	Scales of Independent Behavior	Money & Value
F	Scales of Independent Behavior	Personal Self-Care
F	Scales of Independent Behavior	Time & Punctuality
F	Street Survival Skills Questionnaire	Domestics
F	Vineland Adaptive Behavior Scales–Classroom Edition	Domestic Living Skills
F	Vineland Adaptive Behavior Scales–Classroom Edition	Personal Living Skills
F	Vineland Adaptive Behavior Scales–Interview Edition, Expanded Form	Domestic Living Skills
F	Vineland Adaptive Behavior Scales–Interview Edition, Expanded Form	Personal Living Skills
F	Vineland Adaptive Behavior Scales–Interview Edition, Survey Form	Domestic Living Skills
F	Vineland Adaptive Behavior Scales–Interview Edition, Survey Form	Personal Living Skills

1930 Other Adaptive Behaviors

B	Inventory for Client & Agency Planning	Community Living Skills
F	AAMD Adaptive Behavior Scales	Economic Activity
F	AAMD Adaptive Behavior Scales–Public School Version	Economic Activity/Normal & Special Norms
F	AAMD Adaptive Behavior Scales–School Edition	Economic Activity/Normal & Special Norms
F	Street Survival Skills Questionnaire	Tools

APTITUDE/DEVELOPMENTAL ABILITIES

2000   Overall Aptitude/Developmental Abilities

B	Detroit Tests of Learning Aptitude, 2nd Edition	Attention-Enhanced Quotient
B	Detroit Tests of Learning Aptitude, 2nd Edition	Attention-Reduced Quotient
B	Detroit Tests of Learning Aptitude, 2nd Edition	Conceptual Quotient
B	Detroit Tests of Learning Aptitude, 2nd Edition	General Intelligence Quotient
B	Detroit Tests of Learning Aptitude, 2nd Edition	Motor-Enhanced Quotient
B	Detroit Tests of Learning Aptitude, 2nd Edition	Motor-Reduced Quotient
B	Detroit Tests of Learning Aptitude, 2nd Edition	Nonverbal Quotient
B	Detroit Tests of Learning Aptitude, 2nd Edition	Structural Quotient
B	Detroit Tests of Learning Aptitude, 2nd Edition	Verbal Quotient
B	Detroit Tests of Learning Aptitude, 3rd Edition	Associative Level
B	Detroit Tests of Learning Aptitude, 3rd Edition	Attention-Enhanced Composite
B	Detroit Tests of Learning Aptitude, 3rd Edition	Motor-Enhanced Composite
B	Detroit Tests of Learning Aptitude, 3rd Edition	Nonverbal Composite
B	Detroit Tests of Learning Aptitude, 3rd Edition	Performance Scale
B	Detroit Tests of Learning Aptitude, 3rd Edition	Simultaneous Processing
B	Detroit Tests of Learning Aptitude, 3rd Edition	Successive Processing
B	Detroit Tests of Learning Aptitude–Adult	Associative Level
B	Detroit Tests of Learning Aptitude–Adult	Attention-Enhanced Composite
B	Detroit Tests of Learning Aptitude–Adult	Motor-Enhanced Composite
B	Detroit Tests of Learning Aptitude–Adult	Successive Processing
B	Detroit Tests of Learning Aptitude–Primary	Attention-Enhanced Quotient
B	Detroit Tests of Learning Aptitude–Primary	Attention-Reduced Quotient
B	Detroit Tests of Learning Aptitude–Primary	Conceptual Quotient
B	Detroit Tests of Learning Aptitude–Primary	General Intelligence Quotient
B	Detroit Tests of Learning Aptitude–Primary	Motor-Enhanced Quotient
B	Detroit Tests of Learning Aptitude–Primary	Motor-Reduced Quotient
B	Detroit Tests of Learning Aptitude–Primary	Structural Quotient
B	Detroit Tests of Learning Aptitude–Primary, 2nd Edition	Attention-Enhanced
B	Detroit Tests of Learning Aptitude–Primary, 2nd Edition	Attention-Reduced
B	Detroit Tests of Learning Aptitude–Primary, 2nd Edition	General Mental Ability
B	Detroit Tests of Learning Aptitude–Primary, 2nd Edition	Motor-Enhanced
B	Detroit Tests of Learning Aptitude–Primary, 2nd Edition	Motor-Reduced
B	Developmental Indicators for the Assessment of Learning–Revised	Total
B	Kaufman Assessment Battery for Children	Gestalt Closure
B	Kaufman Assessment Battery for Children	Mental Processing
B	Kaufman Assessment Battery for Children	Sequential Processing
B	Kaufman Assessment Battery for Children	Simultaneous Processing
B	Kaufman Brief Intelligence Test	Total
B	Stanford-Binet Intelligence Scale, 4th Edition	Short-Term Memory
B	Vane Kindergarten Test, The	Total
B	Wide Range Assessment of Memory and Learning	General Memory
B	Wide Range Assessment of Memory and Learning	Learning
B	Woodcock-Johnson Psycho-Educational Battery–Part 1	Concept Formation
B	Woodcock-Johnson Psycho-Educational Battery–Part 1	Mathematics Aptitude Cluster
B	Woodcock-Johnson Psycho-Educational Battery–Part 1	Reading Aptitude Cluster
B	Woodcock-Johnson Psycho-Educational Battery–Part 1	Reasoning Cluster
B	Woodcock-Johnson Psycho-Educational Battery–Part 1	Verbal Cluster
B	Woodcock-Johnson Psycho-Educational Battery–Part 1	Visual-Auditory Learning

B	Woodcock-Johnson Psycho-Educational Battery–Revised–Tests of Cognitive Ability	Early Development Scale
B	Woodcock-Johnson Psycho-Educational Battery–Revised–Tests of Cognitive Ability	Extended Scale
B	Woodcock-Johnson Psycho-Educational Battery–Revised–Tests of Cognitive Ability	Fluid Reasoning
B	Woodcock-Johnson Psycho-Educational Battery–Revised–Tests of Cognitive Ability	Knowledge Aptitude
B	Woodcock-Johnson Psycho-Educational Battery–Revised–Tests of Cognitive Ability	Mathematics Aptitude
B	Woodcock-Johnson Psycho-Educational Battery–Revised–Tests of Cognitive Ability	Oral Language Aptitude
B	Woodcock-Johnson Psycho-Educational Battery–Revised–Tests of Cognitive Ability	Reading Aptitude
B	Woodcock-Johnson Psycho-Educational Battery–Revised–Tests of Cognitive Ability	Standard Scale
B	Woodcock-Johnson Psycho-Educational Battery–Revised–Tests of Cognitive Ability	Written Language Aptitude
F	Bankson Language Screening Test	Total
F	Carrow Auditory-Visual Abilities Test	Entry Test
F	Carrow Auditory-Visual Abilities Test	General Visual Processing
F	Carrow Auditory-Visual Abilities Test	Grammatical Organization
F	Carrow Auditory-Visual Abilities Test	Perceptual-Cognitive Integration
F	Carrow Auditory-Visual Abilities Test	Total
F	Carrow Auditory-Visual Abilities Test	Verbal Reproduction of Auditory Stimuli
F	Carrow Auditory-Visual Abilities Test	Visual Battery
F	Cognitive Levels Test	Memory
F	Computer Aptitude, Literacy & Interest Profile	Logical Structures
F	Computer Aptitude, Literacy & Interest Profile	Series
F	Detroit Tests of Learning Aptitude, 2nd Edition	Oral Directions
F	Developmental Profile II	Academic
F	Illinois Test of Psycholinguistic Abilities	Composite
F	McCarthy Scales of Children's Abilities	Memory
F	Miller Assessment for Preschoolers	Complex Tasks
F	Miller Assessment for Preschoolers	Foundations
F	Miller Assessment for Preschoolers	Total
F	Multiscore Depression Inventory	Cognitive Difficulty
F	Psycholinguistic Rating Scale	Association
F	Psycholinguistic Rating Scale	Closure
F	Psycholinguistic Rating Scale	Expression
F	Psycholinguistic Rating Scale	Memory
F	Psycholinguistic Rating Scale	Nonsymbolic
F	Psycholinguistic Rating Scale	Reception
F	Psycholinguistic Rating Scale	Symbolic
F	Psycholinguistic Rating Scale	Total
F	Psycholinguistic Rating Scale	Visual
F	Pupil Rating Scale–Revised, The	Orientation
F	Purdue Perceptual-Motor Survey, The	Total
F	Wechsler Memory Scale–Revised	Attention/Concentration
F	Wechsler Memory Scale–Revised	Delayed Recall
F	Wechsler Memory Scale–Revised	Verbal Memory
F	Wide Range Assessment of Memory & Learning	Memory Screening Index
F	Woodcock Reading Mastery Tests–Revised	Visual-Auditory Learning
F	Woodcock-Johnson Psycho-Educational Battery–Revised–Tests of Cognitive Ability	Test 14: Concept Formation

2100 Nonverbal Aptitude/Developmental Abilities, General

B	Detroit Tests of Learning Aptitude, 3rd Edition	Fluid Intelligence
B	Detroit Tests of Learning Aptitude–Adult	Fluid Intelligence
B	Detroit Tests of Learning Aptitude–Primary	Nonverbal Quotient
B	Detroit Tests of Learning Aptitude–Primary, 2nd Edition	Nonverbal
B	Developmental Indicators for the Assessment of Learning–Revised	Motor Area
B	Kaufman Assessment Battery for Children	Nonverbal Scale
B	Stanford-Binet Intelligence Scale, 4th Edition	Abstract/Visual Reasoning
B	Wechsler Adult Intelligence Scale–Revised	Performance Scale
B	Wechsler Intelligence Scale for Children–3rd Edition	Performance IQ
B	Wechsler Intelligence Scale for Children–3rd Edition	Perceptual Organization Index
F	Bruininks-Oseretsky Test of Motor Proficiency	Battery Composite
F	Bruininks-Oseretsky Test of Motor Proficiency	Short Form
F	Carrow Auditory-Visual Abilities Test	Auditory Discrimination
F	Carrow Auditory-Visual Abilities Test	Auditory Memory for Sequence
F	Carrow Auditory-Visual Abilities Test	Auditory Memory for Unrelated Stimuli
F	Carrow Auditory-Visual Abilities Test	Short-Term Memory Span
F	Inventory for Client & Agency Planning	Motor Skills
F	Leiter International Performance Scale Handbook, The	Total
F	Luria-Nebraska Neuropsychological Battery: Children's Revision	S1
F	Luria-Nebraska Neuropsychological Battery: Children's Revision	S2
F	Luria-Nebraska Neuropsychological Battery: Children's Revision	S3
F	McCarthy Scales of Children's Abilities	Motor
F	McCarthy Scales of Children's Abilities	Perceptual-Performance
F	Miller Assessment for Preschoolers	Non-Verbal
F	Nonverbal Test of Cognitive Skills	Cognitive Skills Index
F	Psycholinguistic Rating Scale	Manual Expression
F	Wechsler Intelligence Scale for Children–Revised	Performance Scale
F	Wechsler Memory Scale–Revised	Visual Memory
F	Wechsler Preschool & Primary Scale of Intelligence	Performance Scale

2110 Nonverbal Cognition

B	Detroit Tests of Learning Aptitude, 2nd Edition	Symbolic Relations
B	Detroit Tests of Learning Aptitude, 3rd Edition	Symbolic Relations
B	Detroit Tests of Learning Aptitude–Adult	Form Assembly
B	Detroit Tests of Learning Aptitude–Adult	Story Sequences
B	Detroit Tests of Learning Aptitude–Adult	Symbolic Relations
B	Human Figures Drawing Test	Total Score
B	Kaufman Assessment Battery for Children	Matrix Analogies
B	Kaufman Assessment Battery for Children	Photo Series
B	Kaufman Brief Intelligence Test	Matrices
B	Matrix Analogies Test–Short Form	Total
B	Occupational Aptitude Survey & Interest Schedule, 2nd Edition	Aptitude Survey–Spatial Relations
B	Scholastic Abilities Test for Adults	Nonverbal Reasoning
B	Scholastic Aptitude Scale	Nonverbal Reasoning
B	Stanford-Binet Intelligence Scale, 4th Edition	Matrices
B	Test of Nonverbal Intelligence	Quotient
B	Test of Nonverbal Intelligence, 2nd Edition	TONI Quotient
B	Vane Kindergarten Test, The	Man
B	Woodcock-Johnson Psycho-Educational Battery–Part 1	Analysis–Synthesis
F	Cognitive Levels Test	Abstract Reasoning
F	Columbia Mental Maturity Scale	Total

F	Comprehensive Test of Visual Functioning	Nonverbal Visual Reasoning/Memory
F	Computer Aptitude, Literacy & Interest Profile	Graphic Patterns
F	Culture Fair Intelligence Tests	Short Form Scale 2
F	Culture Fair Intelligence Tests	Short Form Scale 3
F	Culture Fair Intelligence Tests	Total Test Scale 2
F	Culture Fair Intelligence Tests	Total Test Scale 3
F	Detroit Tests of Learning Aptitude, 2nd Edition	Conceptual Matching
F	Illinois Test of Psycholinguistic Abilities	Manual Expression
F	Illinois Test of Psycholinguistic Abilities	Visual Association
F	Illinois Test of Psycholinguistic Abilities	Visual Reception
F	Matrix Analogies Test–Expanded Form	Pattern Completion
F	Matrix Analogies Test–Expanded Form	Reasoning by Analogy
F	Matrix Analogies Test–Expanded Form	Serial Reasoning
F	Matrix Analogies Test–Expanded Form	Spatial Visualization
F	Matrix Analogies Test–Expanded Form	Total
F	Occupational Aptitude Survey & Interest Schedule	Aptitude Survey–Spatial Relations/Male & Female Norms
F	Torrance Tests of Creative Thinking	Figural Elaboration
F	Torrance Tests of Creative Thinking	Figural Flexibility
F	Torrance Tests of Creative Thinking	Figural Fluency
F	Torrance Tests of Creative Thinking	Figural Originality
F	Wechsler Adult Intelligence Scale–Revised	Picture Arrangement
F	Wechsler Intelligence Scale for Children–Revised	Picture Arrangement
F	Wechsler Intelligence Scale for Children–Third Edition	Picture Arrangement
F	Wide Range Intelligence–Personality Test	Number Series
F	Wide Range Intelligence–Personality Test	Picture Reasoning
F	Wide Range Intelligence–Personality Test	Space Series
F	Woodcock-Johnson Psycho-Educational Battery–Revised–Tests of Cognitive Ability	Test 19: Spatial Relations

2120 Nonverbal Processing, Auditory Perception

F	Carrow Auditory-Visual Abilities Test	General Auditory Memory
F	Carrow Auditory-Visual Abilities Test	Response by Indication–Auditory Stimuli
F	Luria-Nebraska Neuropsychological Battery: Children's Revision	C2
F	Luria-Nebraska Neuropsychological Battery: Children's Revision	F6

2130 Nonverbal Processing, Visual Perception

F	Carrow Auditory-Visual Abilities Test	General Reproduction
F	Carrow Auditory-Visual Abilities Test	General Visual Memory
F	Carrow Auditory-Visual Abilities Test	Graphic Reproduction of Visual Stimuli
F	Developmental Test of Visual Perception	Perceptual Quotient
F	Motor-Free Visual Perception Test	Total
F	Normative Adaptive Behavior Checklist	Sensory Motor
F	Test of Visual-Perceptual Skills	Perceptual Quotient

2131 Visual Perception, Discrimination

B	Detroit Tests of Learning Aptitude, Third Edition	Picture Fragments
B	Stanford-Binet Intelligence Scale, 4th Edition	Paper Folding & Cutting
B	Wechsler Adult Intelligence Scale–Revised	Picture Completion

B	Wechsler Intelligence Scale for Children–3rd Edition	Picture Completion
B	Woodcock-Johnson Psycho-Educational Battery–Revised–Tests of Cognitive Ability	Visual Processing
F	Carrow Auditory-Visual Abilities Test	Visual Discrimination Matching
F	Comprehensive Test of Visual Functioning	Nonverbal Visual Closure
F	Comprehensive Test of Visual Functioning	Visual Processing/Figure Ground
F	Developmental Test of Visual Perception	Constancy of Shape
F	Developmental Test of Visual Perception	Figure Ground
F	Developmental Test of Visual Perception	Position in Space
F	Illinois Test of Psycholinguistic Abilities	Visual Closure
F	Jordan Left-Right Reversal Test	Level I Total
F	Jordan Left-Right Reversal Test	Level II Total
F	Jordan Left-Right Reversal Test, 1990 Edition	Level I Total
F	Kaufman Assessment Battery for Children	Magic Window
F	Luria-Nebraska Neuropsychological Battery: Children's Revision	C4
F	Occupational Aptitude Survey & Interest Schedule	Aptitude Survey–Word Comparison/Male & Female Norms
F	Pictorial Test of Intelligence	Form Discrimination
F	Sensory Integration & Praxis Tests	Figure-Ground Perception
F	Sensory Integration & Praxis Tests	Motor Accuracy
F	Southern California Sensory Integration Tests–Revised	Figure-Ground Perception
F	Southern California Sensory Integration Tests–Revised	Position in Space
F	Test of Pictures/Forms/Letters/Numbers/Spatial Orientation & Sequencing	Spatial Relationships (Forms)
F	Test of Pictures/Forms/Letters/Numbers/Spatial Orientation & Sequencing	Spatial Relationships (Pictures)
F	Test of Visual-Perceptual Skills	Visual Closure
F	Test of Visual-Perceptual Skills	Visual Discrimination
F	Test of Visual-Perceptual Skills	Visual Figure-Ground
F	Test of Visual-Perceptual Skills	Visual Form Constancy
F	Test of Visual-Perceptual Skills	Visual-Spatial Relations
F	Wechsler Intelligence Scale for Children–Revised	Picture Completion
F	Wechsler Preschool & Primary Scale of Intelligence	Picture Completion
F	Wide Range Intelligence–Personality Test	Space Completion
F	Woodcock-Johnson Psycho-Educational Battery–Part 1	Perceptual Speed Cluster
F	Woodcock-Johnson Psycho-Educational Battery–Part 1	Spatial Relations
F	Woodcock-Johnson Psycho-Educational Battery–Part 1	Visual Matching
F	Woodcock-Johnson Psycho-Educational Battery–Revised–Tests of Cognitive Ability	Test 5: Visual Closure
F	Woodcock-Johnson Psycho-Educational Battery–Revised–Tests of Cognitive Ability	Test 12: Picture Recognition

2132   Visual Perception, Visual-Motor Integration

B	Detroit Tests of Learning Aptitude, 2nd Edition	Design Reproduction
B	Detroit Tests of Learning Aptitude, 3rd Edition	Design Reproduction
B	Detroit Tests of Learning Aptitude, 3rd Edition	Design Sequences
B	Detroit Tests of Learning Aptitude–Adult	Design Reproduction
B	Detroit Tests of Learning Aptitude–Adult	Design Sequences
B	Kaufman Assessment Battery for Children	Triangles
B	Occupational Aptitude Survey & Interest Schedule, 2nd Edition	Aptitude Survey–Making Marks
B	Stanford-Binet Intelligence Scale, 4th Edition	Copying
B	Stanford-Binet Intelligence Scale, 4th Edition	Pattern Analysis
B	Vane Kindergarten Test, The	Perceptual-Motor

B	Watkins Bender-Gestalt Scoring System, The	Total Score
B	Wechsler Adult Intelligence Scale–Revised	Block Design
B	Wechsler Adult Intelligence Scale–Revised	Digit Symbol
B	Wechsler Intelligence Scale for Children–3rd Edition	Picture Arrangement
F	Bender Gestalt Test for Young Children, The	Total
F	Bruininks-Oseretsky Test of Motor Proficiency	Fine Motor Composite
F	Bruininks-Oseretsky Test of Motor Proficiency	Response Speed
F	Bruininks-Oseretsky Test of Motor Proficiency	Upper-Limb Speed & Dexterity
F	Bruininks-Oseretsky Test of Motor Proficiency	Visual-Motor Control
F	Carrow Auditory-Visual Abilities Test	Motor Speed
F	Carrow Auditory-Visual Abilities Test	Visual-Motor Copying
F	Comprehensive Test of Visual Functioning	Spatial Orientation/Motor
F	Comprehensive Test of Visual Functioning	Visual Design/Motor
F	Developmental Test of Visual Perception	Eye-Hand Perception
F	Developmental Test of Visual Perception	Spatial Relations
F	Developmental Test of Visual-Motor Integration	Total Score
F	Luria-Nebraska Neuropsychological Battery: Children's Revision	F4
F	Luria-Nebraska Neuropsychological Battery: Children's Revision	F5
F	Minnesota Percepto-Diagnostic Test	Total
F	Occupational Aptitude Survey & Interest Schedule	Aptitude Survey–Making Marks/Male & Female Norms
F	Primary Visual Motor Test	Total/Normal & Retarded Norms
F	Purdue Perceptual-Motor Survey, The	Chalkboard
F	Purdue Perceptual-Motor Survey, The	Imitation of Movement
F	Purdue Perceptual-Motor Survey, The	Rhythmic Writing
F	Purdue Perceptual-Motor Survey, The	Visual Achievement Forms
F	Sensory Integration & Praxis Tests	Constructional Praxis
F	Sensory Integration & Praxis Tests	Design Copying
F	Sensory Integration & Praxis Tests	Space Visualization
F	Southern California Sensory Integration Tests–Revised	Design Copying
F	Southern California Sensory Integration Tests–Revised	Motor Accuracy
F	Southern California Sensory Integration Tests–Revised	Space Visualization
F	Test of Visual-Motor Skills	Total
F	Wechsler Adult Intelligence Scale–Revised	Object Assembly
F	Wechsler Intelligence Scale for Children–Revised	Block Design
F	Wechsler Intelligence Scale for Children–Revised	Coding
F	Wechsler Intelligence Scale for Children–Revised	Mazes
F	Wechsler Intelligence Scale for Children–Revised	Object Assembly
F	Wechsler Intelligence Scale for Children–3rd Edition	Coding
F	Wechsler Intelligence Scale for Children–3rd Edition	Mazes
F	Wechsler Intelligence Scale for Children–3rd Edition	Object Assembly
F	Wechsler Intelligence Scale for Children–3rd Edition	Symbol Search
F	Wechsler Memory Scale–Revised	Visual Reproduction I
F	Wechsler Memory Scale–Revised	Visual Reproduction II
F	Wechsler Preschool & Primary Scale of Intelligence	Animal House
F	Wechsler Preschool & Primary Scale of Intelligence	Block Design
F	Wechsler Preschool & Primary Scale of Intelligence	Geometric Designs
F	Wechsler Preschool & Primary Scale of Intelligence	Mazes
F	Wide Range Intelligence–Personality Test	Coding
F	Woodcock-Johnson Psycho-Educational Battery–Revised–Tests of Cognitive Ability	Test 10: Cross Out

2133   Visual Perception, Memory

B	Detroit Tests of Learning Aptitude, 2nd Edition	Object Sequences
B	Kaufman Assessment Battery for Children	Spatial Memory
B	Stanford-Binet Intelligence Scale, 4th Edition	Bead Memory
B	Wide Range Assessment of Memory & Learning	Design Memory
B	Wide Range Assessment of Memory & Learning	Finger Windows
B	Wide Range Assessment of Memory & Learning	Picture Memory
B	Wide Range Assessment of Memory & Learning	Visual Learning
B	Wide Range Assessment of Memory & Learning	Visual Memory
F	Carrow Auditory-Visual Abilities Test	Visual Discrimination Memory
F	Carrow Auditory-Visual Abilities Test	Visual-Motor Memory
F	Comprehensive Test of Visual Functioning	Spatial Orientation/Memory/Motor
F	Comprehensive Test of Visual Functioning	Visual Design/Memory/Motor
F	Illinois Test of Psycholinguistic Abilities	Visual Sequential Memory
F	Kaufman Assessment Battery for Children	Face Recognition
F	Kaufman Assessment Battery for Children	Hand Movements
F	Learning Efficiency Test	Visual Memory Ordered Immediate Recall
F	Learning Efficiency Test	Visual Memory Ordered Long Term Recall
F	Learning Efficiency Test	Visual Memory Ordered Short Term Recall
F	Learning Efficiency Test	Visual Memory Unordered Immediate Recall
F	Learning Efficiency Test	Visual Memory Unordered Long Term Recall
F	Learning Efficiency Test	Visual Memory Unordered Short Term Recall
F	Pictorial Test of Intelligence	Immediate Recall
F	Psycholinguistic Rating Scale	Visual Memory
F	Stanford-Binet Intelligence Scale, 4th Edition	Memory for Objects
F	Test of Visual-Perceptual Skills	Visual Memory
F	Test of Visual-Perceptual Skills	Visual-Sequential Memory
F	Wechsler Memory Scale–Revised	Figural Memory
F	Wechsler Memory Scale–Revised	Visual Memory Span
F	Wechsler Memory Scale–Revised	Visual Paired Associates I
F	Wechsler Memory Scale–Revised	Visual Paired Associates II

2134   Visual Perception, Ocular Control

| F | Comprehensive Test of Visual Functioning | Visual Tracking |
| F | Purdue Perceptual-Motor Survey, The | Ocular Control |

2140   Nonverbal Processing, Haptic Perception

F	Luria-Nebraska Neuropsychological Battery: Children's Revision	C1
F	Luria-Nebraska Neuropsychological Battery: Children's Revision	C3
F	Luria-Nebraska Neuropsychological Battery: Children's Revision	F2
F	Luria-Nebraska Neuropsychological Battery: Children's Revision	F7
F	Sensory Integration & Praxis Tests	Finger Identification
F	Sensory Integration & Praxis Tests	Graphesthesia
F	Sensory Integration & Praxis Tests	Kinesthesia
F	Sensory Integration & Praxis Tests	Localization of Tactile Stimulation
F	Southern California Sensory Integration Tests–Revised	Double Tactile Stimuli Perception
F	Southern California Sensory Integration Tests–Revised	Finger Identification
F	Southern California Sensory Integration Tests–Revised	Graphesthesia
F	Southern California Sensory Integration Tests–Revised	Kinesthesia

F   Southern California Sensory Integration Tests–Revised   Localization of Tactile Stimuli
F   Southern California Sensory Integration Tests–Revised   Manual Form Perception

2150   Nonverbal Processing, Gross Motor Abilities

B   Scales of Independent Behavior   Gross Motor
B   Scales of Independent Behavior   Motor Skills
B   Vineland Adaptive Behavior Scales–Interview Edition, Expanded Form   Motor Skills Domain
B   Vineland Adaptive Behavior Scales–Interview Edition, Survey Form   Motor Skills Domain
F   Developmental Profile II   Physical
F   Pupil Rating Scale–Revised, The   Motor Coordination
F   AAMD Adaptive Behavior Scales   Physical Development
F   AAMD Adaptive Behavior Scales–Public School Version   Physical Development/Normal &
                                                                       Special Norms
F   AAMD Adaptive Behavior Scales–School Edition   Physical Development/Normal &
                                                                       Special Norms
F   Bruininks-Oseretsky Test of Motor Proficiency   Gross Motor Competence
F   Devereux Child Behavior Rating Scale   Poor Coordination & Body Tonus
F   Vineland Adaptive Behavior Scales–Classroom Edition   Fine Motor Skills
F   Vineland Adaptive Behavior Scales–Classroom Edition   Gross Motor Skills
F   Vineland Adaptive Behavior Scales–Classroom Edition   Motor Skills Domain
F   Vineland Adaptive Behavior Scales–Interview Edition, Expanded Form   Fine Motor Skills
F   Vineland Adaptive Behavior Scales–Interview Edition, Expanded Form   Gross Motor Skills
F   Vineland Adaptive Behavior Scales–Interview Edition, Survey Form   Fine Motor Skills
F   Vineland Adaptive Behavior Scales–Interview Edition, Survey Form   Gross Motor Skills

2151   Gross Motor Abilities, Balance/Posture

F   Bruininks-Oseretsky Test of Motor Proficiency   Balance
F   Sensory Integration & Praxis Tests   Postural Praxis
F   Sensory Integration & Praxis Tests   Standing & Walking Balance
F   Southern California Sensory Integration Tests–Revised   Imitation of Postures
F   Southern California Sensory Integration Tests–Revised   Standing Balance: Eyes Closed
F   Southern California Sensory Integration Tests–Revised   Standing Balance: Eyes Open

2152   Gross Motor Abilities, Strength/Endurance

F   Bruininks-Oseretsky Test of Motor Proficiency   Strength
F   Purdue Perceptual-Motor Survey, The   Kraus-Weber

2153   Gross Motor Abilities, Coordination

F   Bruininks-Oseretsky Test of Motor Proficiency   Bilateral Coordination
F   Bruininks-Oseretsky Test of Motor Proficiency   Upper-Limb Coordination
F   Luria-Nebraska Neuropsychological Battery: Children's Revision   F3
F   Miller Assessment for Preschoolers   Coordination
F   Purdue Perceptual-Motor Survey, The   Angels-in-the-Snow
F   Purdue Perceptual-Motor Survey, The   Jumping
F   Purdue Perceptual-Motor Survey, The   Obstacle Course
F   Purdue Perceptual-Motor Survey, The   Walking Board
F   Southern California Tests of Sensory Integration–Revised   Bilateral Motor Coordination

F   Test of Gross Motor Development   Gross Motor Development Quotient
F   Test of Gross Motor Development   Locomotor
F   Test of Gross Motor Development   Object Control

2154   Other Gross Motor Abilities

F   Bruininks-Oseretsky Test of Motor Proficiency   Running Speed & Agility
F   Scales of Independent Behavior   Fine Motor
F   Sensory Integration & Praxis Tests   Bilateral Motor Coordination
F   Sensory Integration & Praxis Tests   Manual Form Perception
F   Sensory Integration & Praxis Tests   Oral Praxis
F   Sensory Integration & Praxis Tests   Postrotary Nystagmus
F   Sensory Integration & Praxis Tests   Praxis on Verbal Command
F   Sensory Integration & Praxis Tests   Sequencing Praxis
F   Southern California Sensory Integration Tests–Revised   Crossing Mid-Line of Body
F   Southern California Sensory Integration Tests–Revised   Right-Left Discrimination

2200   Verbal Aptitude/Developmental Abilities, General

A   Test of Early Language Development, 2nd Edition   Total, Forms A & B
B   Clinical Evaluation of Language Functions–Screening Test–Advanced   Total
      Level
B   Clinical Evaluation of Language Functions–Screening Test–   Total
      Elementary Level
B   Clinical Evaluation of Language Fundamentals–Revised (8–16 yrs.) Receptive Language
B   Clinical Evaluation of Language Fundamentals–Revised (8–16 yrs.) Total Language
B   Detroit Tests of Learning Aptitude–Primary   Verbal Quotient
B   Detroit Tests of Learning Aptitude–Primary, 2nd Edition   Verbal
B   Developmental Indicators for the Assessment of Learning–Revised   Concepts Area
B   Screening Children for Related Early Educational Needs   Language
B   Stanford-Binet Intelligence Scale, 4th Edition   Verbal Reasoning
B   Test of Early Language Development   Language Quotient
B   Wide Range Assessment of Memory & Learning   Verbal Memory
B   Woodcock Language Proficiency Battery–Revised   Oral Language
B   Woodcock-Johnson Psycho-Educational Battery–Part 1   Memory Cluster
B   Woodcock-Johnson Psycho-Educational Battery–Revised–Tests of   Long-Term Retrieval
      Cognitive Ability
B   Woodcock-Johnson Psycho-Educational Battery–Revised–Tests of   Oral Language
      Cognitive Ability
B   Woodcock-Johnson Psycho-Educational Battery–Revised–Tests of   Processing Speed
      Cognitive Ability
B   Woodcock-Johnson Psycho-Educational Battery–Revised–Tests of   Short-Term Retrieval
      Cognitive Ability
B   Woodcock-Johnson Psycho-Educational Battery–Revised–Tests of   Test 8: Visual-Auditory Learning
      Cognitive Ability
F   Analysis of the Language of Learning   Total
F   Carrow Auditory-Visual Abilities Test   Auditory Battery
F   Clinical Evaluation of Language Functions–Screening Test–Advanced   Processing Items
      Level
F   Clinical Evaluation of Language Functions–Screening Test–Advanced   Production Items
      Level
F   Clinical Evaluation of Language Functions–Screening Test–   Processing Items
      Elementary Level

F	Clinical Evaluation of Language Functions–Screening Test–Elementary Level	Production Items
F	Language Processing Test	Total
F	McCarthy Scales of Children's Abilities	Verbal
F	Miller Assessment for Preschoolers	Verbal
F	Psycholinguistic Rating Scale	Auditory
F	Psycholinguistic Rating Scale	Auditory Association
F	Psycholinguistic Rating Scale	Auditory Closure
F	Psycholinguistic Rating Scale	Auditory Reception
F	Screening Assessment for Gifted Elementary Students	Program Related–C/Normal & Gifted Norms
F	Screening Test of Adolescent Language	Total
F	Test of Auditory-Perceptual Skills	Auditory Processing
F	Visual Aural Digit Span Test, The	Aural Output
F	Visual Aural Digit Span Test, The	Oral Expression
F	Visual Aural Digit Span Test, The	Total
F	Woodcock-Johnson Psycho-Educational Battery–Revised–Tests of Cognitive Ability	Test 16: Delayed Recall-Visual-Auditory Learning
F	Word Test, The	Total Test
F	Word Test–R: Elementary, The	Total
F	Word Test: Adolescent, The	Total

2210   Verbal Cognition, Reasoning

B	Clinical Evaluation of Language Fundamentals–Revised (8–16 yrs.)	Word Classes
B	Scholastic Abilities Test for Adults	Verbal Reasoning
B	Scholastic Aptitude Scale	Verbal Reasoning
B	Screening Assessment for Gifted Elementary Students	Reasoning/Normal Norms
B	Stanford-Binet Intelligence Scale, 4th Edition	Absurdities
B	Stanford-Binet Intelligence Scale, 4th Edition	Comprehension
B	Stanford-Binet Intelligence Scale, 4th Edition	Verbal Relations
B	Wechsler Adult Intelligence Scale–Revised	Comprehension
B	Woodcock Language Proficiency Battery–Revised	Verbal Analogies
B	Woodcock-Johnson Psycho-Educational Battery–Part 1	Analogies
B	Woodcock-Johnson Psycho-Educational Battery–Revised–Tests of Cognitive Ability	Test 7: Analysis-Synthesis
B	Woodcock-Johnson Psycho-Educational Battery–Revised–Tests of Cognitive Ability	Test 21: Verbal Analogies
F	Career Maturity Inventory Competence Test	Part 5: Problem Solving
F	Cognitive Levels Test	Verbal Reasoning
F	Hahnemann High School Behavior Rating Scale	Reasoning Ability
F	Illinois Test of Psycholinguistic Abilities	Auditory Association
F	Language Processing Test	Associations
F	Language Processing Test	Categorization
F	Language Processing Test	Differences
F	Language Processing Test	Similarities
F	Luria-Nebraska Neuropsychological Battery: Children's Revision	F11
F	Pictorial Test of Intelligence	Similarities
F	Screening Assessment for Gifted Elementary Students	Reasoning/Gifted Norms
F	Screening Test of Adolescent Language	Language Processing
F	Screening Test of Adolescent Language	Proverb Explanation
F	Test of Auditory-Perceptual Skills	Auditory Quotient
F	Test of Language Competence	Composite
F	Test of Language Competence	Making Inferences
F	Test of Language Competence	Partial

F	Test of Language Competence	Recreating Sentences
F	Test of Language Competence	Understanding Ambiguous Sentences
F	Test of Language Competence	Understanding Metaphoric Expressions
F	Test of Problem Solving	Avoiding Problems
F	Test of Problem Solving	Determining Causes
F	Test of Problem Solving	Determining Solutions
F	Test of Problem Solving	Explaining Inferences
F	Test of Problem Solving	Negative Why Questions
F	Test of Problem Solving	Total
F	Wechsler Intelligence Scale for Children–Revised	Comprehension
F	Wechsler Intelligence Scale for Children–3rd Edition	Comprehension
F	Wechsler Preschool & Primary Scales of Intelligence	Comprehension
F	Word Test, The	Associations
F	Word Test, The	Semantic Absurdities
F	Word Test–R: Elementary, The	Associations
F	Word Test: Adolescent, The	Brand Names
F	Word Test: Adolescent, The	Signs of the Times

2220 Verbal Cognition, Creativity

F	Devereux Elementary School Behavior Rating Scale II	Creative Initiative/Involvement
F	Hahnemann Elementary School Behavior Rating Scale	Originality
F	Hahnemann High School Behavior Rating Scale	Originality
F	Screening Assessment for Gifted Elementary Students	Divergent Production/Normal & Gifted Norms
F	Torrance Tests of Creative Thinking	Verbal Flexibility
F	Torrance Tests of Creative Thinking	Verbal Fluency
F	Torrance Tests of Creative Thinking	Verbal Originality

2230 Verbal Cognition, Spoken Language

B	Clinical Evaluation of Language Functions–Diagnostic Test	Processing
B	Clinical Evaluation of Language Functions–Diagnostic Test	Processing Linguistic Concepts
B	Clinical Evaluation of Language Functions–Diagnostic Test	Processing Spoken Paragraphs
B	Clinical Evaluation of Language Functions–Diagnostic Test	Producing Formulated Sentences
B	Clinical Evaluation of Language Functions–Diagnostic Test	Production
B	Clinical Evaluation of Language Fundamentals–Revised (5–7 yrs.)	Expressive Language
B	Clinical Evaluation of Language Fundamentals–Revised (5–7 yrs.)	Receptive Language
B	Clinical Evaluation of Language Fundamentals–Revised (5–7 yrs.)	Total Language
B	Clinical Evaluation of Language Fundamentals–Revised (8–16 yrs.)	Expressive Language
B	Clinical Evaluation of Language Fundamentals–Revised Screening Test	Total
B	Developmental Indicators for the Assessment of Learning–Revised	Language Area
B	Diagnostic Achievement Battery, 2nd Edition	Listening
B	Diagnostic Achievement Battery, 2nd Edition	Speaking
B	Diagnostic Achievement Battery, 2nd Edition	Spoken Language
B	Scales of Independent Behavior	Language Comprehension
B	Scales of Independent Behavior	Language Expression
B	Test for Auditory Comprehension of Language–Revised	Total
B	Test of Adolescent Language, 2nd Edition	Listening
B	Test of Adolescent Language, 2nd Edition	Speaking
B	Test of Adolescent Language, 2nd Edition	Spoken Language
B	Test of Adolescent/Adult Word Finding	Total
B	Test of Language Development–Intermediate	Listening
B	Test of Language Development–Intermediate	Overall Spoken Language

B	Test of Language Development–Intermediate	Speaking
B	Test of Language Development–Intermediate, 2nd Edition	Listening
B	Test of Language Development–Intermediate, 2nd Edition	Short Form
B	Test of Language Development–Intermediate, 2nd Edition	Speaking
B	Test of Language Development–Intermediate, 2nd Edition	Spoken Language
B	Test of Language Development–Primary, 2nd Edition	Listening
B	Test of Language Development–Primary, 2nd Edition	Short Form
B	Test of Language Development–Primary, 2nd Edition	Speaking
B	Test of Language Development–Primary, 2nd Edition	Spoken Language
B	Utah Test of Language Development, 3rd Edition	Language Comprehension
B	Utah Test of Language Development, 3rd Edition	Language Expression
B	Utah Test of Language Development, 3rd Edition	Language Quotient
B	Woodcock Language Proficiency Battery–Revised	Listening Comprehension
F	Analysis of the Language of Learning	Repairing Sentences
F	Basic School Skills Inventory–Diagnostic	Spoken Language
F	Clark-Madison Test of Oral Language	Total
F	Clinical Evaluation of Language Functions–Diagnostic Test	Processing Oral Directions
F	Clinical Evaluation of Language Functions–Diagnostic Test	Processing Relationships & Ambiguities
F	Communication Abilities Diagnostic Test	Language Comprehension
F	Communication Abilities Diagnostic Test	Language Expression
F	Communication Abilities Diagnostic Test	Pragmatics
F	Communication Abilities Diagnostic Test	Total Language
F	Devereux Adolescent Behavior Rating Scale	Bizarre Speech & Cognition
F	Diagnostic Achievement Battery	Listening
F	Diagnostic Achievement Battery	Speaking
F	Diagnostic Achievement Battery	Spoken Language
F	Diagnostic Reading Scales	Potential Level
F	Fluharty Preschool Speech & Language Screening Test	Comprehension
F	Houston Test of Language Development–Revised	Total
F	Kindergarten Language Screening Test	Total
F	Learning Disability Evaluation Scale, The	Listening
F	Learning Disability Evaluation Scale, The	Speaking
F	Luria-Nebraska Neuropsychological Battery: Children's Revision	C5
F	Luria-Nebraska Neuropsychological Battery: Children's Revision	C6
F	Merrill Language Screening Test	Total Score
F	Psycholinguistic Rating Scale	Verbal Expression
F	Psycholinguistic Rating Scale	Visual Association
F	Psycholinguistic Rating Scale	Visual Closure
F	Psycholinguistic Rating Scale	Visual Reception
F	Pupil Rating Scale–Revised, The	Auditory Comprehension
F	Pupil Rating Scale–Revised, The	Spoken Language
F	Pupil Rating Scale–Revised, The	Total Verbal
F	Reynell Developmental Language Scales, U.S. Edition	Expressive Language
F	Reynell Developmental Language Scales, U.S. Edition	Verbal Comprehension
F	Test of Adolescent Language	Listening
F	Test of Adolescent Language	Speaking
F	Test of Adolescent Language	Spoken Language
F	Test of Auditory-Perceptual Skills	Auditory Interpretation of Directions
F	Test of Language Development–Primary	Listening
F	Test of Language Development–Primary	Speaking
F	Test of Language Development–Primary	Spoken Language
F	Test of Relational Concepts	Concept Score
F	Vineland Adaptive Behavior Scales–Classroom Edition	Expressive Communication
F	Vineland Adaptive Behavior Scales–Classroom Edition	Receptive Communication
F	Vineland Adaptive Behavior Scales–Interview Edition, Expanded Form	Expressive Communication

F	Vineland Adaptive Behavior Scales–Interview Edition, Expanded Form	Receptive Communication
F	Vineland Adaptive Behavior Scales–Interview Edition, Survey Form	Expressive Communication
F	Vineland Adaptive Behavior Scales–Interview Edition, Survey Form	Receptive Communication
F	Wechsler Memory Scale–Revised	Logical Memory I
F	Wechsler Memory Scale–Revised	Logical Memory II
F	Woodcock-Johnson Psycho-Educational Battery–Revised–Tests of Cognitive Ability	Test 20: Listening Comprehension

2231 Spoken Language, Vocabulary

B	Clinical Evaluation of Language Functions–Diagnostic Test	Processing Word Classes
B	Clinical Evaluation of Language Functions–Diagnostic Test	Producing Names on Confrontation–Accuracy
B	Clinical Evaluation of Language Functions–Diagnostic Test	Producing Names on Confrontation–Time
B	Clinical Evaluation of Language Functions–Diagnostic Test	Producing Word Series–Time
B	Clinical Evaluation of Language Fundamentals–Revised (5–7 yrs.)	Formulated Sentences
B	Clinical Evaluation of Language Fundamentals–Revised (5–7 yrs.)	Linguistic Concepts
B	Clinical Evaluation of Language Fundamentals–Revised (8–16 yrs.)	Formulated Sentences
B	Clinical Evaluation of Language Fundamentals–Revised (8–16 yrs.)	Semantic Relationships
B	Detroit Tests of Learning Aptitude, 2nd Edition	Word Opposites
B	Detroit Tests of Learning Aptitude, 3rd Edition	Word Opposites
B	Detroit Tests of Learning Aptitude–Adult	Word Opposites
B	Diagnostic Achievement Battery, 2nd Edition	Characteristics
B	Diagnostic Achievement Battery, 2nd Edition	Synonyms
B	Kaufman Assessment Battery for Children	Expressive Vocabulary
B	Kaufman Assessment Battery for Children	Riddles
B	Kaufman Brief Intelligence Test	Vocabulary
B	Peabody Picture Vocabulary Test–Revised	Total Score
B	Stanford-Binet Intelligence Scale, 4th Edition	Vocabulary
B	Test for Auditory Comprehension of Language–Revised	Word Classes & Relations
B	Test of Adolescent Language, 2nd Edition	Listening/Vocabulary
B	Test of Adolescent Language, 2nd Edition	Speaking/Vocabulary
B	Test of Language Development–Intermediate	Characteristics
B	Test of Language Development–Intermediate	Generals
B	Test of Language Development–Intermediate	Semantics
B	Test of Language Development–Intermediate, 2nd Edition	Generals
B	Test of Language Development–Intermediate, 2nd Edition	Malapropisms
B	Test of Language Development–Intermediate, 2nd Edition	Semantics
B	Test of Language Development–Intermediate, 2nd Edition	Vocabulary
B	Test of Language Development–Primary, 2nd Edition	Oral Vocabulary
B	Test of Language Development–Primary, 2nd Edition	Picture Vocabulary
B	Test of Language Development–Primary, 2nd Edition	Semantics
B	Test of Word Finding	Total
B	Wechsler Adult Intelligence Scale–Revised	Similarities
B	Wechsler Adult Intelligence Scale–Revised	Vocabulary
B	Wechsler Intelligence Scale for Children–3rd Edition	Similarities
B	Wechsler Intelligence Scale for Children–3rd Edition	Vocabulary
B	Woodcock Language Proficiency Battery–Revised	Oral Vocabulary
B	Woodcock Language Proficiency Battery–Revised	Picture Vocabulary
B	Woodcock-Johnson Psycho-Educational Battery–Part 1	Antonyms–Synonyms
B	Woodcock-Johnson Psycho-Educational Battery–Part 1	Picture Vocabulary
B	Woodcock-Johnson Psycho-Educational Battery–Revised–Tests of Cognitive Ability	Comprehension-Knowledge

B	Woodcock-Johnson Psycho-Educational Battery–Revised–Tests of Cognitive Ability	Test 13: Oral Vocabulary
F	Analysis of the Language of Learning	Defining Concepts
F	Analysis of the Language of Learning	Generating Concept Examples
F	Analysis of the Language of Learning	Recognizing Concepts
F	Assessing Semantic Skills Through Everyday Themes	Identifying Attributes
F	Assessing Semantic Skills Through Everyday Themes	Identifying Categories
F	Assessing Semantic Skills Through Everyday Themes	Identifying Definitions
F	Assessing Semantic Skills Through Everyday Themes	Identifying Functions
F	Assessing Semantic Skills Through Everyday Themes	Identifying Labels
F	Assessing Semantic Skills Through Everyday Themes	Stating Attributes
F	Assessing Semantic Skills Through Everyday Themes	Stating Categories
F	Assessing Semantic Skills Through Everyday Themes	Stating Definitions
F	Assessing Semantic Skills Through Everyday Themes	Stating Functions
F	Assessing Semantic Skills Through Everyday Themes	Stating Labels
F	Assessing Semantic Skills Through Everyday Themes	Total Expressive
F	Assessing Semantic Skills Through Everyday Themes	Total Receptive
F	Assessing Semantic Skills Through Everyday Themes	Total Test
F	Auditory-Visual, Single-Word Picture Vocabulary Test–Adolescent	Total
F	Bankson-Bernthal Test of Phonology	Word Inventory
F	Boehm Test of Basic Concepts–Revised	Total
F	Carrow Auditory-Visual Abilities Test	Picture Memory
F	Carrow Auditory-Visual Abilities Test	Picture Sequence Selection
F	Clinical Evaluation of Language Functions–Diagnostic Test	Producing Word Associations
F	Clinical Evaluation of Language Functions–Diagnostic Test	Producing Word Series–Accuracy
F	Clinical Evaluation of Language Fundamentals–Revised (5–7 yrs.)	Oral Directions
F	Clinical Evaluation of Language Fundamentals–Revised (8–16 yrs.)	Oral Directions
F	Communication Abilities Diagnostic Test	Semantics
F	Diagnostic Achievement Battery	Characteristics
F	Diagnostic Achievement Battery	Synonyms
F	Expressive One-Word Picture Vocabulary Test	Total
F	Expressive One-Word Picture Vocabulary Test (Revised)	Total
F	Expressive One-Word Picture Vocabulary Test–Upper Extension	Total
F	Fluharty Preschool Speech & Language Screening Test	Identification
F	Goldman-Fristoe-Woodcock Auditory Skills Test Battery	Selective Attention
F	Illinois Test of Psycholinguistic Abilities	Auditory Reception
F	Illinois Test of Psycholinguistic Abilities	Verbal Expression
F	Language Processing Test	Attributes
F	Language Processing Test	Multiple Meanings
F	Normative Adaptive Behavior Checklist	Language/Concepts
F	Peabody Picture Vocabulary Test	Total Score
F	Pictorial Test of Intelligence	Information–Comprehension
F	Pictorial Test of Intelligence	Picture Vocabulary
F	Purdue Perceptual-Motor Survey, The	Identification of Body Parts
F	Quick Test, The	Total
F	Receptive One-Word Picture Vocabulary Test	Total
F	Screening Test of Adolescent Language	Vocabulary
F	Test of Adolescent Language	Listening/Vocabulary
F	Test of Adolescent Language	Speaking/Vocabulary
F	Test of Language Development–Primary	Oral Vocabulary
F	Test of Language Development–Primary	Picture Vocabulary
F	Test of Language Development–Primary	Semantics
F	Vane Kindergarten Test, The	Vocabulary
F	Wechsler Intelligence Scale for Children–Revised	Similarities
F	Wechsler Intelligence Scale for Children–Revised	Vocabulary

F	Wechsler Preschool & Primary Scale of Intelligence	Similarities
F	Wechsler Preschool & Primary Scale of Intelligence	Vocabulary
F	Woodcock-Johnson Psycho-Educational Battery–Revised–Tests of Cognitive Ability	Test 6: Picture Vocabulary
F	Word Test, The	Antonyms
F	Word Test, The	Definitions
F	Word Test, The	Multiple Definitions
F	Word Test, The	Synonyms
F	Word Test–R: Elementary, The	Antonyms
F	Word Test–R: Elementary, The	Definitions
F	Word Test–R: Elementary, The	Multiple Definitions
F	Word Test–R: Elementary, The	Semantic Absurdities
F	Word Test–R: Elementary, The	Synonyms
F	Word Test: Adolescent, The	Definitions
F	Word Test: Adolescent, The	Synonyms

2232   Spoken Language, Grammar

B	Clinical Evaluation of Language Functions–Diagnostic Test	Processing Word & Sentence Structures
B	Clinical Evaluation of Language Functions–Diagnostic Test	Producing Model Sentences
B	Clinical Evaluation of Language Fundamentals–Revised (5–7 yrs.)	Recalling Sentences
B	Clinical Evaluation of Language Fundamentals–Revised (5–7 yrs.)	Sentence Structure
B	Clinical Evaluation of Language Fundamentals–Revised (5–7 yrs.)	Word Structure
B	Clinical Evaluation of Language Fundamentals–Revised (8–16 yrs.)	Recalling Sentences
B	Clinical Evaluation of Language Fundamentals–Revised (8–16 yrs.)	Sentence Assembly
B	Detroit Tests of Learning Aptitude, 2nd Edition	Sentence Imitation
B	Detroit Tests of Learning Aptitude, 3rd Edition	Sentence Imitation
B	Detroit Tests of Learning Aptitude–Adult	Sentence Imitation
B	Diagnostic Achievement Battery, 2nd Edition	Grammatic Completion
B	Stanford-Binet Intelligence Scale, 4th Edition	Memory for Sentences
B	Test for Auditory Comprehension of Language–Revised	Elaborated Sentences
B	Test for Auditory Comprehension of Language–Revised	Grammatic Morphemes
B	Test of Adolescent Language, 2nd Edition	Listening/Grammar
B	Test of Adolescent Language, 2nd Edition	Speaking/Grammar
B	Test of Language Development–Intermediate	Grammatic Completion
B	Test of Language Development–Intermediate	Sentence Combining
B	Test of Language Development–Intermediate	Syntax
B	Test of Language Development–Intermediate	Word Ordering
B	Test of Language Development–Intermediate, 2nd Edition	Grammatic Comprehension
B	Test of Language Development–Intermediate, 2nd Edition	Sentence Combining
B	Test of Language Development–Intermediate, 2nd Edition	Syntax
B	Test of Language Development–Intermediate, 2nd Edition	Word Ordering
B	Test of Language Development–Primary, 2nd Edition	Grammatic Completion
B	Test of Language Development–Primary, 2nd Edition	Grammatic Understanding
B	Test of Language Development–Primary, 2nd Edition	Sentence Imitation
B	Test of Language Development–Primary, 2nd Edition	Syntax
B	Wide Range Assessment of Memory & Learning	Sentence Memory
B	Woodcock Language Proficiency Battery–Revised	Memory for Sentences
F	Carrow Auditory-Visual Abilities Test	Sentence Repetition
F	Carrow Elicited Language Inventory	Adjectives
F	Carrow Elicited Language Inventory	Adverbs
F	Carrow Elicited Language Inventory	Articles
F	Carrow Elicited Language Inventory	Conjunctions
F	Carrow Elicited Language Inventory	Contractions

F	Carrow Elicited Language Inventory	Demonstratives
F	Carrow Elicited Language Inventory	Negatives
F	Carrow Elicited Language Inventory	Noun Plurals
F	Carrow Elicited Language Inventory	Nouns
F	Carrow Elicited Language Inventory	Prepositions
F	Carrow Elicited Language Inventory	Pronouns
F	Carrow Elicited Language Inventory	Total
F	Carrow Elicited Language Inventory	Verbs
F	Communication Abilities Diagnostic Test	Syntax
F	Diagnostic Achievement Battery	Grammatic Completion
F	Fluharty Preschool Speech & Language Screening Test	Repetition
F	Illinois Test of Psycholinguistic Abilities	Grammatic Closure
F	Measurement of Language Development	Expressive
F	Measurement of Language Development	Receptive
F	Miller-Yoder Language Comprehension Test–Clinical Edition	Total
F	Northwestern Syntax Screening Test	Expressive
F	Northwestern Syntax Screening Test	Receptive
F	Rhode Island Test of Language Structure	Total/Hearing & Hearing Impaired Norms
F	Screening Test of Adolescent Language	Auditory Memory Span
F	Test of Adolescent Language	Listening/Grammar
F	Test of Adolescent Language	Speaking/Grammar
F	Test of Auditory-Perceptual Skills	Auditory Sentence Memory
F	Test of Language Development–Primary	Grammatic Completion
F	Test of Language Development–Primary	Grammatic Understanding
F	Test of Language Development–Primary	Sentence Imitation
F	Test of Language Development–Primary	Syntax
F	Wechsler Preschool & Primary Scale of Intelligence	Sentences
F	Woodcock-Johnson Psycho-Educational Battery–Part 1	Memory for Sentences
F	Woodcock-Johnson Psycho-Educational Battery–Revised–Tests of Cognitive Ability	Test 2: Memory for Sentences

2233 Spoken Language, Contextual Speech

B	Detroit Tests of Learning Aptitude, 2nd Edition	Story Construction
B	Detroit Tests of Learning Aptitude, 3rd Edition	Story Construction
B	Detroit Tests of Learning Aptitude, 3rd Edition	Story Sequences
B	Diagnostic Achievement Battery, 2nd Edition	Story Comprehension
B	Wide Range Assessment of Memory & Learning	Story Memory
F	Diagnostic Achievement Battery	Story Comprehension

2240 Verbal Processing, Spoken Words

B	Test of Language Development–Primary, 2nd Edition	Phonology
F	Luria-Nebraska Neuropsychological Battery: Children's Revision	F10
F	Luria-Nebraska Neuropsychological Battery: Children's Revision	F8
F	Luria-Nebraska Neuropsychological Battery: Children's Revision	F9

2241 Spoken Words, Discrimination

B	Test of Language Development–Primary, 2nd Edition	Word Discrimination
F	Auditory Discrimination Test–Revised	Total
F	Clinical Evaluation of Language Functions–Diagnostic Test	Processing Speech Sounds

F	Goldman-Fristoe-Woodcock Auditory Skills Test Battery	Diagnostic Discrimination
F	Goldman-Fristoe-Woodcock Test of Auditory Discrimination	Noise Subtest
F	Goldman-Fristoe-Woodcock Test of Auditory Discrimination	Quiet Subtest
F	Lindamood Auditory Conceptualization Test	Total
F	Test of Auditory-Perceptual Skills	Auditory Word Discrimination
F	Test of Language Development–Primary	Word Discrimination
F	Wepman's Auditory Discrimination Test, 2nd Edition	Total
F	Woodcock-Johnson Psycho-Educational Battery–Revised–Tests of Cognitive Ability	Test 18: Sound Patterns

2242   Spoken Words, Memory

B	Detroit Tests of Learning Aptitude, 2nd Edition	Word Sequences
B	Detroit Tests of Learning Aptitude, 3rd Edition	Reversed Letters
B	Detroit Tests of Learning Aptitude, 3rd Edition	Word Sequences
B	Detroit Tests of Learning Aptitude–Adult	Reversed Letters
B	Detroit Tests of Learning Aptitude–Adult	Word Sequences
B	Kaufman Assessment Battery for Children	Number Recall
B	Kaufman Assessment Battery for Children	Word Order
B	Stanford-Binet Intelligence Scale, 4th Edition	Memory for Digits
B	Wechsler Adult Intelligence Scale–Revised	Digit Span
B	Wechsler Intelligence Scale for Children–Third Edition	Digit Span
B	Wide Range Assessment of Memory & Learning	Number/Letter Memory
B	Wide Range Assessment of Memory & Learning	Verbal Learning
F	Carrow Auditory-Visual Abilities Test	Digit Repetition Backward
F	Carrow Auditory-Visual Abilities Test	Digit Repetition Forward
F	Carrow Auditory-Visual Abilities Test	Word Repetition
F	Children's Auditory Verbal Learning Test	Delayed Recall
F	Children's Auditory Verbal Learning Test	Immediate Memory Span
F	Children's Auditory Verbal Learning Test	Immediate Recall
F	Children's Auditory Verbal Learning Test	Level of Learning
F	Children's Auditory Verbal Learning Test	Recognition Accuracy
F	Children's Auditory Verbal Learning Test	Total Intrusions
F	Goldman-Fristoe-Woodcock Auditory Skills Test Battery	Memory for Content
F	Goldman-Fristoe-Woodcock Auditory Skills Test Battery	Memory for Sequence
F	Goldman-Fristoe-Woodcock Auditory Skills Test Battery	Recognition Memory
F	Illinois Test of Psycholinguistic Ability	Auditory Sequential Memory
F	Learning Efficiency Test	Auditory Memory Ordered Immediate Recall
F	Learning Efficiency Test	Auditory Memory Ordered Long Term Recall
F	Learning Efficiency Test	Auditory Memory Ordered Short Term Recall
F	Learning Efficiency Test	Auditory Memory Unordered Immediate Recall
F	Learning Efficiency Test	Auditory Memory Unordered Long Term Recall
F	Learning Efficiency Test	Auditory Memory Unordered Short Term Recall
F	Psycholinguistic Rating Scale	Auditory Memory
F	Test of Auditory-Perceptual Skills	Auditory Number Memory–Forward
F	Test of Auditory-Perceptual Skills	Auditory Number Memory–Reversed
F	Test of Auditory-Perceptual Skills	Auditory Word Memory
F	Visual Aural Digit Span Test, The	Aural–Oral
F	Wechsler Intelligence Scale for Children–Revised	Digit Span
F	Wechsler Memory Scale–Revised	Digit Span
F	Wechsler Memory Scale–Revised	Verbal Paired Associates I
F	Wechsler Memory Scale–Revised	Verbal Paired Associates II

F   Woodcock-Johnson Psycho-Educational Battery–Part 1   Numbers Reversed
F   Woodcock-Johnson Psycho-Educational Battery–Revised–Tests of   Test 1: Memory for Names
      Cognitive Ability
F   Woodcock-Johnson Psycho-Educational Battery–Revised–Tests of   Test 9: Memory for Words
      Cognitive Ability
F   Woodcock-Johnson Psycho-Educational Battery–Revised–Tests of   Test 15: Delayed Recall-Memory for Names
      Cognitive Ability
F   Woodcock-Johnson Psycho-Educational Battery–Revised–Tests of   Test 17: Numbers Reversed
      Cognitive Ability

2243   Spoken Words, Articulation

B   Test of Language Development–Primary, 2nd Edition   Word Articulation
F   Alpha Test of Phonology, The   Affrication
F   Alpha Test of Phonology, The   Alveolarization
F   Alpha Test of Phonology, The   Backing
F   Alpha Test of Phonology, The   Cluster Reduction
F   Alpha Test of Phonology, The   Cluster Substitution
F   Alpha Test of Phonology, The   Consonant Deletion
F   Alpha Test of Phonology, The   Deaffrication
F   Alpha Test of Phonology, The   Fronting
F   Alpha Test of Phonology, The   Gliding
F   Alpha Test of Phonology, The   Labialization
F   Alpha Test of Phonology, The   Stopping
F   Alpha Test of Phonology, The   Stridency Deletion
F   Alpha Test of Phonology, The   Syllable Deletion
F   Alpha Test of Phonology, The   Total Processes
F   Alpha Test of Phonology, The   Voicing Change
F   Alpha Test of Phonology, The   Vowelization
F   Arizona Articulation Proficiency Scale, 2nd Edition   Total Score
F   Bankson-Bernthal Test of Phonology   Consonants Composite
F   Bankson-Bernthal Test of Phonology   Phonological Process Composite
F   Clinical Evaluation of Language Functions–Diagnostic Test   Producing Speech Sounds
F   Fluharty Preschool Speech & Language Screening Test   Articulation
F   Goldman-Fristoe Test of Articulation   Sounds-in-Sentences
F   Goldman-Fristoe Test of Articulation   Sounds-in-Sentences
F   Goldman-Fristoe Test of Articulation   Sounds-in-Words
F   Goldman-Fristoe Test of Articulation   Sounds-in-Words
F   Goldman-Fristoe Test of Articulation   Stimulability
F   Goldman-Fristoe Test of Articulation   Stimulability
F   Goldman-Fristoe-Woodcock Auditory Skills Test Battery   Sound Mimicry
F   Templin-Darley Test of Articulation–Diagnostic   Total
F   Templin-Darley Test of Articulation–Total   Total
F   Test of Articulation Performance–Screen   Articulation Quotient/Imitation & Picture
                                                                                 Prompt Norms
F   Test of Language Development–Primary   Word Articulation
F   Weiss Comprehensive Articulation Test   Picture Test
F   Weiss Comprehensive Articulation Test   Sentence Test

2244   Other Spoken Words

B   Wide Range Assessment of Memory & Learning   Sound Symbol
B   Woodcock-Johnson Psycho-Educational Battery–Part 1   Blending

B Woodcock-Johnson Psycho-Educational Battery–Revised–Tests of Cognitive Ability Auditory Processing

B Woodcock-Johnson Psycho-Educational Battery–Revised–Tests of Cognitive Ability Test 11: Sound Blending

F Analysis of the Language of Learning Generating Words
F Analysis of the Language of Learning Segmenting Sentences
F Analysis of the Language of Learning Segmenting Words
F Carrow Auditory-Visual Abilities Test Auditory Blending
F Goldman-Fristoe-Woodcock Auditory Skills Test Battery Sound Analysis
F Goldman-Fristoe-Woodcock Auditory Skills Test Battery Sound Blending
F Goldman-Fristoe-Woodcock Auditory Skills Test Battery Sound Recognition
F Illinois Test of Psycholinguistic Abilities Auditory Closure
F Illinois Test of Psycholinguistic Abilities Sound Blending
F Wechsler Memory Scale–Revised Mental Control
F Woodcock-Johnson Psycho-Educational Battery–Revised–Tests of Cognitive Ability Test 4: Incomplete Words

2250 Verbal Processing, Written Words

B Detroit Tests of Learning Aptitude, 2nd Edition Word Fragments
B Detroit Tests of Learning Aptitude, 2nd Edition Letter Sequences
B Occupational Aptitude Survey & Interest Schedule, 2nd Edition Aptitude Survey–Word Comparison
B Woodcock-Johnson Psycho-Educational Battery–Revised–Tests of Cognitive Ability Test 3: Visual Matching

F Test of Academic Performance Copying Rate
F Test of Pictures/Forms/Letters/Numbers/Spatial Orientation & Sequencing Letter Sequencing

F Test of Pictures/Forms/Letters/Numbers/Spatial Orientation & Sequencing Reversed Letter & Number

F Test of Pictures/Forms/Letters/Numbers/Spatial Orientation & Sequencing Reversed Letters from Non-Reversed Letters

F Test of Pictures/Forms/Letters/Numbers/Spatial Orientation & Sequencing Reversed Letters in Words

F Test of Pictures/Forms/Letters/Numbers/Spatial Orientation & Sequencing Reversed Numbers from Non-Reversed Numbers

F Visual Aural Digit Span Test, The Aural–Written
F Visual Aural Digit Span Test, The Intersensory Integration
F Visual Aural Digit Span Test, The Intrasensory Integration
F Visual Aural Digit Span Test, The Visual Input
F Visual Aural Digit Span Test, The Visual–Oral
F Visual Aural Digit Span Test, The Visual–Written
F Visual Aural Digit Span Test, The Written Expression

AFFECT

3000 Overall Affect

B Behavior Evaluation Scale Behavior Quotient
B Behavior Evaluation Scale Inappropriate Behavior
B Behavior Evaluation Scale Learning Problems

B	Behavior Evaluation Scale–2	Inappropriate Behavior
B	Behavior Evaluation Scale–2	Learning Problems
B	Behavior Evaluation Scale–2	Total
B	Behavior Rating Profile	Student Rating Scales–Home
B	Behavior Rating Profile	Student Rating Scales–School
B	Behavior Rating Profile, 2nd Edition	Parent Rating Scale
B	Behavior Rating Profile, 2nd Edition	Student Rating Scales–Home
B	Behavior Rating Profile, 2nd Edition	Student Rating Scales–School
B	Behavior Rating Profile, 2nd Edition	Teacher Rating Scale
B	Children's Apperceptive Story-Telling Test	Adaptive Factor
B	Children's Apperceptive Story-Telling Test	Nonadaptive Factor
B	Children's Apperceptive Story-Telling Test	Positive Operational
B	Index of Personality Characteristics	Academic Scale
B	Index of Personality Characteristics	Acting In Scale
B	Index of Personality Characteristics	Nonacademic Scale
B	Index of Personality Characteristics	Total Test
B	Social-Emotional Dimension Scale	Behavior Quotient
B	Walker-McConnell Scale of Social Competence & School Adjustment	School Adjustment Behavior
B	Walker-McConnell Scale of Social Competence & School Adjustment	Total Score
F	AAMD Adaptive Behavior Scales–School Edition	Factor 5: Personal Adjustment/Normal & Special Norms
F	Adolescent Drinking Index	Total Score
F	Basic School Skills Inventory–Diagnostic	Classroom Behavior
F	Behavior Dimensions Rating Scale	Total/Male & Female Norms
F	Behavior Rating Profile	Parent Rating Scale
F	Behavior Rating Profile	Teacher Rating Scale
F	Childhood Autism Rating Scale, The	Total
F	Children's Apperceptive Story-Telling Test	Negative Affect
F	Children's Apperceptive Story-Telling Test	Negative Operational
F	Children's Apperceptive Story-Telling Test	Negative Preoperational
F	Children's Apperceptive Story-Telling Test	Positive Affect
F	Children's Apperceptive Story-Telling Test	Positive Preoperational
F	Developmental Profile II	Social
F	Differential Test of Conduct & Emotional Problems	Emotional Disturbance
F	Draw A Person	Total
F	Family Apperception Test	Total Dysfunctional Index
F	Personal Experience Inventory	Deviant Behavior/Dependency Group & High School Norms
F	Personal Experience Inventory	Psychological Disturbance/Dependency Group & High School Norms
F	Pupil Rating Scale–Revised, The	Personal-Social Behavior
F	Roberts Apperception Test for Children	Problem Identification
F	Scales of Independent Behavior	General Maladaptive Behavior
F	Scales of Independent Behavior	Internalized Maladaptive Behavior
F	Social Skills Rating System	Parent Form: Internalizing
F	Social Skills Rating System	Parent Form: Total Problem Behavior
F	Social Skills Rating System	Teacher Form: Internalizing
F	Social Skills Rating System	Teacher Form: Total Problem Behavior
F	Social-Emotional Dimension Scale	Inappropriate Behavior
F	Test of Early Socioemotional Development	Parent Rating Scale
F	Test of Early Socioemotional Development	Student Rating Scale
F	Test of Early Socioemotional Development	Teacher Rating Scale
F	Walker Problem Behavior Identification Checklist–Revised	Total

3100   Anxiety

B	Behavior Evaluation Scale	Physical Symptoms/Fears
B	Behavior Evaluation Scale–2	Physical Symptoms/Fears
F	AAMD Adaptive Behavior Scales–School Edition	Symptomatic Behavior/Normal & Special Norms
F	Behavior Dimensions Rating Scale	Fearful/Anxious/Male & Female Norms
F	Burks' Behavior Rating Scales	Excessive Anxiety
F	Children's Apperceptive Story-Telling Test	Inadequacy
F	Comprehensive Behavior Rating Scale for Children	Anxiety/Total, Male & Female Norms
F	Conners' Parent Rating Scales–48	Anxiety
F	Conners' Parent Rating Scales–48	Psychosomatic
F	Conners' Parent Rating Scales–93	Anxious–Shy
F	Conners' Parent Rating Scales–93	Psychosomatic
F	Conners' Teacher Rating Scales–39	Anxious–Passive
F	Devereux Adolescent Behavior Rating Scale	Anxious Self-Blame
F	Devereux Child Behavior Rating Scale	Anxious–Fearful Ideation
F	Devereux Elementary School Behavior Rating Scale II	Failure Anxiety
F	Endler Multidimensional Anxiety Scales	Perception Scales: Total
F	Endler Multidimensional Anxiety Scales	State Scales: Autonomic–Emotional
F	Endler Multidimensional Anxiety Scales	State Scales: Cognitive–Worry
F	Endler Multidimensional Anxiety Scales	State Scales: Total
F	Endler Multidimensional Anxiety Scales	Trait Scales: Ambiguous
F	Endler Multidimensional Anxiety Scales	Trait Scales: Daily Routines
F	Endler Multidimensional Anxiety Scales	Trait Scales: Physical Danger
F	Endler Multidimensional Anxiety Scales	Trait Scales: Social Evaluation
F	Hahnemann Elementary School Behavior Rating Scale	Failure Anxiety
F	Hahnemann High School Behavior Rating Scale	Anxious Producer
F	Hahnemann High School Behavior Rating Scale	General Anxiety
F	Piers-Harris Children's Self-Concept Scale–Revised	Anxiety
F	Roberts Apperception Test for Children	Anxiety
F	School Behavior Checklist	Anxiety
F	Social-Emotional Dimension Scale	Physical/Fear Reaction

3200   Attitudes and Interests, General

No scores reviewed

3210   Academic Attitudes and Interests

B	Woodcock-Johnson Psycho-Educational Battery–Part 3	Language Interest
B	Woodcock-Johnson Psycho-Educational Battery–Part 3	Mathematics Interest
B	Woodcock-Johnson Psycho-Educational Battery–Part 3	Reading Interest
B	Woodcock-Johnson Psycho-Educational Battery–Part 3	Scholastic Interest
F	Devereux Elementary School Behavior Rating Scale II	Positive Toward Teacher
F	Hahnemann Elementary School Behavior Rating Scale	Approach to Teacher
F	Hahnemann High School Behavior Rating Scale	Expressed Inability
F	Test of Mathematical Abilities	Attitude Toward Math

3220   Occupational Attitudes and Interests

B	Occupational Attitude Survey & Interest Schedule, 2nd Edition	Interest Schedule–Accommodating
B	Occupational Attitude Survey & Interest Schedule, 2nd Edition	Interest Schedule–Artistic

B	Occupational Attitude Survey & Interest Schedule, 2nd Edition	Interest Schedule–Business Detail
B	Occupational Attitude Survey & Interest Schedule, 2nd Edition	Interest Schedule–Humanitarian
B	Occupational Attitude Survey & Interest Schedule, 2nd Edition	Interest Schedule–Industrial
B	Occupational Attitude Survey & Interest Schedule, 2nd Edition	Interest Schedule–Leading-Influencing
B	Occupational Attitude Survey & Interest Schedule, 2nd Edition	Interest Schedule–Mechanical
B	Occupational Attitude Survey & Interest Schedule, 2nd Edition	Interest Schedule–Nature
B	Occupational Attitude Survey & Interest Schedule, 2nd Edition	Interest Schedule–Physical Performing
B	Occupational Attitude Survey & Interest Schedule, 2nd Edition	Interest Schedule–Protective
B	Occupational Attitude Survey & Interest Schedule, 2nd Edition	Interest Schedule–Scientific
B	Occupational Attitude Survey & Interest Schedule, 2nd Edition	Interest Schedule–Selling
B	Scales of Independent Behavior	Work Skills
F	Career Decision-Making System	Business
F	Career Decision-Making System	Clerical
F	Career Decision-Making System	Crafts
F	Career Decision-Making System	Scientific
F	Career Decision-Making System	Social
F	Career Decision-Making System	The Arts
F	Career Maturity Inventory	Scale A1
F	Career Maturity Inventory–Competence Test	Part 3: Goal Selection
F	Career Maturity Inventory–Counseling Form, Scale B2	Compromise
F	Career Maturity Inventory–Counseling Form, Scale B2	Decisiveness
F	Career Maturity Inventory–Counseling Form, Scale B2	Independence
F	Career Maturity Inventory–Counseling Form, Scale B2	Involvement
F	Career Maturity Inventory–Counseling Form, Scale B2	Orientation
F	Career Maturity Inventory–Screening Form	Scale A2
F	Computer Aptitude, Literacy, & Interest Profile	Interest/Male & Female Norms
F	Occupational Aptitude Survey & Interest Schedule	Interest Schedule–Accommodating/Male & Female Norms
F	Occupational Aptitude Survey & Interest Schedule	Interest Schedule–Artistic/Male & Female Norms
F	Occupational Aptitude Survey & Interest Schedule	Interest Schedule–Business Detail/Male & Female Norms
F	Occupational Aptitude Survey & Interest Schedule	Interest Schedule–Humanitarian/Male & Female Norms
F	Occupational Aptitude Survey & Interest Schedule	Interest Schedule–Industrial/Male & Female Norms
F	Occupational Aptitude Survey & Interest Schedule	Interest Schedule–Leading-Influencing/Male & Female Norms
F	Occupational Aptitude Survey & Interest Schedule	Interest Schedule–Mechanical/Male & Female Norms
F	Occupational Aptitude Survey & Interest Schedule	Interest Schedule–Nature/Male & Female Norms
F	Occupational Aptitude Survey & Interest Schedule	Interest Schedule–Physical Performing/Male & Female Norms
F	Occupational Aptitude Survey & Interest Schedule	Interest Schedule–Protective/Male & Female Norms
F	Occupational Aptitude Survey & Interest Schedule	Interest Schedule–Scientific/Male & Female Norms
F	Occupational Aptitude Survey & Interest Schedule	Interest Schedule–Selling/Male & Female Norms
F	Wide Range Interest-Opinion Test	Agreement
F	Wide Range Interest-Opinion Test	Ambition
F	Wide Range Interest-Opinion Test	Art
F	Wide Range Interest-Opinion Test	Athletics
F	Wide Range Interest-Opinion Test	Biological Science

F	Wide Range Interest-Opinion Test	Drama
F	Wide Range Interest-Opinion Test	Literature
F	Wide Range Interest-Opinion Test	Machine Operation
F	Wide Range Interest-Opinion Test	Management
F	Wide Range Interest-Opinion Test	Mechanics
F	Wide Range Interest-Opinion Test	Music
F	Wide Range Interest-Opinion Test	Negative
F	Wide Range Interest-Opinion Test	Number
F	Wide Range Interest-Opinion Test	Office Work
F	Wide Range Interest-Opinion Test	Outdoor
F	Wide Range Interest-Opinion Test	Personal Service
F	Wide Range Interest-Opinion Test	Physical Science
F	Wide Range Interest-Opinion Test	Positive
F	Wide Range Interest-Opinion Test	Protective Service
F	Wide Range Interest-Opinion Test	Risk
F	Wide Range Interest-Opinion Test	Sales
F	Wide Range Interest-Opinion Test	Sedentariness
F	Wide Range Interest-Opinion Test	Sex Stereotype
F	Wide Range Interest-Opinion Test	Skill Level
F	Wide Range Interest-Opinion Test	Social Science
F	Wide Range Interest-Opinion Test	Social Service

3230   Other Attitudes and Interests

F	Woodcock-Johnson Psycho-Educational Battery–Part 3	Non-Scholastic Interest
F	Woodcock-Johnson Psycho-Educational Battery–Part 3	Physical Interest
F	Woodcock-Johnson Psycho-Educational Battery–Part 3	Social Interest

3300   Depression

B	Behavior Evaluation Scale	Unhappiness/Depression
B	Behavior Evaluation Scale-2	Unhappiness/Depression
B	Reynolds Adolescent Depression Scale	Total/Total, Male & Female Norms
F	Beck Depression Inventory	Total
F	Emotional & Behavior Problem Scale	Social-Emotional Withdrawal/Depression
F	Multiscore Depression Inventory	Sad Mood
F	Reynolds Child Depression Scale	Total Score/Male & Female Norms
F	Roberts Apperception Test for Children	Depression
F	Social-Emotional Dimension Scale	Depressive Reaction

3400   Interpersonal/Social Relations

B	Adaptive Behavior Inventory	Social Skills/Normal & Retarded Norms
B	Behavior Evaluation Scale	Interpersonal Difficulties
B	Behavior Evaluation Scale-2	Interpersonal Difficulties
B	Behavior Rating Profile	Student Rating Scales–Peer
B	Behavior Rating Profile, 2nd Edition	Student Rating Scales–Peer
B	Index of Personality Characteristics	Perception of Others Scale
B	Vineland Adaptive Behavior Scales–Interview Edition, Expanded Form	Socialization Domain
B	Vineland Adaptive Behavior Scales–Interview Edition, Survey Form	Socialization Domain
B	Walker-McConnell Scale of Social Competence & School Adjustment	Peer-Preferred Social Behavior

B	Walker-McConnell Scale of Social Competence & School Adjustment	Teacher-Preferred Social Behavior
F	AAMD Adaptive Behavior Scales	Inappropriate Interpersonal Manners
F	AAMD Adaptive Behavior Scales	Socialization
F	AAMD Adaptive Behavior Scales	Withdrawal
F	AAMD Adaptive Behavior Scales–Public School Version	Inappropriate Interpersonal Manners/Normal & Special Norms
F	AAMD Adaptive Behavior Scales–Public School Version	Socialization/Normal & Special Norms
F	AAMD Adaptive Behavior Scales–Public School Version	Withdrawal/Normal & Special Norms
F	AAMD Adaptive Behavior Scales–School Edition	Antisocial vs. Social Behavior/Normal & Special Norms
F	AAMD Adaptive Behavior Scales–School Edition	Factor 4: Social Adjustment/Normal & Special Norms
F	AAMD Adaptive Behavior Scales–School Edition	Interpersonal Manners/Normal & Special Norms
F	AAMD Adaptive Behavior Scales–School Edition	Socialization/Normal & Special Norms
F	AAMD Adaptive Behavior Scales–School Edition	Withdrawal vs. Involvement/Normal & Special Norms
F	ADD-H Comprehensive Teacher's Rating Scale	Social Skills
F	Behavior Dimensions Rating Scale	Socially Withdrawn/Male & Female Norms
F	Behavior Rating Profile	Sociogram
F	Behavior Rating Profile, 2nd Edition	Sociogram
F	Burks' Behavior Rating Scales	Excessive Withdrawal
F	Burks' Behavior Rating Scales	Poor Social Conformity
F	Canfield Learning Styles Inventory	Competition
F	Canfield Learning Styles Inventory	Instructor
F	Canfield Learning Styles Inventory	Peer
F	Canfield Learning Styles Inventory	People
F	Children's Apperceptive Story-Telling Test	Affiliation
F	Children's Apperceptive Story-Telling Test	Alienation
F	Children's Apperceptive Story-Telling Test	Interpersonal Conflict
F	Children's Apperceptive Story-Telling Test	Interpersonal Cooperation
F	Children's Version of the Family Environment Scale, The	Cohesion
F	Children's Version of the Family Environment Scale, The	Conflict
F	Comprehensive Behavior Rating Scale for Children	Social Competence/Total, Male & Female Norms
F	Conners' Teaching Rating Scales–39	Asocial
F	Devereux Adolescent Behavior Rating Scale	Domineering–Sadistic
F	Devereux Adolescent Behavior Rating Scale	Heterosexual Interest
F	Devereux Adolescent Behavior Rating Scale	Need Approval, Dependency
F	Devereux Child Behavior Rating Scale	Need for Adult Contact
F	Devereux Child Behavior Rating Scale	Social Integration
F	Devereux Child Behavior Rating Scale	Social Isolation
F	Devereux Elementary School Behavior Rating Scale II	Peer Cooperation
F	Devereux Elementary School Behavior Rating Scale II	Socially Withdrawn
F	Emotional & Behavior Problem Scale	Avoidance/Unresponsive
F	Hahnemann Elementary School Behavior Rating Scale	Critical–Competitive
F	Hahnemann Elementary School Behavior Rating Scale	Disruptive Social Involvement
F	Hahnemann Elementary School Behavior Rating Scale	Holding Back/Withdrawn
F	Hahnemann Elementary School Behavior Rating Scale	Intellectual Dependency with Peers
F	Hahnemann Elementary School Behavior Rating Scale	Involvement
F	Hahnemann Elementary School Behavior Rating Scale	Productive with Peers
F	Hahnemann High School Behavior Rating Scale	Quiet–Withdrawn
F	Hahnemann High School Behavior Rating Scale	Rapport with Teacher
F	Hahnemann High School Behavior Rating Scale	Verbal Interaction

F Inventory for Client & Agency Planning · Social & Communication Skills
F Kohn Problem Checklist/Kohn Social Competence Scale · KPC Apathy–Withdrawal
F Kohn Problem Checklist/Kohn Social Competence Scale · KSC Apathy–Withdrawal
F Multiscore Depression Inventory · Social Introversion
F Normative Adaptive Behavior Checklist · Social Skills
F Personal Experience Inventory · Family Estrangement/Dependency Group & High School Norms
F Personal Experience Inventory · Family Pathology/Dependency Group & High School Norms
F Personal Experience Inventory · Rejecting Conventions/Dependency Group & High School Norms
F Personal Experience Inventory · Social Isolation/Dependency Group & High School Norms
F Personal Experience Inventory · Spiritual Isolation/Dependency Group & High School Norms
F Roberts Apperception Test for Children · Rejection
F Roberts Apperception Test for Children · Reliance on Others
F Roberts Apperception Test for Children · Support–Other
F Scales of Independent Behavior · Social Interaction
F Scales of Independent Behavior · Socially Offensive Behavior
F School Behavior Checklist · Extraversion
F Social Skills Rating System · Parent Form: Assertion
F Social Skills Rating System · Parent Form: Cooperation
F Social Skills Rating System · Parent Form: Total Social Skills
F Social Skills Rating System · Student Form: Assertion
F Social Skills Rating System · Student Form: Cooperation
F Social Skills Rating System · Student Form: Total Social Skills
F Social Skills Rating System · Teacher Form: Assertion
F Social Skills Rating System · Teacher Form: Cooperation
F Social Skills Rating System · Teacher Form: Total Social Skills
F Social-Emotional Dimension Scale · Avoidance of Peer Interaction
F Social-Emotional Dimension Scale · Avoidance of Teacher Interaction
F Temperament Assessment Battery for Children, The · Clinician Form: Approach/Withdrawal
F Temperament Assessment Battery for Children, The · Parent Form: Approach/Withdrawal
F Temperament Assessment Battery for Children, The · Teacher Form: Approach/Withdrawal
F Transition Behavior Scale, The · Interpersonal Relations/Total, Male & Female Norms
F Vineland Adaptive Behavior Scales–Classroom Edition · Interpersonal Relationships
F Vineland Adaptive Behavior Scales–Classroom Edition · Socialization Domain
F Vineland Adaptive Behavior Scales–Interview Edition, Expanded Form · Interpersonal Relationships
F Vineland Adaptive Behavior Scales–Interview Edition, Survey Form · Interpersonal Relationships
F Walker Problem Behavior Identification Checklist–Revised · Disturbed Peer Relationships
F Walker Problem Behavior Identification Checklist–Revised · Withdrawal
F Wide Range Intelligence–Personality Test · Social Concept

3500   Opposition/Conduct Disorder

B Index of Personality Characteristics · Acting Out Scale
F AAMD Adaptive Behavior Scales · Antisocial Behavior
F AAMD Adaptive Behavior Scales · Rebellious Behavior
F AAMD Adaptive Behavior Scales · Violent & Destructive Behavior
F AAMD Adaptive Behavior Scales–Public School Version · Antisocial Behavior/Normal & Special Norms
F AAMD Adaptive Behavior Scales–Public School Version · Rebellious Behavior/Normal & Special Norms

F	AAMD Adaptive Behavior Scales–Public School Version	Violent & Destructive Behavior/Normal & Special Norms
F	AAMD Adaptive Behavior Scales–School Edition	Aggressiveness/Normal & Special Norms
F	AAMD Adaptive Behavior Scales–School Edition	Rebelliousness/Normal & Special Norms
F	ADD-H Comprehensive Teacher's Rating Scale	Oppositional
F	Adolescent Drinking Index	Rebellious Behavior
F	Behavior Dimensions Rating Scale	Aggressive/Acting Out/Male & Female Norms
F	Burks' Behavior Rating Scales	Excessive Aggressiveness
F	Burks' Behavior Rating Scales	Excessive Resistance
F	Comprehensive Behavior Rating Scale for Children	Oppositional-Conduct Disorders/Total, Male & Female Norms
F	Conners' Parent Rating Scales–48	Conduct Problem
F	Conners' Parent Rating Scales–93	Antisocial
F	Conners' Parent Rating Scales–93	Conduct Disorder
F	Conners' Teacher Rating Scales–28	Conduct Problem
F	Conners' Teacher Rating Scales–39	Conduct Problem
F	Devereux Adolescent Behavior Rating Scale	Defiant–Resistive
F	Devereux Elementary School Behavior Rating Scale II	Negative–Aggressive
F	Differential Test of Conduct & Emotional Problems	Conduct Problem
F	Emotional & Behavior Problem Scale	Social Aggression/Conduct Disorder
F	Kohn Problem Checklist/Kohn Social Competence Scale	KPC Anger–Defiance
F	Kohn Problem Checklist/Kohn Social Competence Scale	KSC Anger–Defiance
F	Roberts Apperception Test for Children	Aggression
F	Scales of Independent Behavior	Asocial Maladaptive Behavior
F	Scales of Independent Behavior	Destructive to Property
F	Scales of Independent Behavior	Disruptive Behavior
F	Scales of Independent Behavior	Externalized Maladaptive Behavior
F	Scales of Independent Behavior	Hurtful to Others
F	Scales of Independent Behavior	Uncooperative Behavior
F	School Behavior Checklist	Aggression
F	School Behavior Checklist	Hostile Isolation
F	Social Skills Rating System	Parent Form: Externalizing
F	Social Skills Rating System	Teacher Form: Externalizing
F	Social-Emotional Dimension Scale	Aggressive Interaction
F	Walker Problem Behavior Identification Checklist–Revised	Acting Out

3600   Self-Abuse/Self-Destruction, General

No scores reviewed

3610   Eating Disorders

No scores reviewed

3620   Self-Injury

F	AAMD Adaptive Behavior Scales	Self-Abusive Behavior
F	AAMD Adaptive Behavior Scales–Public School Version	Self-Abusive Behavior/Normal & Special Norms
F	Emotional & Behavior Problem Scale	Aggressive/Self-Destructive
F	Scales of Independent Behavior	Hurtful to Self

3630   Substance Abuse, General

F	Personal Experience Inventory	Effects from Drug Use/Dependency Group & High School Norms
F	Personal Experience Inventory	Loss of Control/Dependency Group & High School Norms
F	Personal Experience Inventory	Peer Chemical Environment/Dependency Group & High School Norms
F	Personal Experience Inventory	Personal Involvement with Chemicals/ Dependency Group & High School Norms
F	Personal Experience Inventory	Polydrug Use/Dependency Group & High School Norms
F	Personal Experience Inventory	Preoccupation with Drugs/Dependency Group & High School Norms
F	Personal Experience Inventory	Psychological Benefits of Drug Use/ Dependency Group & High School Norms
F	Personal Experience Inventory	Sibling Chemical Use/Dependency Group & High School Norms
F	Personal Experience Inventory	Social Benefits of Drug Use/Dependency Group & High School Norms
F	Personal Experience Inventory	Transitional Drug Use/Dependency Group & High School Norms

3631   Alcohol Abuse

F	Adolescent Drinking Index	Self-Medicated Drinking

3632   Other Substance Abuse

No scores reviewed

3640   Suicide

F	Suicidal Ideation Questionnaire	Form HS Total/Total, Male & Female Norms
F	Suicidal Ideation Questionnaire	Form JR Total/Total, Male & Female Norms

3650   Other Self-Abuse/Self-Destruction

No scores reviewed

3700   Self-Esteem, General

B	Index of Personality Characteristics	Perception of Self
B	Self-Esteem Index	Self-Esteem Quotient
F	Burks' Behavior Rating Scales	Poor Sense of Identity
F	Career Maturity Inventory–Competence Test	Part 1: Self-Appraisal
F	Culture-Free Self-Esteem Inventories for Children & Adults	General
F	Culture-Free Self-Esteem Inventories for Children & Adults	Parents
F	Culture-Free Self-Esteem Inventories for Children & Adults	Total

F   Multiscore Depression Inventory   Low Self-Esteem
F   Personal Experience Inventory   Negative Self-Image/Dependency Group &
                                                                                 High School Norms
F   Piers-Harris Children's Self-Concept Scale   Total Score
F   Piers-Harris Children's Self-Concept Scale–Revised   Total Score
F   Self-Description Questionnaire–II   General Self
F   Self-Esteem Inventories–School Form   General Self Subscale
F   Self-Esteem Inventories–School Form   Home-Parents Subscale
F   Self-Esteem Inventories–School Form   Student Short Form Total Self
F   Self-Esteem Inventories–School Form   Total Self

3710   Cognitive Self-Esteem

B   Self-Esteem Index   Academic Competence
F   Burks' Behavior Rating Scales   Poor Academics
F   Burks' Behavior Rating Scales   Poor Intellectuality
F   Culture-Free Self-Esteem Inventories for Children & Adults   Academics
F   Piers-Harris Children's Self-Concept Scale–Revised   Intellectual & School Status
F   Self-Description Questionnaire–II   General School
F   Self-Description Questionnaire–II   Math
F   Self-Description Questionnaire–II   Verbal
F   Self-Esteem Inventories–School Form   School–Academic Subscale

3720   Physical Self-Esteem

F   Burks' Behavior Rating Scales   Poor Coordination
F   Burks' Behavior Rating Scales   Poor Physical Strength
F   Piers-Harris Children's Self-Concept Scale–Revised   Physical Appearance & Attributes
F   Self-Description Questionnaire–II   Physical Abilities
F   Self-Description Questionnaire–II   Physical Appearance

3730   Social Self-Esteem

B   Self-Esteem Index   Familial Acceptance
B   Self-Esteem Index   Peer Popularity
F   Culture-Free Self-Esteem Inventories for Children & Adults   Social
F   Piers-Harris Children's Self-Concept Scale–Revised   Popularity
F   Self-Description Questionnaire–II   Opposite-Sex Relations
F   Self-Description Questionnaire–II   Parent Relations
F   Self-Description Questionnaire–II   Same-Sex Relations
F   Self-Esteem Inventories–School Form   Social Self-Peers Subscale

3740   Other Self-Esteem

B   Self-Esteem Index   Personal Scurity
F   Piers-Harris Children's Self-Concept Scale–Revised   Behavior
F   Piers-Harris Children's Self-Concept Scale–Revised   Happiness & Satisfaction
F   Self-Description Questionnaire–II   Emotional Stability
F   Self-Description Questionnaire–II   Honesty-Trustworthiness

3800   Self-Regulation/Responsibility, General

F   Behavior Dimensions Rating Scale   Irresponsible/Inattentive/Male &
                                                                         Female Norms
F   Comprehensive Behavior Rating Scale for Children   Inattention–Disorganization/Total, Male &
                                                                         Female Norms
F   Conners' Parent Rating Scales–48   Impulsive-Hyperactive
F   Conners' Parent Rating Scales–93   Hyperactive-Immature
F   Conners' Teacher Rating Scales–39   Daydream-Attention Problem
F   Personal Experience Inventory   Absence of Goals/Dependency Group &
                                                                         High School Norms
F   Personal Experience Inventory   Uncontrolled/Dependency Group &
                                                                         High School Norms

3810   Hyperactivity/Hypoactivity

F   AAMD Adaptive Behavior Scales   Hyperactive Tendencies/Normal &
                                                                         Special Norms
F   AAMD Adaptive Behavior Scales–Public School Version   Hyperactive Tendencies/Normal &
                                                                         Special Norms
F   AAMD Adaptive Behavior Scales–School Edition   Activity Level/Normal & Special Norms
F   Aberrant Behavior Checklist   Hyperactivity
F   Aberrant Behavior Checklist   Lethargy
F   ADD-H Comprehensive Teacher's Rating Scale   Hyperactivity
F   Comprehensive Behavior Rating Scale for Children   Motor Hyperactivity/Total, Male &
                                                                         Female Norms
F   Comprehensive Behavior Rating Scale for Children   Sluggish Tempo/Total, Male & Female Norms
F   Conners' Parent Rating Scales–48   Hyperactivity Index
F   Conners' Parent Rating Scales–93   Hyperactivity Index
F   Conners' Teacher Rating Scales–28   Hyperactivity
F   Conners' Teacher Rating Scales–28   Hyperactivity Index
F   Conners' Teacher Rating Scales–39   Hyperactivity
F   Conners' Teacher Rating Scales–39   Hyperactivity Index
F   Devereux Adolescent Behavior Rating Scale   Hyperactive-Expansive
F   Devereux Child Behavior Rating Scale   Unresponsiveness to Stimulation
F   Devereux Elementary School Behavior Rating Scale II   Irrelevant Thinking/Talk
F   Hahnemann Elementary School Behavior Rating Scale   Irrelevant Talk
F   Hahnemann Elementary School Behavior Rating Scale   Disturbance-Restlessness
F   Multiscore Depression Inventory   Low Energy Level
F   Social Skills Rating System   Parent Form: Hyperactivity
F   Social Skills Rating System   Teacher Form: Hyperactivity
F   Temperament Assessment Battery for Children, The   Clinician Form: Activity
F   Temperament Assessment Battery for Children, The   Parent Form: Activity
F   Temperament Assessment Battery for Children, The   Teacher Form: Activity

3820   Attention/Vigilance

F   ADD-H Comprehensive Teacher's Rating Scale   Attention
F   Burks' Behavior Rating Scales   Poor Attention
F   Canfield Learning Styles Inventory   Detail
F   Conners' Teacher Rating Scales–28   Inattentive-Passive
F   Devereux Child Behavior Rating Scale   Distractibility
F   Devereux Elementary School Behavior Rating Scale II   Impatience

F   Devereux Elementary School Behavior Rating Scale II   Inattention
F   Devereux Elementary School Behavior Rating Scale II   Perseverance
F   Hahnemann Elementary School Behavior Rating Scale   Unreflectiveness
F   Scales of Independent Behavior   Withdrawal or Inattentive Behavior
F   Temperament Assessment Battery for Children, The   Clinician Form: Distractibility
F   Temperament Assessment Battery for Children, The   Clinician Form: Persistence
F   Temperament Assessment Battery for Children, The   Parent Form: Persistence
F   Temperament Assessment Battery for Children, The   Teacher Form: Distractibility
F   Temperament Assessment Battery for Children, The   Teacher Form: Persistence
F   Walker Problem Behavior Identification Checklist–Revised   Distractibility

3830   Responsibility/Locus of Control

B   Index of Personality Characteristics   External Locus of Control Scale
B   Index of Personality Characteristics   Internal Locus of Control Scale
F   AAMD Adaptive Behavior Scales   Responsibility
F   AAMD Adaptive Behavior Scales   Self-Direction
F   AAMD Adaptive Behavior Scales   Untrustworthy Behavior
F   AAMD Adaptive Behavior Scales–Public School Version   Responsibility/Normal & Special Norms
F   AAMD Adaptive Behavior Scales–Public School Version   Self-Direction/Normal & Special Norms
F   AAMD Adaptive Behavior Scales–Public School Version   Untrustworthy Behavior/Normal &
                                                                  Special Norms
F   AAMD Adaptive Behavior Scales–School Edition   Responsibility/Normal & Special Norms
F   AAMD Adaptive Behavior Scales–School Edition   Self-Direction/Normal & Special Norms
F   AAMD Adaptive Behavior Scales–School Edition   Trustworthiness/Normal & Special Norms
F   Burks' Behavior Rating Scales   Excessive Dependency
F   Burks' Behavior Rating Scales   Excessive Self-Blame
F   Burks' Behavior Rating Scales   Poor Anger Control
F   Canfield Learning Styles Inventory   Authority
F   Canfield Learning Styles Inventory   Independence
F   Canfield Learning Styles Inventory   Organization
F   Children's Version of the Family Environment Scale, The   Independence
F   Devereux Adolescent Behavior Rating Scale   Unethical Behavior
F   Devereux Child Behavior Rating Scale   Inadequate Need for Independence
F   Devereux Elementary School Behavior Rating Scales II   Blaming
F   Devereux Elementary School Behavior Rating Scales II   Need for Direction in Work
F   Devereux Elementary School Behavior Rating Scales II   Work Organization
F   Hahnemann Elementary School Behavior Rating Scale   Blaming
F   Hahnemann Elementary School Behavior Rating Scale   Independent Learning
F   Hahnemann High School Behavior Rating Scale   Lack of Intellectual Independence
F   Hahnemann High School Behavior Rating Scale   Poor Work Habits
F   Social Skills Rating System   Parent Form: Responsibility
F   Social Skills Rating System   Parent Form: Self-Control
F   Social Skills Rating System   Student Form: Self-Control
F   Social Skills Rating System   Teacher Form: Self-Control

3840   Other Self-Regulation/Responsibility

B   Children's Apperceptive Story-Telling Test   Immature Factor
F   Burks' Behavior Rating Scales   Poor Impulse Control
F   Children's Apperceptive Story-Telling Test   Limits
F   Children's Version of the Family Environment Scale, The   Control

F   Comprehensive Behavior Rating Scale for Children   Daydreaming/Total, Male & Female Norms
F   Conners' Parent Rating Scales–93   Restless–Disorganized
F   Devereux Adolescent Behavior Rating Scale   Bizarre Action
F   Devereux Adolescent Behavior Rating Scale   Inability to Delay
F   Devereux Adolescent Behavior Rating Scale   Poor Emotional Control
F   Devereux Child Behavior Rating Scale   Inability to Delay
F   Devereux Child Behavior Rating Scale   Proneness to Emotional Upset
F   Devereux Child Behavior Rating Scale   "Impulse" Ideation
F   Multiscore Depression Inventory   Instrumental Helplessness
F   Multiscore Depression Inventory   Learned Helplessness
F   Roberts Apperception Test for Children   Limit Setting
F   Vineland Adaptive Behavior Scales–Classroom Edition   Coping Skills
F   Vineland Adaptive Behavior Scales–Interview Edition, Expanded Form   Coping Skills
F   Vineland Adaptive Behavior Scales–Interview Edition, Survey Form   Coping Skills
F   Walker Problem Behavior Identification Checklist–Revised   Immaturity

3900   Other Affective Characteristics

B   Children's Apperceptive Story-Telling Test   Instrumentality
B   Children's Apperceptive Story-Telling Test   Refusal
B   Children's Apperceptive Story-Telling Test   Uninvested Factor
F   AAMD Adaptive Behavior Scales   Psychological Disturbances
F   AAMD Adaptive Behavior Scales   Sexually Aberrant Behavior
F   AAMD Adaptive Behavior Scales   Stereotyped Behavior & Odd Mannerisms
F   AAMD Adaptive Behavior Scales   Unacceptable or Eccentric Habits
F   AAMD Adaptive Behavior Scales   Unacceptable Vocal Habits
F   AAMD Adaptive Behavior Scales–Public School Version   Psychological Disturbances/Normal & Special Norms
F   AAMD Adaptive Behavior Scales–Public School Version   Sexually Aberrant Behaviors/Normal & Special Norms
F   AAMD Adaptive Behavior Scales–Public School Version   Stereotyped Behaviors & Odd Mannerisms/ Normal & Special Norms
F   AAMD Adaptive Behavior Scales–Public School Version   Unacceptable or Eccentric Habits/Normal & Special Norms
F   AAMD Adaptive Behavior Scales–Public School Version   Unacceptable Vocal Habits/Normal & Special Norms
F   AAMD Adaptive Behavior Scales–School Edition   Acceptability of Habits/Normal & Special Norms
F   AAMD Adaptive Behavior Scales–School Edition   Acceptability of Vocal Habits/Normal & Special Norms
F   AAMD Adaptive Behavior Scales–School Edition   Mannerisms/Normal & Special Norms
F   Aberrant Behavior Checklist   Inappropriate Speech
F   Aberrant Behavior Checklist   Irritability
F   Aberrant Behavior Checklist   Stereotypy
F   Beck Hopelessness Scale   Total
F   Burks' Behavior Rating Scales   Excessive Sense of Persecution
F   Burks' Behavior Rating Scales   Excessive Suffering
F   Burks' Behavior Rating Scales   Poor Ego Strength
F   Burks' Behavior Rating Scales   Poor Reality Contact
F   Canfield Learning Styles Inventory   A Expectation
F   Canfield Learning Styles Inventory   B Expectation
F   Canfield Learning Styles Inventory   C Expectation
F   Canfield Learning Styles Inventory   D Expectation

F	Canfield Learning Styles Inventory	Direct Experience
F	Canfield Learning Styles Inventory	Goal Setting
F	Canfield Learning Styles Inventory	Iconic
F	Canfield Learning Styles Inventory	Inanimate
F	Canfield Learning Styles Inventory	Listening
F	Canfield Learning Styles Inventory	Numeric
F	Canfield Learning Styles Inventory	Qualitative
F	Canfield Learning Styles Inventory	Reading
F	Canfield Learning Styles Inventory	Total Expectation
F	Children's Apperceptive Story-Telling Test	Unresolved
F	Children's Version of the Family Environment Scale, The	Achievement Orientation
F	Children's Version of the Family Environment Scale, The	Active–Recreational Orientation
F	Children's Version of the Family Environment Scale, The	Expressiveness
F	Children's Version of the Family Environment Scale, The	Intellectual–Cultural Orientation
F	Children's Version of the Family Environment Scale, The	Moral–Religious Emphasis
F	Conners' Parent Rating Scales-93	Obsessive–Compulsive
F	Conners' Teacher Rating Scales-39	Emotional–Overindulgent
F	Devereux Adolescent Behavior Rating Scale	Emotional Distance
F	Devereux Adolescent Behavior Rating Scale	Paranoid Thinking
F	Devereux Adolescent Behavior Rating Scale	Schizoid Withdrawal
F	Devereux Child Behavior Rating Scale	Emotional Detachment
F	Devereux Child Behavior Rating Scale	Pathological Use of Senses
F	Devereux Elementary School Behavior Rating Scale II	Confusion
F	Hahnemann Elementary School Behavior Rating Scale	Negative Feelings
F	Hahnemann High School Behavior Rating Scale	Dogmatic–Inflexible
F	Hahnemann High School Behavior Rating Scale	Verbal Negativism
F	Multiscore Depression Inventory	Guilt
F	Multiscore Depression Inventory	Irritability
F	Multiscore Depression Inventory	Pessimism
F	Parent Rating of Student Behavior	Social Responsibility
F	Roberts Apperception Test for Children	Resolution 1
F	Roberts Apperception Test for Children	Resolution 2
F	Roberts Apperception Test for Children	Resolution 3
F	Roberts Apperception Test for Children	Unresolved
F	Scales of Independent Behavior	Unusual or Repetitive Habits
F	School Behavior Checklist	Low Need Achievement
F	School Behavior Checklist	Normal Irritability
F	Social Skills Rating System	Student Form: Empathy
F	Temperament Assessment Battery for Children, The	Clinician Form: Adaptability
F	Temperament Assessment Battery for Children, The	Parent Form: Adaptability
F	Temperament Assessment Battery for Children, The	Parent Form: Ease-of-Management-Through-Distraction
F	Temperament Assessment Battery for Children, The	Parent Form: Emotional Intensity
F	Temperament Assessment Battery for Children, The	Teacher Form: Adaptability
F	Temperament Assessment Battery for Children, The	Teacher Form: Emotional Intensity
F	Vineland Adaptive Behavior Scales–Classroom Edition	Play & Leisure Time
F	Vineland Adaptive Behavior Scales–Interview Edition, Expanded Form	Play & Leisure Time
F	Vineland Adaptive Behavior Scales–Interview Edition, Survey Form	Play & Leisure Time

GENERAL INTELLIGENCE

4000   General Intelligence

A	Wechsler Intelligence Scale for Children–3rd Edition	Full Scale IQ
A	Wechsler Intelligence Scale for Children–3rd Edition	Verbal IQ
B	Adaptive Behavior Inventory	Communication Skills/Normal & Retarded Norms
B	Adaptive Behavior Inventory	Total Score–Long Form/Normal & Retarded Norms
B	Adaptive Behavior Inventory	Total Score–Short Form/Normal & Retarded Norms
B	Detroit Tests of Learning Aptitude, 3rd Edition	Attention-Reduced Composite
B	Detroit Tests of Learning Aptitude, 3rd Edition	Cognitive Level
B	Detroit Tests of Learning Aptitude, 3rd Edition	Crystallized Intelligence
B	Detroit Tests of Learning Aptitude, 3rd Edition	General Mental Ability
B	Detroit Tests of Learning Aptitude, 3rd Edition	Motor-Reduced Composite
B	Detroit Tests of Learning Aptitude, 3rd Edition	Verbal Composite
B	Detroit Tests of Learning Aptitude, 3rd Edition	Verbal Scale
B	Detroit Tests of Learning Aptitude–Adult	Attention-Reduced Composite
B	Detroit Tests of Learning Aptitude–Adult	Cognitive Level
B	Detroit Tests of Learning Aptitude–Adult	Crystallized Intelligence
B	Detroit Tests of Learning Aptitude–Adult	General Mental Ability
B	Detroit Tests of Learning Aptitude–Adult	Motor-Reduced Composite
B	Detroit Tests of Learning Aptitude–Adult	Nonverbal Composite
B	Detroit Tests of Learning Aptitude–Adult	Performance Scale
B	Detroit Tests of Learning Aptitude–Adult	Simultaneous Processing
B	Detroit Tests of Learning Aptitude–Adult	Verbal Composite
B	Detroit Tests of Learning Aptitude–Adult	Verbal Scale
B	Diagnostic Achievement Battery, Second Edition	Total Achievement
B	Inventory for Client & Agency Planning	Broad Independence
B	Kaufman Assessment Battery for Children	Achievement Scale
B	Occupational Aptitude Survey & Interest Schedule, 2nd Edition	Aptitude Survey–General Ability
B	Scales of Independent Behavior	Broad Independence
B	Scales of Independent Behavior	Short Form Scale
B	Scales of Independent Behavior	Social Interaction & Communication Skills
B	Scholastic Abilities Test for Adults	General Aptitude
B	Scholastic Abilities Test for Adults	Quantitative
B	Scholastic Abilities Test for Adults	Scholastic Abilities
B	Scholastic Abilities Test for Adults	Verbal
B	Scholastic Aptitude Scale	General Aptitude
B	Screening Assessment for Gifted Elementary Students	Program Related–B/Normal Norms
B	Screening Children for Related Early Educational Needs	Early Achievement Quotient
B	Stanford-Binet Intelligence Scale, 4th Edition	Test Composite
B	Test of Adolescent Language, 2nd Edition	Adolescent Language
B	Test of Adolescent Language, 2nd Edition	Expressive Language
B	Test of Adolescent Language, 2nd Edition	Grammar
B	Test of Adolescent Language, 2nd Edition	Receptive Language
B	Test of Adolescent Language, 2nd Edition	Vocabulary
B	Test of Mathematical Abilities	Total Math Quotient
B	Vineland Adaptive Behavior Scales–Interview Edition, Expanded Form	Adaptive Behavior Composite
B	Vineland Adaptive Behavior Scales–Interview Edition, Expanded Form	Communication Domain

B	Vineland Adaptive Behavior Scales–Interview Edition, Survey Form	Adaptive Behavior Composite
B	Vineland Adaptive Behavior Scales–Interview Edition, Survey Form	Communication Domain
B	Wechsler Adult Intelligence Scale–Revised	Full Scale
B	Wechsler Adult Intelligence Scale–Revised	Verbal Scale
B	Wechsler Intelligence Scale for Children–3rd Edition	Freedom from Distractibility Index
B	Wechsler Intelligence Scale for Children–3rd Edition	Verbal Comprehension Index
B	Woodcock Language Proficiency Battery–Revised	Broad English Ability–Ed
B	Woodcock Language Proficiency Battery–Revised	Broad English Ability–Standard
B	Woodcock-Johnson Psycho-Educational Battery–Part 1	Brief Scale Cluster
B	Woodcock-Johnson Psycho-Educational Battery–Part 1	Full Scale Cluster
B	Woodcock-Johnson Psycho-Educational Battery–Part 1	Knowledge Aptitude Cluster
B	Woodcock-Johnson Psycho-Educational Battery–Part 1	Written Language Aptitude Cluster
F	AAMD Aptitude Behavior Scales	Language Development
F	AAMD Adaptive Behavior Scales–Public School Version	Language Development/Normal & Special Norms
F	AAMD Adaptive Behavior Scales–School Edition	Language Development/Normal & Special Norms
F	Basic School Skills Inventory–Diagnostic	Total Score
F	Cognitive Levels Test	Abstract Quantitative Reasoning
F	Cognitive Levels Test	Best G Index
F	Cognitive Levels Test	Cognitive Index
F	Cognitive Levels Test	Rapid Cognitive Index
F	Comprehensive Behavior Rating Scale for Children	Cognitive Deficits
F	Comprehensive Behavior Rating Scale for Children	Total/Total, Male & Female Norms
F	Computer Aptitude, Literacy & Interest Profile	Total
F	Developmental Profile II	Communication
F	Developmental Profile II	IQ Equivalence
F	Devereux Adolescent Behavior Rating Scale	Physical Inferiority/Timidity
F	Diagnostic Achievement Battery	Total Achievement
F	Gifted Evaluation Scale, The	Academic Aptitude
F	Gifted Evaluation Scale, The	Creativity
F	Gifted Evaluation Scale, The	Intellectual
F	Gifted Evaluation Scale, The	Leadership Ability
F	Gifted Evaluation Scale, The	Performing & Visual Arts
F	Gifted Evaluation Scale, The	Total
F	Kindergarten Readiness Test	Total
F	Learning Disability Rating Procedure	Total
F	Luria-Nebraska Neuropsychological Battery: Children's Revision	C11
F	Luria-Nebraska Neuropsychological Battery: Children's Revision	F1
F	McCarthy Scales of Children's Abilities	General Cognitive Index
F	McCarthy Scales of Children's Abilities	Quantitative
F	Multiscore Depression Inventory	Full Scale
F	Multiscore Depression Inventory	Short Form
F	Normative Adaptive Behavior Checklist	Total Test
F	Occupational Aptitude Survey & Interest Schedule	Aptitude Survey–General Ability/Male & Female Norms
F	Parent Rating of Student Behavior	Personal Independence
F	Parent Rating of Student Behavior	Total
F	Pictorial Test of Intelligence	Deviation Quotient
F	Pictorial Test of Intelligence	Short Form
F	Pupil Rating Scale–Revised, The	Total Scale
F	School Behavior Checklist	School Disturbance
F	School Behavior Checklist	Total Disability
F	Screening Assessment for Gifted Elementary Students	Program Related–A/Normal & Gifted Norms
F	Screening Assessment for Gifted Elementary Students	Program Related–B/Gifted Norms

F   Screening Assessment for Gifted Elementary Students   Program Related–D/Normal & Gifted Norms
F   Slosson Intelligence Test for Children & Adults–Revised 1985   Total
F   Slosson Intelligence Test for Children & Adults–Revised 1991   Total
F   Stanford-Binet Intelligence Scale, 1972 Norms Edition   Total
F   Test of Adolescent Language   Adolescent Language
F   Test of Adolescent Language   Expressive Language
F   Test of Adolescent Language   Grammar
F   Test of Adolescent Language   Receptive Language
F   Test of Adolescent Language   Vocabulary
F   Transition Behavior Scale, The   Social/Community Expectations/Total, Male
                                                                      & Female Norms
F   Transition Behavior Scale, The   Total/Total, Male & Female Norms
F   Transition Behavior Scale, The   Work Related
F   Utah Test of Language Development–Revised Edition   Total
F   Vineland Adaptive Behavior Scales–Classroom Edition   Adaptive Behavior Composite
F   Vineland Adaptive Behavior Scales–Classroom Edition   Communication Domain
F   Wechsler Intelligence Scale for Children–Revised   Full Scale
F   Wechsler Intelligence Scale for Children–Revised   Verbal Scale
F   Wechsler Memory Scale–Revised   General Memory
F   Wechsler Preschool & Primary Scale of Intelligence   Full Scale
F   Wechsler Preschool & Primary Scale of Intelligence   Verbal Scale
F   Wide Range Intelligence–Personality Test   Intelligence Score
F   Woodcock Reading Mastery Tests–Revised   Readiness Cluster

---

UNCLASSIFIED ATTRIBUTES

5000 Unclassified Attributes

B   Detroit Tests of Learning Aptitude–Adult   Optimal Composite
B   Woodcock-Johnson Psycho-Educational Battery–Revised–Tests of   Test 30: Humanities
        Achievement
F   Comprehensive Test of Visual Functioning   Visual Acuity
F   Diagnostic Screening Test: Achievement   Literature & the Arts

APPENDIX C

**CONSUMER'S GUIDE
REVIEW BOARD**

Ralph F. Blanco, PhD
  Professor, Department of School Psychology
  Temple University (Philadelphia, Pennsylvania)
Sharon Bradley-Johnson, EdD
  Professor, Department of Psychology
  Central Michigan University (Mount Pleasant)
Linda Brown, PhD
  Austin, Texas
Brian R. Bryant, PhD
  Boca Raton, Florida
Berttram Chiang, PhD
  Associate Professor
  University of Wisconsin–Oshkosh
Maggie Coleman, PhD
  Department of Special Education
  The University of Texas at Austin
Jack A. Cummings, PhD
  Assistant Professor, Department of Educational
    Psychology
  Indiana University (Bloomington)
Elizabeth Delaney, PhD
  Associate Professor, Division of Teacher Education
  Sam Houston State University (Huntsville, Texas)
Caroline Dunn, PhD
  Assistant Professor, Department of Special Education
  Auburn University (Auburn, Alabama)
Larry Evans, MA ·
  Doctoral Student, Department of Psychology
  Central Michigan University (Mount Pleasant)
Rebecca R. Fewell, PhD
  Mailman Center for Child Development
  University of Miami (Miami, Florida)
Laura Fowler, BS
  PRO-ED, Inc. (Austin, Texas)
Douglas Fuchs, PhD
  Associate Professor, John F. Kennedy Center for
    Research in Education and Human Development
  Peabody College of Vanderbilt University (Nashville,
    Tennessee)
Lynn Fuchs, PhD
  Associate Professor, John F. Kennedy Center for
    Research in Education and Human Development
  Peabody College of Vanderbilt University (Nashville,
    Tennessee)
Frank M. Gresham, PhD
  Professor, Department of Education
  University of California–Riverside
Donald D. Hammill, EdD
  President
  PRO-ED, Inc. (Austin, Texas)
William R. Harmer, PhD
  Professor of Education
  The University of Texas at Austin

M. Suzanne Hasenstab, PhD
  Director, Preschool Clinical Educational Services
  University of Virginia (Charlottesville)
Gary L. Hessler, PhD
  Diagnostic Consultant
  Macomb Intermediate School District (Mount Clemens,
    Michigan)
Cheryl Hiltebeitel, PhD
  University of Texas Health Science Center (Dallas)
E. Scott Huebner, PhD
  Project Coordinator, Rural School Psychology Project
  Indiana University (Bloomington)
William A. Horn, EdD
  Diagnostician
  Fort Stewart Dependent Schools (Fort Stewart, Georgia)
Kathleen Kelley, MA
  Speech/Language Pathologist
  Cherry Creek Public Schools (Englewood, Colorado)
Judi Lesiak, PhD
  Professor, Department of Psychology
  Central Michigan University (Mount Pleasant)
Rena B. Lewis, PhD
  Associate Professor, Department of Special Education
  San Diego State University (San Diego, California)
Robin Locke, PhD
  Austin, Texas
Doris A. Lohry, EdD
  School Psychologist
  Western Hills Area Education Agency (Sioux City,
    Iowa)
Robert Lowe, MEd
  Assistant Professor, Department of Communication
    Disorders
  University of South Dakota (Vermillion)
Judy Montgomery, PhD
  Director of Special Services
  Fountain Valley School District (Fountain Valley,
    California)
Deborah Muscella, PhD
  Staff Associate, Biological Sciences Curriculum Study
  The Colorado College (Colorado Springs)
Anne O. Netick, PhD
  Professor of Special Education
  University of Louisville (Louisville, Kentucky)
Randall M. Parker, PhD
  Professor of Special Education
  The University of Texas at Austin
James E. Reese, MS
  Appraisal and Learning Disabilities Consultant
  Iowa Department of Public Instruction (Des Moines)
Cecil R. Reynolds, PhD
  Professor of Educational Psychology
  Texas A & M University (College Station)

Ben Wallace, PhD
   Baytown, Texas

James E. Ysseldyke, PhD
   Professor of Education
   University of Minnesota (Minneapolis)

APPENDIX D

TESTS REVIEWED IN THE CONSUMER'S GUIDE

AAMD Adaptive Behavior Scales. (1969). K. Nihira, R. Foster, M. Shellhaas, & H. Leland. American Association on Mental Deficiency.

AAMD Adaptive Behavior Scales–Public School Version. (1974). N. Lambert, M. Windmiller, L. Cole, & R. Figueroa. American Association on Mental Deficiency.

AAMD Adaptive Behavior Scales–School Edition. (1981). N. Lambert. CTB/McGraw-Hill.

Aberrant Behavior Checklist. (1986). M. G. Aman & N. N. Singh. Slosson Educational Publications.

Adaptive Behavior Inventory. (1986). L. Brown & J. E. Leigh. PRO-ED.

ADD-H Comprehensive Teacher's Rating Scale. (1988). R. K. Ullmann, E. K. Sleator, & R. L. Sprague. MetriTech.

Adolescent Drinking Index. (1989). A. V. Harrell & P. W. Wirtz. Psychological Assessment Resources.

The Alpha Test of Phonology. (1986). R. J. Lowe. LinguiSystems.

Analysis of the Language of Learning. (1987). E. G. Blodgett & E. B. Cooper. LinguiSystems.

Arizona Articulation Proficiency Scale (2nd ed.). (1986). J. B. Fudala & W. R. Reynolds. Western Psychological Services.

Assessing Semantic Skills Through Everyday Themes. (1986). M. Barrett, L. Zachman, & R. Huisingh. LinguiSystems.

Auditory Discrimination Test–Revised. (1973). J. M. Wepman. Western Psychological Services.

Auditory-Visual, Single-Word Picture Vocabulary Test–Adolescent. (1986). M. F. Gardner. Psychological and Educational Publications.

Bankson-Bernthal Test of Phonology. (1990). N. W. Bankson & J. E. Bernthal. Special Press.

Bankson Language Screening Test. (1977). N. W. Bankson. PRO-ED.

Basic Achievement Skills Individual Screener. (1983). The Psychological Corporation.

Basic School Skills Inventory–Diagnostic. (1983). D. D. Hammill & J. E. Leigh. PRO-ED.

Beck Depression Inventory. (1987). A. T. Beck & R. A. Steer. The Psychological Corporation.

Beck Hopelessness Scale. (1988). A. T. Beck & R. A. Steer. The Psychological Corporation.

Behavior Dimensions Rating Scale. (1989). L. M. Bullock & M. J. Wilson. DLM/Teaching Resources.

Behavior Evaluation Scale. (1983). S. B. McCarney, J. E. Leigh, & J. A. Cornbleet. Educational Services.

Behavior Evaluation Scale-2. (1990). S. B. McCarney & J. E. Leigh. Educational Services.

Behavior Rating Profile. (1983). L. Brown & D. D. Hammill. PRO-ED.

Behavior Rating Profile, 2nd Edition. (1990). L. Brown & D. D. Hammill. PRO-ED.

The Bender Gestalt Test for Young Children. (1975). E. M. Koppitz. The Psychological Corporation.

Boder Test of Reading and Spelling Patterns. (1982). E. Boder & S. Jarrico. Grune & Stratton.

Boehm Test of Basic Concepts–Revised. (1986). A. E. Boehm. The Psychological Corporation.

Bruininks-Oseretsky Test of Motor Proficiency. (1978). R. H. Bruininks. American Guidance Service.

Burks' Behavior Rating Scale. (1977). H. F. Burks. Western Psychological Services.

Canfield Learning Styles Inventory. (1988). A. A. Canfield. Western Psychological Services.

Career Decision-Making System. (1982). T. F. Harrington & A. J. O'Shea. American Guidance Service.

Career Maturity Inventory. (1978). J. O. Crites. CTB/McGraw-Hill.

Carrow Auditory-Visual Abilities Test. (1981). E. Carrow-Woolfolk. DLM/Teaching Resources.

Carrow Elicited Language Inventory. (1974). E. Carrow. DLM/Teaching Resources.

The Childhood Autism Rating Scale. (1988). E. Schopler, R. J. Reichler, & B. R. Renner. Western Psychological Services.

Children's Apperceptive Story-Telling Test. (1989). M. F. Schneider. PRO-ED.

Children's Auditory Verbal Learning Test. (1990). J. L. Talley. Psychological Assessment Resources.

The Children's Version of the Family Environment Scale. (1984). C. J. Pino, N. Simons, & M. J. Slawinowski. Slosson Educational Publications.

Clark-Madison Test of Oral Language. (1986). J. B. Clark & C. L. Madison. PRO-ED.

Clinical Evaluation of Language Functions. (1980). E. M. Semel & E. H. Wiig. The Psychological Corporation.

Clinical Evaluation of Language Fundamentals–Revised. (1987). E. Semel, E. H. Wiig, & W. Secord. The Psychological Corporation.

Clinical Evaluation of Language Fundamentals–Revised Screening Test. (1989). E. Semel, E. H. Wiig, & W. Secord. The Psychological Corporation.

Cognitive Levels Test. (1988). B. Algozzine, R. C. Eaves, L. Mann, & H. R. Vance. ARETE.

Columbia Mental Maturity Scale. (1972). B. B. Burgemeister, L. H. Blum, & I. Lorge. Harcourt Brace Jovanovich.

Communication Abilities Diagnostic Test. (1990). E. B. Johnston & A. V. Johnston. Special Press.

Comprehensive Behavior Rating Scale for Children. (1990). R. Neeper, B. B. Lahey, & P. J. Frick. The Psychological Corporation.

Comprehensive Test of Visual Functioning. (1990). S. L. Larson, E. Buethe, & G. J. Vitali. Slosson Educational Publications.

Computer Aptitude, Literacy, and Interest Profile. (1984). M. S. Poplin, D. E. Drew, & R. S. Gable. PRO-ED.

Conners' Parent Rating Scales-48. (1990). C. K. Conners. Multi-Health Systems.

Conners' Parent Rating Scales–93. (1990). C. K. Conners. Multi-Health Systems.

Conners' Teacher Rating Scales–28. (1990). C. K. Conners. Multi-Health Systems.

Conners' Teacher Rating Scales–39. (1990). C. K. Conners. Multi-Health Systems.

Culture Fair Intelligence Tests. (1973). Institute for Personality and Ability Testing.

Culture-Free Self-Esteem Inventories for Children and Adults. (1981). J. Battle. Special Child Publications.

Detroit Tests of Learning Aptitude, 2nd Edition. (1985). D. D. Hammill. PRO-ED.

Detroit Tests of Learning Aptitude, 3rd Edition. (1991). D. D. Hammill. PRO-ED.

Detroit Tests of Learning Aptitude–Adult. (1991). D. D. Hammill & B. R. Bryant. PRO-ED.

Detroit Tests of Learning Aptitude–Primary. (1986). D. D. Hammill & B. R. Bryant. PRO-ED.

Detroit Tests of Learning Aptitude–Primary, 2nd Edition. (1991). D. D. Hammill & B. R. Bryant. PRO-ED.

Developmental Indicators for the Assessment of Learning–Revised. (1990). C. Mardel-Czudnowski & D. S. Goldenberg. American Guidance Service.

Developmental Profile II. (1986). G. Alpern, T. Boll, & M. Shearer. Western Psychological Services.

Developmental Test of Visual-Motor Integration. (1982). K. E. Beery. Modern Curriculum Press.

Developmental Test of Visual Perception. (1966). M. Frostig, W. Lefever, & J. R. B. Whittlesey. Consulting Psychologists Press.

Devereux Adolescent Behavior Rating Scale. (1967). G. Spivack, P. Haimes, & J. Spotts. Devereux Foundation.

Devereux Child Behavior Rating Scale. (1966). G. Spivack & J. Spotts. Devereux Foundation.

Devereux Elementary School Behavior Rating Scale II. (1982). G. Spivack & M. Swift. Devereux Foundation.

Diagnostic Achievement Battery. (1984). P. L. Newcomer & D. Curtis. PRO-ED.

Diagnostic Achievement Battery, 2nd Edition. (1990). P. L. Newcomer. PRO-ED.

Diagnostic Achievement Test for Adolescents. (1986). P. L. Newcomer & B. R. Bryant. PRO-ED.

Diagnostic Analysis of Reading Errors. (1979). J. Gillespie & J. Shomet. Jastak Assessment Systems.

Diagnostic Reading Scales. (1981). G. D. Spache. CTB/McGraw-Hill.

Diagnostic Screening Test: Achievement. (1977). T. D. Gnagey & P. A. Gnagey. Slosson Educational Publications.

Diagnostic Screening Test: Language, 2nd Edition. (1980). T. D. Gnagey & P. A. Gnagey. Slosson Educational Publications.

Diagnostic Screening Test: Math, 3rd Edition. (1980). T. D. Gnagey. Slosson Educational Publications.

Diagnostic Screening Test: Reading, 3rd Edition. (1982). T. D. Gnagey & P. A. Gnagey. Slosson Educational Publications.

Diagnostic Screening Test: Spelling, 3rd Edition. (1982). T. D. Gnagey & P. A. Gnagey. Slosson Educational Publications.

Diagnostic Spelling Potential Test. (1982). J. Arena. Academic Therapy Publications.

Differential Test of Conduct and Emotional Problems. (1990). E. J. Kelly. Slosson Educational Publications.

Draw A Person. (1991). J. A. Naglieri, T. J. McNeish, & A. N. Bardos. PRO-ED.

Emotional and Behavior Problem Scale. (1989). F. Wright. Hawthorne Educational Services.

Endler Multidimensional Anxiety Scales. (1991). N. S. Endler, J. M. Edwards, & R. Vitello. Western Psychological Services.

Expressive One-Word Picture Vocabulary Test. (1979). M. F. Gardner. Academic Therapy Publications.

Expressive One-Word Picture Vocabulary Test (Revised). (1990). M. F. Gardner. Academic Therapy Publications.

Expressive One-Word Picture Vocabulary Test–Upper Extension. (1983). M. F. Gardner. Academic Therapy Publications.

Family Apperception Test. (1988). W. M. Sotile, A. Julian, S. E. Henry, & M. O. Sotile. Western Psychological Services.

Fluharty Preschool Speech and Language Screening Test. (1968). N. B. Fluharty. DLM/Teaching Resources.

Formal Reading Inventory. (1986). J. L. Wiederholt. PRO-ED.

The Gifted Evaluation Scale. (1987). S. B. McCarney. Hawthorne Educational Services.

Gilmore Oral Reading Test. (1968). J. V. Gilmore & E. C. Gilmore. Harcourt Brace Jovanovich.

Goldman-Fristoe Test of Articulation. (1972). R. Goldman & M. Fristoe. American Guidance Service.

Goldman-Fristoe Test of Articulation. (1986). R. Goldman & M. Fristoe. American Guidance Service.

Goldman-Fristoe-Woodcock Auditory Skills Test Battery. (1976). R. W. Woodcock. American Guidance Service.

Goldman-Fristoe-Woodcock Test of Auditory Discrimination. (1970). R. Goldman, M. Fristoe, & R. W. Woodcock. American Guidance Service.

Gray Oral Reading Test. (1967). W. S. Gray & H. M. Robinson (Eds.). PRO-ED.

Gray Oral Reading Tests–Revised. (1986). J. L. Wiederholt & B. R. Bryant. PRO-ED.

Hahnemann Elementary School Behavior Rating Scale. (1975). G. Spivack & M. Swift. Hahnemann University.

Hahnemann High School Behavior Rating Scale. (1971). G. Spivack & M. Swift. Hahnemann University.

Houston Test of Language Development–Revised. (1978). M. Crabtree. Stoelting.

Human Figures Drawing Test. (1986). E. Gonzalez. PRO-ED.

Illinois Test of Psycholinguistic Abilities. (1968). S. A. Kirk, J. J. McCarthy, & W. D. Kirk. University of Illinois Press.

Index of Personality Characteristics. (1988). L. Brown & M. Coleman. PRO-ED.

Inventory for Client and Agency Planning. (1986). R. H. Bruininks, B. K. Hill, R. F. Weatherman, & R. W. Woodcock. DLM/Teaching Resources.

Jordan Left-Right Reversal Test. (1980). B. T. Jordan. Academic Therapy Publications.

Jordan Left-Right Reversal Test, 1990 Edition. (1990). B. T. Jordan. Academic Therapy Publications.

Kaufman Assessment Battery for Children. (1983). A. S. Kaufman & N. L. Kaufman. American Guidance Service.

Kaufman Brief Intelligence Test. (1990). A. S. Kaufman & N. L. Kaufman. American Guidance Service.

Kaufman Test of Educational Achievement–Brief Form. (1985). A. S. Kaufman & N. L. Kaufman. American Guidance Service.

Kaufman Test of Educational Achievement–Comprehensive Form. (1985). A. S. Kaufman & N. L. Kaufman. American Guidance Service.

KeyMath Diagnostic Arithmetic Test. (1971). A. Connolly, W. Nachtman, & E. M. Pritchett. American Guidance Service.

KeyMath–Revised. (1988). A. J. Connolly. American Guidance Service.

Kindergarten Language Screening Test. (1983). S. V. Gauthier & C. L. Madison. PRO-ED.

Kindergarten Readiness Test. (1988). S. L. Larson & G. J. Vitali. Slosson Educational Publications.

Kohn Problem Checklist/Kohn Social Competence Scale. (1988). M. Kohn. The Psychological Corporation.

Language Processing Test. (1985). G. Richard & M. A. Hanner. LinguiSystems.

The Learning Disability Evaluation Scale. (1983). S. B. McCarney. Hawthorne Educational Services.

Learning Disability Rating Procedure. (1981). G. J. Spadafore & S. J. Spadafore. Academic Therapy Publications.

Learning Efficiency Test. (1981). R. E. Webster. Academic Therapy Publications.

The Leiter International Performance Scale Handbook. (1982). M. N. Levine. Western Psychological Services.

Lindamood Auditory Conceptualization Test. (1971). C. Lindamood & P. Lindamood. DLM/Teaching Resources.

Luria-Nebraska Neuropsychological Battery: Children's Revision. (1987). C. J. Golden. Western Psychological Services.

Matrix Analogies Test-Expanded Form. (1985). J. A. Naglieri. The Psychological Corporation.

Matrix Analogies Test-Short Form. (1985). J. A. Naglieri. The Psychological Corporation.

McCarthy Scales of Children's Abilities. (1972). D. McCarthy. The Psychological Corporation.

Measurement of Language Development. (1975). C. R. Melnick. Stoelting.

Merrill Language Screening Test. (1980). M. Mumm, W. Secord, & K. Dykstra. The Psychological Corporation.

Miller Assessment for Preschoolers. (1988). L. J. Miller. The Psychological Corporation.

Miller-Yoder Language Comprehension Test–Clinical Edition. (1984). J. F. Miller & D. E. Yoder. PRO-ED.

Minnesota Percepto-Diagnostic Test. (1982). G. B. Fuller. Clinical Psychology Publishing Company.

Motor-Free Visual Perception Test. (1972). R. P. Colarusso & D. D. Hammill. Academic Therapy Publications.

Multiscore Depression Inventory. (1986). D. J. Berndt. Western Psychological Services.

Nonverbal Test of Cognitive Skills. (1981). G. O. Johnson & H. F. Boyd. The Psychological Corporation.

Normative Adaptive Behavior Checklist. (1986). G. L. Adams. The Psychological Corporation.

Northwestern Syntax Screening Test. (1971). L. Lee. Northwestern University Press.

Occupational Aptitude Survey and Interest Schedule. (1983). R. M. Parker. PRO-ED.

Occupational Aptitude Survey and Interest Schedule, 2nd Edition. (1991). R. M. Parker. PRO-ED.

Parent Rating of Student Behavior. (1987). S. B. McCarney. Hawthorne Educational Services.

Peabody Individual Achievement Test. (1970). L. M. Dunn & F. C. Markwardt. American Guidance Service.

Peabody Individual Achievement Test–Revised. (1989). F. C. Markwardt. American Guidance Service.

Peabody Picture Vocabulary Test. (1965). L. M. Dunn & L. Dunn. American Guidance Service.

Peabody Picture Vocabulary Test–Revised. (1981). L. M. Dunn & L. Dunn. American Guidance Service.

Personal Experience Inventory. (1989). K. C. Winters & G. A. Henly. Western Psychological Services.

Pictorial Test of Intelligence. (1964). J. L. French. Houghton Mifflin.

Piers-Harris Children's Self-Concept Scale. (1969). E. V. Piers. Western Psychological Services.

Piers-Harris Children's Self-Concept Scale–Revised Manual 1984. (1984). E. V. Piers. Western Psychological Services.

Prescriptive Reading Performance Test. (1978). J. B. Fudala. Western Psychological Services.

Primary Visual Motor Test. (1970). M. R. Haworth. Grune & Stratton.

Psycholinguistic Rating Scale. (1982). K. L. Hobby. Western Psychological Services.

The Pupil Rating Scale, Revised. (1981). H. R. Myklebust. The Psychological Corporation.

The Purdue Perceptual-Motor Survey. (1966). E. G. Roach & N. C. Kephart. The Psychological Corporation.

Quick-Score Achievement Test. (1987). D. D. Hammill, J. J. Ammer, M. E. Cronin, L. H. Mandlebaum, & S. S. Quinby. PRO-ED.

The Quick Test. (1962). R. B. Ammons & C. H. Ammons. Psychological Test Specialists.

Receptive One-Word Picture Vocabulary Test. (1985). M. F. Gardner. Academic Therapy Publications.

Responsibility and Independence Scale for Adolescents. (1990). J. Salvia, J. T. Neisworth, & M. W. Schmidt. DLM/Teaching Resources.

Reynell Developmental Language Scales, U.S. Edition. (1990). J. K. Reynell & C. P. Gruber. Western Psychological Services.

Reynolds Adolescent Depression Scale. (1987). W. M. Reynolds. Psychological Assessment Resources.

Reynolds Child Depression Scale. (1989). W. M. Reynolds. Psychological Assessment Resources.

Rhode Island Test of Language Structure. (1983). E. Engen & T. Engen. PRO-ED.

Roberts Apperception Test for Children. (1982). G. E. Roberts & D. S. McArthur. Western Psychological Services.

Scales of Independent Behavior. (1985). R. H. Bruininks, R. W. Woodcock, R. F. Weatherman, & B. K. Hill. DLM/Teaching Resources.

Scholastic Abilities Test for Adults. (1991). B. R. Bryant, J. R. Patton, & C. Dunn. PRO-ED.

Scholastic Aptitude Scale. (1991). B. R. Bryant & P. L. Newcomer. PRO-ED.

School Behavior Checklist. (1981). L. C. Miller. Western Psychological Services.

Schubert General Ability Battery. (1986). H. J. P. Schubert. Slosson Educational Publications.

Screening Assessment for Gifted Elementary Students. (1987). S. K. Johnsen & A. L. Corn. PRO-ED.

Screening Children for Related Early Educational Needs. (1988). W. P. Hresko, D. K. Reid, D. D. Hammill, H. P. Ginsburg, & A. J. Baroody. PRO-ED.

Screening Test of Adolescent Language. (1980). E. M. Prather, S. V. A. Breecher, M. L. Stafford, & E. M. Wallace. University of Washington Press.

Self-Description Questionnaire–II. (1990). H. W. Marsh. The Psychological Corporation.

Self-Esteem Index. (1991). L. Brown & J. Alexander. PRO-ED.

Self-Esteem Inventories–School Form. (1984). S. Coopersmith. Consulting Psychologists Press.

Sensory Integration & Praxis Test. (1989). A. J. Ayres. Western Psychological Services.

Sequential Assessment of Mathematics Inventories. (1985). F. K. Reisman & T. A. Hutchinson. The Psychological Corporation.

Slosson Intelligence Test for Children and Adults–Revised. (1985). R. L. Slosson. Slosson Educational Publications.

Slosson Intelligence Test for Children and Adults–Revised. (1991). R. L. Slosson, revised by C. L. Nicholson & T. H. Hibpshman. Slosson Educational Publications.

Slosson Oral Reading Test, Revised. (1990). R. L. Slosson, revised by C. L. Nicholson. Slosson Educational Publications.

Social-Emotional Dimension Scale. (1986). J. B. Hutton & T. G. Roberts. PRO-ED.

Social Skills Rating System. (1990). F. M. Gresham & S. N. Elliott. American Guidance Service.

Southern California Sensory Integration Tests–Revised. (1980). A. J. Ayres. Western Psychological Services.

Stanford-Binet Intelligence Scale, 4th Edition. (1986). R. L. Thorndike, E. P. Hagen, & J. M. Sattler. Riverside Publishing.

Stanford-Binet Intelligence Scale, 1972 Norms Edition. (1973). L. M. Terman & M. A. Merrill. Houghton Mifflin.

Street Survival Skills Questionnaire. (1980). D. Linkenhoker & L. McCarron. McCarron-Dial Systems.

Suicidal Ideation Questionnaire. (1988). W. M. Reynolds. Psychological Assessment Resources.

The Temperament Assessment Battery for Children. (1988). R. P. Martin. Clinical Psychology Publishing.

Templin-Darley Tests of Articulation. (1969). M. C. Templin & F. L. Darley. University of Iowa Bureau of Educational Research and Service.

Test for Auditory Comprehension of Language–Revised. (1985). E. Carrow-Woolfolk. DLM/Teaching Resources.

Test of Academic Performance. (1989). W. Adams, D. Sheslow, & L. Erb. The Psychological Corporation.

Test of Adolescent/Adult Word Finding. (1990). D. J. German. DLM/Teaching Resources.

Test of Adolescent Language. (1980) D. D. Hammill, V. L. Brown, S. C. Larsen, & J. L. Wiederholt. PRO-ED.

Test of Adolescent Language, 2nd Edition. (1987). D. D. Hammill, V. L. Brown, S. C. Larsen, & J. L. Wiederholt. PRO-ED.

Test of Articulation Performance–Screen. (1983). B. R. Bryant & D. L. Bryant. PRO-ED.

Test of Auditory-Perceptual Skills. (1985). M. F. Gardner. Psychological and Educational Publications.

Test of Early Language Development. (1981). W. P. Hresko, D. K. Reid, & D. D. Hammill. PRO-ED.

Test of Early Language Development, 2nd Edition. (1991). W. P. Hresko, D. K. Reid, & D. D. Hammill. PRO-ED.

Test of Early Mathematics Ability. (1983). H. P. Ginsburg & A. J. Baroody. PRO-ED.

Test of Early Mathematics Ability, 2nd Edition. (1990). H. P. Ginsburg & A. J. Baroody. PRO-ED.

Test of Early Reading Ability. (1981). D. K. Reid, W. P. Hresko, & D. D. Hammill. PRO-ED.

Test of Early Reading Ability, 2nd Edition. (1989). D. K. Reid, W. P. Hresko, & D. D. Hammill. PRO-ED.

Test of Early Reading Ability–Deaf or Hard of Hearing. (1991). D. K. Reid, W. P. Hresko, D. D. Hammill, & S. Wiltshire. PRO-ED.

Test of Early Socioemotional Development. (1984). W. P. Hresko & L. Brown. PRO-ED.

Test of Early Written Language. (1988). W. P. Hresko. PRO-ED.

Test of Gross Motor Development. (1985). D. A. Ulrich. PRO-ED.

Test of Language Competence. (1985). E. H. Wiig & W. Secord. The Psychological Corporation.

Test of Language Development–Intermediate. (1982) D. D. Hammill & P. L. Newcomer. PRO-ED.

Test of Language Development–Intermediate, 2nd Edition. (1988). D. D. Hammill & P. L. Newcomer. PRO-ED.

Test of Language Development–Primary. (1982). P. L. Newcomer & D. D. Hammill. PRO-ED.

Test of Language Development–Primary, 2nd Edition. (1988). P. L. Newcomer & D. D. Hammill. PRO-ED.

Test of Legible Handwriting. (1989). S. C. Larsen & D. D. Hammill. PRO-ED.

Test of Mathematical Abilities. (1984). V. L. Brown & E. McEntire. PRO-ED.

Test of Nonverbal Intelligence. (1982). L. Brown, R. J. Sherbenou, & S. K. Johnsen. PRO-ED.

Test of Nonverbal Intelligence, 2nd Edition. (1991). L. Brown, R. J. Sherbenou, & S. K. Johnsen. PRO-ED.

Test of Pictures/Forms/Letters/Numbers/Spatial Orientation & Sequencing Skills. (1991). M. F. Gardner. Psychological and Educational Publications.

Test of Practical Knowledge. (1983). J. L. Wiederholt & S. C. Larsen. PRO-ED.

Test of Problem Solving. (1984). L. Zachman, C. Jorgensen, R. Huisingh, & M. Barrett. LinguiSystems.

Test of Reading Comprehension. (1978). V. L. Brown, D. D. Hammill, & J. L. Wiederholt. PRO-ED.

Test of Reading Comprehension–Revised. (1986). V. L. Brown, D. D. Hammill, & J. L. Wiederholt. PRO-ED.

Test of Relational Concepts. (1988). N. K. Edmonston & N. L. Thane. PRO-ED.

Test of Visual-Motor Skills. (1986). M. F. Gardner. Psychological and Educational Publications.

Test of Visual-Perceptual Skills. (1982). M. F. Gardner. Psychological and Educational Publications.

Test of Word Finding. (1986). D. G. German. DLM/Teaching Resources.

Test of Written Language. (1983). D. D. Hammill & S. C. Larsen. PRO-ED.

Test of Written Language, 2nd Edition. (1988). D. D. Hammill & S. C. Larsen. PRO-ED.

Test of Written Spelling. (1976). S. C. Larsen & D. D. Hammill. PRO-ED.

Test of Written Spelling, 2nd Edition. (1986). S. C. Larsen & D. D. Hammill. PRO-ED.

Tests for Everyday Living. (1979). A. S. Halpern, L. K. Irvin, & J. T. Landman. CTB/McGraw Hill.

Torrance Tests of Creative Thinking. (1974). E. P. Torrance. Scholastic Testing Service.

The Transition Behavior Scale. (1989). S. B. McCarney. Hawthorne Educational Services.

Utah Test of Language Development–Revised Edition. (1978). M. J. Mecham & J. D. Jones. PRO-ED.

Utah Test of Language Development, 3rd Edition. (1989). M. J. Mecham. PRO-ED.

The Vane Kindergarten Test. (1984). J. R. Vane. Clinical Psychology Publishing.

Vineland Adaptive Behavior Scales–Classroom Edition. (1985). S. S. Sparrow, D. A. Balla, & D. V. Cicchetti. American Guidance Service.

Vineland Adaptive Behavior Scales–Interview Edition, Expanded Form. (1984). S. S. Sparrow, D. A. Balla, & D. V. Cicchetti. American Guidance Service.

Vineland Adaptive Behavior Scales–Interview Edition, Survey Form. (1984). S. S. Sparrow, D. A. Balla, & D. V. Cicchetti. American Guidance Service.

The Visual Aural Digit Span Test. (1977). E. M. Koppitz. Grune & Stratton.

Walker-McConnell Scale of Social Competence and School Adjustment. (1988). H. M. Walker & S. R. McConnell. PRO-ED.

Walker Problem Behavior Identification Checklist–Revised 1983. (1983). H. M. Walker. Western Psychological Services.

The Watkins Bender-Gestalt Scoring System. (1976). E. O. Watkins. Academic Therapy Publications.

Wechsler Adult Intelligence Scale–Revised. (1981). D. Wechsler. The Psychological Corporation.

Wechsler Intelligence Scale for Children–Revised. (1974). D. Wechsler. The Psychological Corporation.

Wechsler Intelligence Scale for Children–3rd Edition. (1992). D. Wechsler. The Psychological Corporation.

Wechsler Memory Scale–Revised. (1987). D. Wechsler. The Psychological Corporation.

Wechsler Preschool and Primary Scale of Intelligence. (1967). D. Wechsler. The Psychological Corporation.

Weiss Comprehensive Articulation Test. (1980). C. E. Weiss. DLM/Teaching Resources.

Wepman's Auditory Discrimination Test–2nd Edition. (1987). W. M. Reynolds. Western Psychological Services.

Wide Range Achievement Test. (1978). J. Jastak & S. Jastak. Jastak Assessment Systems.

Wide Range Achievement Test–Revised. (1984). J. Jastak & G. S. Wilkinson. Jastak Assessment Systems.

Wide Range Assessment of Memory and Learning. (1990). D. Sheslow & W. Adams. Jastak Assessment Systems.

Wide Range Intelligence-Personality Test. (1978). J. F. Jastak. Jastak Assessment Systems.

Wide Range Interest-Opinion Test. (1979). J. F. Jastak. Jastak Assessment Systems.

Woodcock-Johnson Psycho-Educational Battery. (1977). R. W. Woodcock. DLM/Teaching Resources.

Woodcock-Johnson Psycho-Educational Battery–Revised. (1989). R. W. Woodcock & W. B. Johnson. DLM/Teaching Resources.

Woodcock Language Proficiency Battery–Revised. (1991). R. W. Woodcock. DLM/Teaching Resources.

Woodcock Reading Mastery Tests. (1973). R. W. Woodcock. American Guidance Service.

Woodcock Reading Mastery Tests–Revised. (1988). R. W. Woodcock. American Guidance Service.

The Word Test. (1981). C. Jorgensen, M. Barrett, R. Huisingh, & L. Zachman. LinguiSystems.

The Word Test: Adolescent. (1989). L. Zachman, R. Huisingh, M. Barrett, J. Orman, & C. Blagden. LinguiSystems.

The Word Test–R: Elementary. (1990). R. Huisingh, M. Barrett, L. Zachman, C. Blagden, & J. Orman. LinguiSystems.

Written Language Assessment. (1989). J. J. Grill & M. M. Kirwin. Academic Therapy Publications.

APPENDIX E

**PUBLISHERS OF TESTS
REVIEWED IN THE
CONSUMER'S GUIDE**

Academic Therapy Publications
20 Commercial Boulevard
Novato, CA 94947-6191
American Association on Mental Deficiency
5101 Wisconsin Avenue, NW
Washington, DC 20016
American Guidance Service
Publishers' Building
Circle Pines, MN 55014
ARETE, Inc.
540 Swede Street
Norristown, PA 19401
Clinical Psychology Publishing Company, Inc.
4 Conant Square
Brandon, VT 05733
Consulting Psychologists Press
577 College Avenue
Palo Alto, CA 94306
CTB/McGraw-Hill
2500 Garden Road
Del Monte Research Park
Monterey, CA 93940
Devereux Foundation
19 South Waterloo Road
P.O. Box 400
Devon, PA 19333
DLM/Teaching Resources
P.O. Box 4000
One DLM Park
Allen, TX 75002
Educational Assessment Service, Inc.
Route One, Box 139-A
Watertown, WI 53094
Educational Services
P.O. Box 1835
Columbia, MO 65205
Grune & Stratton, Inc.
Orlando, FL 32887-0018
Hahnemann University
Preventive Intervention Research Center
Philadelphia, PA 19102
Harcourt Brace Jovanovich, Inc.
757 Third Avenue
New York, NY 10017
Hawthorne Educational Services
P.O. Box 7570
Columbia, MO 65205
Houghton Mifflin Company
1 Beacon Street
Boston, MA 02108
Institute for Personality and Ability Testing
1602 Coronado Drive
Champaign, IL 61820

Jastak Assessment Systems
1526 Gilpin Avenue
Wilmington, DE 19806
LinguiSystems, Inc.
716 17th Street
Moline, IL 61265
McCarron-Dial Systems
P.O. Box 45628
Dallas, TX 75245
MetriTech, Inc.
111 North Market Street
Champaign, IL 61820
Modern Curriculum Press
13900 Prospect Road
Cleveland, OH 44136
Multi-Health Systems, Inc.
908 Niagara Falls Boulevard
North Tonawanda, NY 14120-2060
Northwestern University Press
Department SLD-82
1735 Benson Avenue
Evanston, IL 60201
PRO-ED, Inc.
8700 Shoal Creek Boulevard
Austin, TX 78758
Psychological Assessment Resources, Inc.
P.O. Box 998
Odessa, FL 33556
The Psychological Corporation
555 Academic Court
San Antonio, TX 78204
Psychological and Educational Publications, Inc.
1477 Rollins Road
Burlingame, CA 94010
Psychological Test Specialists
Box 9229
Missoula, MT 59807
Riverside Publishing Company
8420 Bryn Mawr Avenue
Chicago, IL 60631
Scholastic Testing Service
480 Meyer Road
Bensenville, IL 60106
Slosson Educational Publications, Inc.
P.O. Box 280
East Aurora, NY 14052
Special Child Publications
4535 Union Bay Place NE
Seattle, WA 98105
Special Press, Inc.
11230 West Avenue, Suite 3250
San Antonio, TX 78213

Stoelting
  1350 S. Kostner Avenue
  Chicago, IL 60623
University of Illinois Press
  54 East Gregory Drive
  Box 5081, Station A
  Champaign, IL 61820
University of Iowa Bureau of Educational Research
      and Service
  University of Iowa
  Iowa City, IA 52240

University of Minnesota Press
  P.O. Box 1416
  Minneapolis, MN 61820
University of Washington Press
  P.O. Box C-50096
  4045 Brooklyn Avenue, NE
  Seattle, WA 98105
Western Psychological Services
  12031 Wilshire Boulevard
  Los Angeles, CA 90025

APPENDIX F

CONSUMER'S GUIDE
REVIEWER EVALUATION FORM

Reviewer _____

CONSUMER'S GUIDE REVIEWER EVALUATION FORM

Test Name (Date of Publication) _____ (_____)

Test Author(s) _____

Publisher, City, State _____

Test Score Being Reviewed _____

Taxonomy Classification _____

Administration and Scoring Characteristics

Administration: _____ Group or individual

_____ Individual only

Time required for administration: _____

Scores are interpreted in terms of:

_____ Age equivalents

_____ Grade equivalents

_____ Percentile ranks or related scores

_____ Standard scores

_____ Other (specify: _____)

Test may be administered to subjects in grades _____ through _____ or subjects ages _____ through _____ years.

Format Characteristics

_____ The respondent is not the target student but a third party such as a teacher, parent, or peer.

_____ The respondent is the target student, and the format requires the respondent to:

Input	**Output**
_____ Listen	_____ Make one-word responses
_____ Read print, including letters, words, and numbers	_____ Make multiple-word responses
_____ Look at stimuli (pictures, objects)	_____ Manipulate objects
_____ Other (specify: _____)	_____ Mark an answer sheet
	_____ Point
	_____ Draw
	_____ Write print
	_____ Other (specify: _____)

Examiner Characteristics

_____ The test is easily administered after reading the manual.

_____ Administration requires special training beyond familiarity with the test manual.

_____ Administration is restricted to examiners with specified certificates or licenses.

Determining the Overall Consumer's Guide Rating

Norms Rating _____

Reliability Rating _____

Validity Rating _____

Overall Rating _____

Norms

A. Normative Scores

_____ No normative scores are reported; only age or grade equivalents are reported; or only ratio IQs or scores are available.

_____ Percentile ranks, quartiles, deciles, centiles, or dichotomous standard scores are reported.

_____ Standard scores are reported.

B. Size of the Normative Group

_____ The size of the normative group is not specified or does not meet the criteria below.

_____ The normative group contains 75 or more subjects in most one-year age intervals or academic grade levels with which the test is intended to be used. In addition, there are 750 or more subjects in the total sample.

_____ The normative group contains 100 or more subjects in every one-year age interval or academic grade level with which the test is intended to be used. In addition, there are 1,000 or more subjects in the total sample.

C. Demographic Characteristics of the Normative Group

_____ The characteristics of the normative group are not specified or do not meet the criteria below.

_____ The characteristics of the normative group correspond approximately to the known characteristics of the specified population on three or four of the following variables: gender, domicile, parental education, parental occupation, geographic region, race, ethnicity, intelligence, socioeconomic status, or other relevant variables (specify: _____).

_____ The characteristics of the normative group correspond approximately to the known characteristics of the specified population on five or more of the following variables: gender, domicile, parental education, parental occupation, geographic region, race, ethnicity, intelligence, socioeconomic status, or other relevant variables (specify: _____).

D. Recency of Normative Data

Normative data were gathered in

_____ 1975 or before.

_____ 1976–1985.

_____ 1986 or after.

Norms Rating: _____

Reliability

A. Internal Consistency Reliability

Internal consistency reliability

_____ Is not reported; is below .80 at most ages; or is reported with no apparent controls for the effects of age.

_____ Is .80 or above at most ages when reported for two or more age intervals spanning no more than three years each; is .80–.89 for a single group when evidence is presented to demonstrate that the test is not significantly related to age; or is .80 or above when the effects of age are controlled statistically.

_____ Is .90 or above at most ages when reported for two or more age intervals spanning no more than three years each; or is .90 or above for a single group when evidence is presented to demonstrate that the test is not significantly related to age.

B. Stability Reliability

Stability reliability

_____ Is not reported; is below .80 at most ages; or is reported with no apparent controls for the effects of age.

_____ Is .80 or above at most ages when reported for two or more age intervals spanning no more than three years each; is .80–.89 for a single group when evidence is presented to demonstrate that the test is not significantly related to age; or is .80 or above when the effects of age are controlled statistically.

_____ Is .90 or above at most ages when reported for two or more age intervals spanning no more than three years each; or is .90 or above for a single group when evidence is presented to demonstrate that the test is not significantly related to age.

Reliability Rating: _____

Validity

_____ Validity is not reported; validity studies are not acceptable in design; validity studies do not yield significant results as hypothesized; or validity is supported exclusively by nonempirical evidence of content validity.

_____ Validity is supported by studies that provide appropriate evidence that the test score

_____ is related as hypothesized to age or grade.

_____ correlates as hypothesized with measures of achievement.

_____ correlates as hypothesized with measures of aptitude/developmental abilities or general intelligence.

_____ correlates as hypothesized with measures of affect.

_____ produces hypothesized multiple correlation/regression results.

_____ has hypothesized factor structures.

_____ predicts appropriately over time.

_____ distinguishes between specified groups.

_____ intercorrelates as hypothesized with the test's other scores.

_____ has appropriate item-total correlations, item discriminating power, or evidence of another appropriate data-based approach to item selection.

_____ discriminates as hypothesized on the basis of gender, race, ethnicity, or other demographic variables.

_____ other (specify: _____).

Validity Rating: _____

Personal Comments

_____

_____

_____

_____